# Programming Languages: Theory and Practice

# Programming Languages: Theory and Practice

Editor: Katy Spalding

NY Research Press
New York

Published by NY Research Press
118-35 Queens Blvd., Suite 400,
Forest Hills, NY 11375, USA
www.nyresearchpress.com

Programming Languages: Theory and Practice
Edited by Katy Spalding



International Standard Book Number: 978-1-64725-371-4 (Hardback)



**Cataloging-in-publication Data**

Programming languages : theory and practice / edited by Katy Spalding.
p. cm.
Includes bibliographical references and index.
ISBN 978-1-64725-371-4
1. Programming languages (Electronic computers). 2. Electronic data processing. I. Spalding, Katy.
QA76.7 .P76 2023
005.13--dc23

# Contents

# Preface

It is often said that books are a boon to mankind. They document every progress and pass on the knowledge from one generation to the other. They play a crucial role in our lives. Thus I was both excited and nervous while editing this book. I was pleased by the thought of being able to make a mark but I was also nervous to do it right because the future of students depends upon it. Hence, I took a few months to research further into the discipline, revise my knowledge and also explore some more aspects. Post this process, I begun with the editing of this book.

A programming language refers to a set of rules for converting strings or graphical program elements to several types of machine code output. They are used to implement algorithms in computer programming. The description of a programming language is typically divided into two components, which include semantics and syntax, that are normally defined by a formal language. Specification document defines the programming language in certain cases, while some languages have dominant implementation which is treated as reference. Some languages have both, where basic language is defined by a standard and extensions derived from the dominant implementation. Programming language theory is a sub discipline of computer science concerned with the design, implementation, characterization, development, analysis and categorization of programming languages. This book is a valuable compilation of topics, ranging from the basic to the most complex advancements related to the theoretical and practical aspects of programming languages. It is appropriate for students seeking detailed information in this area of computer science as well as for experts.

I thank my publisher with all my heart for considering me worthy of this unparalleled opportunity and for showing unwavering faith in my skills. I would also like to thank the editorial team who worked closely with me at every step and contributed immensely towards the successful completion of this book. Last but not the least, I wish to thank my friends and colleagues for their support.

**Editor**

1

# Counters in Kappa: Semantics, Simulation and Static Analysis

Pierre Boutillier[1], Ioana Cristescu[2], and Jérôme Feret[3](✉)

[1] Harvard Medical School, Boston, USA
Pierre_Boutillier@hms.harvard.edu
[2] Inria Rennes - Bretagne Atlantique, Rennes, France
ioana-domnina.cristescu@inria.fr
[3] DI-ENS (INRIA/ÉNS/CNRS/PSL*), Paris, France
feret@ens.fr

**Abstract.** Site-graph rewriting languages, such as Kappa or BNGL, offer parsimonious ways to describe highly combinatorial systems of mechanistic interactions among proteins. These systems may be then simulated efficiently. Yet, the modeling mechanisms that involve counting (a number of phosphorylated sites for instance) require an exponential number of rules in Kappa. In BNGL, updating the set of the potential applications of rules in the current state of the system comes down to the sub-graph isomorphism problem (which is NP-complete).

In this paper, we extend Kappa to deal both parsimoniously and efficiently with counters. We propose a single push-out semantics for Kappa with counters. We show how to compile Kappa with counters into Kappa without counters (without requiring an exponential number of rules). We design a static analysis, based on affine relationships, to identify the meaning of counters and bound their ranges accordingly.

## 1 Introduction

Site-graph rewriting is a paradigm for modeling mechanistic interactions among proteins. In Kappa [18] and BNGL [3,40], rewriting rules describe how instances of proteins may bind and unbind, and how each protein may activate the interaction sites of each others, by changing their properties. Sophisticated signaling cascades may be described. The long term behavior of such models usually emerges from competition against shared-resources, proteins with multiple-phosphorylation sites, scaffolds, separation of scales, and non-linear feedback loops.

It is often desirable to add more structure to states in order to describe generic mechanisms more compactly. In this paper, we consider extending Kappa with counters with numerical values. As opposed to the properties of classical Kappa sites, which offer no structure, counters allow for expressive preconditions (such as the value of a counter is less than 2), but also for generic update functions (such as incrementing or decrementing the current value of a counter by a given value independently of its current value). Without counters, such

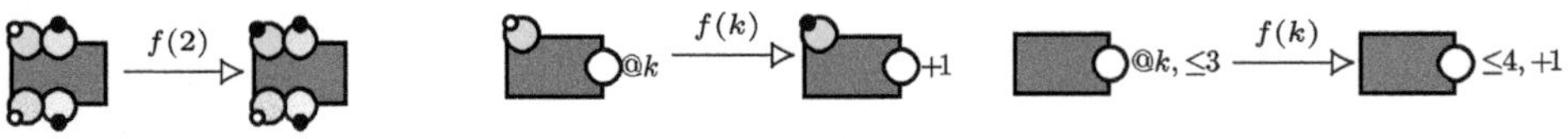


(a) With phosphorylation sites only.

(b) With a counter and phosphorylation sites

(c) With a counter only

**Fig. 1.** Three representations for the phosphorylation of a site. We assume that the rate of phosphorylation of a site in a protein in which exactly $k$ sites are already phosphorylated, is equal to the value $f(k)$. The function $f$ is left as a parameter of the model. In (a), we do not use counters. In order to get the number of sites that are already phosphorylated, we have to document the state of all the sites of the protein. In this rule, there are exactly 2 sites already phosphorylated, thus the rate of the rule is equal to $f(2)$. In (b), we use a counter to encode the number of sites already phosphorylated. The variable $k$, that is introduced by the notation $@k$, contains the number of sites that are phosphorylated before the application of the rule. Thus, the rate of the rule is equal to $f(k)$. In the right hand side, the notation $+1$ indicates that the counter is incremented at each application of the rule. The rule in (b) summarizes exactly 8 rules of the kind of the one in (a) (it defines the phosphorylation of the site $a$ regardless of the states of the three other phosphorylation sites). In (c), we abstract away the sites and keep only the counter. The notation $@k$ binds the variable $k$ to the value of the counter. The left hand side also indicates that the rule may be applied only if the value of the counter is less than or equal to 3 (so that at least one site is not already phosphorylated). The right hand side specifies that the value of the counter is incremented at each application of the rule and that after the application of a rule, the value of the counter is always less than or equal to 4. The rule in (c) stands for 32 rules of the kind of the one in (a) (it depends neither on which site is phosphorylated, nor on the state of the three other sites).

update functions would require one rule per potential value of the counter. This raises efficiency issues for the simulation and also blurs any potential reasoning on the causality of the system.

However adding counters cannot be done without consequences. The efficiency of Kappa simulations mainly relies on two ingredients. Firstly, Kappa graphs are rigid [16, 39]: an embedding from a connected site-graph into a site-graph, when it exists, is fully determined by the image of one node. Thanks to rigidity, searching for the occurrences of a sub-graph into another graph (up-to isomorphism) may be done without backtracking (once a first node has been placed), and embeddings can be described in memory very concisely. Secondly, the representation of the set of potential applications of rules relies on a categorical construction [6] that optimizes sharing among patterns. Yet this construction cannot cope with the more expressive patterns that involve counters. In order to efficiently simulate models with counters, we need an efficient encoding that preserves rigidity and that use classical site-graph patterns.

Let us consider a case study so as to illustrate the need for counters in Kappa. This example is inspired from the behavior of the protein *KaiC* that is involved in the synchronization of the proteins in the circadian clock. We consider one kind of protein with $n$ identified sites that can get phosphorylated. Indeed, $n$ is equal to 6 in the protein *KaiC*. We take $n$ equal to 4 to make graphical representation lighter. We will make $n$ diverge towards the infinity so as to empirically estimate the combinatorial complexity of several encoding schemes.

The rate of phosphorylation/dephosphorylation of each site, depends on the number of sites that are already phosphorylated. In Fig. 1(a), we provide the example of a rule that phosphorylates the site $a$ of the protein, assuming that the sites $b$ and $c$ are already phosphorylated and that the site $d$ is not. Proteins are depicted as rectangles. Sites are depicted clockwise from the site $a$ to the site $d$ starting at the top left corner of the protein. Phosphorylation states are depicted with a black mark when the site is phosphorylated, and with a white mark otherwise. To fully encode this model in Kappa, we would require $n \cdot 2^n$ rules. Indeed, we need to decide whether this is a phosphorylation or a dephosphorylation (2 possibilities), then on which site to apply the transformation ($n$ possibilities), then what the state of the other sites is ($2^{n-1}$ possibilities). This combinatorial complexity may be reduced by the means of counters. We consider a fresh site (this site is depicted on the right of the protein) and we assume that this site takes numerical values. Writing each rule carefully, we can enforce that the value of this site is always equal to the number of the sites that are phosphorylated in the protein instance. Thanks to this invariant, describing our model requires $2{\cdot}n$ rules according to whether we describe a phosphorylation or a dephosphorylation (2 possibilities) and to which site the transformation is applied ($n$ possibilities). An example of rule for the phosphorylation of the site $a$ is given in Fig. 1(b). The notation $@k$ assigns the value of the counter before the application of the rule to the variable $k$. Then the rate of the rule may depend on the value of $k$. This way, we can make the rate of phosphorylation depend on the number of sites already phosphorylated in the protein. Since there are only $n$ sites that may be phosphorylated, it is straightforward to see that the counter may range only between the values 0 and $n$.

If only the number of phosphorylated sites matters, we can go even further: we need just one counter and two rules, one for phosphorylating a new site (e. g. see Fig. 1(c)) and one for dephosphorylating it. The value of the counter is no longer related explicitly to a number of phosphorylated sites, thus we need another way to specify that the value of the counter is bounded. We do this, by specifying in the precondition of the rule that the phosphorylation rule may be applied only if the value of the counter is less or equal to $n-1$, which entails that the value of the counter may range only between the values 0 and $n$.

Not only parsimonious description of the mechanistic interactions in a model eases the process of writing a model, enhances readability and leads to more efficient simulation, but also it may provide better grain of observation of the system behavior. In Fig. 2, we illustrate this by looking at three causal traces that denote the same execution, but for three different encodings. Intuitively, causal traces [14,15] are inspired by event structures [43]. They describe sets of traces seen up to permutation of concurrent computation steps. The level of representation for the potential configurations of each protein impacts the way causality is defined, because what is tested in rules depends on the representation level. In our case study, the phosphorylation of each site is intuitively causally independent: one site may be phosphorylated whatever the state of the other sites is. Without counters, the only way to specify that the rate of phosphorylation depends on the number of the sites that are already phosphorylated, is to detail the state of every site of the protein in the precondition of the rule. This induces spurious causal relations (e. g. see Fig. 2(a)). Utilizing counters relaxes this constraint. However it is important to equip counters with arithmetic. Without arithmetic, a rule may only set the value of a counter to a constant value. Thus for implementing counter increment, rules have to enumerate the potential values of the counter before their applications, and set the value of this counter accordingly. This induces again spurious causal relations (e. g. see Fig. 2(b)). With arithmetic, incrementing counters becomes a generic operation that may be applied independently of the current value of the counter. As a result the phosphorylation of the four sites can be seen as causally independent (e. g. see Fig. 2(c)). This faithfully represents the fact that the phosphorylation of the four sites may happen in arbitrary order.

*Contribution.* Now we describe the main contributions of this paper.

In Sect. 2, we formalize a single push-out (SPO) semantics for Kappa with counters. Having a categorical framework dealing with counters, as opposed to implementing counters as syntactic sugar, is important. Firstly, this semantics will serve as a reference for the formal specification of the behavior of counters. Secondly, the categorical setting of Kappa provides efficient ways to define causality [14,15], symmetries [25], and some sound symbolic reasonings on the behavior of the number of occurrences of patterns [1,26] that are used in model reduction. Including counters in the categorical semantics of Kappa allows for extending the definition of these concepts to Kappa with counters for free.

Yet different encodings of counters may be necessary to extend other tools for Kappa. In Sect. 3, we propose a couple of translations from Kappa with counters into Kappa without counters. The goal is to simulate models with counters efficiently without modifying the implementation of the Kappa simulator, KaSim [17]. The first encoding requires counters to be bounded from below and it supports only two kinds of preconditions over counters: a rule may require the value of a counter to be equal to a given value, or to be greater than a given value. Requiring the value of a counter to be less than a given value is not supported. The second encoding supports equality and inequality (in both directions) tests. But it requires the value of each counter to be bounded also from above.

Static analysis is needed not only to prove these requirements, but also to retrieve the meaning of counters. In Sect. 4, we introduce a generic abstract interpretation framework [9] to infer the properties of reachable states of a model. This framework is parametric with respect to a class of properties. In Sect. 5, we instantiate this framework with a relational numerical analysis aiming at relating the value of each counter to its interpretation with respect to the state of the other sites. This is used to detect and prove bounds on the range of counters.

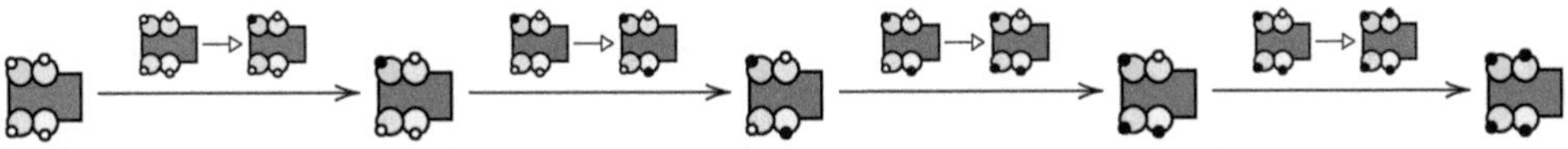

(a) Causal trace for the representation without counters.

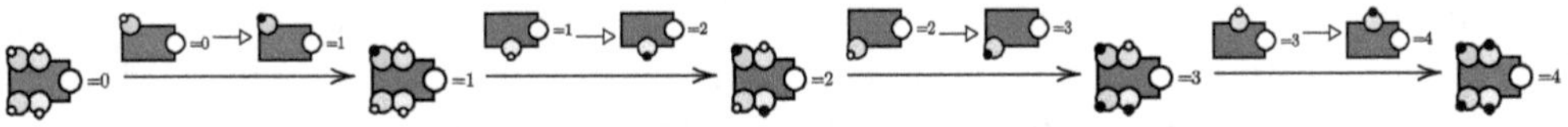


(b) Causal trace for the representation with flat counters.

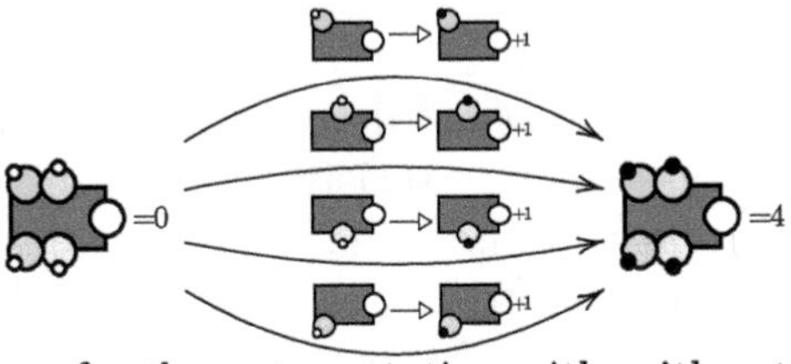


(c) Causal trace for the representation with arithmetical counters.

**Fig. 2.** Three causal traces. Each causal trace is made of a set of partially ordered computation steps. Roughly speaking, a computation step precedes another one, if the former is necessary to perform the later. Each computation step is denoted as an arrow labeled with the rule that implements it. In (a), counters are not used. Every rule tests the full configuration of the protein. At this level of representation, the $k$-th phosphorylation causally precedes the $k+1$-th one, whatever the order in which the sites have been phosphorylated. In (b), an additional site is used to record the number of phosphorylated sites in its internal state. With this encoding, the number of phosphorylated sites cannot be incremented without testing explicitly the internal state of the additional site. As a consequence, here again, at this level of representation, each phosphorylation causally depends on the previous one. In (c), we use the expressiveness of arithmetic. We use generic rules to increment the counter regardless of its current value. Hence, at this level of representation, the phosphorylation of the four sites become independent, which flatten the causal trace.

*Related Works.* Many modeling languages support arbitrary data-types. In Spatial-Kappa [41], counters encode the discrete position of agents. More generally, in Chromar [29] and in colored Petri nets [30,35], agents may be tagged with values in arbitrary auxiliary programming languages. In ML-Rules [28], agents with attributes continuously diffuse within compartments and collide to interact.

We have different motivations. Our goal is to enrich the state of proteins with some redundant information, so as to reduce the number of rules that are necessary to describe their mechanistic interactions. Also we want to avoid too expressive data-types, which could not be integrated within simulation, causality analysis, and static analysis tools, without altering their performance. For instance, analysis of colored Petri nets usually relies on unfolding them into classical ones. Unfolding rule sets into classical ones does not scale because the number of rules would become intractable. Thus we need tools which deal directly with counters.

An encoding of two-counter machines has been proposed to show that most problems in Kappa are undecidable [19, 34]. We represent counters the same way in our first encoding, but we provide atomic implementation for more primitives.

The number of isomorphic classes of connected components that may occur in Kappa models during simulation is usually huge (if not infinite), which prevents from using agent-centric approaches [4]. For instance, one of the first non-toy model written in Kappa was involving more than $10^{19}$ kinds of bio-molecular complexes [16, 26]. Kappa follows a rule-centric approach which allows for the description and the execution of models independently from the number of potential complexes. Also, Kappa disallows to describe diffusion of molecules. Instead the state of the system is assumed to satisfy the well-mixed assumption. This provides efficient ways to represent and update the distribution of potential computation steps, along a simulation [6, 17].

Equivalent sites [3] or hyperlinks [31] offer promising solutions to extend the decision procedures to extract minimal causal traces in the case of counters, but the rigidity of graphs is lost. Our encodings rely neither on the use of equivalent sites, nor on expanding the rules into more refined and more numerous ones. Hence our encodings preserve the efficiency of the simulation.

Our analysis is based on the use of affine relationships [32]. It relates counter values to the state of the other variables. Such relationships look like the ones that help understanding and proving the correctness of semaphores [20, 21]. We use the decision procedure that is described in [23, 24] to deduce bounds on the values of counters from the affine relationships. The cost of each atomic computation is cubic with respect to the number of variables. Abstract multi-sets [27, 38] may succeed in expressing the properties of interest, but they require a parameter setting a bound on the values that can abstract precisely. In practice, their time-cost is exponential as soon as this bound is not chosen big enough. Our abstraction has an infinite height. It uses widening [11] and reduction [12] to discover the bounds of interest automatically. Octagons [36, 37] have a cubic complexity, but they cannot express the properties involving more than two variables which are required in our context. Polyhedra [13] express all the properties needed for an exponential time-cost in practice.

## 2 Kappa

In this section, we enrich the syntax and the operational semantics of Kappa so as to cope with counters. We focus on the single push-out (SPO) semantics.

### 2.1 Signature

Firstly we define the signature of a model.

**Definition 1 (signature).** *The signature of a model is defined as a tuple* $\Sigma = (\Sigma_{ag}, \Sigma_{site}, \Sigma_{int}, \Sigma_{ag\text{-}st}^{int}, \Sigma_{ag\text{-}st}^{lnk}, \Sigma_{ag\text{-}st}^{\$}, Prop_{\$}, Update_{\$})$ *where:*

1. *$\Sigma_{ag}$ is a finite set of agent types,*
2. *$\Sigma_{site}$ is a finite set of site identifiers,*
3. *$\Sigma_{int}$ is a finite set of internal state identifiers,*
4. *$\Sigma^{lnk}_{ag\text{-}st}$, $\Sigma^{int}_{ag\text{-}st}$, and $\Sigma^{\$}_{ag\text{-}st}$ are three site maps (from $\Sigma_{ag}$ into $\wp(\Sigma_{site})$)*
5. *$Prop_{\$}$ is a potentially infinite set of non-empty subsets of $\mathbb{Z}$,*
6. *$Update_{\$}$ is a potentially infinite set of functions from $\mathbb{Z}$ to $\mathbb{Z}$ containing the identity function.*

*For every $G \in Prop_{\$}$, we assume that for every function $f \in Update_{\$}$, the set $\{f(k) \mid k \in G\}$ belongs to the set $Prop_{\$}$, and that for every element $k \in G$, the set $\{k\}$ belongs to the set $Prop_{\$}$ as well.*

Agent types in $\Sigma_{ag}$ denote the agents of interest, the different kinds of proteins for instance. A site identifier in $\Sigma_{site}$ represents an identified locus for a capability of interaction. Each agent type $A \in \Sigma_{ag}$ is associated with a set of sites $\Sigma^{int}_{ag\text{-}st}(A)$ with an internal state (i.e. a property), a set of sites $\Sigma^{lnk}_{ag\text{-}st}(A)$ which may be linked, and a set of sites $\Sigma^{\$}_{ag\text{-}st}(A)$ with a counter. We assume without any loss of generality that the three sets $\Sigma^{lnk}_{ag\text{-}st}(A)$, $\Sigma^{int}_{ag\text{-}st}(A)$, and $\Sigma^{\$}_{ag\text{-}st}(A)$ are disjoint pairwise. The set $Prop_{\$}$ contains the set of valid conditions that may be checked on the value of counters, whereas the set $Update_{\$}$ contains all the possible update functions for the value of counters. We assume that every singleton that is included in a valid condition is a valid condition as well. In this way, a valid condition may be refined to a fully specified value. Additionally, the image of a valid condition is required to be valid, so that the post-condition obtained by applying an update function to a valid precondition, is valid as well.

*Example 1 (running example). We define the signature for our case study as the tuple $(\Sigma_{ag}, \Sigma_{site}, \Sigma_{int}, \Sigma^{int}_{ag\text{-}st}, \Sigma^{lnk}_{ag\text{-}st}, \Sigma^{\$}_{ag\text{-}st}, Prop_{\$}, Update_{\$})$ where:*

1. *$\Sigma_{ag} := \{P\}$;*
2. *$\Sigma_{site} := \{a, b, c, d, x\}$;*
3. *$\Sigma_{int} := \{\circ, \bullet\}$;*
4. *$\Sigma^{int}_{ag\text{-}st} := [P \mapsto \{a, b, c, d\}]$;*
5. *$\Sigma^{lnk}_{ag\text{-}st} := [P \mapsto \emptyset]$;*
6. *$\Sigma^{\$}_{ag\text{-}st} := [P \mapsto \{x\}]$;*
7. *$Prop_{\$}$ is the set of all the convex parts of $\mathbb{Z}$;*
8. *$Update_{\$}$ contains the function mapping each integer $n \in \mathbb{Z}$ to its successor, and the function mapping each integer $n \in \mathbb{Z}$ to its predecessor.*

*The agent type $P$ denotes the only kind of proteins. It has four sites $a$, $b$, $c$, $d$ carrying an internal state and one site $x$ carrying a counter.* □

Until the rest of the paper, we assume given a signature $\Sigma$.

## 2.2 Site-Graphs

Site-graphs describe both patterns and chemical mixtures. Their nodes are typed agents with some sites which may carry internal and binding states, and counters.

(a) $G_1$. (b) $G_2$. (c) $G_3$. (d) $G_4$.

**Fig. 3.** Four site-graphs $G_1$, $G_2$, $G_3$, and $G_4$.

**Definition 2 (site-graph).** *A site-graph is a tuple $G = (\mathcal{A}, type, \mathcal{S}, \mathcal{L}, p\kappa, c\kappa)$ where:*

1. *$\mathcal{A}$ is a finite set of agents,*
2. *$type : \mathcal{A} \to \Sigma_{ag}$ is a function mapping each agent to its type,*
3. *$\mathcal{S}$ is a set of sites satisfying the following property:*

$$\mathcal{S} \subseteq \{(n,i) \mid n \in \mathcal{A}, i \in \Sigma_{ag\text{-}st}(type(n))\},$$

4. *$\mathcal{L}$ maps the set:*

$$\{(n,i) \in \mathcal{S} \mid i \in \Sigma^{lnk}_{ag\text{-}st}(type(n))\}$$

*to the set:*

$$\{(n,i) \in \mathcal{S} \mid i \in \Sigma^{lnk}_{ag\text{-}st}(type(n))\} \cup \{\dashv, -\},$$

*such that:*
   *(a) for any site $(n,i) \in \mathcal{S}$, we have $\mathcal{L}(n,i) \neq (n,i)$;*
   *(b) for any two sites $(n,i), (n',i') \in \mathcal{S}$, we have $(n',i') = \mathcal{L}(n,i)$ if and only if $(n,i) = \mathcal{L}(n',i')$;*
5. *$p\kappa$ maps the set $\{(n,i) \in \mathcal{S} \mid i \in \Sigma^{int}_{ag\text{-}st}(type(n))\}$ to the set $\Sigma_{int}$;*
6. *$c\kappa$ maps the set $\{(n,i) \in \mathcal{S} \mid i \in \Sigma^{\$}_{ag\text{-}st}(type(n))\}$ to the set $Prop_{\$}$.*

For a site-graph $G$, we write as $\mathcal{A}_G$ its set of agents, $type_G$ its typing function, $\mathcal{S}_G$ its set of sites, and $\mathcal{L}_G$ its set of links. Given a site-graph $G$, we write as $\mathcal{S}^{lnk}_G$ (resp. $\mathcal{S}^{int}_G$, resp. $\mathcal{S}^{\$}_G$) its set of binding sites (resp. property sites, resp. counters) that is to say the set of the sites $(n,i)$ such that $i \in \Sigma^{lnk}_{ag\text{-}st}(type_G(n))$ (resp. $i \in \Sigma^{int}_{ag\text{-}st}(type_G(n))$, resp. $i \in \Sigma^{\$}_{ag\text{-}st}(type_G(n))$).

Let us consider a binding site $(n,i) \in \mathcal{S}^{lnk}_G$. Whenever $\mathcal{L}_G(n,i) = \dashv$, the site $(n,i)$ is free. Various levels of information may be given about the sites that are bound. Whenever $\mathcal{L}_G(n,i) = -$, the site $(n,i)$ is bound to an unspecified site. Whenever $\mathcal{L}_G(n,i) = (n',i')$ (and hence $\mathcal{L}_G(n',i') = (n,i)$), the sites $(n,i)$ and $(n',i')$ are bound together.

A *chemical mixture* is a site-graph in which the state of each site is fully specified. Formally, a site-graph $G$ is a chemical mixture, if and only if, the three following properties:

1. the set $\mathcal{S}_G$ is equal to the set $\{(n,i) \mid n \in \mathcal{A}_G,\ i \in \Sigma_{ag\text{-}st}(type_G(n))\}$;
2. every binding site is free or bound to another binding site (i. e. for every $(n,i) \in \mathcal{S}_G \cap \Sigma^{lnk}_{ag\text{-}st}(type_G(n))$, $\mathcal{L}_G(n,i) \neq -$);

3. every counter has a single value (i. e. for every $(n,i) \in \Sigma^{\$}_{ag\text{-}st}$, $c\kappa_G(n,i)$ is a singleton);

are satisfied.

*Example 2 (running example). In Fig. 3, we give a graphical representation of the four site-graphs, $G_1$, $G_2$, $G_3$, and $G_4$ that are defined as follows:*

1. (a) $\mathcal{A}_{G_1} = \{1\}$,
   (b) $type_{G_1} = [1 \mapsto P]$,
   (c) $\mathcal{S}_{G_1} = \{(1,a),(1,x)\}$,
   (d) $\mathcal{L}_{G_1} = \emptyset$,
   (e) $p\kappa_{G_1} = [(1,a) \mapsto \circ]$,
   (f) $c\kappa_{G_1} = [(1,x) \mapsto \{k \in \mathbb{Z} \mid k \leq 2\}]$;
2. (a) $\mathcal{A}_{G_2} = \{1\}$,
   (b) $type_{G_2} = [1 \mapsto P]$,
   (c) $\mathcal{S}_{G_2} = \{(1,x)\}$,
   (d) $\mathcal{L}_{G_2} = \emptyset$,
   (e) $p\kappa_{G_2} = []$,
   (f) $c\kappa_{G_2} = [(1,x) \mapsto \{k \in \mathbb{Z} \mid k \leq 2\}]$;
3. (a) $\mathcal{A}_{G_3} = \{1\}$,
   (b) $type_{G_3} = [1 \mapsto P]$,
   (c) $\mathcal{S}_{G_3} = \{(1,a),(1,x)\}$,
   (d) $\mathcal{L}_{G_3} = \emptyset$,
   (e) $p\kappa_{G_3} = [(1,a) \mapsto \bullet]$,
   (f) $c\kappa_{G_3} = [(1,x) \mapsto \{k \in \mathbb{Z} \mid k \leq 3\}]$;
4. (a) $\mathcal{A}_{G_4} = \{1\}$,
   (b) $type_{G_4} = [1 \mapsto P]$,
   (c) $\mathcal{S}_{G_4} = \{(1,a),(1,b),(1,c),(1,d),(1,x)\}$,
   (d) $\mathcal{L}_{G_4} = \emptyset$,
   (e) $p\kappa_{G_4} = [(1,a) \mapsto \circ, (1,b) \mapsto \bullet, (1,c) \mapsto \bullet, (1,d) \mapsto \circ]$,
   (f) $c\kappa_{G_4} = [(1,x) \mapsto \{2\}]$;

*The white site on the side of proteins is always the site $x$. The other sites, starting from the top-left one denote the sites $a$, $b$, $c$, and $d$ clockwise.* □

## 2.3 Sliding Embeddings

In classical Kappa, two site-graphs may be related by structure-preserving injections, which are called embeddings. Here, we extend their definition to cope with counters. There are two main issues: a rule may require the value of a given counter to belong to a non-singleton set; also updating counters may involve arithmetic computations. The smaller the set of the potential values for a counter is, the more information we have. Thus, embeddings may map the potential values of a given counter into a subset. In order to cope with update functions, we equip embeddings with some arithmetic functions which explain how to get from the value of the counter in the source of the embedding to its value in the target. This way, our embeddings not only define instances of site-graphs, but they also contain the information to compute the values of counters.

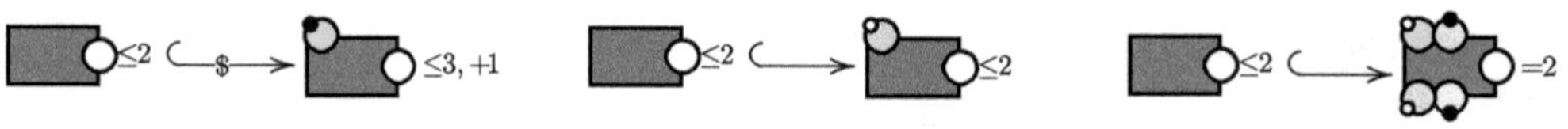


(a) A sliding embedding. (b) A pure embedding. (c) A pure embedding.

**Fig. 4.** Three sliding embeddings from the $G_2$ respectively into the site-graphs $G_3$, $G_1$, and $G_4$. Only the second and the third embeddings are pure.

**Definition 3 (sliding embedding).** *A* sliding embedding $h : G \overset{\$}{\hookrightarrow} H$ *from a site-graph $G$ into a site-graph $H$ is a pair $(h_e, h_\$)$ where $h_e$ is a function of agents $h_e : \mathcal{A}_G \to \mathcal{A}_H$ and $h_\$$ is a function mapping the counters of the site-graph $G$ to update functions $h_\$ : \mathcal{S}^\$_G \to Update_\$$ such that for all agent identifiers $m$, $n$, $n' \in \mathcal{A}_G$ and for all site identifiers $i \in \Sigma_{ag\text{-}st}(type_G(n))$, $i' \in \Sigma_{ag\text{-}st}(type_G(n'))$, the following properties are satisfied:*

1. *if $m \neq n$, then $h_e(m) \neq h_e(n)$;*
2. *$type_G(n) = type_H(h_e(n))$;*
3. *if $(n,i) \in \mathcal{S}_G$, then $(h_e(n), i) \in \mathcal{S}_H$;*
4. *if $(n,i) \in \mathcal{S}^{lnk}_G$ and $\mathcal{L}_G(n,i) = (n', i')$, then $\mathcal{L}_H(h_e(n), i) = (h_e(n'), i')$;*
5. *if $(n,i) \in \mathcal{S}^{lnk}_G$ and $\mathcal{L}_G(n,i) = \dashv$, then $\mathcal{L}_H(h_e(n), i) = \dashv$;*
6. *if $(n,i) \in \mathcal{S}^{lnk}_G$ and $\mathcal{L}_G(n,i) = -$, then $\mathcal{L}_H(h_e(n), i) \in \{-\} \cup \mathcal{S}_H$;*
7. *if $(n,i) \in \mathcal{S}^{int}_G$ and $p\kappa_G(n,i) = \iota$, then $p\kappa_H(h_e(n), i) = \iota$;*
8. *if $(n,i) \in \mathcal{S}^\$_G$, then $c\kappa_H(h(n), i) \subseteq \{h_\$(k) \mid k \in c\kappa_G(n,i)\}$.*

Two sliding embeddings between site-graphs, from $E$ to $F$, and from $F$ to $G$ respectively, compose to form a sliding embedding from $E$ to $G$ (functions compose pair-wise). A sliding embedding $(h_e, h_\$)$ such that $h_\$$ maps each counter to the identity function is called a *pure embedding.* A pure embedding from $E$ to $F$ is denoted as $E \hookrightarrow F$. Pure embeddings compose. Two site-graphs $E$ and $F$ are isomorphic if and only if there exist a pure embedding from $E$ to $F$ and a pure embedding from $F$ to $E$. A pure embedding between two isomorphic site-graphs is called an isomorphism. When it exists, the unique pure embedding $(h_e, h_\$)$ from a site-graph $E$ into the site-graph $F$ such that $\mathcal{A}_E \subseteq \mathcal{A}_F$ and $h_e(n) = n$ for every agent $n \in \mathcal{A}_E$, is called the *inclusion* from $E$ to $F$ and is denoted as $i_{E,F}$ or as $E \overset{\subseteq}{\hookrightarrow} F$. In such a case, we say that the site-graph $E$ is included in the site-graph $F$. The inclusion from a site-graph into itself always exists and is called an identity embedding.

*Example 3 (running example). We show in Fig. 4 three sliding embeddings from the site-graph $G_2$ respectively into the site-graphs $G_3$, $G_1$, and $G_4$. The first of these three sliding embeddings is assumed to increment the value of the counter of the site $x$. The last two embeddings are pure.* □

Let $L$, $R$, and $D$ be three site-graphs, such that $R$ is included in $D$, and let $\phi$ be a sliding embedding from $L$ into $D$. Then there exist a site graph $D'$ that is included in $L$ and a sliding embedding $\psi$ from $D'$ to $R$ such that $i_{R,D}\psi = \phi i_{D',L}$ and such that $D'$ is *maximal* (w.r.t. inclusion among site-graphs) for this property. The pair $(D', i_{D',L}, \psi)$ is called the *pull-pack* of the pair $(\phi, i_{R,D})$.

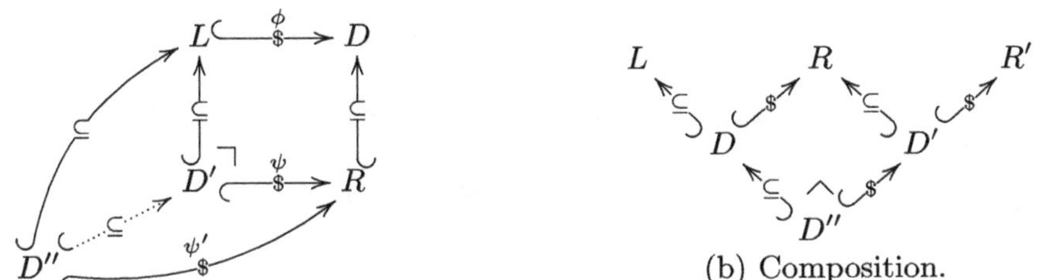

(a) Pull-back.

(b) Composition.

**Fig. 5.** Composition of partial sliding embeddings.

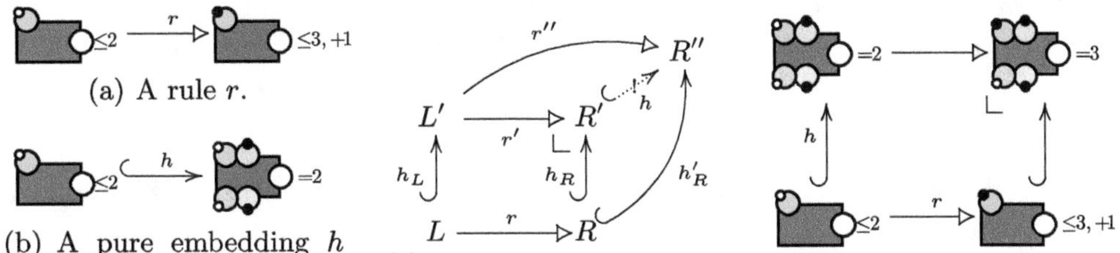

(a) A rule $r$.

(b) A pure embedding $h$ from the lhs of the rule $r$ to the site-graph $G_4$.

(c) Universal construction

(d) Application of the rule $r$ on the site-graph $G_4$.

**Fig. 6.** Rule application.

Let $L$, $R$, and $D$ be three site-graphs such that $D$ is included in $L$. A *partial sliding embedding* from $L$ into $R$ is defined as a pair made of the inclusion $i_{D,L}$ and a sliding embedding from $D$ to $R$. Sliding embeddings may be considered as partial sliding embeddings with the inclusion as the identity embedding. Partial sliding embeddings compose by the means of a pull-back (e.g. see Fig. 5(b)).

### 2.4 Rules

Rules represent transformations between site-graphs. For the sake of simplicity, we only use a fragment of Kappa (we assume here that there are no *side effects*). Rules may break and create bonds between pairs of sites, change the properties of sites, update the value of counters. They may also create and remove agents. When an agent is created, all its sites must be fully specified: binding sites may be either free, or bound to a specific site, and the value of counters must be singletons. So as to ensure that there is no side-effect when an agent is removed, we also assume that the binding sites of removed agents are fully specified. These requirements are formalized as follows:

**Definition 4 (rule).** *A* rule *is a partial sliding embedding* $L \twoheadleftarrow\supseteq\hookleftarrow D \xhookrightarrow[\$]{(h_e,h_\$)} R$ *such that:*

1. *(modified agents) for all agents* $n \in \mathcal{A}_D$ *such that* $h_e(n) \in \mathcal{A}_R$ *and for every site identifier* $i \in \Sigma_{site}(type_L(n))$,

(a) *the site* $(n,i)$ *belongs to the set* $\mathcal{S}_L$ *if and only if* $(h_e(n),i)$ *belongs to set* $\mathcal{S}_R$*;*
(b) *if the site* $(n,i)$ *belongs to the set* $\mathcal{S}_L^{lnk}$*, then either* $\mathcal{L}_L(n,i) = -$ *and* $\mathcal{L}_R(h_e(n),i) = -$*, or* $\mathcal{L}_L(n,i) \in \mathcal{S}_L^{lnk} \cup \{\dashv\}$ *and* $\mathcal{L}_R(h_e(n),i) \in \mathcal{S}_R^{lnk} \cup \{\dashv\}$*;*
(c) *if the site* $(n,i)$ *belongs to the set* $\mathcal{S}_L^{\$}$*, then the sets* $c\kappa_R(h_e(n),i)$ *and* $\{h_\$(v) \mid v \in c\kappa_L(n,i)\}$ *are equal.*

2. *(removed agents) for all agents* $n \in \mathcal{A}_L$ *such that* $n \notin \mathcal{A}_D$*, for every site identifier* $i \in \Sigma_{ag\text{-}st}^{lnk}(type_L(n))$*,* $(n,i) \in \mathcal{S}_L^{lnk}$ *and* $\mathcal{L}_L(n,i) \in \mathcal{S}_L^{lnk} \cup \{\dashv\}$*.*
3. *(created agents) for all agents* $n \in \mathcal{A}_R$ *for which there exists no* $n' \in \mathcal{A}_D$ *such that* $n = h_e(n')$*, and for every site identifier* $i \in \Sigma_{site}(type_R(n))$*,*
   (a) *the site* $(n,i)$ *belongs to the set* $\mathcal{S}_R$*;*
   (b) *if the site* $(n,i)$ *belongs to the set* $\mathcal{S}_R^{lnk}$*, then the binding state* $\mathcal{L}_R(n,i)$ *belong to the set* $\mathcal{S}_R^{lnk} \cup \{\dashv\}$*;*
   (c) *if the site* $(n,i)$ *belongs to the set* $\mathcal{S}_R^{\$}$*, then* $c\kappa_R(n,i)$ *is a singleton.*

In Definition 4, each agent that is *modified* occurs on both hand sides of a rule. Constraint 1a ensures that they document the same sites. Constraint 1b ensures that, if the binding state of a site is modified, then it has to be fully specified (either free, or bound to a specific site) in both hand sides of the rule. Constraint 1c ensures that the post-condition associated to a counter is the direct image of its precondition by its update function. Constraint 2 ensures that the agents that are *removed* have their binding sites fully specified. Constraint 3a ensures that, in the agents that are *created*, all the sites are documented. Beside, constraint 3b requires that the state of their binding site is either free or bound to a specific site. Constraint 3c ensures that their counters have a single value.

An example of a rule is given in Fig. 6(a).

A rule $L \xleftarrow{\supseteq} D \xhookrightarrow{\$} R$ is usually denoted as $L \twoheadrightarrow R$ (leaving the common region and the sliding embedding implicit). Rules are applied to site-graphs via pure embeddings using the *single push-out* construction [22].

**Definition 5 (rule application** [14]**).** *Let* $r$ *be a rule* $L \twoheadrightarrow R$*,* $L'$ *be a site-graph, and* $h_L$ *be a pure embedding from* $L$ *to* $L'$*. Then, there exists a rule* $r' : L' \twoheadrightarrow R'$ *and a pure embedding* $h_R : R \hookrightarrow R'$ *such that the following properties are satisfied (e. g. see Fig. 6(c)):*

1. $h_R r = r' h_L$*;*
2. *for all rules* $r''$ *between the site-graph* $L'$ *and a site-graph* $R''$ *and all embeddings* $h'_R$ *from* $R$ *into* $R''$ *such that* $h'_R r = r'' h_L$*, there exists a unique pure embedding* $h$ *from* $R'$ *into* $R''$ *such that* $r'' = h r'$ *and* $h'_R = h h_R$*.*

*Moreover, whenever the site-graph* $L'$ *is a chemical mixture, the site-graph* $R'$ *is a chemical mixture as well.*

We write $L' \xrightarrow{r} R'$ for a transition from the state $L'$ into the state $R'$ via an application of a rule $r$. Usually transition labels also mention the pure embedding ($h_L$ here), but we omit it since we do not use it in the rest of the paper.

*Example 4 (running example). An example of rule application is depicted in Fig. 6. We consider the rule r that takes a protein with the site a unphosphorylated and a counter with a value at least equal to 2, and that phosphorylates the site a while incrementing the counter by 1 (e. g. see Fig. 6(a)). Note that the update function of the counter is written next to its post-condition in the right hand side of the rule. We apply the rule to a protein with the sites b and c phosphorylated, the site d unphosphorylated, and the counter equal to 2 (e. g. see Fig. 6(b)). The result is a protein with the sites a, b, and c phosphorylated, the site d unphosphorylated and the counter equal to 3 (e. g. see Fig. 6(d)).* □

*A model $\mathcal{M}$ over a given signature $\Sigma$* is defined as the pair $(G_0, \mathcal{R})$ where $G_0$ is a chemical mixture, representing the initial state, and $\mathcal{R}$ is a set of rules. Each rule is associated with a functional rate which maps each potential tuple of values for the counters of the left hand side of the rule to a non negative real number. We write $\mathcal{C}(\mathcal{M})$ for the set of states obtained from $G_0$ by applying a potentially empty sequence of rules in $\mathcal{R}$.

## 3 Encoding Counters

In this section, we introduce two encodings from Kappa with counters into Kappa without counters. As explained in Sect. 1, our goal is to preserve the rigidity of site-graphs and to avoid the blow-up of the number of rules in the target model. This is mandatory to preserve the good performances of the Kappa simulator. Both encodings rely on syntactic restrictions over the preconditions and the update functions that may be applied to counters and on semantics ones about the potential range of counters. In Sects. 4 and 5, we provide a static analysis to check whether, or not, these semantics assumptions hold.

### 3.1 Encoding the Value of Counters as Unbounded Chains of Agents

In this encoding, each counter is bound to a chain of fictitious agents the length of which minus 1 denotes the value of the counter (another encoding not requiring the subtraction is possible but it would require side-effects). Encoding counters as chains of agents has already been used in the implementation of two-counter machines in Kappa [19,34]. We slightly extend these works to implement more atomic operations over counters. We assume that the value of counters is bounded from below. For the sake of simplicity, we assume that counters range in $\mathbb{N}$, but arbitrary lower bounds may be considered by shifting each value accordingly. We denote by $\Omega_1$ the set of the site-graphs that have a counter with a negative value. They are considered as erroneous states, since they may not be encoded with chains of agents.

Only two kinds of guards are handled. A rule may require the value of a counter to be equal to a given number or that the value of a counter is greater than a given number. Rules testing whether a value is less than a given number

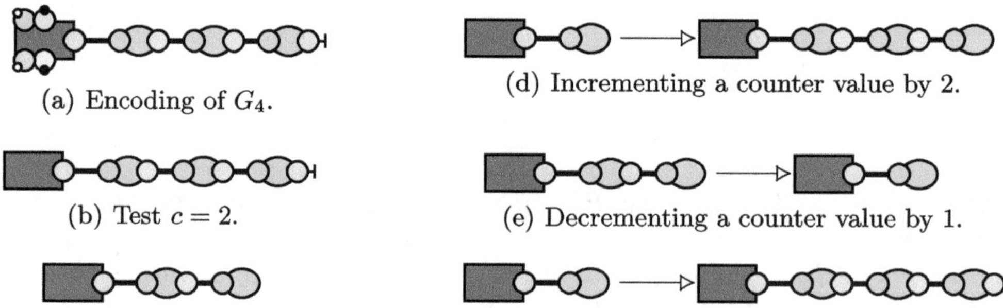

(a) Encoding of $G_4$.

(b) Test $c = 2$.

(c) Test $c \geq 1$.

(d) Incrementing a counter value by 2.

(e) Decrementing a counter value by 1.

(f) Assigning 2 to a counter.

**Fig. 7.** Encoding the value of counters as unbounded chains of agents.

require unfolding each such rule into several ones (one per potential value). Also when the rate of a rule depends on the value of some counters, we unfold each rule according to the value of these counters, so that the rate of each unfolded rule is a constant (the Kappa simulator requires all the instances of a given rule in a given simulation state to have the same rate, for efficiency concerns). For update functions, we only consider constant functions and the functions that increase/decrease the value of counters by a fixed value. Testing whether the value of a counter is equal to (resp. greater than) $n$, can be done by requiring the corresponding chain to contain exactly (resp. at least) $n+1$ agents (e. g. see Figs. 7(b) and (c)). Incrementing (resp. decrementing) the value of a counter is modeled by inserting (resp. removing) agents at the beginning its chain (e. g. see Fig. 7(d), resp. Fig. 7(e)). Setting a counter to a fixed value, requires to detach its full chain in order to create a new one of the appropriate length (e. g. see Fig. 7(f)). In such a case, the former chain remains as a junk. Thus the state of the model must be understood up to insertion of junk agents. We introduce the function $gc_1$ that removes every chain of spurious agents not bound to any counter. We denote as $[\![G]\!]_1^g$ (resp. $[\![r]\!]_1^r$) the encoding of a site-graph $G$ (resp. of a rule $r$).

### 3.2 Encoding the Value of Counters as Circular Lists of Agents

In this second encoding, each counter is bound to a ring of agents. Each such agent has three binding sites *zero*, *pred*, and *next*, and a property site *value* which may be activated, or not. In a ring, agents are connected circularly through their site *pred* and *next*. Exactly one agent per ring is bound to a counter and exactly one agent per ring has the site *value* activated. The value of the counter is encoded by the distance between the agent bound to the counter and the agent that is activated, scanning the agents by following the direction given by the site *next* of each agent (clock-wisely in the graphical representation). We have to consider that counter values are bounded from above and below. Without any loss of generality, we assume that the length of each ring is the same, that is to say that counters range from 0 to $n-1$, for a given $n \in \mathbb{N}$. We denote by $\Omega_2$ the set of the site-graphs with at least one counter not satisfying these bounds.

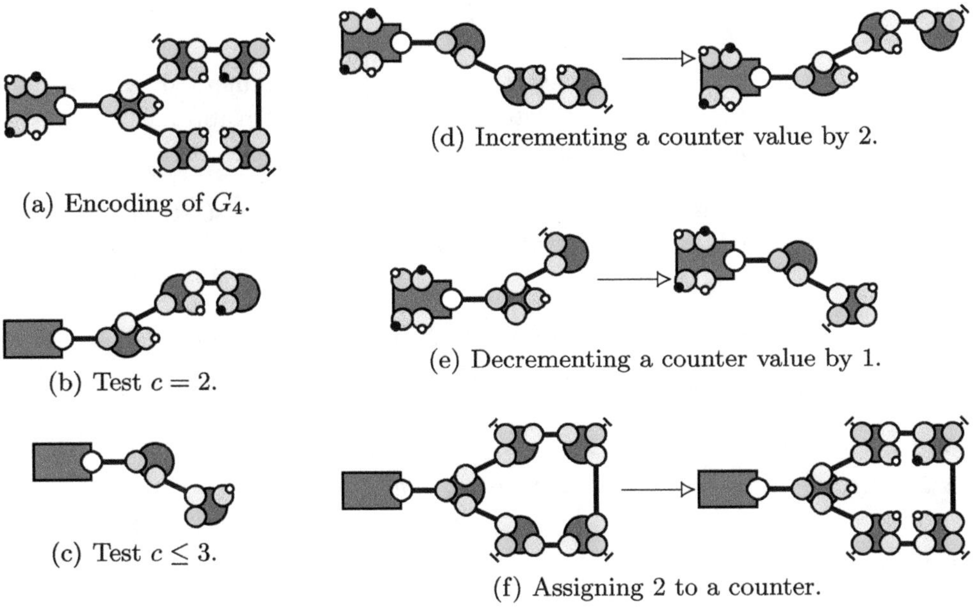

(a) Encoding of $G_4$.

(b) Test $c = 2$.

(c) Test $c \leq 3$.

(d) Incrementing a counter value by 2.

(e) Decrementing a counter value by 1.

(f) Assigning 2 to a counter.

**Fig. 8.** Encoding the value of counters as circular lists of agents.

Compared to the first encoding, this one may additionally cope with testing that a counter has a value less than a given constant without having to unfold the rule. Both encodings may deal with the same update functions. Testing whether a counter is equal to a value is done by requiring that the activated agent is at the appropriate distance of the agent that is connected to the counter (e. g. see Fig. 8(b)). It is worth noting that the intermediary agents are required to be not activated. This is not mandatory for the soundness of the encoding, this is an optimization that helps the simulator for detecting early that no embedding may associate a given agent of the left hand side of a rule to a given agent in the current state of the system. Inequalities are handled by checking that enough agents starting from the one that is connected to the counter and in the direction specified by the direction of the inequality, are not activated (e. g. see Fig. 8(c)). Incrementing/decrementing the value of a counter is modeled by making counter glide along the ring (e. g. see Figs. 8(d) and (e)). Special care has to be taken to ensure that the activated agent never crosses the agent linked to the counter (which would cause a numerical wrap-around). Assigning a given value to a counter requires to entirely remove the ring and to replace it with a fresh one (e. g. see Fig. 8(f)). It may be efficiently implemented without memory allocation. As in the first encoding, when the rate of a rule depends on the value of some counters, we unfold each rule according to the value of these counters, so that the rate of each unfolded rule is constant.

We introduce the function $gc_2$ as the identity function over site-graphs (there are no junk agent in this encoding). We denote as $[\![G]\!]^g_2$ (resp. $[\![r]\!]^r_2$) the encoding without counter of a site-graph $G$ (resp. of a rule $r$).

### 3.3 Correspondence

The following theorem states that, whenever there is no numerical overflow and providing that junk agents are neglected, the semantics of Kappa with counters and the semantics of their encodings are in bisimulation.

**Theorem 1 (correspondence).** *Let $i$ be either 1 or 2. Let $G$ be a fully specified site-graph such that $G \notin \Omega_i$ and $r$ be a rule. Both following properties are satisfied:*

1. *whenever there exists a site-graph $G'$ such that $G \xrightarrow{r} G'$ and $G' \notin \Omega_i$, there exists a site-graph $G'_{\$}$, such that $[\![G]\!]_i^g \xrightarrow{[\![r]\!]_i^r} G'_{\$}$ and $[\![G']\!]_i^g = gc_i(G'_{\$})$;*
2. *whenever there exists a site-graph $G'_{\$}$ such that $[\![G]\!]_i^g \xrightarrow{[\![r]\!]_i^r} G'_{\$}$, there exists a site-graph $G'$ such that $G \xrightarrow{r} G'$, $G' \notin \Omega_i$, and $[\![G']\!]_i^g = gc_i(G'_{\$})$.*

### 3.4 Benchmarks

The experimental evaluation of the impact of both encodings to the performance of the simulator KaSim [6,17] is presented in Fig. 9. We focus on the example that has been presented in Sect. 1. We plot the number of events that are simulated per second of CPU. For the sake of comparison, we also provide the simulation efficiency of the simulator NFSim [40] on the models written in BNGL with equivalent sites (with a linear number of rules only).

We notice that, with KaSim, the direct approach (without counter) is the most efficient when there are less than 9 phosphorylation sites. We explain this overhead, by the fact that each encoding utilizes spurious agents that have to be allocated in memory and relies on rules with bigger left hand sides. Nevertheless this overhead is reasonable if we consider the gain in conciseness in the description of the models. The versions of models with counters rely on a linear number of rules, which make models easier to read, document, and update. For more phosphorylation sites, simulation time for models written without counters blow up very quickly, due to the large number of rules. The simulation of the models with counters scales much better for both encodings.

Models can be concisely described in BNGL without using counters, by the means of equivalent sites. Each version of the model uses $n$ indistinguishable sites and only a linear number of rules is required. However, detecting the potential applications of rules in the case of equivalent sites relies on the sub-graph isomorphism problem on general graphs, which prevent the approach to scale to large value of $n$. We observe that the efficiency of NFSim on this family of examples is not as good as the ones of KaSim (whatever which of the three modeling methods is used). We also observe a very quick deterioration of the performances starting at $n$ equal to 5.

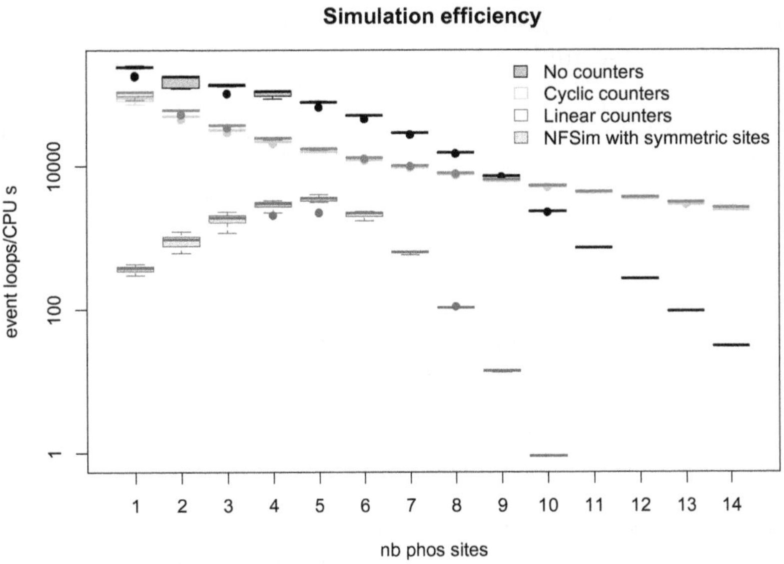


**Fig. 9.** Efficiency of the simulation for the example in Sect. 1 with $n$ ranging between 1 and 14. We test the simulator KaSim with a version of the models written without counters and versions of the models according to both encodings (including the $n$ phosphorylation sites). For the sake of comparison, we also compare with the efficiency of the simulator NFSim with the same model but written in BNGL by the means of equivalent sites. For each version of the model and each simulation method, we run 15 simulations of $10^5$ events on an initial state made of 100 agents and we plot the number of computation steps computed in average per second of CPU on a log scale. Every simulation has been performed on 4 processors: Intel(R) Xeon(R) CPU E5-2609 0 @ 2.40 GHz 126 GB of RAM, running ubuntu 18.04.

## 4 Generic Abstraction of Reachable States

So far, we have provided two encodings to compile Kappa with counters into Kappa without counters. These encodings are sound under some assumptions over the range of counters. Now we propose a static analysis not only to check that these conditions are satisfied, but also to infer the meaning of the counters (in our case study, that they are equal to the number of phosphorylated sites).

Firstly, we provide a generic abstraction to capture the properties of the states that a Kappa model may potentially take. Our abstraction is parametric with respect to the class of properties. It will be instantiated in Sect. 5. Our analysis is not complete: not all the properties of the program are discovered; nevertheless, the result is sound: all the properties that are captured, are correct.

### 4.1 Collecting Semantics

Let $\mathcal{Q}$ be the set of all the site-graphs. We are interested in the set $\mathcal{C}(\mathcal{M})$ of all the states that a model $\mathcal{M} = (G_0, \mathcal{R})$ may take in 0, 1, or more computation steps. This is the collecting semantics [7]. By [33], it may be expressed as the least fixpoint of the $\cup$-complete endomorphism $\mathbb{F}$ on the complete lattice $\wp(\mathcal{Q})$ that is defined as $\mathbb{F}(X) = \{G_0\} \cup \{q' \mid \exists q \in X, r \in \mathcal{R} \text{ such that } q \xrightarrow{r} q'\}$. By [42], the collecting semantics is also equal to the meet of all the post-fixpoints of the function $\mathbb{F}$ (i. e. $\mathcal{C}(\mathcal{M}) = \bigcap\{X \in \wp(\mathcal{Q}) \mid \mathbb{F}(X) \subseteq X\}$), that is to say the strongest inductive invariant of our model that is satisfied by the initial state.

### 4.2 Generic Abstraction

The collecting semantics is usually not decidable. We use the Abstract Interpretation framework [9, 10] to compute a sound approximation of it.

**Definition 6 (abstraction).** *A tuple $\mathcal{A} = (\mathcal{Q}^\sharp, \sqsubseteq, \gamma, \sqcup, \bot, \mathcal{I}^\sharp, t^\sharp, \nabla)$ is called an abstraction when all following conditions are satisfied:*

1. *the pair $(\mathcal{Q}^\sharp, \sqsubseteq)$ is a pre-order of abstract properties;*
2. *the component $\gamma : \mathcal{Q}^\sharp \to \wp(\mathcal{Q})$ is a monotonic map (i. e. for every two abstract elements $q_1^\sharp$, $q_2^\sharp \in \mathcal{Q}^\sharp$ such that $q_1^\sharp \sqsubseteq q_2^\sharp$, we have $\gamma(q_1^\sharp) \subseteq \gamma(q_2^\sharp)$);*
3. *the component $\sqcup$ maps each finite set of abstract properties $X^\sharp \in \wp_{finite}(\mathcal{Q}^\sharp)$ to an abstract property $\sqcup(X^\sharp) \in \mathcal{Q}^\sharp$ such that for each abstract property $q^\sharp \in X^\sharp$, we have: $q^\sharp \sqsubseteq \sqcup(X^\sharp)$;*
4. *the component $\bot \in \mathcal{Q}^\sharp$ is an abstract property such that $\gamma(\bot) = \emptyset$;*
5. *the component $\mathcal{I}^\sharp$ is an element of the set $\mathcal{Q}^\sharp$ such that $\{G_0\} \subseteq \gamma(\mathcal{I}^\sharp)$;*
6. *the component $t^\sharp$ is a function mapping each pair $(q, r) \in \mathcal{Q}^\sharp \times \mathcal{R}$ to an abstract property $t^\sharp(q, r) \in \mathcal{Q}^\sharp$ such that: $\forall q^\sharp \in \mathcal{Q}^\sharp$, $\forall q \in \gamma(q^\sharp)$, $\forall r \in \mathcal{R}$, $\forall q' \in \mathcal{Q}$, we have $q' \in \gamma(t^\sharp(q^\sharp))$ whenever $q \xrightarrow{r} q'$;*
7. *the component $\nabla : \mathcal{Q}^\sharp \times \mathcal{Q}^\sharp \to \mathcal{Q}^\sharp$ satisfies both following properties:*
   *(a) $\forall q_1^\sharp$, $q_2^\sharp \in \mathcal{Q}^\sharp$, $q_1^\sharp \sqsubseteq q_1^\sharp \nabla q_2^\sharp$ and $q_2^\sharp \sqsubseteq q_1^\sharp \nabla q_2^\sharp$,*
   *(b) $\forall (q_n^\sharp)_{n\in\mathbb{N}} \in \left(\mathcal{Q}^\sharp\right)^{\mathbb{N}}$, the sequence $(q_n^\nabla)_{n\in\mathbb{N}}$ that is defined as $q_0^\nabla = q_0^\sharp$ and $q_{n+1}^\nabla = q_n^\nabla \nabla q_{n+1}^\sharp$ for every integer $n \in \mathbb{N}$, is ultimately stationary.*

The set $\mathcal{Q}^\sharp$ is an abstract domain. It captures the properties of interest, and abstracts away the others. Each property $q^\sharp \in \mathcal{Q}^\sharp$ is mapped to the set of the concrete states $\gamma(q^\sharp)$ which satisfy this property by the means of the concretization function $\gamma$. The pre-order $\sqsubseteq$ describes the amount of information which is known about the properties that we approximate. We use a pre-order to allow some concrete properties to be described by several unrelated abstract elements. The abstract union $\sqcup$ is used to gather the information described by a finite number of abstract elements. It may not necessarily compute the least upper bound of a finite set of abstract elements (this least bound may not even exist). The abstract element $\bot$ provides the basis for abstract iterations. The concretization function is strict which means that it maps the element $\bot$ to the empty set. The abstract property $\mathcal{I}^\sharp$ is satisfied by the initial state. The function $t^\sharp$ is used to mimic concrete rewriting steps in the abstract. The operator $\nabla$ is called a widening. It ensures the convergence of the analysis in finitely many iterations.

Given an abstraction $(\mathcal{Q}^\sharp, \sqsubseteq, \gamma, \sqcup, \bot, \mathcal{I}^\sharp, t^\sharp, \nabla)$, the abstract counterpart $\mathbb{F}^\sharp$ to $\mathbb{F}$ is defined as $\mathbb{F}^\sharp(q^\sharp) = \sqcup^\sharp \left(\{q^\sharp, \mathcal{I}^\sharp\} \cup \{t^\sharp(q^\sharp, r) \mid r \in \mathcal{R}\}\right)$. The function $\mathbb{F}^\sharp$ satisfies the soundness condition $\forall q^\sharp \in \mathcal{Q}^\sharp$, $[\mathbb{F} \circ \gamma](q^\sharp) \subseteq [\gamma \circ \mathbb{F}^\sharp](q^\sharp)$. Following [7], we compute a sound and decidable approximation of our abstract semantics by using the widening operator $\nabla$. The abstract iteration [10,11] of $\mathbb{F}^\sharp$ is defined by the following induction: $\mathbb{F}_0^\nabla = \bot$ and, for each integer $n \in \mathbb{N}$, $\mathbb{F}_{n+1}^\nabla = \mathbb{F}_n^\nabla$ whenever $\mathbb{F}^\sharp(\mathbb{F}_n^\nabla) \sqsubseteq \mathbb{F}_n^\nabla$, and $\mathbb{F}_{n+1}^\nabla = \mathbb{F}_n^\nabla \nabla \mathbb{F}^\sharp(\mathbb{F}_n^\nabla)$ otherwise.

**Theorem 2 (Termination and soundness).** *The abstract iteration is ultimately stationary and its limit $\mathbb{F}^\nabla$ satisfies $\mathcal{C}(\mathcal{M}) \subseteq \gamma(\mathbb{F}^\nabla)$.*

*Proof.* By construction, $\mathbb{F}^\sharp(\mathbb{F}^\nabla) \sqsubseteq \mathbb{F}^\nabla$. Since $\gamma$ is monotonic, it follows that: $\gamma(\mathbb{F}^\sharp(\mathbb{F}^\nabla)) \subseteq \gamma(\mathbb{F}^\nabla)$. Since, $\mathbb{F} \circ \gamma \dot{\subseteq} \gamma \circ \mathbb{F}^\sharp$, $\mathbb{F}(\gamma(\mathbb{F}^\nabla)) \subseteq \gamma(\mathbb{F}^\nabla)$. So $\gamma(\mathbb{F}^\nabla)$ is a post-fixpoint of $\mathbb{F}$. By [42], we have *lfp* $\mathbb{F} \subseteq \gamma(\mathbb{F}^\nabla)$. □

### 4.3 Coalescent Product

Two abstractions may be combined pair-wise to form a new one. The result is a coalescent product that defines a mutual induction over both abstractions.

**Definition 7 (coalescent product).** *The coalescent product between two abstractions $(\mathcal{Q}_1^\sharp, \sqsubseteq_1, \gamma_1, \sqcup_1, \bot_1, \mathcal{I}_1^\sharp, t_1^\sharp, \nabla_1)$ and $(\mathcal{Q}_2^\sharp, \sqsubseteq_2, \gamma_2, \sqcup_2, \bot_2, \mathcal{I}_2^\sharp, t_2^\sharp, \nabla_2)$ is defined as the tuple $(\mathcal{Q}^\sharp, \sqsubseteq, \gamma, \sqcup, \bot, \mathcal{I}^\sharp, t^\sharp, \nabla)$ where*

1. *$\mathcal{Q}^\sharp = \mathcal{Q}_1^\sharp \times \mathcal{Q}_2^\sharp$;*
2. *$\sqsubseteq$, $\sqcup$, $\bot$, and $\nabla$ are defined pair-wise;*
3. *$\gamma$ maps every pair $(q_1^\sharp, q_2^\sharp)$ to the meet $\gamma_1(q_1^\sharp) \cap \gamma_2(q_2^\sharp)$ of their respective concretization;*
4. *$\mathcal{I}^\sharp = (\mathcal{I}_1^\sharp, \mathcal{I}_2^\sharp)$;*
5. *$t^\sharp$ maps every pair $((q_1^\sharp, q_2^\sharp), r) \in \mathcal{Q}^\sharp \times \mathcal{R}$ made of a pair of abstract properties and a rule to the abstract property $(t_1^\sharp(q_1^\sharp, r), t_2^\sharp(q_2^\sharp, r))$ whenever $t_1^\sharp(q_1^\sharp, r) \neq \bot_1$ and $t_2^\sharp(q_2^\sharp, r) \neq \bot_2$, and to the pair $(\bot_1, \bot_2)$ otherwise.*

**Theorem 3 (Soundness of the coalescent product).** *The coalescent product of two abstractions is an abstraction as well.*

We notice that if either of both abstractions proves that the precondition of a rule is not satisfiable, then this rule is discarded in the other abstraction (hence the term coalescent). By mutual induction, the composite abstraction may detect which rules may be safely discarded along the iterations of the analysis.

We may now define an analysis modularly with respect to the class of considered properties. We use the coalescent product to extend the existing static analyzer KaSa [5] with a new abstraction dedicated to the range of counters.

# 5 Numerical Abstraction

Now we specialize our generic abstraction to detect and prove safe bounds to the range of counters. In general, this requires to relate the value of the counters to the state of others sites. Our approach consists in translating each protein configuration into a vector of relative numbers and in abstracting each rule by its potential effect on these vectors. We obtain an integer linear programming problem that we will solve by choosing an appropriate abstract domain.

The set of convex parts of $\mathbb{Z}$ is written as $\mathcal{I}_{\mathbb{Z}}$. We assume that guards on counters are element of $\mathcal{I}_{\mathbb{Z}}$ and that each update function either set counters to a constant value, or increment/decrement counters by a constant value.

## 5.1 Encoding States and Preconditions

We propose to translate each agent into a set of numerical constraints. A protein of type $A$ is associated with one variable $\chi_i^\lambda$ for each binding site $i$ and each binding state $\lambda$, one variable $\chi_i^\iota$ for each property site $i$ and each internal state identifier $\iota$, and one variable $val_i$ for each counter in $i$.

**Definition 8 (numerical variables).** *Let $A \in \Sigma_{ag}$ be an agent type. We define the set $\mathcal{V}ar_A$ as the set of variables $\mathcal{V}ar_A^{lnk} \cup \mathcal{V}ar_A^{int} \cup \mathcal{V}ar_A^{\$}$ where:*

1. $\mathcal{V}ar_A^{lnk} = \{\chi_i^\lambda \mid i \in \Sigma_{ag\text{-}st}^{lnk}(A), \lambda \in \{\dashv\} \cup \{(A', i') \mid A' \in \Sigma_{ag}, i' \in \Sigma_{ag\text{-}st}^{lnk}(A')\}\}$;
2. $\mathcal{V}ar_A^{int} = \{\chi_i^\iota \mid i \in \Sigma_{ag\text{-}st}^{int}(A), \iota \in \Sigma_{int}\}$;
3. $\mathcal{V}ar_A^{\$} = \{val_i \mid i \in \Sigma_{ag\text{-}st}^{\$}\}$.

Intuitively, variables of the form $\chi_i^\lambda$ (resp. $\chi_i^\iota$) take the value 1 if the binding (resp. internal) state of the site $i$ is $\lambda$ (resp. $\iota$), whereas the variables of the form $val_i$ takes the value of the counter $i$.

Each agent of type $A$ may be translated into a function mapping each variable in the set $\mathcal{V}ar_A$ into a subset of the set $\mathbb{Z}$. Such a function is called a guard.

**Definition 9 (Encoding of agents).** *Let $G$ be a site-graph and $n$ be an agent in $\mathcal{A}_G$. We denote by $A$ the type $type_G(n)$. We define as follows the function $guard_G(n)$ from the set $\mathcal{V}ar_A$ into the set $\mathcal{I}_{\mathbb{Z}}$:*

1. *$guard_G(n)(\chi_i^\dashv)$ is equal to the singleton $\{1\}$ whenever $(n,i) \in \mathcal{S}_G^{lnk}(A)$ and $\mathcal{L}_G(n,i) = \dashv$, to the singleton $\{0\}$ whenever $(n,i) \in \mathcal{S}_G^{lnk}(A)$ and $\mathcal{L}_G(n,i) \neq \dashv$, and to the set $\{0,1\}$ whenever $(n,i) \notin \mathcal{S}_G^{lnk}(A)$;*
2. *$guard_G(n)(\chi_i^{(A',i')})$ is equal to the singleton $\{1\}$ whenever $(n,i) \in \mathcal{S}_G^{lnk}(A)$ and there exists $n' \in \mathcal{A}_G$ such that both conditions $type_G(n') = A'$ and $\mathcal{L}_G(n,i) = (n',i')$ are satisfied, to the singleton $\{0\}$ whenever $(n,i) \in \mathcal{S}_G^{lnk}(A)$ and either $\mathcal{L}_G(n,i) = \dashv$, or there exist an agent identifier $n'' \in \mathcal{A}_G$ and a site name $i'' \in \Sigma_{site}$ such that $(type_G(n''), i'') \neq (A',i')$, and to the set $\{0,1\}$ whenever $(n,i) \notin \mathcal{S}_G^{lnk}(A)$ or $\mathcal{L}_G(n,i) = -$;*
3. *$guard_G(n)(\chi_i^\iota)$ is equal to the singleton $\{1\}$ whenever $(n,i) \in \mathcal{S}_G^{int}(A)$ and $p\kappa_G(n,i) = \iota$; to the singleton $\{0\}$ whenever $(n,i) \in \mathcal{S}_G^{int}(A)$ and $p\kappa_G(n,i) \neq \iota$; and to set $\{0,1\}$ whenever $(n,i) \notin \mathcal{S}_G^{int}(A)$.*

*4. $guard_G(n)(val_i)$ is equal to the set $c\kappa_G(c)$ whenever $(n,i) \in \mathcal{S}_G^{\$}$ and to the set $\mathbb{Z}$ otherwise.*

The variable $\chi_i^{\dashv}$ takes the value $\{1\}$ if we know that the site $i$ is free, the value $\{0\}$ if we know that it is bound, and the value $\{0,1\}$ if we do not know whether the site is free or not. This is the same for binding type, the variable $\chi_i^{(A',i')}$ takes the value $\{1\}$ if we know that the site is bound to the site $i'$ of an agent of type $A'$, the value $\{0\}$ if we know that this is not the case, and the value $\{0,1\}$ otherwise. Property sites work the same way. Lastly, the variable $val_i$ takes as value the set attached to the counter or the value $\mathbb{Z}$ if the site is not mentioned in the agent. We notice that when $n$ is a fully-specified agent of type $A$, the function $guard_G(n)$ maps every variable in the set $\mathcal{V}ar_A$ to a singleton.

*Example 5 (running example).* We provide the translation of the unique agent of the site-graph $G_1$ (e. g. see Fig. 3(a)) and the one of the unique agent of the site-graph $G_4$ (e. g. see Fig. 3(d)).

The agent of the site-graph $G_1$ is translated as follows:

$$\left\{\begin{array}{l} \chi_a^{\circ} = \{1\}; \chi_a^{\bullet} = \{0\}; \\ \chi_b^{\circ} = \{0,1\}; \chi_b^{\bullet} = \{0,1\}; \\ \chi_c^{\circ} = \{0,1\}; \chi_c^{\bullet} = \{0,1\}; \\ \chi_d^{\circ} = \{0,1\}; \chi_d^{\bullet} = \{0,1\}; \\ val_x = \{z \in \mathbb{Z} \mid z \leq 2\} \end{array}\right\}.$$

According to the first two constraints, the site $a$ is unphosphorylated. According to the next six ones, the sites $b$, $c$, and $d$ have an unspecified state. According to the last constraint, the value of the counter must be less than or equal to 2.

The translation of the agent of the site-graph $G_4$ is obtained the same way:

$$\left\{\begin{array}{l} \chi_a^{\circ} = \{1\}; \chi_a^{\bullet} = \{0\}; \\ \chi_b^{\circ} = \{0\}; \chi_b^{\bullet} = \{1\}; \\ \chi_c^{\circ} = \{0\}; \chi_c^{\bullet} = \{1\}; \\ \chi_d^{\circ} = \{1\}; \chi_d^{\bullet} = \{0\}; \\ val_x = \{2\} \end{array}\right\}.$$

This means that the sites $b$ and $c$ are phosphorylated while the sites $a$ and $d$ are not. According to the last constraint, the value of the counter is equal to 2.

### 5.2 Encoding Rules

In Kappa, a rule may be applied only when its precondition is satisfied. Moreover, the application of a rule modifies the state of some sites in agents. We translate each rule into a tuple of guards that encodes its precondition, a set of non-invertible assignments (when a site is given a new state that does not depend on the former one), and a set of invertible assignments (when the new state of a site depends on the previous one). Such a distinction is important as we want to establish relationships among the value of some variables [32]: a non-invertible assignment completely hides the former value of a variable. This is not the case with invertible assignments for which relationships may be propagated more easily. The agents that are created (which have no precondition) and the ones that are removed (which disappear), have a special treatment.

**Definition 10 (Encoding of rules).** *Each rule* $r : L \leftarrow\!\supseteq\!\!\rightharpoonup D \overset{(h_e,h_\$)}{\underset{\$}{\hookrightarrow}} R$ *is associated with the tuple* $(pre_r, not\text{-}invert_r, invert_r, new_r)$ *where:*

1. $pre_r$ *maps every agent* $n \in \mathcal{A}_L$ *in the left hand side of the rule* $r$ *to its guard* $guard_L(n)$*;*
2. $not\text{-}invert_r$ *maps every agent* $n \in \mathcal{A}_D$ *and every variable* $v \in \mathcal{V}ar_{type_D(n)}$ *such that the set* $guard_R(h_e(n))(v)$ *is a singleton and* $guard_R(h_e(n))(v) \neq guard_L(n)(v)$ *to the unique element of the set* $guard_R(h_e(n))(v)$*.*
3. $invert_r$ *maps every agent* $n \in \mathcal{A}_D$ *and every variable* $v \in \mathcal{V}ar_{type_D(n)}$ *such that the set* $guard_R(h_e(n))(v)$ *is not a singleton and* $h_\$(n,i)$ *is a function of the form* $[z \in \mathbb{Z} \mapsto z + c]$ *with* $c \in \mathbb{Z}$*, to the relative number* $c$*.*
4. $new_r$ *maps every agent* $n' \in \mathcal{A}_R$ *such that there is no agent* $n \in \mathcal{A}_D$ *satisfying* $h_e(n) = n'$ *to the guard* $guard_R(n')$*.*

*Example 6 (running example).* The encoding of the rule of Fig. 6(a) is given as follows:

- the function $pre_r$ maps the agent 1 to the following set of constraints:

$$\left\{\begin{array}{l} \chi_a^\circ = \{1\}; \chi_a^\bullet = \{0\}; \\ \chi_b^\circ = \{0,1\}; \chi_b^\bullet = \{0,1\}; \\ \chi_c^\circ = \{0,1\}; \chi_c^\bullet = \{0,1\}; \\ \chi_d^\circ = \{0,1\}; \chi_d^\bullet = \{0,1\}; \\ val_x = \{z \in \mathbb{Z} \mid z \leq 2\} \end{array}\right\};$$

- the function $not\text{-}invert_r$ maps the pair $(1, \chi_a^\circ)$ to the value 0, and the pair $(1, \chi_a^\bullet)$ to the value 1;
- the function $invert_r$ maps the pair $(1, x)$ to the successor function;
- the function $new_r$ is the function with the empty domain.

The guard specifies that the site $a$ must be unphosphorylated and the value of the counter less or equal to 2. Applying the rule modifies the value of three variables. The site $a$ gets phosphorylated. This is a non-invertible modification that sets the variable $\chi_a^\circ$ to the constant value 0 and the variable $\chi_a^\bullet$ to the constant value 1. The counter $x$ is incremented. This is an invertible modification that is encoded by incrementing the value of the variable $val_x$.

### 5.3 Generic Numerical Abstract Domain

We are now ready to define a generic numerical abstraction.

**Definition 11 (Numerical domain).** *A numerical abstract domain is a family* $(\mathcal{A}_A^\mathcal{N})_{A \in \Sigma_{ag}}$ *of tuples* $(\mathcal{D}_A^\mathcal{N}, \sqsubseteq_A^\mathcal{N}, \gamma_A, \sqcup_A^\mathcal{N}, \bot_A^\mathcal{N}, \top_A^\mathcal{N}, g_A^\mathcal{N}, forget_A^\mathcal{N}, \delta_A^\mathcal{N}, \nabla_A^\mathcal{N})$ *that satisfy the following conditions, for every agent type* $A \in \Sigma_{ag}$*:*

1. *the pair* $(\mathcal{D}_A^{\mathcal{N}}, \sqsubseteq_A^{\mathcal{N}})$ *is a pre-order;*
2. *the component* $\gamma_A^{\mathcal{N}} : \mathcal{D}_A^{\mathcal{N}} \rightarrow \wp(\mathbb{Z}^{\mathcal{V}ar_A})$ *is a monotonic function;*
3. *the component* $\sqcup_A^{\mathcal{N}} : \wp_{finite}(\mathcal{D}_A^{\mathcal{N}}) \rightarrow \mathcal{D}_A^{\mathcal{N}}$ *is an operator such that* $\forall X^\sharp \in \wp_{finite}(\mathcal{D}_A^{\mathcal{N}})$, $\forall \rho^\sharp \in X^\sharp$, $\rho^\sharp \sqsubseteq \sqcup(X^\sharp)$;
4. *the component* $\bot_A^{\mathcal{N}}$ *is an element in the set* $\mathcal{D}_A^{\mathcal{N}}$ *such that* $\gamma_A^{\mathcal{N}}(\bot_A^{\mathcal{N}}) = \emptyset$;
5. *the component* $\top_A^{\mathcal{N}}$ *is an element in the set* $\mathcal{D}_A^{\mathcal{N}}$ *such that* $\gamma_A^{\mathcal{N}}(\top_A^{\mathcal{N}}) = \mathbb{Z}^{\mathcal{V}ar_A}$;
6. *the component* $g_A^{\mathcal{N}}$ *is a function mapping each pair* $(g, \rho^\sharp)$ *where* $g$ *is a guard and* $\rho^\sharp$ *an abstract property in* $\mathcal{D}_A^{\mathcal{N}}$ *to an abstract element in* $\mathcal{D}_A^{\mathcal{N}}$ *such that the set* $\gamma_A^{\mathcal{N}}(g_A^{\mathcal{N}}(g, \rho^\sharp))$ *contains at least each function* $\rho \in \gamma_A^{\mathcal{N}}(\rho^\sharp)$ *that verifies the condition* $\rho(v) \in \rho^\sharp(v)$ *for every variable* $v \in \mathcal{V}ar_A$;
7. *the component* $forget_A^{\mathcal{N}}$ *maps each pair* $(V, \rho^\sharp) \in \wp(\mathcal{V}ar_A) \times \mathcal{D}_A^{\mathcal{N}}$ *to an abstract property* $forget_A^{\mathcal{N}}(V, \rho^\sharp) \in \mathcal{D}_A^{\mathcal{N}}$, *the concretization* $\gamma(forget_A^{\mathcal{N}}(V, \rho^\sharp))$ *of which contains at least each function* $\rho \in \mathbb{Z}^{\mathcal{V}ar_A}$ *such that there exists a function* $\rho' \in \gamma_A^{\mathcal{N}}(\rho^\sharp)$ *satisfying* $\rho(v) = \rho'(v)$ *for each variable* $v \in \mathcal{V}ar_A \setminus V$;
8. *the component* $\delta_A^{\mathcal{N}}$ *maps each pair* $(t, \rho^\sharp) \in \mathbb{Z}^{\mathcal{V}ar_A} \times \mathcal{D}_A^{\mathcal{N}}$ *to an abstract property* $\delta_A^{\mathcal{N}}(t, \rho^\sharp) \in \mathcal{D}_A^{\mathcal{N}}$, *such for each function* $\rho \in \gamma_A^{\mathcal{N}}(\rho^\sharp)$, *the function mapping each variable* $v \in \mathcal{V}ar_A$ *to the value* $\rho(v) + t(v)$ *belongs to the set* $\gamma_A^{\mathcal{N}}(\delta_A^{\mathcal{N}}(t, \rho^\sharp))$;
9. *the component* $\nabla^{\mathcal{N}}$ *is a widening operator satisfies both following properties:*
   (a) $\forall \rho_1^\sharp, \rho_2^\sharp \in \mathcal{D}_A^{\mathcal{N}}$, $\rho_1^\sharp \sqsubseteq_A^{\mathcal{N}} \rho_1^\sharp \nabla^{\mathcal{N}} \rho_2^\sharp$ *and* $\rho_2^\sharp \sqsubseteq_A^{\mathcal{N}} \rho_1^\sharp \nabla^{\mathcal{N}} \rho_2^\sharp$,
   (b) $\forall (\rho_n^\sharp)_{n\in\mathbb{N}} \in (\mathcal{D}_A^{\mathcal{N}})^{\mathbb{N}}$, *the sequence* $(\rho_n^\nabla)_{n\in\mathbb{N}}$ *that is defined as* $\rho_0^\nabla = \rho_0^\sharp$ *and* $\rho_{n+1}^\nabla = \rho_n^\nabla \nabla^{\mathcal{N}} \rho_{n+1}^\sharp$ *for every integer* $n \in \mathbb{N}$, *is ultimately stationary.*

### 5.4 Numerical Abstraction

The following theorem explains how to build an abstraction (as defined in Sect. 4) from a numerical abstract domain. We introduce an operator $\uparrow$ to extend the domain of functions with default values. Given a function $f$, a value $v$ and a super-set $X$ of the domain of $f$, we write $\uparrow_X^v f$ the extension of the function $f$ that maps each element $x \in X \setminus Dom\ (f)$ to the value $v$. We also write $set_A$ for the function mapping pairs $(f, X^\sharp)$ where $f$ is a partial function from the set $\mathcal{V}ar_A$ into the set of the convex parts of $\mathbb{Z}$ and $X^\sharp$ an abstract property in $\mathcal{D}_A^{\mathcal{N}}$, to the abstract property: $g_A^{\mathcal{N}}(\uparrow_{\mathcal{V}ar_A}^{\mathbb{Z}} f, forget_A^{\mathcal{N}}(dom(f), X^\sharp))$. The function $set_A$ forgets all the information about the variables in the domain of the function $f$, and reassign their range to their image by $f$ in the abstract.

**Theorem 4.** *Let* $(\mathcal{D}_A^{\mathcal{N}}, \sqsubseteq_A^{\mathcal{N}}, \gamma_A, \sqcup_A^{\mathcal{N}}, \bot_A^{\mathcal{N}}, \top_A^{\mathcal{N}}, g_A^{\mathcal{N}}, forget_A^{\mathcal{N}}, \delta_A^{\mathcal{N}}, \nabla_A^{\mathcal{N}})_{A\in\Sigma_{ag}}$ *be a numerical abstract domain. The tuple* $(\mathcal{Q}^\sharp, \sqsubseteq, \gamma, \sqcup, \bot, \mathcal{I}^\sharp, t^\sharp, \nabla)$ *that is defined by:*

1. *the component* $\mathcal{Q}^\sharp$ *is the set of the functions mapping each agent type* $A \in \Sigma_{ag}$ *to an abstract property in the set* $\mathcal{D}_A^{\mathcal{N}}$;
2. *the component* $\gamma$ *is the function mapping a function* $X^\sharp \in \mathcal{Q}^\sharp$, *to the set of the fully specified site-graph* $G$ *such that for each agent* $n \in \mathcal{A}_G$, *we have* $guard_G(n) \in \gamma_{type_G(n)}(X^\sharp(type_G(n)))$;
3. *the components* $\sqsubseteq$, $\sqcup$, $\bot$ *are defined component-wise;*

4. *the component $\mathcal{I}^\sharp$ maps each agent type $A \in \Sigma_{ag}$ to the abstract property $\sqcup^{\mathcal{N}}_A\{g^{\mathcal{N}}_A(guard_{G_0}(n), \top^{\mathcal{N}}_A) \mid n \in \mathcal{A}_{G_0}\}$;*
5. *the component $t^\sharp$ is a function mapping each pair $(X^\sharp, r) \in \mathcal{Q}^\sharp \times \mathcal{R}$ (we write $r : L \twoheadleftarrow\!\supseteq\!\hookrightarrow D \hookrightarrow\!\$\!\twoheadrightarrow R$) to the element $\bot^{\mathcal{N}}_A$ whenever there exists an agent $n$ in $\mathcal{A}_L$ such that $g^{\mathcal{N}}_A(pre_r(n), X^\sharp(type_L(n))) = \bot^{\mathcal{N}}_A$, and, otherwise, to the function mapping each agent type $A$ to the numerical property:*

$$\sqcup^{\mathcal{N}}_A(\{X^\sharp(A)\} \cup \mathit{fresh}(r, A) \cup \mathit{updated}(r, A, X^\sharp)),$$

*with:*

- *$\mathit{fresh}(r, A)$ the set of the numerical abstract elements $g^{\mathcal{N}}_A(new_r n, \top^{\mathcal{N}}_A)$ for every $n \in dom(new_r)$ such that $type_R(n) = A$;*
- *and $\mathit{updated}(r, A, X^\sharp)$ the set of the elements:*
  $$set_A(not\text{-}invert_r(n), \delta^{\mathcal{N}}_A(\uparrow^0_A invert_r(n), g^{\mathcal{N}}_A(pre_r(n), X^\sharp(A))))$$
  *for each agent $n \in \mathcal{A}_D$ with $type_D(n) = A$;*

*is a generic abstraction.*

Most of the constructions of the abstraction are standard. The expression $g^{\mathcal{N}}_A(pre_r(n), X^\sharp(type_L(n)))$ refines the abstract information about the potential configurations of the $n$-th agent in the left hand side of the rule, by taking into account its precondition. Whenever a bottom element is obtained for at least one agent, the precondition of the rule is not satisfiable and the rule is discarded at this moment of the iteration. Otherwise, the information about each agent is updated. Starting from the result of the refinement of the abstract element by the precondition, the function $\delta^{\mathcal{N}}_A$ applies the invertible transformations $\uparrow^0_A invert_r(n)$ (the function $\uparrow^0_A$ extends the domain of the function $invert_r(n)$ by specifying that the variables not in the domain of this function remain unchanged), and the function $set_A$ applies non invertible one $not\text{-}invert_r(n)$.

The domain of intervals [8] and the one of affine relationships [32] provide all the primitives requested by Definition 11. We use a product of them, when all primitives are defined pair-wise, except the guards which refine its output by using the algorithm that is described in [23]. We use widening with thresholds [2] for intervals so as to avoid infinite bounds when possible. This way we obtain a domain, where all operations are cubic with respect to the number of variables.

This is a very good trade-off. A relational domain is required. Other relational domain are either too imprecise [37], or to costly [13], or both [27,38].

### 5.5 Benchmarks

We run our analysis on the family of models of Sect. 1 for $n$ ranging between 1 and 25. For each version of the model, the protein is made of $n$ phosphorylation sites and a counter. Moreover, our analysis always discover that the counter ranges between 0 and $n$. CPU time is plot in Fig. 10.

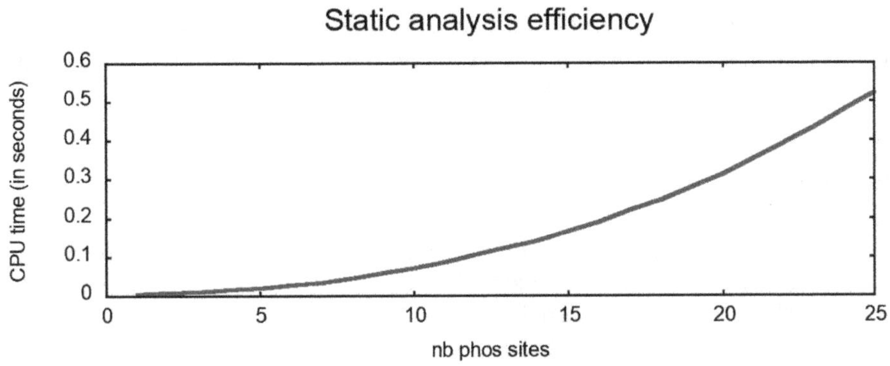


**Fig. 10.** Efficiency of the static analysis for the example in Sect. 1 with $n$ ranging between 1 and 25. Every analysis has successfully computed the exact range of the counter. The analysis has been performed on a MacBook Pro on a 2.8 GHz intel Core i7, 16 GB of RAM, running under macOS High Sierra version 10.13.6.

## 6 Conclusion

When potential protein transformations depend on the number of sites satisfying a given property, counters offer a convenient way to describe generic mechanisms while avoiding the explosion in the number of rules. We have extended the semantics of Kappa to deal with counters. We have proposed some encodings to remove counters while preserving the performance of the Kappa simulator. In particular, graphs remain rigid and the number of rules remain the same. Then, we have introduced a static analysis to bound the range of counters.

It is quite common to find proteins with more than 40 phosphorylation sites. Without our contributions, the modeler has no choice but to assume these proteins to be active only when all their sites are phosphorylated. This is a harsh simplification. Modeling simplifications are usually done not only because detailed knowledge is missing, but also because corresponding models cannot be described, executed, or analyzed efficiently. Yet these simplifications are done without any clue of their impact on the behavior of the systems. By providing ways of describing and handling some complex details, we offer the modelers the means to incorporate these details and to test empirically their impact.

Our framework is fully integrated within the Kappa modeling platform which is open-source and usable online (https://kappalanguage.org). It is worth noting that we have taken two radically different approaches to deal with counters in simulation and in static analysis. Encodings are good for simulation, but they tend to obfuscate the properties of interest, hence damaging drastically the capability of the static analysis to infer useful properties about them. The extension of the categorical semantics provides a parsimonious definition of causality between computation steps, as well as means to reason symbolically on the behavior of the number of occurrences of patterns. For further works, we will extend existing decision procedures [14, 15] that compute minimal causal traces to cope with counters. It is very likely that a third approach will be required. We suggest to use the traces obtained by simulation, then translate the counters in these traces thanks to equivalent sites, and apply existing decision procedures the traces that will be obtained this way.

## References

1. Behr, N., Danos, V., Garnier, I.: Stochastic mechanics of graph rewriting. In: Grohe, M., Koskinen, E., Shankar, N. (eds.) Proceedings of the 31st Annual ACM/IEEE Symposium on Logic in Computer Science (LICS 2016), New York, NY, USA, pp. 46–55. ACM (2016)
2. Blanchet, B., et al.: A static analyzer for large safety-critical software. In: Proceedings of the ACM SIGPLAN 2003 Conference on Programming Language Design and Implementation (PLDI 2003), San Diego, California, USA, 7–14 June 2003, pp. 196–207. ACM Press (2003)
3. Blinov, M.L., Faeder, J.R., Goldstein, B., Hlavacek, W.S.: BioNetGen: software for rule-based modeling of signal transduction based on the interactions of molecular domains. Bioinformatics **20**(17), 3289–3291 (2004)
4. Bortolussi, L., et al.: CARMA: collective adaptive resource-sharing Markovian agents. In: Bertrand, N., Tribastone, M. (eds.) Proceedings of the Thirteenth Workshop on Quantitative Aspects of Programming Languages and Systems (QAPL 2015), London, UK. EPTCS, vol. 194, pp. 16–31 (2015)
5. Boutillier, P., et al.: KaSa: a static analyzer for Kappa. In: Češka, M., Šafránek, D. (eds.) CMSB 2018. LNCS, vol. 11095, pp. 285–291. Springer, Cham (2018). https://doi.org/10.1007/978-3-319-99429-1_17
6. Boutillier, P., Ehrhard, T., Krivine, J.: Incremental update for graph rewriting. In: Yang, H. (ed.) ESOP 2017. LNCS, vol. 10201, pp. 201–228. Springer, Heidelberg (2017). https://doi.org/10.1007/978-3-662-54434-1_8
7. Cousot, P.: Semantic foundations of program analysis. In: Muchnick, S.S., Jones, N.D. (eds.) Program Flow Analysis: Theory and Applications, vol. 10. Prentice-Hall Inc., Englewood Cliffs (1981)
8. Cousot, P., Cousot, R.: Static determination of dynamic properties of programs. In: Proceedings of the Second International Symposium on Programming, pp. 106–130. Dunod, Paris (1976)
9. Cousot, P., Cousot, R.: Abstract interpretation: a unified lattice model for static analysis of programs by construction or approximation of fixpoints. In: Proceedings of POPL 1977. ACM Press (1977)
10. Cousot, P., Cousot, R.: Abstract interpretation frameworks. J. Logic Comput. **2**(4), 511–547 (1992)
11. Cousot, P., Cousot, R.: Comparing the Galois connection and widening/narrowing approaches to abstract interpretation. In: Bruynooghe, M., Wirsing, M. (eds.) PLILP 1992. LNCS, vol. 631, pp. 269–295. Springer, Heidelberg (1992). https://doi.org/10.1007/3-540-55844-6_142
12. Cousot, P., et al.: Combination of abstractions in the ASTRÉE static analyzer. In: Okada, M., Satoh, I. (eds.) ASIAN 2006. LNCS, vol. 4435, pp. 272–300. Springer, Heidelberg (2007). https://doi.org/10.1007/978-3-540-77505-8_23
13. Cousot, P., Halbwachs, N.: Automatic discovery of linear restraints among variables of a program. In: Aho, A.V., Zilles, S.N., Szymanski, T.G. (eds.) Conference Record of the Fifth Annual ACM Symposium on Principles of Programming Languages, Tucson, Arizona, USA, January 1978, pp. 84–96. ACM Press (1978)

14. Danos, V., et al.: Graphs, rewriting and pathway reconstruction for rule-based models. In: D'Souza, D., Kavitha, T., Radhakrishnan, J. (eds.) IARCS Annual Conference on Foundations of Software Technology and Theoretical Computer Science, FSTTCS 2012, Hyderabad, India, 15–17 December 2012. LIPIcs, vol. 18, pp. 276–288. Schloss Dagstuhl - Leibniz-Zentrum fuer Informatik (2012)
15. Danos, V., Feret, J., Fontana, W., Harmer, R., Krivine, J.: Rule-based modelling of cellular signalling. In: Caires, L., Vasconcelos, V.T. (eds.) CONCUR 2007. LNCS, vol. 4703, pp. 17–41. Springer, Heidelberg (2007). https://doi.org/10.1007/978-3-540-74407-8_3
16. Danos, V., Feret, J., Fontana, W., Harmer, R., Krivine, J.: Abstracting the differential semantics of rule-based models: exact and automated model reduction. In: Jouannaud, J.-P. (ed.) Proceedings of the Twenty-Fifth Annual IEEE Symposium on Logic in Computer Science, LICS 2010, Edinburgh, UK, 11–14 July 2010, pp. 362–381. IEEE Computer Society (2010)
17. Danos, V., Feret, J., Fontana, W., Krivine, J.: Scalable simulation of cellular signaling networks. In: Shao, Z. (ed.) APLAS 2007. LNCS, vol. 4807, pp. 139–157. Springer, Heidelberg (2007). https://doi.org/10.1007/978-3-540-76637-7_10
18. Danos, V., Laneve, C.: Formal molecular biology. Theor. Comput. Sci. **325**(1), 69–110 (2004)
19. Delzanno, G., Di Giusto, C., Gabbrielli, M., Laneve, C., Zavattaro, G.: The *kappa*-lattice: decidability boundaries for qualitative analysis in biological languages. In: Degano, P., Gorrieri, R. (eds.) CMSB 2009. LNCS, vol. 5688, pp. 158–172. Springer, Heidelberg (2009). https://doi.org/10.1007/978-3-642-03845-7_11
20. Dijkstra, E.W.: Over de sequentialiteit van procesbeschrijvingen. circulated privately, 1962 or 1963
21. Dijkstra, E.W.: Cooperating sequential processes. Technical report EWD-123 (1965)
22. Ehrig, H., et al.: Algebraic approaches to graph transformation. Part II: single pushout approach and comparison with double pushout approach. In: Handbook of Graph Grammars and Computing by Graph Transformation, pp. 247–312. Springer-Verlag, New York Inc., Secaucus (1997)
23. Feret, J.: Occurrence counting analysis for the pi-calculus. Electron. Notes Theor. Comput. Sci. **39**(2), 1–18 (2001). Workshop on GEometry and Topology in COncurrency theory, PennState, USA, August 21, 2000
24. Feret, J.: Abstract interpretation of mobile systems. J. Log. Algebr. Program. **63**(1), 59–130 (2005)
25. Feret, J.: An algebraic approach for inferring and using symmetries in rule-based models. Electron. Notes Theor. Comput. Sci. **316**, 45–65 (2015)
26. Feret, J., Danos, V., Harmer, R., Fontana, W., Krivine, J.: Internal coarse-graining of molecular systems. PNAS **106**(16), 6453–6458 (2009)
27. Hansen, R.R., Jensen, J.G., Nielson, F., Nielson, H.R.: Abstract interpretation of mobile ambients. In: Cortesi, A., Filé, G. (eds.) SAS 1999. LNCS, vol. 1694, pp. 134–148. Springer, Heidelberg (1999). https://doi.org/10.1007/3-540-48294-6_9
28. Helms, T., Warnke, T., Maus, C., Uhrmacher, A.M.: Semantics and efficient simulation algorithms of an expressive multilevel modeling language. ACM Trans. Model. Comput. Simul. **27**(2), 8:1–8:25 (2017)
29. Honorato-Zimmer, R., Millar, A.J., Plotkin, G.D., Zardilis, A.: Chromar, a language of parameterised agents. Theor. Comput. Sci. (2017)
30. Jensen, K.: Coloured Petri Nets: Basic Concepts, Analysis Methods and Practical Use: Basic Concepts, Analysis Methods and Practical Use. Volume 1. Monographs

in Theoretical Computer Science. An EATCS Series, 2nd edn. Springer, Heidelberg (1996). https://doi.org/10.1007/978-3-662-03241-1
31. John, M., Lhoussaine, C., Niehren, J., Versari, C.: Biochemical reaction rules with constraints. In: Barthe, G. (ed.) ESOP 2011. LNCS, vol. 6602, pp. 338–357. Springer, Heidelberg (2011). https://doi.org/10.1007/978-3-642-19718-5_18
32. Karr, M.: Affine relationships among variables of a program. Acta Informatica **6**(2), 133–151 (1976)
33. Kleene, S.C.: Introduction to Mathematics. ISHI Press International, New York (1952)
34. Kreyßig, P.: Chemical organisation theory beyond classical models: discrete dynamics and rule-based models. Ph.D. thesis, Friedrich-Schiller-University Jena (2015)
35. Liu, F., Blätke, M.A., Heiner, M., Yang, M.: Modelling and simulating reaction-diffusion systems using coloured petri nets. Comput. Biol. Med. **53**, 297–308 (2014)
36. Miné, A.: A new numerical abstract domain based on difference-bound matrices. In: Danvy, O., Filinski, A. (eds.) PADO 2001. LNCS, vol. 2053, pp. 155–172. Springer, Heidelberg (2001). https://doi.org/10.1007/3-540-44978-7_10
37. Miné, A.: The octagon abstract domain. Higher-Order Symbolic Comput. (HOSC) **19**(1), 31–100 (2006)
38. Nielson, H.R., Nielson, F.: Shape analysis for mobile ambients. In: Proceedings of POPL 2000. ACM Press (2000)
39. Petrov, T., Feret, J., Koeppl, H.: Reconstructing species-based dynamics from reduced stochastic rule-based models. In: Laroque, C., Himmelspach, J., Pasupathy, R., Rose, O., Uhrmacher, A.M. (eds.) Winter Simulation Conference, WSC 2012 (2012)
40. Sneddon, M.W., Faeder, J.R., Emonet, T.: Efficient modeling, simulation and coarse-graining of biological complexity with NFsim. Nat. Methods **8**(2), 177–183 (2011)
41. Stewart, D.: Spatial biomodelling. Master thesis, School of Informatics, University of Edinburgh (2010)
42. Tarski, A.: A lattice-theoretical fixpoint theorem and its applications. Pac. J. Math. **5**(2), 285 (1955)
43. Winskel, G.: Event structures. In: Brauer, W., Reisig, W., Rozenberg, G. (eds.) ACPN 1986. LNCS, vol. 255, pp. 325–392. Springer, Heidelberg (1987). https://doi.org/10.1007/3-540-17906-2_31

# 2

# Incremental λ-Calculus in Cache-Transfer Style Static Memoization by Program Transformation

Paolo G. Giarrusso[1(✉)], Yann Régis-Gianas[2], and Philipp Schuster[3]

[1] LAMP—EPFL, Lausanne, Switzerland
[2] IRIF, University of Paris Diderot, Inria, Paris, France
[3] University of Tübingen, Tübingen, Germany

**Abstract.** Incremental computation requires propagating changes and reusing intermediate results of base computations. Derivatives, as produced by static differentiation [7], propagate changes but do not reuse intermediate results, leading to wasteful recomputation. As a solution, we introduce conversion to *Cache-Transfer-Style*, an additional program transformations producing purely incremental functional programs that create and maintain nested tuples of intermediate results. To prove CTS conversion correct, we extend the correctness proof of static differentiation from STLC to untyped λ-calculus via *step-indexed logical relations*, and prove sound the additional transformation via simulation theorems.

To show ILC-based languages can improve performance relative to from-scratch recomputation, and that CTS conversion can extend its applicability, we perform an initial performance case study. We provide derivatives of primitives for operations on collections and incrementalize selected example programs using those primitives, confirming expected asymptotic speedups.

## 1 Introduction

After computing a base output from some base input, we often need to produce updated outputs corresponding to updated inputs. Instead of rerunning the same *base program* on the updated input, incremental computation transforms the input change to an output change, potentially reducing asymptotic time complexity and significantly improving efficiency, especially for computations running on large data sets.

Incremental λ-Calculus (ILC) [7] is a recent framework for *higher-order* incremental computation. ILC represents changes from a base value $v_1$ to an updated value $v_2$ as a first-class *change value* $dv$. Since functions are first-class values, change values include *function changes*.

ILC also statically transforms *base programs* to *incremental programs* or *derivatives*, that are functions mapping input changes to output changes. Incremental language designers can then provide their language with (higher-order) primitives (with their derivatives) that efficiently encapsulate incrementalizable computation skeletons (such as tree-shaped folds), and ILC will incrementalize higher-order programs written in terms of these primitives.

Alas, ILC only incrementalizes efficiently *self-maintainable computations* [7, Sect. 4.3], that is, computations whose output changes can be computed using only input changes, but not the inputs themselves [11]. Few computations are self-maintainable: for instance, mapping self-maintainable functions on a sequence is self-maintainable, but dividing numbers is not! We elaborate on this problem in Sect. 2.1. In this paper, we extend ILC to non-self-maintainable computations. To this end, we must enable derivatives to reuse intermediate results created by the base computation.

Many incrementalization approaches remember intermediate results through dynamic memoization: they typically use hashtables to memoize function results, or dynamic dependence graphs [1] to remember a computation trace. However, looking up intermediate results in such dynamic data structure has a runtime cost that is hard to optimize; and reasoning on dynamic dependence graphs and computation traces is often complex. Instead, ILC produces purely functional programs, suitable for further optimizations and equational reasoning.

To that end, we replace dynamic memoization with *static memoization*: following Liu and Teitelbaum [20], we transform programs to *cache-transfer style (CTS)*. A CTS function outputs their primary result along with *caches* of intermediate results. These caches are just nested tuples whose structure is derived from code, and accessing them does not involve looking up keys depending on inputs. Instead, intermediate results can be fetched from these tuples using statically known locations. To integrate CTS with ILC, we extend differentiation to produce *CTS derivatives*: these can extract from caches any intermediate results they need, and produce updated caches for the next computation step.

The correctness proof of static differentiation in CTS is challenging. First, we must show a forward simulation relation between two triples of reduction traces (the first triple being made of the source base evaluation, the source updated evaluation and the source derivative evaluation; the second triple being made of the corresponding CTS-translated evaluations). Dealing with six distinct evaluation environments at the same time was error prone on paper and for this reason, we conducted the proof using Coq [26]. Second, the simulation relation must not only track values but also caches, which are only partially updated while in the middle of the evaluation of derivatives. Finally, we study the translation for an untyped $\lambda$-calculus, while previous ILC correctness proofs were restricted to simply-typed $\lambda$-calculus. Hence, we define which changes are valid via a *logical relation* and show its *fundamental property*. Being in an untyped setting, our logical relation is not indexed by types, but *step-indexed*. We study an untyped language, but our work also applies to the erasure of typed languages. Formalizing a type-preserving translation is left for future work because giving a type to CTS programs is challenging, as we shall explain.

In addition to the correctness proof, we present preliminary experimental results from three case studies. We obtain efficient incremental programs even on non self-maintainable functions.

We present our contributions as follows. First, we summarize ILC and illustrate the need to extend it to remember intermediate results via CTS (Sect. 2). Second, in our mechanized formalization (Sect. 3), we give a novel proof of correctness for ILC differentiation for untyped λ-calculus, based on step-indexed logical relations (Sect. 3.4). Third, building on top of ILC differentiation, we show how to transform untyped higher-order programs to CTS (Sect. 3.5) and we show that CTS functions and derivatives *simulate* correctly their non-CTS counterparts (Sect. 3.7). Finally, in our case studies (Sect. 4), we compare the performance of the generated code to the base programs. Section 4.4 discusses limitations and future work. Section 5 discusses related work and Sect. 6 concludes. Our mechanized proof in Coq, the case study material, and the extended version of this paper with appendixes are available online at https://github.com/yurug/cts.

## 2 ILC and CTS Primer

In this section we exemplify ILC by applying it on an average function, show why the resulting incremental program is asymptotically inefficient, and use CTS conversion and differentiation to incrementalize our example efficiently and speed it up asymptotically (as confirmed by benchmarks in Sect. 4.1). Further examples in Sect. 4 apply CTS to higher-order programs and suggest that CTS enables incrementalizing efficiently some core database primitives such as joins.

### 2.1 Incrementalizing *average* via ILC

Our example computes the average of a bag of numbers. After computing the *base output* $y_1$ of the average function on the *base input* bag $xs_1$, we want to update the output in response to a stream of updates to the input bag. Here and throughout the paper, we contrast *base* vs *updated* inputs, outputs, values, computations, and so on. For simplicity, we assume we have two *updated inputs* $xs_2$ and $xs_3$ and want to compute two *updated outputs* $y_2$ and $y_3$. We express this program in Haskell as follows:

$$\begin{aligned}
&average && :: Bag\ \mathbb{Z} \rightarrow \mathbb{Z}\\
&average\ xs && = \mathbf{let}\ s = sum\ xs; n = length\ xs; r = div\ s\ n\ \mathbf{in}\ r\\
&average_3 && = \mathbf{let}\ y_1 = average\ xs_1; y_2 = average\ xs_2; y_3 = average\ xs_3\\
& && \quad\ \mathbf{in}\ (y_1, y_2, y_3)
\end{aligned}$$

To compute the updated outputs $y_2$ and $y_3$ in $average_3$ faster, we try using ILC. For that, we assume that we receive not only updated inputs $xs_2$ and $xs_3$ but also *input change* $dxs_1$ from $xs_1$ to $xs_2$ and input change $dxs_2$ from $xs_2$ to $xs_3$. A change $dx$ from $x_1$ to $x_2$ describes the changes from base value $x_1$ to updated value $x_2$, so that $x_2$ can be computed via the *update operator* $\oplus$ as $x_1 \oplus dx$. A nil change $\mathbf{0}_x$ is a change from base value $x$ to updated value $x$ itself.

ILC differentiation automatically transforms the *average* function to its derivative $daverage :: Bag\ \mathbb{Z} \to \Delta(Bag\ \mathbb{Z}) \to \Delta\mathbb{Z}$. A derivative maps input changes to output changes: here, $dy_1 = daverage\ xs_1\ dxs_1$ is a change from base output $y_1 = average\ xs_1$ to updated output $y_2 = average\ xs_2$, hence $y_2 = y_1 \oplus dy_1$.

Thanks to *daverage*'s correctness, we can rewrite $average_3$ to avoid expensive calls to *average* on updated inputs and use *daverage* instead:

$$
\begin{aligned}
&incrementalAverage_3 :: (\mathbb{Z}, \mathbb{Z}, \mathbb{Z})\\
&incrementalAverage_3 =\\
&\quad \mathbf{let}\ y_1 = average\ xs_1;\ dy_1 = daverage\ xs_1\ dxs_1\\
&\qquad\ \ y_2 = y_1 \oplus dy_1;\ dy_2 = daverage\ xs_2\ dxs_2\\
&\qquad\ \ y_3 = y_2 \oplus dy_2\\
&\quad \mathbf{in}\ \ (y_1, y_2, y_3)
\end{aligned}
$$

In general, also the value of a function $f :: A \to B$ can change from a base value $f_1$ to an updated value $f_2$, mainly when $f$ is a closure over changing data. In that case, the change from base output $f_1\ x_1$ to updated output $f_2\ x_2$ is given by $df\ x_1\ dx$, where $df :: A \to \Delta A \to \Delta B$ is now a *function change* from $f_1$ to $f_2$. Above, *average* exemplifies the special case where $f_1 = f_2 = f$: then the function change $df$ is a nil change, and $df\ x_1\ dx$ is a change from $f_1\ x_1 = f\ x_1$ and $f_2\ x_2 = f\ x_2$. That is, a nil function change for $f$ is a derivative of $f$.

## 2.2 Self-maintainability and Efficiency of Derivatives

Alas, derivatives are efficient only if they are *self-maintainable*, and *daverage* is not, so $incrementalAverage_3$ is no faster than $average_3$! Consider the result of differentiating *average*:

$$
\begin{aligned}
&daverage :: Bag\ \mathbb{Z} \to \Delta(Bag\ \mathbb{Z}) \to \Delta\mathbb{Z}\\
&daverage\ xs\ dxs = \mathbf{let}\ s = sum\ xs;\ ds = dsum\ xs\ dxs;\\
&\qquad\qquad\qquad\qquad\quad n = length\ xs;\ dn = dlength\ xs\ dxs;\\
&\qquad\qquad\qquad\qquad\quad r = div\ s\ n;\ dr = ddiv\ s\ ds\ n\ dn\\
&\qquad\qquad\qquad\quad\ \ \mathbf{in}\ dr
\end{aligned}
$$

Just like *average* combines *sum*, *length*, and *div*, its derivative *daverage* combines those functions and their derivatives. *daverage* recomputes base intermediate results $s$, $n$ and $r$ exactly as done in *average*, because they might be needed as base inputs of derivatives. Since $r$ is unused, its recomputation can be dropped during later optimizations, but expensive intermediate results $s$ and $n$ are used by *ddiv*:

$$
\begin{aligned}
&ddiv :: \mathbb{Z} \to \Delta\mathbb{Z} \to \mathbb{Z} \to \Delta\mathbb{Z} \to \Delta\mathbb{Z}\\
&ddiv\ a\ da\ b\ db = div\ (a \oplus da)\ (b \oplus db) - div\ a\ b
\end{aligned}
$$

Function *ddiv* computes the difference between the updated and the original result, so it needs its base inputs $a$ and $b$. Hence, *daverage* must recompute $s$ and $n$ and will be slower than *average*!

Typically, ILC derivatives are only efficient if they are *self-maintainable*: a self-maintainable derivative does not inspect its base inputs, but only its change inputs, so recomputation of its base inputs can be elided. Cai et al. [7] leave efficient support for non-self-maintainable derivatives for future work.

But this problem is fixable: executing $daverage\ xs\ dxs$ will compute exactly the same $s$ and $n$ as executing $average\ xs$, so to avoid recomputation we must simply save $s$ and $n$ and reuse them. Hence, we CTS-convert each function $f$ to a *CTS function* $fC$ and a *CTS derivative* $dfC$: CTS function $fC$ produces, together with its final result, a *cache* containing intermediate results, that the caller must pass to CTS derivative $dfC$.

CTS-converting our example produces the following code, which requires no wasteful recomputation.

$$
\begin{array}{l}
\textbf{type}\ AverageC = (\mathbb{Z}, SumC, \mathbb{Z}, LengthC, \mathbb{Z}, DivC) \\
averageC :: Bag\ \mathbb{Z} \to (\mathbb{Z}, AverageC) \\
averageC\ xs = \\
\quad \textbf{let}\ (s, cs_1) = sumC\ xs; (n, cn_1) = lengthC\ xs; (r, cr_1) = divC\ s\ n \\
\quad \textbf{in}\ \ (r, (s, cs_1, n, cn_1, r, cr_1)) \\
daverageC :: Bag\ \mathbb{Z} \to \Delta(Bag\ \mathbb{Z}) \to AverageC \to (\Delta\mathbb{Z}, AverageC) \\
daverageC\ xs\ dxs\ (s, cs_1, n, cn_1, r, cr_1) = \\
\quad \textbf{let}\ (ds, cs_2)\ \ = dsumC\ xs\ dxs\ cs_1 \\
\qquad\ \ (dn, cn_2) = dlengthC\ xs\ dxs\ cn_1 \\
\qquad\ \ (dr, cr_2)\ \ = ddivC\ s\ ds\ n\ dn\ cr_1 \\
\quad \textbf{in}\ \ (dr, ((s \oplus ds), cs_2, (n \oplus dn), cn_2, (r \oplus dr), cr_2))
\end{array}
$$

For each function $f$, we introduce a type $FC$ for its cache, such that a CTS function $fC$ has type $A \to (B, FC)$ and CTS derivative $dfC$ has type $A \to \Delta A \to FC \to (\Delta B, FC)$. Crucially, CTS derivatives like *daverageC* must return an updated cache to ensure correct incrementalization, so that application of further changes works correctly. In general, if $(y_1, c_1) = fC\ x_1$ and $(dy, c_2) = dfC\ x_1\ dx\ c_1$, then $(y_1 \oplus dy, c_2)$ must equal the result of the base function $fC$ applied to the updated input $x_1 \oplus dx$, that is $(y_1 \oplus dy, c_2) = fC\ (x_1 \oplus dx)$.

For CTS-converted functions, the cache type $FC$ is a tuple of intermediate results and caches of subcalls. For primitive functions like *div*, the cache type *DivC* could contain information needed for efficient computation of output changes. In the case of *div*, no additional information is needed. The definition of *divC* uses *div* and produces an empty cache, and the definition of *ddivC* follows the earlier definition for *ddiv*, except that we now pass along an empty cache.

$$
\begin{array}{l}
\textbf{data}\ DivC = DivC \\
divC :: \mathbb{Z} \to \mathbb{Z} \to (\mathbb{Z}, DivC) \\
divC\ a\ b = (div\ a\ b, DivC) \\
ddivC :: \mathbb{Z} \to \Delta\mathbb{Z} \to \mathbb{Z} \to \Delta\mathbb{Z} \to DivC \to (\Delta\mathbb{Z}, DivC) \\
ddivC\ a\ da\ b\ db\ DivC = (div\ (a \oplus da)\ (b \oplus db) - div\ a\ b, DivC)
\end{array}
$$

Finally, we can rewrite $average_3$ to incrementally compute $y_2$ and $y_3$:

$$
\begin{array}{l}
ctsIncrementalAverage_3 :: (\mathbb{Z}, \mathbb{Z}, \mathbb{Z}) \\
ctsIncrementalAverage_3 = \\
\quad \textbf{let } (y_1, c_1) = averageC\ xs_1; (dy_1, c_2) = daverageC\ xs_1\ dxs_1\ c_1 \\
\qquad\quad y_2 = y_1 \oplus dy_1; (dy_2, c_3) = daverageC\ xs_2\ dxs_2\ c_2 \\
\qquad\quad y_3 = y_2 \oplus dy_2 \\
\quad \textbf{in } (y_1, y_2, y_3)
\end{array}
$$

Since functions of the same type translate to CTS functions of different types, in a higher-order language CTS translation is not always type-preserving; however, this is not a problem for our case studies (Sect. 4); Sect. 4.1 shows how to map such functions, and we return to this problem in Sect. 4.4.

## 3 Formalization

We now formalize CTS-differentiation for an untyped Turing-complete $\lambda$-calculus, and formally prove it sound with respect to differentiation. We also give a novel proof of correctness for differentiation itself, since we cannot simply adapt Cai et al. [7]'s proof to the new syntax: Our language is untyped and Turing-complete, while Cai et al. [7]'s proof assumed a strongly normalizing simply-typed $\lambda$-calculus and relied on its naive set-theoretic denotational semantics. Our entire formalization is mechanized using Coq [26]. For reasons of space, some details are deferred to the appendix.

| | | | |
|---|---|---|---|
| | ***Terms*** | | ***Closed values*** |
| $a_t ::= \textbf{let}\, a_p = a_t\, \textbf{in}\, a_t$ | *Let* | $a_v ::= a_E[\lambda \overline{a_p}.\, a_t]$ | *Closure* |
| $\mid\ a_T$ | *Tuple* | $\mid\ (\overline{a_v})$ | *Tuple* |
| $\mid\ f\ \overline{x}$ | *Application* | $\mid\ \ell$ | *Literal* |
| | ***Nested tuples*** | $\mid\ \mathbf{p}$ | *Primitive* |
| $a_T ::= x$ | *Variable* | $\mid\ 0_{\mathbf{p}}$ | *Nil change for primitive* |
| $\mid\ x \oplus dx$ | *Update* | $\mid\ !a_v$ | *Replacement change* |
| $\mid\ (\overline{a_T})$ | *Tuple* | | ***Value environments*** |
| | ***Patterns*** | $a_E ::= \bullet$ | *Empty* |
| $a_p ::= x$ | *Variable* | $\mid\ a_E; x = a_v$ | *Value binding* |
| $\mid\ (\overline{a_p})$ | *Tuple* | $j, k, n \in \mathbb{N}$ | ***Step indexes*** |

**Fig. 1.** Our language $\lambda_L$ of lambda-lifted programs. Tuples can be nullary.

*Transformations.* We introduce and prove sound three term transformations, namely differentiation, CTS translation and CTS differentiation, that take a function to its corresponding (non-CTS) derivative, CTS function and CTS derivative. Each CTS function produces a base output and a cache from a base input, while each CTS derivative produces an output change and an updated cache from an input, an input change and a base cache.

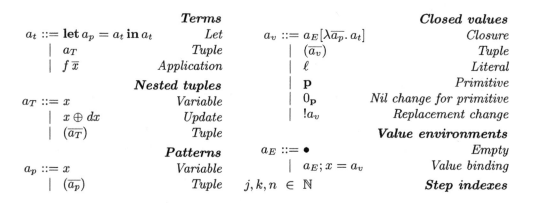

*Proof technique.* To show soundness, we prove that CTS functions and derivatives simulate respectively non-CTS functions and derivatives. In turn, we formalize (non-CTS) differentiation as well, and we prove differentiation sound with respect to non-incremental evaluation. Overall, this shows that CTS functions and derivatives are sound relatively to non-incremental evaluation. Our presentation proceeds in the converse order: first, we present differentiation, formulated as a variant of Cai et al. [7]'s definition; then, we study CTS differentiation.

By using logical relations, we simplify significantly the setup of Cai et al. [7]. To handle an untyped language, we employ *step-indexed* logical relations. Besides, we conduct our development with big-step operational semantics because that choice simplifies the correctness proof for CTS conversion. Using big-step semantics for a Turing complete language restricts us to terminating computations. But that is not a problem: to show incrementalization is correct, we need only consider computations that terminate on both old and new inputs, following Acar et al. [3] (compared with in Sect. 5).

*Structure of the formalization.* Section 3.1 introduces the syntax of the language $\lambda_L$ we consider in this development, and introduces its four sublanguages $\lambda_{AL}$, $\lambda_{IAL}$, $\lambda_{CAL}$ and $\lambda_{ICAL}$. Section 3.2 presents the syntax and the semantics of $\lambda_{AL}$, the source language for our transformations. Section 3.3 defines differentiation and its target language $\lambda_{IAL}$, and Sect. 3.4 proves differentiation correct. Section 3.5 defines CTS conversion, comprising CTS translation and CTS differentiation, and their target languages $\lambda_{CAL}$ and $\lambda_{ICAL}$. Section 3.6 presents the semantics of $\lambda_{CAL}$. Finally, Sect. 3.7 proves CTS conversion correct.

*Notations.* We write $\overline{X}$ for a sequence of $X$ of some unspecified length $X_1, \ldots, X_m$.

### 3.1 Syntax for $\lambda_L$

*A superlanguage.* To simplify our transformations, we require input programs to have been lambda-lifted [15] and converted to A'-normal form (A'NF). Lambda-lifted programs are convenient because they allow us to avoid a specific treatment for free variables in transformations. A'NF is a minor variant of ANF [24], where every result is bound to a variable before use; unlike ANF, we also bind the result of the tail call. Thus, every result can thus be stored in a cache by CTS conversion and reused later (as described in Sect. 2). This requirement is not onerous: A'NF is a minimal variant of ANF, and lambda-lifting and ANF conversion are routine in compilers for functional languages. Most examples we show are in this form.

In contrast, our transformation's outputs are lambda-lifted but not in A'NF. For instance, we restrict base functions to take exactly one argument—a base input. As shown in Sect. 2.1, CTS functions take instead two arguments—a base input and a cache—and CTS derivatives take three arguments—an input, an input change, and a cache. We could normalize transformation outputs to inhabit the source language and follow the same invariants, but this would complicate our proofs for little benefit. Hence, we do not *prescribe* transformation outputs to satisfy the same invariants, and we rather *describe* transformation outputs through separate grammars.

As a result of this design choice, we consider languages for base programs, derivatives, CTS programs and CTS derivatives. In our Coq mechanization, we formalize those as four separate languages, saving us many proof steps to check the validity of required structural invariants. For simplicity, in this paper we define a single language called $\lambda_L$ (for $\lambda$-Lifted). This language satisfies invariants common to all these languages (including some of the A'NF invariants). Then, we define *sublanguages* of $\lambda_L$. We describe the semantics of $\lambda_L$ informally, and we only formalize the semantics of its sublanguages.

*Syntax for terms.* The $\lambda_L$ language is a relatively conventional lambda-lifted $\lambda$-calculus with a limited form of pattern matching on tuples. The syntax for terms and values is presented in Fig. 1. We separate terms and values in two distinct syntactic classes because we use big-step operational semantics. Our **let**-bindings are non-recursive as usual, and support shadowing. Terms cannot contain $\lambda$-expressions directly, but only refer to closures through the environment, and similarly for literals and primitives; we elaborate on this in Sect. 3.2. We do not introduce case expressions, but only bindings that destructure tuples, both in **let**-bindings and $\lambda$-expressions of closures. Our semantics does not assign meaning to match failures, but pattern-matchings are only used in generated programs and our correctness proofs ensure that the matches always succeed. We allow tuples to contain terms of form $x \oplus dx$, which update base values $x$ with changes in $dx$, because A'NF-converting these updates is not necessary to the transformations. We often inspect the result of a function call "$f\ x$", which is not a valid term in our syntax. Hence, we write "$@(f, x)$" as a syntactic sugar for "$\textbf{let}\ y = f\ x\ \textbf{in}\ y$" with $y$ chosen fresh.

*Syntax for closed values.* A closed value is either a closure, a tuple of values, a literal, a primitive, a nil change for a primitive or a replacement change. A closure is a pair of an evaluation environment $E$ and a $\lambda$-abstraction closed with respect to $E$. The set of available literals $\ell$ is left abstract. It may contain usual first-order literals like integers. We also leave abstract the primitives $\mathbf{p}$ like `if-then-else` or projections of tuple components. Each primitive $\mathbf{p}$ comes with a nil change, which is its derivative as explained in Sect. 2. A change value can also represent a replacement by some closed value $a_v$. Replacement changes are not produced by static differentiation but are useful for clients of derivatives: we include them in the formalization to make sure that they are not incompatible with our system. As usual, environments $E$ map variables to closed values.

*Sublanguages of $\lambda_L$.* The source language for all our transformations is a sublanguage of $\lambda_L$ named $\lambda_{AL}$, where A stands for A'NF. To each transformation we associate a target language, which matches the transformation image. The target language for CTS conversion is named $\lambda_{CAL}$, where "C" stands for CTS. The target languages of differentiation and CTS differentiation are called, respectively, $\lambda_{IAL}$ and $\lambda_{ICAL}$, where the "I" stands for incremental.

### 3.2 The Source Language $\lambda_{AL}$

We show the syntax of $\lambda_{AL}$ in Fig. 2. As said above, $\lambda_{AL}$ is a sublanguage of $\lambda_L$ denoting lambda-lifted base terms in A'NF. With no loss of generality, we assume that all bound variables in $\lambda_{AL}$ programs and closures are distinct. The step-indexed big-step semantics (Fig. 3) for base terms is defined by the judgment written $E \vdash t \Downarrow_n v$ (where $n$ can be omitted) and pronounced "Under environment $E$, base term $t$ evaluates to closed value $v$ in $n$ steps." Intuitively, our step-indexes count the number of "nodes" of a big-step derivation.[1] As they are relatively standard, we defer the explanations of these rules to Appendix B.

**Term differentiation** $\boxed{dt = \mathcal{D}^\iota(t)}$

$$\begin{aligned}
\mathcal{D}^\iota(x) &= dx \\
\mathcal{D}^\iota(\mathbf{let}\ y = f\ x\ \mathbf{in}\ t) &= \\
&\mathbf{let}\ y = f\ x, dy = df\ x\ dx\ \mathbf{in}\ \mathcal{D}^\iota(t) \\
\mathcal{D}^\iota(\mathbf{let}\ y = (\overline{x})\ \mathbf{in}\ t) &= \\
&\mathbf{let}\ y = (\overline{x}), dy = (\overline{dx})\ \mathbf{in}\ \mathcal{D}^\iota(t)
\end{aligned}$$

**Value differentiation** $\boxed{dv = \mathcal{D}^\iota(v)}$

$$\begin{aligned}
\mathcal{D}^\iota((\overline{v})) &= (\overline{\mathcal{D}^\iota(v)}) \\
\mathcal{D}^\iota(E_f[\lambda x.\, t]) &= \mathcal{D}^\iota(E_f)[\lambda x\ dx.\, \mathcal{D}^\iota(t)] \\
\mathcal{D}^\iota(\ell) &= \mathbf{nil}\ \ell \\
\mathcal{D}^\iota(\mathbf{p}) &= 0_{\mathbf{p}}
\end{aligned}$$

**Environment differentiation** $\boxed{dE = \mathcal{D}^\iota(E)}$

$$\begin{aligned}
\mathcal{D}^\iota(\bullet) &= \bullet \\
\mathcal{D}^\iota(E; x = v) &= \mathcal{D}^\iota(E); x = v; dx = \mathcal{D}^\iota(v)
\end{aligned}$$

**Base/updated environment** $\boxed{E = \lfloor dE \rfloor_i}$

$$\begin{aligned}
\lfloor \bullet \rfloor_i &= \bullet \qquad \mathrm{i} = 1, 2 \\
\lfloor dE; x = v; dx = dv \rfloor_i &= \lfloor dE \rfloor_i; x = v' \\
&\quad v' = v \text{ if } i = 1 \text{ or} \\
&\quad v' = v \oplus dv \text{ if } i = 2
\end{aligned}$$

**$\lambda_{IAL}$ change terms**

$$\begin{aligned}
dt ::=\ & dx \\
|\ & \mathbf{let}\ y = f\ x, dy = df\ x\ dx \\
& \mathbf{in}\ dt \\
|\ & \mathbf{let}\ y = (\overline{x}), dy = (\overline{dx}) \\
& \mathbf{in}\ dt
\end{aligned}$$

**$\lambda_{IAL}$ change values**

$$\begin{aligned}
dv ::=\ & (\overline{dv}) \mid dE[\lambda x\ dx.\, dt] \mid \\
& d\ell \mid 0_{\mathbf{p}} \mid\ !v
\end{aligned}$$

**$\lambda_{IAL}$ change environments**

$$dE ::= \bullet \mid dE; x = v; dx = dv$$

**$\lambda_{AL}$ base terms**

$$\begin{aligned}
t ::=\ & x \mid \mathbf{let}\ y = f\ x\ \mathbf{in}\ t \mid \\
& \mathbf{let}\ y = (\overline{x})\ \mathbf{in}\ t
\end{aligned}$$

**$\lambda_{AL}$ closed values**

$$v ::= (\overline{v}) \mid E[\lambda x.\, t] \mid \ell \mid \mathbf{p}$$

**$\lambda_{AL}$ value environments**

$$E ::= \bullet \mid E; x = v$$

**Fig. 2.** Static differentiation $\mathcal{D}^\iota(-)$; syntax of its target language $\lambda_{IAL}$, tailored to the output of differentiation; syntax of its source language $\lambda_{AL}$. We assume that in $\lambda_{IAL}$ the same **let** binds both $y$ and $dy$ and that $\alpha$-renaming preserves this invariant. We also define the *base environment* $\lfloor dE \rfloor_1$ and the *updated environment* $\lfloor dE \rfloor_2$ of a change environment $dE$.

*Expressiveness.* A closure in the base environment can be used to represent a top-level definition. Since environment entries can point to primitives, we need no syntax to directly represent calls of primitives in the syntax of base terms. To encode in our syntax a program with top-level definitions and a term to be evaluated representing the entry point, one can produce a term $t$ representing the

[1] It is more common to count instead small-step evaluation steps [3,4], but our choice simplifies some proofs and makes a minor difference in others.

$$\frac{[\text{SVar}]}{E \vdash x \Downarrow_1 E(x)} \qquad \frac{\begin{array}{c}[\text{STuple}]\\ E; y = (E(\overline{x})) \vdash t \Downarrow_n v\end{array}}{E \vdash \mathbf{let}\, y = (\overline{x})\, \mathbf{in}\, t \Downarrow_{n+1} v} \qquad \frac{\begin{array}{c}[\text{SPrimitiveCall}]\\ E(f) = \mathbf{p}\\ E; y = \delta_{\mathbf{p}}(E(x)) \vdash t \Downarrow_n v\end{array}}{E \vdash \mathbf{let}\, y = f\, x\, \mathbf{in}\, t \Downarrow_{n+1} v}$$

$$\frac{\begin{array}{c}[\text{SClosureCall}]\\ E(f) = E_f[\lambda x.\, t_f] \qquad E_f; x = E(x) \vdash t_f \Downarrow_m v_y \qquad E; y = v_y \vdash t \Downarrow_n v\end{array}}{E \vdash \mathbf{let}\, y = f\, x\, \mathbf{in}\, t \Downarrow_{m+n+1} v}$$

**Fig. 3.** Step-indexed big-step semantics for base terms of source language $\lambda_{AL}$.

entry point together with an environment $E$ containing as values any top-level definitions, primitives and literals used in the program. Semi-formally, given an environment $E_0$ mentioning needed primitives and literals, and a list of top-level function definitions $D = \overline{f = \lambda x.\, t}$ defined in terms of $E_0$, we can produce a base environment $E = \mathcal{L}(D)$, with $\mathcal{L}$ defined by:

$$\mathcal{L}(\bullet) = E_0 \text{ and } \mathcal{L}(D, f = \lambda x.\, t) = E, f = E[\lambda x.\, t] \text{ where } \mathcal{L}(D) = E$$

Correspondingly, we extend all our term transformations to values and environments to transform such encoded top-level definitions.

Our mechanization can encode $n$-ary functions "$\lambda(x_1, x_2, \ldots, x_n).\, t$" through unary functions that accept tuples; we encode partial application using a **curry** primitive such that, essentially, $\mathbf{curry}\, f\, x\, y = f\,(x, y)$; suspended partial applications are represented as closures. This encoding does not support currying efficiently, we further discuss this limitation in Sect. 4.4.

Control operators, like recursion combinators or branching, can be introduced as primitive operations as well. If the branching condition changes, expressing the output change in general requires replacement changes. Similarly to branching we can add tagged unions.

To check the assertions of the last two paragraphs, the Coq development contains the definition of a **curry** primitive as well as a primitive for a fixpoint combinator, allowing general recursion and recursive data structures as well.

### 3.3 Static Differentiation from $\lambda_{AL}$ to $\lambda_{IAL}$

Previous work [7] defines static differentiation for simply-typed $\lambda$-calculus terms. Figure 2 transposes differentiation as a transformation from $\lambda_{AL}$ to $\lambda_{IAL}$ and defines $\lambda_{IAL}$'s syntax.

Differentiating a base term $t$ produces a change term $\mathcal{D}^{\iota}(t)$, its *derivative*. Differentiating final result variable $x$ produces its change variable $dx$. Differentiation copies each binding of an intermediate result $y$ to the output and adds a new binding for its change $dy$. If $y$ is bound to tuple $(\overline{x})$, then $dy$ will be bound to the change tuple $(\overline{dx})$. If $y$ is bound to function application "$f\ x$", then $dy$ will be bound to the application of function change $df$ to input $x$ and its change $dx$. We explain differentiation of environments $\mathcal{D}^{\iota}(E)$ later in this section.

$$\frac{[\text{SDVar}]}{dE \vdash dx \Downarrow_1 dE(dx)}$$

$$\frac{[\text{SDTuple}] \quad dE(\overline{x}, \overline{dx}) = \overline{v_x}, \overline{dv_x} \quad dE; y = (\overline{v_x}); dy = (\overline{dv_x}) \vdash dt \Downarrow_n dv}{dE \vdash \textbf{let}\, y = (\overline{x}), dy = (\overline{dx})\, \textbf{in}\, dt \Downarrow_{n+1} dv}$$

$$\frac{[\text{SDReplaceCall}] \quad \lfloor dE \rfloor_1 \vdash @(f, x) \Downarrow_m v_y \quad \lfloor dE \rfloor_2 \vdash @(f, x) \Downarrow_n v_y{}' \quad dE(df) = !v_f \quad dE; y = v_y; dy = !v_y{}' \vdash dt \Downarrow_p dv}{dE \vdash \textbf{let}\, y = f\, x, dy = df\, x\, dx\, \textbf{in}\, dt \Downarrow_{m+n+p+1} dv}$$

$$\frac{[\text{SDPrimitiveNil}] \quad dE(f, df) = \mathbf{p}, 0_{\mathbf{p}} \quad dE(x, dx) = v_x, dv_x \quad dE; y = \delta_{\mathbf{p}}(v_x); dy = \Delta_{\mathbf{p}}(v_x, dv_x) \vdash dt \Downarrow_n dv}{dE \vdash \textbf{let}\, y = f\, x, dy = df\, x\, dx\, \textbf{in}\, dt \Downarrow_{n+1} dv}$$

$$\frac{[\text{SDClosureChange}] \quad dE(f, df) = E_f[\lambda x.\, t_f], dE_f[\lambda x\, dx.\, dt_f] \quad dE(x, dx) = v_x, dv_x \quad E_f; x = v_x \vdash t_f \Downarrow_m v_y \quad dE_f; x = v_x; dx = dv_x \vdash dt_f \Downarrow_n dv_y \quad dE; y = v_y; dy = dv_y \vdash dt \Downarrow_p dv}{dE \vdash \textbf{let}\, y = f\, x, dy = df\, x\, dx\, \textbf{in}\, dt \Downarrow_{m+n+p+1} dv}$$

**Fig. 4.** Step-indexed big-step semantics for the change terms of $\lambda_{IAL}$.

Evaluating $\mathcal{D}^{\iota}(t)$ recomputes all intermediate results computed by $t$. This recomputation will be avoided through cache-transfer style in Sect. 3.5. A comparison with the original static differentiation [7] can be found in Appendix A.

*Semantics for* $\lambda_{IAL}$. We move on to define how $\lambda_{IAL}$ change terms evaluate to change values. We start by defining necessary definitions and operations on changes, such as define *change values* $dv$, *change environments* $dE$, and the *update operator* $\oplus$.

Closed change values $dv$ are particular $\lambda_L$ values $a_v$. They are either a closure change, a tuple change, a literal change, a replacement change or a primitive nil change. A closure change is a closure containing a change environment $dE$ and a $\lambda$-abstraction expecting a value and a change value as arguments to evaluate a change term into an output change value. An evaluation environment $dE$ follows the same structure as **let**-bindings of change terms: it binds variables to closed values and each variable $x$ is immediately followed by a binding for its associated change variable $dx$. As with **let**-bindings of change terms, $\alpha$-renamings in an environment $dE$ must rename $dx$ into $dy$ if $x$ is renamed into $y$. We define the *update operator* $\oplus$ to update a value with a change. This operator is a partial function written "$v \oplus dv$", defined as follows:

$$\begin{aligned}
v_1 \oplus {!v_2} &= v_2 \\
\ell \oplus d\ell &= \delta_\oplus(\ell, d\ell) \\
E[\lambda x.\, t] \oplus dE[\lambda x\; dx.\, dt] &= (E \oplus dE)[\lambda x.\, t] \\
(v_1, \ldots, v_n) \oplus (dv_1, \ldots, dv_n) &= (v_1 \oplus dv_1, \ldots, v_n \oplus dv_n) \\
\mathbf{p} \oplus 0_{\mathbf{p}} &= \mathbf{p}
\end{aligned}$$

where $(E; x = v) \oplus (dE; x = v; dx = dv) = ((E \oplus dE); x = (v \oplus dv))$.

Replacement changes can be used to update all values (literals, tuples, primitives and closures), while tuple changes can only update tuples, literal changes can only update literals, primitive nil can only update primitives and closure changes can only update closures. A replacement change overrides the current value $v$ with a new one $v'$. On literals, $\oplus$ is defined via some interpretation function $\delta_\oplus$, which takes a literal and a literal change to produce an updated literal. Change update for a closure ignores $dt$ instead of computing something like $dE[t \oplus dt]$. This may seem surprising, but we only need $\oplus$ to behave well for valid changes (as shown by Theorem 3.1): for valid closure changes, $dt$ must behave anyway similarly to $\mathcal{D}^\iota(t)$, which Cai et al. [7] show to be a nil change. Hence, $t \oplus \mathcal{D}^\iota(t)$ and $t \oplus dt$ both behave like $t$, so $\oplus$ can ignore $dt$ and only consider environment updates. This definition also avoids having to modify terms at runtime, which would be difficult to implement safely. We could also implement $f \oplus df$ as a function that invokes both $f$ and $df$ on its argument, as done by Cai et al. [7], but we believe that would be less efficient when $\oplus$ is used at runtime. As we discuss in Sect. 3.4, we restrict validity to avoid this runtime overhead.

Having given these definitions, we show in Fig. 4 a step-indexed big-step semantics for change terms, defined through judgment $dE \vdash dt \Downarrow_n dv$ (where $n$ can be omitted). This judgment is pronounced "Under the environment $dE$, the change term $dt$ evaluates into the closed change value $dv$ in $n$ steps." Rules [SDVar] and [SDTuple] are unsurprising. To evaluate function calls in **let**-bindings "**let** $y = f\ x, dy = df\ x\ dx$ **in** $dt$" we have three rules, depending on the shape of $dE(df)$. These rules all recompute the value $v_y$ of $y$ in the original environment, but compute differently the change $dy$ to $y$. If $dE(df)$ replaces the value of $f$, [SDReplaceCall] recomputes $v'_y = f\ x$ from scratch in the new environment, and bind $dy$ to $!v'_y$ when evaluating the **let** body. If $dE(df)$ is the nil change for primitive $\mathbf{p}$, [SDPrimitiveNil] computes $dy$ by running $\mathbf{p}$'s derivative through function $\Delta_{\mathbf{p}}(-)$. If $dE(df)$ is a closure change, [SDClosureChange] invokes it normally to compute its change $dv_y$. As we show, if the closure change is valid, its body behaves like $f$'s derivative, hence incrementalizes $f$ correctly.

Closure changes with non-nil environment changes represent partial application of derivatives to non-nil changes; for instance, if $f$ takes a pair and $dx$ is a non-nil change, $0_{\mathbf{curry}}\, f\ df\ x\ dx$ constructs a closure change containing $dx$, using the derivative of **curry** mentioned in Sect. 3.2. In general, such closure changes do not arise from the rules we show, only from derivatives of primitives.

### 3.4 A New Soundness Proof for Static Differentiation

In this section, we show that static differentiation is sound (Theorem 3.3) and that Eq. (1) holds:

$$f\ a_2 = f\ a_1 \oplus \mathcal{D}^{\iota}(f)\ a_1\ da \tag{1}$$

whenever $da$ is a valid change from $a_1$ to $a_2$ (as defined later). One might want to prove this equation assuming only that $a_1 \oplus da = a_2$, but this is false in general. A direct proof by induction on terms fails in the case for application (ultimately because $f_1 \oplus df = f_2$ and $a_1 \oplus da = a_2$ do not imply that $f_1\ a_1 \oplus df\ a_1\ da = f_2\ a_2$). As usual, this can be fixed by introducing a logical relation. We call ours *validity*: a function change is valid if it turns valid input changes into valid output changes.

- $d\ell \rhd_n \ell \hookrightarrow \delta_\oplus(\ell, d\ell)$ • $!v_2 \rhd_n v_1 \hookrightarrow v_2$ • $0_{\mathbf{p}} \rhd_n \mathbf{p} \hookrightarrow \mathbf{p}$
- $(dv_1, \ldots, dv_m) \rhd_n (v_1, \ldots, v_m) \hookrightarrow (v'_1, \ldots, v'_m)$
  if and only if $(v_1, \ldots, v_m) \oplus (dv_1, \ldots, dv_m) = (v'_1, \ldots, v'_m)$
  and $\forall k < n,\ \forall i \in [1 \ldots m],\ dv_i \rhd_k v_i \hookrightarrow v'_i$
- $dE[\lambda x\ dx.\ dt] \rhd_n E_1[\lambda x.\ t] \hookrightarrow E_2[\lambda x.\ t]$
  if and only if $E_2 = E_1 \oplus dE$ and
  $\forall k < n, v_1, dv, v_2,$
  if $dv \rhd_k v_1 \hookrightarrow v_2$ then
  $(dE; x = v_1; dx = dv \vdash dt) \blacktriangleright_k (E_1; x = v_1 \vdash t) \hookrightarrow (E_2; x = v_2 \vdash t)$
- $(dE \vdash dt) \blacktriangleright_n (E_1 \vdash t_1) \hookrightarrow (E_2 \vdash t_2)$
  if and only if $\forall k < n, v_1, v_2,$
  $E_1 \vdash t_1 \Downarrow_k v_1$ and $E_2 \vdash t_2 \Downarrow v_2$ implies that
  $\exists dv, dE \vdash dt \Downarrow dv \wedge dv \rhd_{n-k} v_1 \hookrightarrow v_2$

**Fig. 5.** Step-indexed validity, through judgments for values and for terms.

Static differentiation is only sound on input changes that are *valid*. Cai et al. [7] show soundness for a strongly normalizing simply-typed λ-calculus using denotational semantics. Using an operational semantics, we generalize this result to an untyped and Turing-complete language, so we must turn to a *step-indexed* logical relation [3,4].

*Validity as a step-indexed logical relation.* We say that "$dv$ is a valid change from $v_1$ to $v_2$, up to $k$ steps" and write

$$dv \rhd_k v_1 \hookrightarrow v_2$$

to mean that $dv$ is a change from $v_1$ to $v_2$ and that $dv$ is a *valid* description of the differences between $v_1$ and $v_2$, with validity tested with up to $k$ steps. This relation *approximates* validity; if a change $dv$ is valid at all approximations, it is simply valid (between $v_1$ and $v_2$); we write then $dv \rhd v_1 \hookrightarrow v_2$ (omitting the step-index $k$) to mean that validity holds at all step-indexes. We similarly omit step-indexes $k$ from other step-indexed relations when they hold for all $k$.

To justify this intuition of validity, we show that a valid change from $v_1$ to $v_2$ goes indeed from $v_1$ to $v_2$ (Theorem 3.1), and that if a change is valid up to $k$ steps, it is also valid up to fewer steps (Lemma 3.2).

**Theorem 3.1 ($\oplus$ agrees with validity)**
*If $dv \rhd_k v_1 \hookrightarrow v_2$ holds for all $k > 0$, then $v_1 \oplus dv = v_2$.*

**Lemma 3.2 (Downward-closure)**
*If $N \geq n$, then $dv \rhd_N v_1 \hookrightarrow v_2$ implies $dv \rhd_n v_1 \hookrightarrow v_2$.*

Crucially, Theorem 3.1 enables (a) computing $v_2$ from a valid change and its source, and (b) showing Eq. (1) through validity. As discussed, $\oplus$ ignores changes to closure bodies to be faster, which is only sound if those changes are nil; to ensure Theorem 3.1 still holds, validity on closure changes must be adapted accordingly and forbid non-nil changes to closure bodies. This choice, while unusual, does not affect our results: if input changes do not modify closure bodies, intermediate changes will not modify closure bodies either. Logical relation experts might regard this as a domain-specific invariant we add to our relation. Alternatives are discussed by Giarrusso [10, Appendix C].

As usual with step-indexing, validity is defined by well-founded induction over naturals ordered by $<$; to show well-foundedness we observe that evaluation always takes at least one step.

Validity for values, terms and environments is formally defined by cases in Fig. 5. First, a literal change $d\ell$ is a valid change from $\ell$ to $\ell \oplus d\ell = \delta_{\oplus}(\ell, d\ell)$. Since the function $\delta_{\oplus}$ is partial, the relation only holds for the literal changes $d\ell$ which are valid changes for $\ell$. Second, a replacement change $!v_2$ is always a valid change from any value $v_1$ to $v_2$. Third, a primitive nil change is a valid change between any primitive and itself. Fourth, a tuple change is valid up to step $n$, if each of its components is valid up to any step strictly less than $n$. Fifth, we define validity for closure changes. Roughly speaking, this statement means that a closure change is valid if (i) its environment change $dE$ is valid for the original closure environment $E_1$ and for the new closure environment $E_2$; and (ii) when applied to related values, the closure *bodies* $t$ are related by $dt$, as defined by the auxiliary judgment $(dE \vdash dt) \blacktriangleright_n (E_1 \vdash t_1) \hookrightarrow (E_2 \vdash t_2)$ for validity between terms under related environments (defined in Appendix C). As usual with step-indexed logical relations, in the definition for this judgment about terms, the number $k$ of steps required to evaluate the term $t_1$ is subtracted from the number of steps $n$ that can be used to relate the outcomes of the term evaluations.

*Soundness of differentiation.* We can state a soundness theorem for differentiation without mentioning step-indexes; thanks to this theorem, we can compute the updated result $v_2$ not by rerunning a computation, but by updating the base result $v_1$ with the result change $dv$ that we compute through a derivative on the input change. A corollary shows Eq. (1).

**Theorem 3.3 (Soundness of differentiation in $\lambda_{AL}$).** *If $dE$ is a valid change environment from base environment $E_1$ to updated environment $E_2$, that is $dE \rhd E_1 \hookrightarrow E_2$, and if $t$ converges both in the base and updated environment, that is $E_1 \vdash t \Downarrow v_1$ and $E_2 \vdash t \Downarrow v_2$, then $\mathcal{D}^{\iota}(t)$ evaluates under the change environment $dE$ to a valid change $dv$ between base result $v_1$ and updated result $v_2$, that is $dE \vdash \mathcal{D}^{\iota}(t) \Downarrow dv$, $dv \rhd v_1 \hookrightarrow v_2$ and $v_1 \oplus dv = v_2$.*

We must first show that derivatives map input changes valid up to $k$ steps to output changes valid up to $k$ steps, that is, the *fundamental property* of our step-indexed logical relation:

**Lemma 3.4 (Fundamental Property)**
*For each $n$, if $dE \rhd_n E_1 \hookrightarrow E_2$ then $(dE \vdash \mathcal{D}^{\iota}(t)) \blacktriangleright_n (E_1 \vdash t) \hookrightarrow (E_2 \vdash t)$.*

**Translation of terms** $\boxed{M = \mathcal{T}_t(t')}$

$$\begin{aligned}\mathcal{T}_t(\mathbf{let}\, y = f\, x\, \mathbf{in}\, t') &= \mathbf{let}\, y, c^y_{fx} = f\, x\, \mathbf{in}\, \mathcal{T}_t(t')\\ \mathcal{T}_t(\mathbf{let}\, y = (\overline{x})\, \mathbf{in}\, t') &= \mathbf{let}\, y = (\overline{x})\, \mathbf{in}\, \mathcal{T}_t(t')\\ \mathcal{T}_t(x) &= (x, \mathcal{C}(t))\end{aligned}$$

**Cache of a term** $\boxed{C = \mathcal{C}(t)}$

$$\begin{aligned}\mathcal{C}(\mathbf{let}\, y = f\, x\, \mathbf{in}\, t) &= ((\mathcal{C}(t), y), c^y_{fx})\\ \mathcal{C}(\mathbf{let}\, y = (\overline{x})\, \mathbf{in}\, t) &= (\mathcal{C}(t), y)\\ \mathcal{C}(x) &= ()\end{aligned}$$

**Translation of values** $\boxed{V = \mathcal{T}(v)}$

$$\begin{aligned}\mathcal{T}((\overline{v})) &= (\overline{\mathcal{T}(v)})\\ \mathcal{T}(E[\lambda x.\, t]) &= \mathcal{T}(E)[\lambda x.\, \mathcal{T}_t(t)]\\ \mathcal{T}(\ell) &= \ell\\ \mathcal{T}(\mathbf{p}) &= \mathbf{p}\end{aligned}$$

**Base terms**

$$\begin{aligned}M ::= &\ \mathbf{let}\, y, c^y_{fx} = f\, x\, \mathbf{in}\, M\\ \mid &\ \mathbf{let}\, y = (\overline{x})\, \mathbf{in}\, M\\ \mid &\ (x, C)\end{aligned}$$

**Cache terms/patterns**

$$C ::= (C, c^y_{fx}) \mid (C, x) \mid ()$$

**Closed values**

$$V ::= (\overline{V}) \mid F[\lambda x.\, M] \mid \ell \mid \mathbf{p}$$

**Cache values**

$$V_c ::= () \mid (V_c, V_c) \mid (V_c, V)$$

**Evaluation environments**

$$F ::= \bullet \mid F; D_v$$

**Base environment entries**

$$D_v ::= x = V \mid c^y_{fx} = V_c$$

**Fig. 6.** Cache-Transfer Style translation and syntax of its target language $\lambda_{CAL}$.

### 3.5 CTS Conversion

Figures 6 and 7 define both the syntax of $\lambda_{CAL}$ and $\lambda_{ICAL}$ and CTS conversion. The latter comprises CTS differentiation $\mathcal{D}(-)$, from $\lambda_{AL}$ to $\lambda_{ICAL}$, and CTS translation $\mathcal{T}(-)$, from $\lambda_{AL}$ to $\lambda_{CAL}$.

*Syntax definitions for the target languages* $\lambda_{CAL}$ *and* $\lambda_{ICAL}$. Terms of $\lambda_{CAL}$ follow again λ-lifted A'NF, like $\lambda_{AL}$, except that a **let**-binding for a function application "$f\ x$" now binds an extra *cache identifier* $c^y_{fx}$ besides output $y$. Cache identifiers have non-standard syntax: it can be seen as a triple that refers to the value identifiers $f$, $x$ and $y$. Hence, an $\alpha$-renaming of one of these three identifiers must refresh the cache identifier accordingly. Result terms explicitly return cache $C$ through syntax $(x, C)$. Caches are encoded through nested tuples, but they are in fact a tree-like data structure that is isomorphic to an execution trace. This trace contains both immediate values and the execution traces of nested function calls.

The syntax for $\lambda_{ICAL}$ matches the image of the CTS derivative and witnesses the CTS discipline followed by the derivatives: to determine $dy$, the derivative of $f$ evaluated at point $x$ with change $dx$ expects the cache produced by evaluating $y$ in the base term. The derivative returns the updated cache which contains the intermediate results that would be gathered by the evaluation of $f\ (x \oplus dx)$. The result term of every change term returns the computed change and a cache update $dC$, where each value identifier $x$ of the input cache is updated with its corresponding change $dx$.

**Differentiation of terms** $\boxed{dM = \mathcal{D}_t(t')}$

$$\begin{aligned}
\mathcal{D}_t(\mathbf{let}\ y = f\ x\ \mathbf{in}\ t') &= \mathbf{let}\ dy, c^y_{fx} = df\ x\ dx\ c^y_{fx}\ \mathbf{in} \\
&\quad\ \mathcal{D}_t(t') \\
\mathcal{D}_t(\mathbf{let}\ y = (\overline{x})\ \mathbf{in}\ t') &= \mathbf{let}\ dy = (\overline{dx})\ \mathbf{in}\ \mathcal{D}_t(M') \\
\mathcal{D}_t(x) &= (dx, \mathcal{U}(t))
\end{aligned}$$

**Cache update of a term** $\boxed{dC = \mathcal{U}(t)}$

$$\begin{aligned}
\mathcal{U}(\mathbf{let}\ y = f\ x\ \mathbf{in}\ t) &= ((\mathcal{U}(t), y \oplus dy), c^y_{fx}) \\
\mathcal{U}(\mathbf{let}\ y = (\overline{x})\ \mathbf{in}\ t) &= (\mathcal{U}(t), y \oplus dy) \\
\mathcal{U}(x) &= ()
\end{aligned}$$

**Differentiation of change values** $\boxed{dV = \mathcal{T}(dv)}$

$$\begin{aligned}
\mathcal{T}((\overline{dv})) &= (\overline{\mathcal{T}(dv)}) \\
\mathcal{T}(dE[\lambda x\ dx.\, \mathcal{D}^\iota(t)]) &= \mathcal{T}(dE)[\lambda x\ dx\ (\mathcal{C}(t)).\, \mathcal{D}_t(t)] \\
\mathcal{T}(!v) &= !\mathcal{T}(v) \\
\mathcal{T}(d\ell) &= d\ell \\
\mathcal{T}(0_{\mathbf{p}}) &= 0_{\mathbf{p}}
\end{aligned}$$

**Change terms**

$$\begin{aligned}
dM ::= &\ \mathbf{let}\ dy, c^y_{fx} = df\ x\ dx\ c^y_{fx} \\
&\ \mathbf{in}\ dM \\
|&\ \mathbf{let}\ dy = (\overline{dx})\ \mathbf{in}\ dM \\
|&\ (dx, dC)
\end{aligned}$$

**Cache updates**

$$dC ::= (dC, c^y_{fx}) \mid (dC, x \oplus dx) \mid ()$$

**Change values**

$$dV ::= (\overline{dV}) \mid dF[\lambda x\ dx\ C.\ dM] \mid d\ell \mid 0_{\mathbf{p}} \mid !V$$

**Change environments**

$$dF ::= \bullet \mid dF; dD_v$$

**Change environment entries**

$$dD_v ::= D_v \mid dx = dV$$

**Fig. 7.** CTS differentiation and syntax of its target language $\lambda_{ICAL}$. Beware $\mathcal{T}(dE[\lambda x\ dx.\, \mathcal{D}^\iota(t)])$ applies a left-inverse of $\mathcal{D}^\iota(t)$ during pattern matching.

*CTS conversion and differentiation.* These translations use two auxiliary functions: $\mathcal{C}(t)$ which computes the cache term of a $\lambda_{AL}$ term $t$, and $\mathcal{U}(t)$, which computes the cache update of $t$'s derivative.

CTS translation on terms, $\mathcal{T}_t(t')$, accepts as inputs a *global* term $t$ and a subterm $t'$ of $t$. In tail position ($t' = x$), the translation generates code to return both the result $x$ and the cache $\mathcal{C}(t)$ of the global term $t$. When the transformation visits **let**-bindings, it outputs extra bindings for caches $c^y_{fx}$ on function calls and visits the **let**-body.

Similarly to $\mathcal{T}_t(t')$, CTS derivation $\mathcal{D}_t(t')$ accepts a global term $t$ and a subterm $t'$ of $t$. In tail position, the translation returns both the result change $dx$ and the cache update $\mathcal{U}(t)$. On **let**-bindings, it *does not* output bindings for $y$ but for $dy$, it outputs extra bindings for $c^y_{fx}$ as in the previous case and visits the **let**-body.

To handle function definitions, we transform the base environment $E$ through $\mathcal{T}(E)$ and $\mathcal{T}(\mathcal{D}^{\iota}(E))$ (translations of environments are done pointwise, see Appendix D). Since $\mathcal{D}^{\iota}(E)$ includes $E$, we describe $\mathcal{T}(\mathcal{D}^{\iota}(E))$ to also cover $\mathcal{T}(E)$. Overall, $\mathcal{T}(\mathcal{D}^{\iota}(E))$ CTS-converts each source closure $f = E[\lambda x.\, t]$ to a CTS-translated function, with body $\mathcal{T}_t(t)$, and to the CTS derivative $df$ of $f$. This CTS derivative pattern matches on its input cache using cache pattern $\mathcal{C}(t)$. That way, we make sure that the shape of the cache expected by $df$ is consistent with the shape of the cache produced by $f$. The body of derivative $df$ is computed by CTS-deriving $f$'s body via $\mathcal{D}_t(t)$.

### 3.6 Semantics of $\lambda_{CAL}$ and $\lambda_{ICAL}$

An evaluation environment $F$ of $\lambda_{CAL}$ contains both values and cache values. Values $V$ resemble $\lambda_{AL}$ values $v$, cache values $V_c$ match cache terms $C$ and change values $dV$ match $\lambda_{IAL}$ change values $dv$. Evaluation environments $dF$ for change terms must also bind change values, so functions in change closures take not just a base input $x$ and an input change $dx$, like in $\lambda_{IAL}$, but also an input cache $C$. By abuse of notation, we reuse the same syntax $C$ to both deconstruct and construct caches.

Base terms of the language are evaluated using a conventional big-step semantics, consisting of two judgments. Judgment "$F \vdash M \Downarrow (V, V_c)$" is read "Under evaluation environment $F$, base term $M$ evaluates to value $V$ and cache $V_c$". The semantics follows the one of $\lambda_{AL}$; since terms include extra code to produce and carry caches along the computation, the semantics evaluates that code as well. For space reasons, we defer semantic rules to Appendix E. Auxiliary judgment "$F \vdash C \Downarrow V_c$" evaluates cache terms into cache values: It traverses a cache term and looks up the environment for the values to be cached.

Change terms of $\lambda_{ICAL}$ are also evaluated using a big-step semantics, which resembles the semantics of $\lambda_{IAL}$ and $\lambda_{CAL}$. Unlike those semantics, evaluating cache updates $(dC, x \oplus dx)$ is evaluated using the $\oplus$ operator (overloaded on $\lambda_{CAL}$ values and $\lambda_{ICAL}$ changes). By lack of space, its rules are deferred to Appendix E. This semantics relies on three judgments. Judgment "$dF \vdash dM \Downarrow (dV, V_c)$" is read "Under evaluation environment $F$, change term $dM$ evaluates to change value $dV$ and updated cache $V_c$". The first auxiliary judgment "$dF \vdash dC \Downarrow V_c$" defines evaluation of cache update terms. The final auxiliary judgment "$V_c \sim C \rightarrow dF$" describes a limited form of pattern matching used by CTS derivatives: namely, how a cache pattern $C$ matches a cache value $V_c$ to produce a change environment $dF$.

### 3.7 Soundness of CTS Conversion

The proof is based on a simulation in lock-step, but two subtle points emerge. First, we must relate $\lambda_{AL}$ environments that do not contain caches, with $\lambda_{CAL}$ environments that do. Second, while evaluating CTS derivatives, the evaluation environment mixes caches from the base computation and updated caches computed by the derivatives.

Theorem 3.7 follows because differentiation is sound (Theorem 3.3) and evaluation commutes with CTS conversion; this last point requires two lemmas. First, CTS translation of base terms commutes with our semantics:

**Lemma 3.5 (Commutation for base evaluations)**
*For all* $E, t$ *and* $v$*, if* $E \vdash t \Downarrow v$*, there exists* $V_c$*,* $\mathcal{T}(E) \vdash \mathcal{T}_t(t) \Downarrow (\mathcal{T}(v), V_c)$.

Second, we need a corresponding lemma for CTS translation of differentiation results: intuitively, evaluating a derivative and CTS translating the resulting change value must give the same result as evaluating the CTS derivative. But to formalize this, we must specify which environments are used for evaluation, and this requires two technicalities.

Assume derivative $\mathcal{D}^\iota(t)$ evaluates correctly in some environment $dE$. Evaluating CTS derivative $\mathcal{D}_t(t)$ requires cache values from the base computation, but they are not in $\mathcal{T}(dE)$! Therefore, we must introduce a judgment to complete a CTS-translated environment with the appropriate caches (see Appendix F).

Next, consider evaluating a change term of the form $dM = \mathbb{C}[dM']$, where $\mathbb{C}$ is a standard single-hole change-term context—that is, for $\lambda_{ICAL}$, a sequence of **let**-bindings. When evaluating $dM$, we eventually evaluate $dM'$ in a change environment $dF$ updated by $\mathbb{C}$: the change environment $dF$ contains both the updated caches coming from the evaluation of $\mathbb{C}$ and the caches coming from the base computation (which will be updated by the evaluation of $dM$). Again, a new judgment, given in Appendix F, is required to model this process.

With these two judgments, the second key Lemma stating the commutation between evaluation of derivatives and evaluation of CTS derivatives can be stated. We give here an informal version of this Lemma, the actual formal version can be found in Appendix F.

**Lemma 3.6 (Commutation for derivatives evaluation)**
*If the evaluation of* $\mathcal{D}^\iota(t)$ *leads to an environment* $dE_0$ *when it reaches the differentiated context* $\mathcal{D}^\iota(\mathbb{C})$ *where* $t = \mathbb{C}[t']$*, and if the CTS conversion of* $t$ *under this environment completed with base (resp. changed) caches evaluates into a base value* $\mathcal{T}(v)$ *(resp. a changed value* $\mathcal{T}(v')$*) and a base cache value* $V_c$ *(resp. an updated cache value* $V_c'$*), then under an environment containing the caches already updated by the evaluation of* $\mathcal{D}^\iota(\mathbb{C})$ *and the base caches to be updated, the CTS derivative of* $t'$ *evaluates to* $\mathcal{T}(dv)$ *such that* $v \oplus dv = v'$ *and to the updated cache* $V_c'$.

Finally, we can state soundness of CTS differentiation. This theorem says that CTS derivatives not only produce valid changes for incrementalization but that they also correctly consume and update caches.

**Theorem 3.7 (Soundness of CTS differentiation)**
*If the following hypotheses hold:*

1. $dE \rhd E \hookrightarrow E'$
2. $E \vdash t \Downarrow v$
3. $E' \vdash t \Downarrow v'$

*then there exists* $dv$, $V_c$, $V_c'$ *and* $F_0$ *such that:*

1. $\mathcal{T}(E) \vdash \mathcal{T}(t) \Downarrow (\mathcal{T}(v), V_c)$
2. $\mathcal{T}(E') \vdash \mathcal{T}(t) \Downarrow (\mathcal{T}(v'), V_c')$
3. $\mathcal{C}(t) \sim V_c \rightarrow F_0$
4. $\mathcal{T}(dE); F_0 \vdash \mathcal{D}_t(t) \Downarrow (\mathcal{T}(dv), V_c')$
5. $v \oplus dv = v'$

# 4 Incrementalization Case Studies

In this section, we investigate two questions: whether our transformations can target a typed language like Haskell and whether automatically transformed programs can perform well. We implement by hand primitives on sequences, bags and maps in Haskell. The input terms in all case studies are written in a deep embedding of $\lambda_{AL}$ into Haskell. The transformations generate Haskell code that uses our primitives and their derivatives.

We run the transformations on three case studies: a computation of the average value of a bag of integers, a nested loop over two sequences and a more involved example inspired by Koch et al. [17]'s work on incrementalizing database queries. For each case study, we make sure that results are consistent between from scratch recomputation and incremental evaluation; we measure the execution time for from scratch recomputation and incremental computation as well as the space consumption of caches. We obtain efficient incremental programs, that is ones for which incremental computation is faster than from scratch recomputation. The measurements indicate that we do get the expected asymptotic improvement in time of incremental computation over from scratch recomputation by a linear factor while the caches grows in a similar linear factor.

Our benchmarks were compiled by GHC 8.2.2 and run on a 2.20 GHz hexa core Intel(R) Xeon(R) CPU E5-2420 v2 with 32 GB of RAM running Ubuntu 14.04. We use the *criterion* [21] benchmarking library.

## 4.1 Averaging Bags of Integers

Section 2.1 motivates our transformation with a running example of computing the average over a bag of integers. We represent bags as maps from elements to (possibly negative) multiplicities. Earlier work [7,17] represents bag changes as bags of removed and added elements. We use a different representation of bag changes that takes advantage of the changes to elements and provide primitives on bags and their derivatives. The CTS variant of *map*, that we call *mapC*, takes a function *fC* in CTS and a bag *as* and produces a bag and a cache. The cache stores for each invocation of *fC*, and therefore for each distinct element in *as*, the result of *fC* of type *b* and the cache of type *c*.

Inspired by Rossberg et al. [23], all higher-order functions (and typically, also their caches) are parametric over cache types of their function arguments. Here, functions *mapC* and *dmapC* and cache type *MapC* are parametric over the cache type *c* of *fC* and *dfC*.

$$
\begin{aligned}
&map :: (a \to b) \to Bag\ a \to Bag\ b \\
&\textbf{data}\ MapC\ a\ b\ c = MapC\ (Map\ a\ (b, c)) \\
&mapC :: (a \to (b, c)) \to Bag\ a \to (Bag\ b, MapC\ a\ b\ c) \\
&dmapC :: (a \to (b, c)) \to (a \to \Delta a \to c \to (\Delta b, c)) \to Bag\ a \to \Delta(Bag\ a) \to \\
&\quad MapC\ a\ b\ c \to (\Delta(Bag\ b), MapC\ a\ b\ c)
\end{aligned}
$$

We wrote the *length* and *sum* functions used in our benchmarks in terms of primitives *map* and *foldGroup* and had their CTS function and CTS derivative generated automatically.

We evaluate whether we can produce an updated result with *daverageC* shown in Sect. 2.1 faster than by from scratch recomputation with *average*. We expect the speedup of *daverageC* to depend on the size of the input bag $n$. We fix an input bag of size $n$ as the bag containing the numbers from 1 to $n$. We define a change that inserts the integer 1 into the bag. To measure execution time of from scratch recomputation, we apply *average* to the input bag updated with the change. To measure execution time of the CTS function *averageC*, we apply *averageC* to the input bag updated with the change. To measure execution time of the CTS derivative *daverageC*, we apply *daverageC* to the input bag, the change and the cache produced by *averageC* when applied to the input bag. In all three cases we ensure that all results and caches are fully forced so as to not hide any computational cost behind laziness.

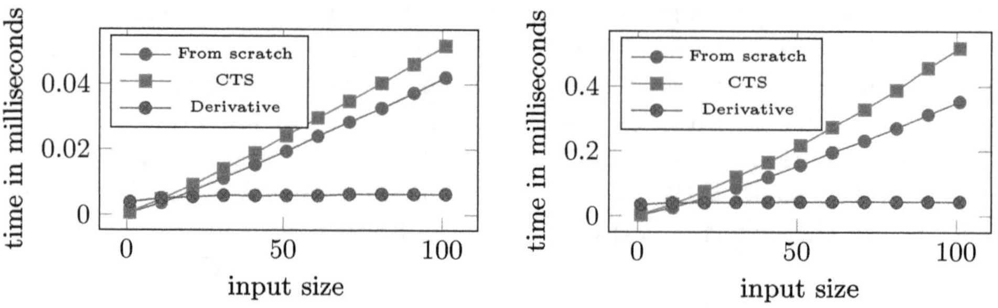


(a) Benchmark results for *average* (b) Benchmark results for *totalPrice*

**Fig. 8.** Benchmark results for *average* and *totalPrice*

The plot in Fig. 8a shows execution time versus the size $n$ of the base input. To produce the base result and cache, the CTS transformed function *averageC* takes longer than the original *average* function takes to produce just the result. Producing the updated result incrementally is slower than from scratch recomputation for small input sizes, but because of the difference in time complexity becomes faster as the input size grows. The size of the cache grows linearly with the size of the input, which is not optimal for this example. We leave optimizing the space usage of examples like this to future work.

### 4.2 Nested Loops over Two Sequences

Next, we consider CTS differentiation on a higher-order example. To incrementalize this example efficiently, we have to enable detecting nil function changes at runtime by representing function changes as closures that can be inspected by incremental programs. Our example here is the Cartesian product of two sequences computed in terms of functions *map* and *concat*.

$$\begin{aligned}
&\mathit{cartesianProduct} :: \mathit{Sequence}\ a \to \mathit{Sequence}\ b \to \mathit{Sequence}\ (a, b)\\
&\mathit{cartesianProduct}\ xs\ ys = \mathit{concatMap}\ (\lambda x \to \mathit{map}\ (\lambda y \to (x, y))\ ys)\ xs\\
&\mathit{concatMap} :: (a \to \mathit{Sequence}\ b) \to \mathit{Sequence}\ a \to \mathit{Sequence}\ b\\
&\mathit{concatMap}\ f\ xs = \mathit{concat}\ (\mathit{map}\ f\ xs)
\end{aligned}$$

We implemented incremental sequences and related primitives following Firsov and Jeltsch [9]: our change operations and first-order operations (such as *concat*) reuse their implementation. On the other hand, we must extend higher-order operations such as *map* to handle non-nil function changes and caching. A correct and efficient CTS derivative *dmapC* has to work differently depending on whether the given function change is nil or not: For a non-nil function change it has to go over the input sequence; for a nil function change it has to avoid that.

Cai et al. [7] use static analysis to conservatively approximate nil function changes as changes to terms that are closed in the original program. But in this example the function argument $(\lambda y \to (x, y))$ to *map* in *cartesianProduct* is not a closed term. It is, however, crucial for the asymptotic improvement that we avoid looping over the inner sequence when the change to the free variable $x$ in the change environment is $\mathbf{0}_x$.

To enable runtime nil change detection, we apply closure conversion to the original program and explicitly construct closures and changes to closures. While the only valid change for closed functions is their nil change, for closures we can have non-nil function changes. A function change *df*, represented as a closure change, is nil exactly when all changes it closes over are nil.

We represent closed functions and closures as variants of the same type. Correspondingly we represent changes to a closed function and changes to a closure as variants of the same type of function changes. We inspect this representation at runtime to find out if a function change is a nil change.

$$\begin{aligned}
&\textbf{data}\ \mathit{Fun}\ a\ b\ c\ \textbf{where}\\
&\quad \mathit{Closed} :: (a \to (b, c)) \to \mathit{Fun}\ a\ b\ c\\
&\quad \mathit{Closure} :: (e \to a \to (b, c)) \to e \to \mathit{Fun}\ a\ b\ c\\
&\textbf{data}\ \Delta(\mathit{Fun}\ a\ b\ c)\ \textbf{where}\\
&\quad \mathit{DClosed} :: (a \to \Delta a \to c \to (\Delta b, c)) \to \Delta(\mathit{Fun}\ a\ b\ c)\\
&\quad \mathit{DClosure} :: (e \to \Delta e \to a \to \Delta a \to c \to (\Delta b, c)) \to e \to \Delta e \to \Delta(\mathit{Fun}\ a\ b\ c)
\end{aligned}$$

We use the same benchmark setup as in the benchmark for the average computation on bags. The input of size $n$ is a pair of sequences $(xs, ys)$. Each sequence initially contains the integers from 1 to $n$. Updating the result in reaction to a change $dxs$ to the outer sequence $xs$ takes less time than updating the result in reaction to a change $dys$ to the inner sequence $ys$. While a change to the outer sequence $xs$ results in an easily located change in the output sequence, a change for the inner sequence $ys$ results in a change that needs a lot more calculation to find the elements it affects. We benchmark changes to the outer sequence $xs$ and the inner sequence $ys$ separately where the change to one sequence is the insertion of a single integer 1 at position 1 and the change for the other one is the nil change.

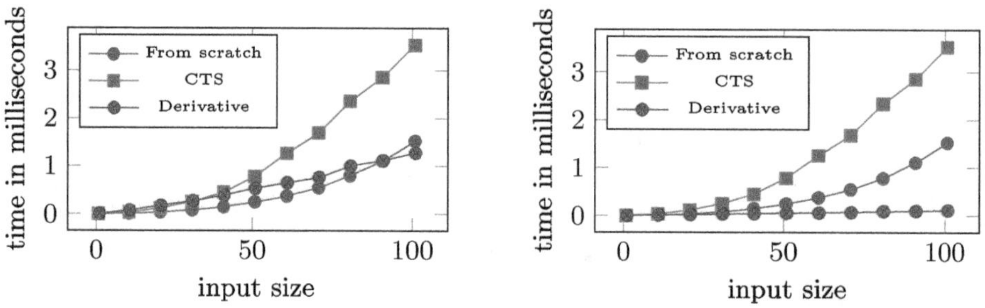


(a) Benchmark results for Cartesian product changing *inner* sequence.

(b) Benchmark results for Cartesian product changing *outer* sequence.

**Fig. 9.** Benchmark results for *cartesianProduct*

Figure 9 shows execution time versus input size. In this example again preparing the cache takes longer than from scratch recomputation alone. The speedup of incremental computation over from scratch recomputation increases with the size of the base input sequences because of the difference in time complexity. Eventually we do get speedups for both kinds of changes (to the inner and to the outer sequence), but for changes to the outer sequence we get a speedup earlier, at a smaller input size. The size of the cache grows super linearly in this example.

### 4.3 Indexed Joins of Two Bags

Our goal is to show that we can compose primitive functions into larger and more complex programs and apply CTS differentiation to get a fast incremental program. We use an example inspired from the DBToaster literature [17]. In this example we have a bag of orders and a bag of line items. An order is a pair of an order key and an exchange rate. A line item is a pair of an order key and a price. We build an index mapping each order key to the sum of all exchange rates of the orders with this key and an index from order key to the sum of the prices of all line items with this key. We then merge the two maps by key, multiplying corresponding sums of exchange rates and sums of prices. We compute the total price of the orders and line items as the sum of those products.

$\mathbf{type}\ Order = (\mathbb{Z}, \mathbb{Z})$
$\mathbf{type}\ LineItem = (\mathbb{Z}, \mathbb{Z})$
$totalPrice :: Bag\ Order \rightarrow Bag\ LineItem \rightarrow \mathbb{Z}$
$totalPrice\ orders\ lineItems = \mathbf{let}$
$\quad orderIndex = groupBy\ fst\ orders$
$\quad orderSumIndex = Map.map\ (Bag.foldMapGroup\ snd)\ orderIndex$
$\quad lineItemIndex = groupBy\ fst\ lineItems$
$\quad lineItemSumIndex = Map.map\ (Bag.foldMapGroup\ snd)\ lineItemIndex$
$\quad merged = Map.merge\ orderSumIndex\ lineItemSumIndex$
$\quad total = Map.foldMapGroup\ multiply\ merged$
$\quad \mathbf{in}\ total$
$groupBy :: (a \rightarrow k) \rightarrow Bag\ a \rightarrow Map\ k\ (Bag\ a)$
$groupBy\ keyOf\ bag =$
$\quad Bag.foldMapGroup\ (\lambda a \rightarrow Map.singleton\ (keyOf\ a)\ (Bag.singleton\ a))\ bag$

Unlike DBToaster, we assume our program is already transformed to explicitly use indexes, as above. Because our indexes are maps, we implemented a change structure, CTS primitives and their CTS derivatives for maps.

To build the indexes, we use a *groupBy* function built from primitive functions *foldMapGroup* on bags and *singleton* for bags and maps respectively. The CTS function *groupByC* and the CTS derivative *dgroupByC* are automatically generated. While computing the indexes with *groupBy* is self-maintainable, merging them is not. We need to cache and incrementally update the intermediately created indexes to avoid recomputing them.

We evaluate the performance in the same way we did in the other case studies. The input of size $n$ is a pair of bags where both contain the pairs $(i, i)$ for $i$ between 1 and $n$. The change is an insertion of the order $(1, 1)$ into the orders bag. For sufficiently large inputs, our CTS derivative of the original program produces updated results much faster than from scratch recomputation, again because of a difference in time complexity as indicated by Fig. 8b. The size of the cache grows linearly with the size of the input in this example. This is unavoidable, because we need to keep the indexes.

### 4.4 Limitations and Future Work

*Typing of CTS programs.* Functions of the same type $f_1, f_2 :: A \rightarrow B$ can be transformed to CTS functions $f_1 :: A \rightarrow (B, C_1), f_2 :: A \rightarrow (B, C_2)$ with different cache types $C_1, C_2$, since cache types depend on the implementation. This heterogeneous typing of translated functions poses difficult typing issues, e.g. what is the translated type of a *list* $(A \rightarrow B)$? We cannot hide cache types behind existential quantifiers because they would be too abstract for derivatives, which only work on very specific cache types. We can fix this problem with some runtime overhead by using a single type *Cache*, defined as a tagged union of all cache types or, maybe with more sophisticated type systems—like first-class translucent sums, open existentials or Typed Adapton's refinement types [12]—that could be able to correctly track down cache types properly.

In any case, we believe that these machineries would add a lot of complexity without helping much with the proof of correctness. Indeed, the simulation relation is more handy here because it maintains a global invariant about the whole evaluations (typically the consistency of cache types between base computations and derivatives), not many local invariants about values as types would.

One might wonder why caches could not be totally hidden from the programmer by embedding them in the derivatives themselves; or in other words, why we did not simply translate functions of type $A \to B$ into functions of type $A \to B \times (\Delta A \to \Delta B)$. We tried this as well; but unlike automatic differentiation, we must remember and update caches according to input changes (especially when receiving a sequence of such changes as in Sect. 2.1). Returning the updated cache to the caller works; we tried closing over the caches in the derivative, but this ultimately fails (because we could receive function changes to the original function, but those would need access to such caches).

*Comprehensive performance evaluation.* This paper focuses on theory and we leave benchmarking in comparison to other implementations of incremental computation to future work. The examples in our case study were rather simple (except perhaps for the indexed join). Nevertheless, the results were encouraging and we expect them to carry over to more complex examples, but not to all programs. A comparison to other work would also include a comparison of space usage for auxiliary data structure, in our case the caches.

*Cache pruning via absence analysis.* To reduce memory usage and runtime overhead, it should be possible to automatically remove from transformed programs any caches or cache fragments that are not used (directly or indirectly) to compute outputs. Liu [19] performs this transformation on CTS programs by using *absence analysis*, which was later extended to higher-order languages by Sergey et al. [25]. In lazy languages, absence analysis removes thunks that are not needed to compute the output. We conjecture that the analysis could remove unused caches or inputs, if it is extended to *not* treat caches as part of the output.

*Unary vs n-ary abstraction.* We only show our transformation correct for unary functions and tuples. But many languages provide efficient support for applying curried functions such as $div :: \mathbb{Z} \to \mathbb{Z} \to \mathbb{Z}$. Naively transforming such a curried function to CTS would produce a function $divC$ of type $\mathbb{Z} \to (\mathbb{Z} \to (\mathbb{Z}, DivC_2)), DivC_1$ with $DivC_1 = ()$, which adds excessive overhead. In Sect. 2 and our evaluation we use curried functions and never need to use this naive encoding, but only because we always invoke functions of known arity.

## 5 Related Work

*Cache-transfer-style.* Liu [19]'s work has been the fundamental inspiration to this work, but her approach has no correctness proof and is restricted to a first-order untyped language. Moreover, while the idea of cache-transfer-style is similar, it's unclear if her approach to incrementalization would extend to higher-order programs. Firsov and Jeltsch [9] also approach incrementalization by code transformation, but their approach does not deal with changes to functions. Instead of transforming functions written in terms of primitives, they provide combinators to write CTS functions and derivatives together. On the other hand, they extend their approach to support mutable caches, while restricting to immutable ones as we do might lead to a logarithmic slowdown.

*Finite differencing.* Incremental computation on collections or databases by finite differencing has a long tradition [6,22]. The most recent and impressive line of work is the one on DBToaster [16,17], which is a highly efficient approach to incrementalize queries over bags by combining iterated finite differencing with other program transformations. They show asymptotic speedups both in theory and through experimental evaluations. Changes are only allowed for datatypes that form groups (such as bags or certain maps), but not for instance for lists or sets. Similar ideas were recently extended to higher-order and nested computation [18], though only for datatypes that can be turned into groups. Koch et al. [18] emphasize that iterated differentiation is necessary to obtain efficient derivatives; however, ANF conversion and remembering intermediate results appear to address the same problem, similarly to the field of automatic differentiation [27].

*Logical relations.* To study correctness of incremental programs we use a logical relation among base values $v_1$, updated values $v_2$ and changes $dv$. To define a logical relation for an untyped λ-calculus we use a *step-indexed* logical relation, following Ahmed [4], Appel and McAllester [5]; in particular, our definitions are closest to the ones by Acar et al. [3], who also work with an untyped language, big-step semantics and (a different form of) incremental computation. However, they do not consider first-class changes. Technically, we use environments rather than substitution, and index our big-step semantics differently.

*Dynamic incrementalization.* The approaches to incremental computation with the widest applicability are in the family of self-adjusting computation [1,2], including its descendant Adapton [14]. These approaches incrementalize programs by combining memoization and change propagation: after creating a trace of base computations, updated inputs are compared with old ones in $O(1)$ to find corresponding outputs, which are updated to account for input modifications. Compared to self-adjusting computation, Adapton only updates results that are demanded. As usual, incrementalization is not efficient on arbitrary programs, but only on programs designed so that input changes produce small changes to the computation trace; refinement type systems have been designed to assist in this task [8,12]. To identify matching inputs, Nominal Adapton [13] replaces input comparisons by pointer equality with first-class labels, enabling more reuse.

# 6 Conclusion

We have presented a program transformation which turns a functional program into its derivative and efficiently shares redundant computations between them thanks to a statically computed cache.

Although our first practical case studies show promising results, this paper focused on putting CTS differentiation on solid theoretical ground. For the moment, we only have scratched the surface of the incrementalization opportunities opened by CTS primitives and their CTS derivatives: in our opinion, exploring the design space for cache data structures will lead to interesting new results in purely functional incremental programming.

**Acknowledgments.** We are grateful to anonymous reviewers: they made important suggestions to help us improve our technical presentation. We also thank Cai Yufei, Tillmann Rendel, Lourdes del Carmen González Huesca, Klaus Ostermann, Sebastian Erdweg for helpful discussions on this project. This work was partially supported by DFG project 282458149 and by SNF grant No. 200021_166154.

# References

1. Acar, U.A.: Self-adjusting computation. Ph.D. thesis, Carnegie Mellon University (2005)
2. Acar, U.A.: Self-adjusting computation: (an overview). In: PEPM, pp. 1–6. ACM (2009)
3. Acar, U.A., Ahmed, A., Blume, M.: Imperative self-adjusting computation. In: Proceedings of the 35th Annual ACM SIGPLAN-SIGACT Symposium on Principles of Programming Languages, POPL 2008, pp. 309–322. ACM, New York (2008). https://doi.acm.org/10.1145/1328438.1328476
4. Ahmed, A.: Step-indexed syntactic logical relations for recursive and quantified types. In: Sestoft, P. (ed.) ESOP 2006. LNCS, vol. 3924, pp. 69–83. Springer, Heidelberg (2006). https://doi.org/10.1007/11693024_6
5. Appel, A.W., McAllester, D.: An indexed model of recursive types for foundational proof-carrying code. ACM Trans. Program. Lang. Syst. **23**(5), 657–683 (2001). https://doi.acm.org/10.1145/504709.504712
6. Blakeley, J.A., Larson, P.A., Tompa, F.W.: Efficiently updating materialized views. In: SIGMOD, pp. 61–71. ACM (1986)
7. Cai, Y., Giarrusso, P.G., Rendel, T., Ostermann, K.: A theory of changes for higher-order languages—incrementalizing λ-calculi by static differentiation. In: Proceedings of the 35th ACM SIGPLAN Conference on Programming Language Design and Implementation, PLDI 2014, pp. 145–155. ACM, New York (2014). https://doi.acm.org/10.1145/2594291.2594304
8. Çiçek, E., Paraskevopoulou, Z., Garg, D.: A type theory for incremental computational complexity with control flow changes. In: Proceedings of the 21st ACM SIGPLAN International Conference on Functional Programming, ICFP 2016, pp. 132–145. ACM, New York (2016)

9. Firsov, D., Jeltsch, W.: Purely functional incremental computing. In: Castor, F., Liu, Y.D. (eds.) SBLP 2016. LNCS, vol. 9889, pp. 62–77. Springer, Cham (2016). https://doi.org/10.1007/978-3-319-45279-1_5
10. Giarrusso, P.G.: Optimizing and incrementalizing higher-order collection queries by AST transformation. Ph.D. thesis, University of Tübingen (2018). Defended. http://inc-lc.github.io/
11. Gupta, A., Mumick, I.S.: Maintenance of materialized views: problems, techniques, and applications. In: Gupta, A., Mumick, I.S. (eds.) Materialized Views, pp. 145–157. MIT Press (1999)
12. Hammer, M.A., Dunfield, J., Economou, D.J., Narasimhamurthy, M.: Typed adapton: refinement types for incremental computations with precise names. October 2016 arXiv:1610.00097 [cs]
13. Hammer, M.A., et al.: Incremental computation with names. In: Proceedings of the 2015 ACM SIGPLAN International Conference on Object-Oriented Programming, Systems, Languages, and Applications, OOPSLA 2015, pp. 748–766. ACM, New York (2015). https://doi.acm.org/10.1145/2814270.2814305
14. Hammer, M.A., Phang, K.Y., Hicks, M., Foster, J.S.: Adapton: composable, demand-driven incremental computation. In: Proceedings of the 35th ACM SIGPLAN Conference on Programming Language Design and Implementation, PLDI 2014, pp. 156–166. ACM, New York (2014)
15. Johnsson, T.: Lambda lifting: transforming programs to recursive equations. In: Jouannaud, J.-P. (ed.) FPCA 1985. LNCS, vol. 201, pp. 190–203. Springer, Heidelberg (1985). https://doi.org/10.1007/3-540-15975-4_37
16. Koch, C.: Incremental query evaluation in a ring of databases. In: Symposium Principles of Database Systems (PODS), pp. 87–98. ACM (2010)
17. Koch, C., et al.: DBToaster: higher-order delta processing for dynamic, frequently fresh views. VLDB J. **23**(2), 253–278 (2014). https://doi.org/10.1007/s00778-013-0348-4
18. Koch, C., Lupei, D., Tannen, V.: Incremental view maintenance for collection programming. In: Proceedings of the 35th ACM SIGMOD-SIGACT-SIGAI Symposium on Principles of Database Systems, PODS 2016, pp. 75–90. ACM, New York (2016)
19. Liu, Y.A.: Efficiency by incrementalization: an introduction. HOSC **13**(4), 289–313 (2000)
20. Liu, Y.A., Teitelbaum, T.: Caching intermediate results for program improvement. In: Proceedings of the 1995 ACM SIGPLAN Symposium on Partial Evaluation and Semantics-based Program Manipulation, PEPM 1995, pp. 190–201. ACM, New York (1995). https://doi.acm.org/10.1145/215465.215590
21. O'Sullivan, B.: criterion: a Haskell microbenchmarking library (2014). http://www.serpentine.com/criterion/
22. Paige, R., Koenig, S.: Finite differencing of computable expressions. TOPLAS **4**(3), 402–454 (1982)
23. Rossberg, A., Russo, C.V., Dreyer, D.: F-ing modules. In: Proceedings of the 5th ACM SIGPLAN Workshop on Types in Language Design and Implementation, TLDI 2010, pp. 89–102. ACM, New York (2010)
24. Sabry, A., Felleisen, M.: Reasoning about programs in continuation-passing style. LISP Symb. Comput. **6**(3–4), 289–360 (1993)
25. Sergey, I., Vytiniotis, D., Peyton Jones, S.: Modular, higher-order cardinality analysis in theory and practice. In: Proceedings of the 41st ACM SIGPLAN-SIGACT Symposium on Principles of Programming Languages, POPL 2014, pp. 335–347. ACM, New York (2014)

26. The Coq Development Team: The Coq proof assistant reference manual, version 8.8 (2018). http://coq.inria.fr
27. Wang, F., Wu, X., Essertel, G., Decker, J., Rompf, T.: Demystifying differentiable programming: shift/reset the penultimate backpropagator. Technical report (2018). https://arxiv.org/abs/1803.10228

# 3

# Safe Deferred Memory Reclamation with Types

Ismail Kuru[✉] and Colin S. Gordon

Drexel University, Philadelphia, USA
{ik335,csgordon}@drexel.edu

**Abstract.** Memory management in lock-free data structures remains a major challenge in concurrent programming. Design techniques including read-copy-update (RCU) and hazard pointers provide workable solutions, and are widely used to great effect. These techniques rely on the concept of a grace period: nodes that should be freed are not deallocated immediately, and all threads obey a protocol to ensure that the deallocating thread can detect when all possible readers have completed their use of the object. This provides an approach to safe deallocation, but only when these subtle protocols are implemented correctly.

We present a static type system to ensure correct use of RCU memory management: that nodes removed from a data structure are always scheduled for subsequent deallocation, and that nodes are scheduled for deallocation at most once. As part of our soundness proof, we give an abstract semantics for RCU memory management primitives which captures the fundamental properties of RCU. Our type system allows us to give the first proofs of memory safety for RCU linked list and binary search tree implementations without requiring full verification.

## 1 Introduction

For many workloads, lock-based synchronization – even fine-grained locking – has unsatisfactory performance. Often lock-free algorithms yield better performance, at the cost of more complex implementation and additional difficulty reasoning about the code. Much of this complexity is due to memory management: developers must reason about not only other threads violating local assumptions, but whether other threads are *finished accessing* nodes to deallocate. At the time a node is unlinked from a data structure, an unknown number of additional threads may have already been using the node, having read a pointer to it before it was unlinked in the heap.

A key insight for manageable solutions to this challenge is to recognize that just as in traditional garbage collection, the unlinked nodes need not be reclaimed immediately, but can instead be reclaimed later after some protocol finishes running. Hazard pointers [29] are the classic example: all threads actively collaborate on bookkeeping data structures to track who is using a certain reference. For structures with read-biased workloads, Read-Copy-Update (RCU) [23] provides an appealing alternative. The programming style resembles a combination of reader-writer locks and lock-free programming. Multiple concurrent readers perform minimal bookkeeping – often nothing they wouldn't already do. A single writer at a time runs in parallel with readers, performing additional work to track which readers may have observed a node they wish to deallocate. There are now RCU implementations of many common tree data structures [3,5,8,19,24,33], and RCU plays a key role in Linux kernel memory management [27].

However, RCU primitives remain non-trivial to use correctly: developers must ensure they release each node exactly once, from exactly one thread, *after* ensuring other threads are finished with the node in question. Model checking can be used to validate correctness of implementations for a mock client [1,7,17,21], but this does not guarantee correctness of arbitrary client code. Sophisticated verification logics can prove correctness of the RCU primitives and clients [12,15,22,32]. But these techniques require significant verification expertise to apply, and are specialized to individual data structures or implementations. One important reason for the sophistication in these logics stems from the complexity of the underlying memory reclamation model. However, Meyer and Wolff [28] show that a suitable abstraction enables separating verifying *correctness* of concurrent data structures from its underlying reclamation model under the assumption of *memory safety*, and study proofs of correctness assuming memory safety.

We propose a type system to ensure that RCU client code uses the RCU primitives safely, ensuring memory safety for concurrent data structures using RCU memory management. We do this in a general way, not assuming the client implements any specific data structure, only one satisfying some basic properties common to RCU data structures (such as having a *tree* memory footprint). In order to do this, we must also give a formal operational model of the RCU primitives that abstracts many implementations, without assuming a particular implementation of the RCU primitives. We describe our RCU semantics and type system, prove our type system sound against the model (which ensures memory is reclaimed correctly), and show the type system in action on two important RCU data structures.

Our contributions include:

- A general (abstract) operational model for RCU-based memory management
- A type system that ensures code uses RCU memory management correctly, which is significantly simpler than full-blown verification logics
- Demonstration of the type system on two examples: a linked-list based bag and a binary search tree
- A proof that the type system guarantees memory safety when using RCU primitives.

## 2 Background and Motivation

In this section, we recall the general concepts of read-copy-update concurrency. We use the RCU linked-list-based bag [25] from Fig. 1 as a running example. It includes annotations for our type system, which will be explained in Sect. 4.2.

```
struct BagNode{
  int data;
  BagNode<rcuItr> Next;
}
BagNode<rcuRoot> head;
void add(int toAdd){
WriteBegin;
BagNode nw = new;
{nw: rcuFresh{}}
nw.data = toAdd;
{head: rcuRoot, par: undef, cur: undef}
BagNode<rcuItr> par,cur = head;
{head: rcuRoot, par: rcuItrε{}}
{cur: rcuItrε{}}
cur = par.Next;
{cur: rcuItrNext{}}
{par: rcuItrε{Next ↦ cur}}
while(cur.Next != null){
  {cur: rcuItr(Next)^k.Next{}}
  {par: rcuItr(Next)^k{Next ↦ cur}}
  par = cur;
  cur = par.Next;
  {cur: rcuItr(Next)^k.Next.Next{}}
  {par: rcuItr(Next)^k.Next{Next ↦ cur}}
}
{nw: rcuFresh{}}
{cur: rcuItr(Next)^k.Next{Next ↦ null}}
{par: rcuItr(Next)^k{Next ↦ cur}}
nw.Next= null;
{nw: rcuFresh{Next ↦ null}}
{cur: rcuItr(Next)^k.Next{Next ↦ null}}
cur.Next=nw;
{nw: rcuItr(Next)^k.Next.Next{Next ↦ null}}
{cur: rcuItr(Next)^k.Next{Next ↦ nw}}
WriteEnd;
}
```

```
void remove(int toDel){
WriteBegin;
{head: rcuRoot, par : undef, cur: undef}
BagNode<rcuItr> par,cur = head;
{head: rcuRoot, par: rcuItrε{}, cur: rcuItrε{}}
cur = par.Next;
{cur: rcuItrNext{}}
{par: rcuItrε{Next ↦ cur}}
while(cur.Next != null&&cur.data != toDel)
{
  {cur: rcuItr(Next)^k.Next{}}
  {par: rcuItr(Next)^k{Next ↦ cur}}
  par = cur;
  cur = par.Next;
  {cur: rcuItr(Next)^k.Next.Next{}}
  {par: rcuItr(Next)^k.Next{Next ↦ cur}}
}
{nw: rcuFresh{}}
{par: rcuItr(Next)^k{Next ↦ cur}}
{cur: rcuItr(Next)^k.Next{}}
BagNode<rcuItr> curl = cur.Next;
{cur: rcuItr(Next)^k.Next{Next ↦ curl}}
{curl: rcuItr(Next)^k.Next.Next{}}
par.Next = curl;
{par: rcuItr(Next)^k{Next ↦ curl}}
{cur: unlinked}
{cur: rcuItr(Next)^k.Next{}}
SyncStart;
SyncStop;
{cur: freeable}
Free(cur);
{cur: undef}
WriteEnd;
}
```

**Fig. 1.** RCU client: singly linked list based bag implementation.

As with concrete RCU implementations, we assume threads operating on a structure are either performing read-only traversals of the structure—*reader threads*—or are performing an update—*writer threads*—similar to the use of many-reader single-writer reader-writer locks.[1] It differs, however, in that readers may execute concurrently with the (single) writer.

This distinction, and some runtime bookkeeping associated with the read- and write-side critical sections, allow this model to determine at modest cost when a node unlinked by the writer can safely be reclaimed.

Figure 1 gives the code for adding and removing nodes from a bag. Type checking for all code, including membership queries for bag, can be found in our technical report [20]. Algorithmically, this code is nearly the same as any sequential implementation. There are only two differences. First, the read-side critical section in `member` is indicated by the use of `ReadBegin` and `ReadEnd`; the write-side critical section is between `WriteBegin` and `WriteEnd`. Second, rather than immediately reclaiming the memory for the unlinked node, `remove` calls

[1] RCU implementations supporting multiple concurrent writers exist [3], but are the minority.

`SyncStart` to begin a *grace period*—a wait for reader threads that may still hold references to unlinked nodes to finish their critical sections. `SyncStop` blocks execution of the writer thread until these readers exit their read critical section (via `ReadEnd`). These are the essential primitives for the implementation of an RCU data structure.

These six primitives together track a critical piece of information: which reader threads' critical sections overlapped the writer's. Implementing them efficiently is challenging [8], but possible. The Linux kernel for example finds ways to reuse existing task switch mechanisms for this tracking, so readers incur no additional overhead. The reader primitives are semantically straightforward – they atomically record the start, or completion, of a read-side critical section.

The more interesting primitives are the write-side primitives and memory reclamation. `WriteBegin` performs a (semantically) standard mutual exclusion with regard to other writers, so only one writer thread may modify the structure *or the writer structures used for grace periods.*

`SyncStart` and `SyncStop` implement *grace periods* [31]: a mechanism to wait for readers to finish with any nodes the writer may have unlinked. A grace period begins when a writer requests one, and finishes when all reader threads active *at the start of the grace period* have finished their current critical section. Any nodes a writer unlinks before a grace period are physically unlinked, but not logically unlinked until after one grace period.

An attentive reader might already realize that our usage of logical/physical unlinking is different than the one used in data-structures literature where typically a *logical deletion* (e.g., marking) is followed by a *physical deletion* (unlinking). Because all threads are forbidden from holding an interior reference into the data structure after leaving their critical sections, waiting for active readers to finish their critical sections ensures they are no longer using any nodes the writer unlinked prior to the grace period. This makes actually freeing an unlinked node after a grace period safe.

`SyncStart` conceptually takes a snapshot of all readers active when it is run. `SyncStop` then blocks until all those threads in the snapshot have finished at least one critical section. `SyncStop` does not wait for *all* readers to finish, and does not wait for all overlapping readers to simultaneously be out of critical sections.

To date, every description of RCU semantics, most centered around the notion of a grace period, has been given algorithmically, as a specific (efficient) implementation. While the implementation aspects are essential to real use, the lack of an abstract characterization makes judging the correctness of these implementations – or clients – difficult in general. In Sect. 3 we give formal *abstract*, *operational* semantics for RCU implementations – inefficient if implemented directly, but correct from a memory-safety and programming model perspective, and not tied to specific low-level RCU implementation details. To use these semantics or a concrete implementation correctly, client code must ensure:

- Reader threads never modify the structure
- No thread holds an interior pointer into the RCU structure across critical sections

- Unlinked nodes are always freed by the unlinking thread *after* the unlinking, *after* a grace period, and *inside* the critical section
- Nodes are freed at most once

In practice, RCU data structures typically ensure additional invariants to simplify the above, e.g.:

- The data structure is always a tree
- A writer thread unlinks or replaces only one node at a time.

and our type system in Sect. 4 guarantees these invariants.

## 3 Semantics

In this section, we outline the details of an abstract semantics for RCU implementations. It captures the core client-visible semantics of most RCU primitives, but not the implementation details required for efficiency [27]. In our semantics, shown in Fig. 2, an abstract machine state, $\mathsf{MState}$, contains:

- A stack $s$, of type $\mathsf{Var} \times \mathsf{TID} \rightharpoonup \mathsf{Loc}$
- A heap, $h$, of type $\mathsf{Loc} \times \mathsf{FName} \rightharpoonup \mathsf{Val}$
- A lock, $l$, of type $\mathsf{TID} \uplus \{\mathsf{unlocked}\}$
- A root location $rt$ of type $\mathsf{Loc}$
- A read set, $R$, of type $\mathcal{P}(\mathsf{TID})$ and
- A bounding set, $B$, of type $\mathcal{P}(\mathsf{TID})$

The lock $l$ enforces mutual exclusion between write-side critical sections. The root location $rt$ is the root of an RCU data structure. We model only a single global RCU data structure; the generalization to multiple structures is straightforward but complicates formal development later in the paper. The reader set $R$ tracks the thread IDs (TIDs) of all threads currently executing a read block. The bounding set $B$ tracks which threads the writer is *actively* waiting for during a grace period—it is empty if the writer is not waiting.

Figure 2 gives operational semantics for *atomic* actions; conditionals, loops, and sequencing all have standard semantics, and parallel composition uses sequentially-consistent interleaving semantics.

The first few atomic actions, for writing and reading fields, assigning among local variables, and allocating new objects, are typical of formal semantics for heaps and mutable local variables. `Free` is similarly standard. A writer thread's critical section is bounded by `WriteBegin` and `WriteEnd`, which acquire and release the lock that enforces mutual exclusion between writers. `WriteBegin` only reduces (acquires) if the lock is $\mathsf{unlocked}$.

Standard RCU APIs include a primitive `synchronize_rcu()` to wait for a grace period for the current readers. We decompose this here into two actions, `SyncStart` and `SyncStop`. `SyncStart` initializes the blocking set to the current set of readers—the threads that may have already observed any nodes the writer has unlinked. `SyncStop` blocks until the blocking set is emptied by completing

$$\alpha ::= \mathsf{skip} \mid \mathsf{x.f} = \mathsf{y} \mid \mathsf{y} = \mathsf{x} \mid \mathsf{y} = \mathsf{x.f} \mid \mathsf{y} = \mathsf{new} \mid \mathsf{Free(x)} \mid \mathsf{Sync} \qquad \mathsf{Sync} \triangleq \mathsf{SyncStart;SyncStop}$$

$$\begin{array}{llll}
(\text{RCU-WBEGIN}) & [\![\texttt{WriteBegin}]\!]\ (s, h, \mathsf{unlocked}, rt, R, B) & \Downarrow_{tid}(s, h, l, rt, R, B) & \\
(\text{RCU-WEND}) & [\![\texttt{WriteEnd}]\!]\ (s, h, l, rt, R, B) & \Downarrow_{tid}(s, h, \mathsf{unlocked}, rt, R, B) & \\
(\text{RCU-RBEGIN}) & [\![\texttt{ReadBegin}]\!]\ (s, h, tid, rt, R, B) & \Downarrow_{tid}(s, h, tid, rt, R \uplus \{tid\}, B) & tid \neq l \\
(\text{RCU-REND}) & [\![\texttt{ReadEnd}]\!]\ (s, h, tid, rt, R \uplus \{tid\}, B) & \Downarrow_{tid}(s, h, l, rt, R, B \setminus \{tid\}) & tid \neq l \\
(\text{RCU-SSTART}) & [\![\texttt{SyncStart}]\!]\ (s, h, l, rt, R, \emptyset) & \Downarrow_{tid}(s, h, l, rt, R, R) & \\
(\text{RCU-SSTOP}) & [\![\texttt{SyncStop}]\!]\ (s, h, l, rt, R, \emptyset) & \Downarrow_{tid}(s, h, l, rt, R, \emptyset) & \\
(\text{FREE}) & [\![\texttt{Free}(x)]\!]\ (s, h, l, rt, R, \emptyset) & \Downarrow_{tid}(s, h', l, rt, R, \emptyset) &
\end{array}$$

$$\text{provided } \forall_{f,o'}.\ rt \neq s(x, tid) \text{ and } o' \neq s(x, tid) \implies h(o', f) = h'(o', f) \text{ and } \forall_f.\ h'(o, f) = \mathsf{undef}$$

$$\begin{array}{ll}
(\text{HUPDT}) & [\![\texttt{x.f=y}]\!]\ (s, h, l, rt, R, B) \Downarrow_{tid}(s, h[s(x, tid), f \mapsto s(y, tid)], l, rt, R, B) \\
(\text{HREAD}) & [\![\texttt{y=x.f}]\!]\ (s, h, l, rt, R, B) \Downarrow_{tid}(s[(y, tid) \mapsto h(s(x, tid), f)], h, l, rt, R, B) \\
(\text{SUPDT}) & [\![\texttt{y=x}]\!]\ (s, h, l, rt, R, B) \Downarrow_{tid}(s[(y, tid) \mapsto (x, tid)], h, l, rt, R, B) \\
(\text{HALLOC}) & [\![\texttt{y=new}]\!]\ (s, h, l, rt, R, B) \Downarrow_{tid}(s, h[\ell \mapsto \mathsf{nullmap}], l, rt, R, B)
\end{array}$$

$$\text{provided } rt \neq s(y, tid) \text{ and } s[(y, tid) \mapsto \ell], \text{ and}$$
$$h[\ell \mapsto \mathsf{nullmap}] \stackrel{\text{def}}{=} \lambda(o', f).\ \text{if } o = o' \text{ then } skip \text{ else } h(o', f)$$

**Fig. 2.** Operational semantics for RCU.

reader threads. However, it does not wait for *all* readers to finish, and does not wait for all overlapping readers to simultaneously be out of critical sections. If two reader threads $A$ and $B$ overlap some `SyncStart-SyncStop`'s critical section, it is possible that $A$ may exit and re-enter a read-side critical section before $B$ exits, and vice versa. Implementations must distinguish subsequent read-side critical sections from earlier ones that overlapped the writer's initial request to wait: since `SyncStart` is used *after* a node is physically removed from the data structure and readers may not retain RCU references across critical sections, $A$ re-entering a fresh read-side critical section will not permit it to re-observe the node to be freed.

Reader thread critical sections are bounded by `ReadBegin` and `ReadEnd`. `ReadBegin` simply records the current thread's presence as an active reader. `ReadEnd` removes the current thread from the set of active readers, and also removes it (if present) from the blocking set—if a writer was waiting for a certain reader to finish its critical section, this ensures the writer no longer waits once that reader has finished its current read-side critical section.

Grace periods are implemented by the combination of `ReadBegin`, `ReadEnd`, `SyncStart`, and `SyncStop`. `ReadBegin` ensures the set of active readers is known. When a grace period is required, `SyncStart;SyncStop;` will store (in $B$) the active readers (which may have observed nodes before they were unlinked), and wait for reader threads to record when they have completed their critical section (and implicitly, dropped any references to nodes the writer wants to free) via `ReadEnd`.

These semantics do permit a reader in the blocking set to finish its read-side critical section and enter a *new* read-side critical section before the writer wakes. In this case, *the writer waits only for the first critical section of that reader to complete*, since entering the new critical section adds the thread's ID back to $R$, but not $B$.

# 4 Type System and Programming Language

In this section, we present a simple imperative programming language with two block constructs for modeling RCU, and a type system that ensures proper (memory-safe) use of the language. The type system ensures memory safety by enforcing these sufficient conditions:

- A heap node can only be freed if it is no longer accessible from an RCU data structure or from local variables of other threads. To achieve this we ensure the reachability and access which can be suitably restricted. We explain how our types support a delayed ownership transfer for the deallocation.
- Local variables may not point inside an RCU data structure unless they are inside an RCU read or write block.
- Heap mutations are *local*: each unlinks or replaces exactly one node.
- The RCU data structure remains a tree. While not a fundamental constraint of RCU, it is a common constraint across known RCU data structures because it simplifies reasoning (by developers or a type system) about when a node has become unreachable in the heap.

We also demonstrate that the type system is not only sound, but useful: we show how it types Fig. 1's list-based bag implementation [25]. We also give type checked fragments of a binary search tree to motivate advanced features of the type system; the full typing derivation can be found in our technical report [20] Appendix B. The BST requires type narrowing operations that refine a type based on dynamic checks (e.g., determining which of several fields links to a node). In our system, we presume all objects contain all fields, but the number of fields is finite (and in our examples, small). This avoids additional overhead from tracking well-established aspects of the type system—class and field types and presence, for example—and focus on checking correct use of RCU primitives. Essentially, we assume the code our type system applies to is already type-correct for a system like C or Java's type system.

## 4.1 RCU Type System for Write Critical Section

Section 4.1 introduces RCU types and the need for subtyping. Section 4.2, shows how types describe program states, through code for Fig. 1's list-based bag example. Section 4.3 introduces the type system itself.

**RCU Types.** There are six types used in Write critical sections

$$\tau ::= \mathsf{rcuItr}\ \rho\ \mathcal{N} \mid \mathsf{rcuFresh}\ \mathcal{N} \mid \mathsf{unlinked} \mid \mathsf{undef} \mid \mathsf{freeable} \mid \mathsf{rcuRoot}$$

*rcuItr* is the type given to references pointing into a shared RCU data structure. A rcuItr type can be used in either a write region or a read region (without the additional components). It indicates both that the reference points into the shared RCU data structure and that the heap location referenced by rcuItr reference is reachable by following the path $\rho$ from the root. A component $\mathcal{N}$ is a set of field mappings taking the field name to local variable names. Field maps are extended when the referent's fields are read. The field map and path components track reachability from the root, and local reachability between nodes. These are used to ensure the structure remains acyclic, and for the type system to recognize exactly when unlinking can occur.

Read-side critical sections use rcultr without path or field map components. These components are both unnecessary for readers (who perform no updates) and would be invalidated by writer threads anyways. Under the assumption that reader threads do not hold references across critical sections, the read-side rules essentially only ensure the reader performs no writes, so we omit the reader critical section type rules. They can be found in our technical report [20] Appendix E.

*unlinked* is the type given to references to unlinked heap locations—objects previously part of the structure, but now unreachable via the heap. A heap location referenced by an unlinked reference may still be accessed by reader threads, which may have acquired their own references before the node became unreachable. Newly-arrived readers, however, will be unable to gain access to these referents.

*freeable* is the type given to references to an unlinked heap location that is safe to reclaim because it is known that no concurrent readers hold references to it. Unlinked references become freeable after a writer has waited for a full grace period.

*undef* is the type given to references where the content of the referenced location is inaccessible. A local variable of type freeable becomes undef after reclaiming that variable's referent.

*rcuFresh* is the type given to references to freshly allocated heap locations. Similar to rcultr type, it has field mappings set $\mathcal{N}$. We set the field mappings in the set of an existing rcuFresh reference to be the same as field mappings in the set of rcultr reference when we replace the heap referenced by rcultr with the heap referenced by rcuFresh for memory safe replacement.

*rcuRoot* is the type given to the fixed reference to the root of the RCU data structure. It may not be overwritten.

**Subtyping.** It is sometimes necessary to use imprecise types—mostly for control flow joins. Our type system performs these abstractions via subtyping on individual types and full contexts, as in Fig. 3.

Figure 3 includes four judgments for subtyping. The first two—$\vdash \mathcal{N} \prec: \mathcal{N}'$ and $\vdash \rho \prec: \rho'$—describe relaxations of field maps and paths respectively. $\vdash \mathcal{N} \prec: \mathcal{N}'$ is read as "the field map $\mathcal{N}$ is more precise than $\mathcal{N}'$" and similarly for paths. The third judgment $\vdash T \prec: T'$ uses path and field map subtyping to give subtyping among rcultr types—one rcultr is a subtype of another if its paths

$$\mathcal{N} = \{f_0|\dots|f_n \rightharpoonup \{y\} \mid f_i \in \mathsf{FName} \wedge\ 0 \le i \le n \wedge\ (y \in \mathsf{Var} \vee y \in \{null\})\} \quad \mathcal{N}_{f,\emptyset} = \mathcal{N} \setminus \{f \rightharpoonup \_\}$$

$$\mathcal{N}_\emptyset = \{\} \quad \mathcal{N}(\cup_{f \rightharpoonup y}) = \mathcal{N} \cup \{f \rightharpoonup y\} \quad \mathcal{N}(\setminus_{f \rightharpoonup y}) = \mathcal{N} - \{f \rightharpoonup y\}$$

$$\mathcal{N}([f \rightharpoonup y]) = \mathcal{N} \text{ where } f \rightharpoonup y \in \mathcal{N} \quad \mathcal{N}(f \rightharpoonup x \setminus y) = \mathcal{N} \setminus \{f \rightharpoonup x\} \cup \{f \rightharpoonup y\}$$

$$\boxed{\vdash \mathcal{N} \prec: \mathcal{N}'} \qquad \text{(T-NSUB3)}\ \frac{}{\vdash \mathcal{N}_{f,\emptyset} \prec: \mathcal{N}([f \rightharpoonup y])} \qquad \text{(T-NSUB4)}\ \frac{}{\vdash \mathcal{N}_\emptyset \prec: \mathcal{N}} \qquad \text{(T-NSUB5)}\ \frac{}{\vdash \mathcal{N} \prec: \mathcal{N}}$$

$$\text{(T-NSUB2)}\ \frac{}{\vdash \mathcal{N}([f_2 \rightharpoonup y]) \prec: \mathcal{N}([f_1|f_2 \rightharpoonup y])} \qquad \text{(T-NSUB1)}\ \frac{}{\vdash \mathcal{N}([f_1 \rightharpoonup y]) \prec: \mathcal{N}([f_1|f_2 \rightharpoonup y])}$$

$$\boxed{\vdash \rho \prec: \rho'} \quad \text{(T-PSUB1)}\ \frac{}{\vdash \rho.f_1 \prec: \rho.f_1|f_2} \qquad \text{(T-PSUB2)}\ \frac{}{\vdash \rho.f_2 \prec: \rho.f_1|f_2} \qquad \text{(T-PSUB3)}\ \frac{}{\vdash \rho \prec: \rho}$$

$$\boxed{\vdash T \prec: T'} \qquad \text{(T-TSUB2)}\ \frac{}{\vdash \mathsf{rcultr} \prec: \mathsf{rcultr}} \qquad \text{(T-TSUB)}\ \frac{}{\vdash \mathsf{rcultr}\ \_ \prec: \mathsf{undef}} \qquad \text{(T-TSUB1)}\ \frac{\vdash \rho \prec: \rho' \qquad \vdash \mathcal{N} \prec: \mathcal{N}'}{\vdash \mathsf{rcultr}\ \rho\, \mathcal{N} \prec: \mathsf{rcultr}\ \rho'\, \mathcal{N}'}$$

$$\boxed{\vdash \Gamma \prec: \Gamma'} \quad \text{(T-CSUB1)}\ \frac{\vdash \Gamma \prec: \Gamma' \quad \vdash \mathrm{T} \prec: \mathrm{T'}}{\vdash \Gamma, x : \mathrm{T} \prec: \Gamma', x : \mathrm{T'}} \qquad \text{(T-CSUB)}\ \frac{}{\vdash \Gamma \prec: \Gamma}$$

**Fig. 3.** Subtyping rules.

$$\boxed{\Gamma \vdash_{M,R} C \dashv \Gamma'} \qquad \text{(T-REINDEX)}\ \frac{}{\Gamma \vdash C_k \dashv \Gamma[\rho.f^k/\rho.f^k.f]} \qquad \text{(T-LOOP1)}\ \frac{\Gamma(x) = \mathsf{bool} \qquad \Gamma \vdash C \dashv \Gamma}{\Gamma \vdash \mathsf{while}(x)\{C\} \dashv \Gamma}$$

$$\text{(T-BRANCH1)}\ \frac{\Gamma, x : \mathsf{rcultr}\ \rho \mathcal{N}([f_1 \rightharpoonup z]) \vdash C_1 \dashv \Gamma_4 \qquad \Gamma, x : \mathsf{rcultr}\ \rho \mathcal{N}([f_2 \rightharpoonup z]) \vdash C_2 \dashv \Gamma_4}{\Gamma, x : \mathsf{rcultr}\ \rho \mathcal{N}([f_1 \mid f_2 \rightharpoonup z]) \vdash \mathsf{if}(x.f_1 == z)\ \mathsf{then}\ C_1\ \mathsf{else}\ C_2 \dashv \Gamma_4}$$

$$\text{(T-BRANCH3)}\ \frac{\Gamma, x : \mathsf{rcultr}\ \rho \mathcal{N}([f \rightharpoonup y \setminus \mathsf{null}]) \vdash C_1 \dashv \Gamma' \qquad \Gamma, x : \mathsf{rcultr}\ \rho \mathcal{N}([f \rightharpoonup y]) \vdash C_2 \dashv \Gamma'}{\Gamma, x : \mathsf{rcultr}\ \rho \mathcal{N}([f \rightharpoonup y]) \vdash \mathsf{if}(x.f == \mathsf{null})\ \mathsf{then}\ C_1\ \mathsf{else}\ C_2 \dashv \Gamma'}$$

$$\text{(T-LOOP2)}\ \frac{\Gamma, x : \mathsf{rcultr}\ \rho\ \mathcal{N}([f \rightharpoonup \_]) \vdash C \dashv \Gamma, x : \mathsf{rcultr}\ \rho'\ \mathcal{N}([f \rightharpoonup \_])}{\Gamma, x : \mathsf{rcultr}\ \rho\ \mathcal{N}([f \rightharpoonup \_]) \vdash \mathsf{while}(x.f \neq \mathsf{null})\{C\} \dashv x : \mathsf{rcultr}\ \rho'\ \mathcal{N}([f \rightharpoonup \mathsf{null}]), \Gamma}$$

$$\text{(T-BRANCH2)}\ \frac{\Gamma(x) = \mathsf{bool} \qquad \Gamma \vdash C_1 \dashv \Gamma' \qquad \Gamma \vdash C_2 \dashv \Gamma'}{\Gamma \vdash \mathsf{if}(x)\ \mathsf{then}\ C_1\ \mathsf{else}\ C_2 \dashv \Gamma'}$$

**Fig. 4.** Type rules for control-flow.

and field maps are similarly more precise—and to allow rcultr references to be "forgotten"—this is occasionally needed to satisfy non-interference checks in the type rules. The final judgment $\vdash \Gamma \prec: \Gamma'$ extends subtyping to all assumptions in a type context.

It is often necessary to abstract the contents of field maps or paths, without simply forgetting the contents entirely. In a binary search tree, for example, it may be the case that one node is a child of another, but *which* parent field points to the child depends on which branch was followed in an earlier conditional (consider the lookup in a BST, which alternates between following left and right children). In Fig. 5, we see that `cur` aliases different fields of `par` – either $Left$ or $Right$ – in different branches of the conditional. The types after the conditional must overapproximate this, here as $Left|Right \mapsto cur$ in `par`'s field map, and a similar path disjunction in `cur`'s path. This is reflected in Fig. 3's T-NSUB1-5 and T-PSUB1-2 – within each branch, each type is coerced to a supertype to validate the control flow join.

Another type of control flow join is handling loop invariants – where paths entering the loop meet the back-edge from the end of a loop back to the start for repetition. Because our types include paths describing how they are reachable from the root, some abstraction is required to give loop invariants that work for any number of iterations – in a loop traversing a linked list, the iterator pointer would naïvely have different paths from the root on each iteration, so the exact path is not loop invariant. However, the paths explored by a loop are regular, so we can abstract the paths by permitting (implicitly) existentially quantified indexes on path fragments, which express the existence of *some* path, without saying *which* path. The use of an explicit abstract repetition allows the type system to preserve the fact that different references have common path prefixes, even after a loop.

Assertions for the `add` function in lines 19 and 20 of Fig. 1 show the *loop*'s effects on paths of iterator references used inside the loop, `cur` and `par`. On line 20, `par`'s path contains has $(Next)^k$. The $k$ in the $(Next)^k$ abstracts the number of loop iterations run, implicitly assumed to be non-negative. The trailing $Next$ in `cur`'s path on line 19 – $(Next)^k.Next$ – expresses the relationship between `cur` and `par`: `par` is reachable from the root by following $Next$ $k$ times, and `cur` is reachable via one additional $Next$. The types of 19 and 20, however, are not the same as lines 23 and 24, so an additional adjustment is needed for the types to become loop-invariant. *Reindexing* (T-REINDEX in Fig. 4) effectively increments an abstract loop counter, contracting $(Next)^k.Next$ to $Next^k$ everywhere in a type environment. This expresses the same relationship between `par` and `cur` as before the loop, but the choice of $k$ to make these paths accurate after each iteration would be one larger than the choice before. Reindexing the type environment of lines 23–24 yields the type environment of lines 19–20, making the types loop invariant. The reindexing essentially chooses a new value for the abstract $k$. This is sound, because the uses of framing in the heap mutation related rules of the type system ensure uses of any indexing variable are never separated – either all are reindexed, or none are.

While abstraction is required to deal with control flow joins, reasoning about whether and which nodes are unlinked or replaced, and whether cycles are created, requires precision. Thus the type system also includes means (Fig. 4) to refine imprecise paths and field maps. In Fig. 5, we see a conditional with the condition $par.Left == cur$. The type system matches this condition to the imprecise types in line 1's typing assertion, and refines the initial type assumptions in each branch accordingly (lines 2 and 7) based on whether execution reflects the truth or falsity of that check. Similarly, it is sometimes required to check – and later remember – whether a field is null, and the type system supports this.

```
{cur : rcultr Left|Right {},  par : rcultr ε {Left|Right ↦ cur}}
if(par.Left == cur){
  {cur : rcultr Left {},  par : rcultr ε {Left ↦ cur}}
  par = cur;
  cur = par.Left;
  {cur : rcultr Left.Left {},  par : rcultr Left {Left ↦ cur}}
}else{
  {cur : rcultr Right {},  par : rcultr ε {Right ↦ cur}}
  par = cur;
  cur = par.Right;
  {cur : rcultr Right.Right {},  par : rcultr Right {Right ↦ cur}}
}
{cur : rcultr Left|Right.Left|Right {},  par : rcultr Left|Right {Left|Right ↦ cur}}
```

**Fig. 5.** Choosing fields to read.

### 4.2 Types in Action

The system has three forms of typing judgement: $\Gamma \vdash C$ for standard typing outside RCU critical sections; $\Gamma \vdash_R C \dashv \Gamma'$ for reader critical sections, and $\Gamma \vdash_M C \dashv \Gamma'$ for writer critical sections. The first two are straightforward, essentially preventing mutation of the data structure, and preventing nesting of a writer critical section inside a reader critical section. The last, for writer critical sections, is flow sensitive: the types of variables may differ before and after program statements. This is required in order to reason about local assumptions at different points in the program, such as recognizing that a certain action may unlink a node. Our presentation here focuses exclusively on the judgment for the write-side critical sections.

Below, we explain our types through the list-based bag implementation [25] from Fig. 1, highlighting how the type rules handle different parts of the code. Figure 1 is annotated with "assertions" – local type environments – in the style of a Hoare logic proof outline. As with Hoare proof outlines, these annotations can be used to construct a proper typing derivation.

**Reading a Global RCU Root.** All RCU data structures have fixed roots, which we characterize with the rcuRoot type. Each operation in Fig. 1 begins by reading the root into a new rcultr reference used to begin traversing the structure. After each initial read (line 12 of `add` and line 4 of `remove`), the path of `cur` reference is the empty path ($\epsilon$) and the field map is empty ($\{\}$), because it is an alias to the root, and none of its field contents are known yet.

**Reading an Object Field and a Variable.** As expected, we explore the heap of the data structure via reading the objects' fields. Consider line 6 of `remove` and its corresponding pre- and post- type environments. Initially `par`'s field map is empty. After the field read, its field map is updated to reflect that its *Next* field is aliased in the local variable `cur`. Likewise, after the update, `cur`'s path is *Next* ($= \epsilon \cdot Next$), extending the par node's path by the field read. This introduces field aliasing information that can subsequently be used to reason about unlinking.

**Unlinking Nodes.** Line 24 of `remove` in Fig. 1 unlinks a node. The type annotations show that before that line `cur` is in the structure (rcultr), while afterwards its type is unlinked. The type system checks that this unlink disconnects only one node: note how the types of `par`, `cur`, and `curl` just before line 24 completely describe a section of the list.

**Grace and Reclamation.** After the referent of `cur` is unlinked, concurrent readers traversing the list may still hold references. So it is not safe to actually reclaim the memory until after a grace period. Lines 28–29 of `remove` initiate a grace period and wait for its completion. At the type level, this is reflected by the change of `cur`'s type from unlinked to freeable, reflecting the fact that the grace period extends until any reader critical sections that might have observed the node in the structure have completed. This matches the precondition required by our rules for calling `Free`, which further changes the type of `cur` to undef reflecting that `cur` is no longer a valid reference. The type system also ensures no local (writer) aliases exist to the freed node and understanding this enforcement is twofold. First, the type system requires that only unlinked heap nodes can be freed. Second, framing relations in rules related to the heap mutation ensure no local aliases still consider the node linked.

**Fresh Nodes.** Some code must also allocate new nodes, and the type system must reason about how they are incorporated into the shared data structure. Line 8 of the add method allocates a new node `nw`, and lines 10 and 29 initialize its fields. The type system gives it a fresh type while tracking its field contents, until line 32 inserts it into the data structure. The type system checks that nodes previously reachable from `cur` remain reachable: note the field maps of `cur` and `nw` in lines 30–31 are equal (trivially, though in general the field need not be null).

### 4.3 Type Rules

Figure 6 gives the primary type rules used in checking write-side critical section code as in Fig. 1.

T-Root reads a root pointer into an rcultr reference, and T-ReadS copies a local variable into another. In both cases, the free variable condition ensures that updating the modified variable does not invalidate field maps of other variables in $\Gamma$. These free variable conditions recur throughout the type system, and we will not comment on them further. T-Alloc and T-Free allocate and reclaim objects. These rules are relatively straightforward. T-ReadH reads a field into a local variable. As suggested earlier, this rule updates the post-environment to reflect that the overwritten variable $z$ holds the same value as $x.f$. T-WriteFH updates a field of a *fresh* (thread-local) object, similarly tracking the update in the fresh object's field map at the type level. The remaining rules are a bit more involved, and form the heart of the type system.

**Grace Periods.** T-Sync gives pre- and post-environments to the compound statement `SyncStart;SyncStop` implementing grace periods. As mentioned earlier, this updates the environment afterwards to reflect that any nodes unlinked before the wait become freeable afterwards.

$$\boxed{\Gamma \vdash_M \alpha \dashv \Gamma'} \quad (\text{T-ROOT})\ \frac{y \notin \mathsf{FV}(\Gamma)}{\Gamma, r{:}\mathsf{rcuRoot}, y{:}\mathsf{undef} \vdash y = r \dashv y{:}\mathsf{rcultr}\epsilon\mathcal{N}_{\emptyset}, r{:}\mathsf{rcuRoot}, \Gamma}$$

$$(\text{T-READS})\ \frac{z \notin \mathsf{FV}(\Gamma)}{\Gamma, z:\_, x:\mathsf{rcultr}\ \rho\ \mathcal{N} \vdash z = x \dashv x:\mathsf{rcultr}\ \rho\ \mathcal{N}, z:\mathsf{rcultr}\ \rho\ \mathcal{N}, \Gamma}$$

$$(\text{T-ALLOC})\ \frac{}{\Gamma, x{:}\mathsf{undef} \vdash x = \mathtt{new} \dashv x{:}\mathsf{rcuFresh}\mathcal{N}_{\emptyset}, \Gamma} \qquad (\text{T-FREE})\ \frac{}{x{:}\mathsf{freeable} \vdash \mathsf{Free}(x) \dashv x{:}\mathsf{undef}}$$

$$(\text{T-READH})\ \frac{\rho.f = \rho' \qquad z \notin \mathsf{FV}(\Gamma)}{\Gamma, z:\_, x{:}\mathsf{rcultr}\rho\mathcal{N} \vdash z = x.f \dashv x{:}\mathsf{rcultr}\rho\mathcal{N}([f \rightharpoonup z]), z{:}\mathsf{rcultr}\rho'\mathcal{N}_{\emptyset}, \Gamma}$$

(T-WRITEFH)

$$\frac{z:\mathsf{rcultr}\rho.f\_ \qquad \mathcal{N}(f) = z \qquad f \notin dom(\mathcal{N}')}{\Gamma, p{:}\mathsf{rcuFresh}\mathcal{N}', x{:}\mathsf{rcultr}\rho\mathcal{N} \vdash_M p.f = z \dashv p{:}\mathsf{rcuFresh}\mathcal{N}'([f \rightharpoonup z]), x{:}\mathsf{rcultr}\rho\mathcal{N}([f \rightharpoonup z]), \Gamma}$$

$$(\text{T-SYNC})\ \frac{}{\Gamma \vdash \mathsf{SyncStart};\ \mathsf{SyncStop} \dashv \Gamma[\overline{x{:}\mathsf{freeable}/x{:}\mathsf{unlinked}}]}$$

(T-UNLINKH)

$$\frac{\begin{array}{c} \mathcal{N}(f_1) = z \qquad \rho.f_1 = \rho_1 \qquad \rho_1.f_2 = \rho_2 \\ \mathcal{N}' = \mathcal{N}([f_1 \rightharpoonup z \setminus r]) \qquad \forall_{f \in dom(\mathcal{N}_1)}.\ f \neq f_2 \implies (\mathcal{N}_1(f) = \mathsf{null}) \qquad \mathcal{N}(f_1) = z \qquad \mathcal{N}_1(f_2) = r \\ \forall_{n \in \Gamma, m, \mathcal{N}_3, p_3, f}.\ n{:}\mathsf{rcultr}\ \rho_3\ \mathcal{N}_3([f \rightharpoonup m]) \implies \left\{ \begin{array}{l} ((\neg\mathsf{MayAlias}(\rho_3, \{\rho, \rho_1, \rho_2\})) \wedge (m \notin \{z, r\})) \\ \wedge(\forall_{\rho_4 \neq \epsilon}.\ \neg\mathsf{MayAlias}(\rho_3, \rho_2.\rho_4)) \end{array} \right. \end{array}}{\Gamma, x{:}\mathsf{rcultr}\rho\mathcal{N}, z{:}\mathsf{rcultr}\rho_1\mathcal{N}_1, r{:}\mathsf{rcultr}\rho_2\mathcal{N}_2 \vdash x.f_1 = r \dashv z{:}\mathsf{unlinked}, x{:}\mathsf{rcultr}\rho\mathcal{N}', r{:}\mathsf{rcultr}\rho_1\mathcal{N}_2, \Gamma}$$

(T-REPLACE)

$$\frac{\begin{array}{c} \mathcal{N}(f) = o \qquad \mathcal{N}' = \mathcal{N}([f \rightharpoonup o \setminus n]) \qquad \rho.f = \rho_1 \qquad \mathcal{N}_1 = \mathcal{N}_2 \qquad \mathsf{FV}(\Gamma) \cap \{p, o, n\} = \emptyset \\ \forall_{x \in \Gamma, \mathcal{N}_3, \rho_2, f_1, y}.\ (x{:}\mathsf{rcultr}\ \rho_2\ \mathcal{N}_3([f_1 \rightharpoonup y])) \implies (\neg\mathsf{MayAlias}(\rho_2, \{\rho, \rho_1\}) \wedge (y \neq o)) \end{array}}{\Gamma, p{:}\mathsf{rcultr}\rho\mathcal{N}, o{:}\mathsf{rcultr}\rho_1\mathcal{N}_1, n{:}\mathsf{rcuFresh}\mathcal{N}_2 \vdash p.f = n \dashv p{:}\mathsf{rcultr}\rho\mathcal{N}', n{:}\mathsf{rcultr}\rho_1\mathcal{N}_2, o{:}\mathsf{unlinked}, \Gamma}$$

(T-INSERT)

$$\frac{\begin{array}{c} \mathcal{N}' = \mathcal{N}([f \rightharpoonup o \setminus n]) \qquad \rho.f = \rho_1 \qquad \rho_1.f_4 = \rho_2 \\ \mathcal{N}(f) = \mathcal{N}_1(f_4) \qquad \forall_{f_2 \in dom(\mathcal{N}_1)}.\ f_4 \neq f_2 \implies \mathcal{N}_1(f_2) = \mathsf{null} \qquad \mathsf{FV}(\Gamma) \cap \{p, o, n\} = \emptyset \\ \forall_{x \in \Gamma, \mathcal{N}_3, \rho_3, f_1, y}.\ (x:\mathsf{rcultr}\ \rho_3\ \mathcal{N}_3([f_1 \rightharpoonup y])) \implies (\forall_{\rho_4 \neq \epsilon}.\ \neg\mathsf{MayAlias}(\rho_3, \rho.\rho_4)) \end{array}}{\Gamma, p{:}\mathsf{rcultr}\rho\mathcal{N}, o{:}\mathsf{rcultr}\rho_1\mathcal{N}_2, n{:}\mathsf{rcuFresh}\mathcal{N}_1 \vdash p.f = n \dashv p{:}\mathsf{rcultr}\rho\mathcal{N}', n{:}\mathsf{rcultr}\rho_1\mathcal{N}_1, o{:}\mathsf{rcultr}\rho_2\mathcal{N}_2, \Gamma}$$

$$\boxed{\Gamma \vdash_M C \dashv \Gamma'} \quad (\text{TORCUWRITE})\ \frac{\begin{array}{c} \mathsf{NoFresh}(\Gamma') \qquad \mathsf{NoUnlinked}(\Gamma') \qquad \mathsf{NoFreeable}(\Gamma') \\ \Gamma, y{:}\mathsf{rcultr}\_ \vdash_M C \dashv \Gamma' \qquad \mathsf{FType}(f) = \mathsf{RCU} \end{array}}{\Gamma \vdash \mathsf{RCUWrite}\ x.f\ \mathsf{as}\ y\ \mathsf{in}\ \{C\}}$$

**Fig. 6.** Type rules for write side critical section.

**Unlinking.** T-UNLINKH type checks heap updates that remove a node from the data structure. The rule assumes three objects $x$, $z$, and $r$, whose identities we will conflate with the local variable names in the type rule. The rule checks the case where $x.f_1 == z$ and $z.f_2 == r$ initially (reflected in the path and field map components, and a write $x.f_1 = r$ removes $z$ from the data structure (we assume, and ensure, the structure is a tree).

The rule must also avoid unlinking multiple nodes: this is the purpose of the first (smaller) implication: it ensures that beyond the reference from $z$ to $r$, all fields of $z$ are null.

Finally, the rule must ensure that no types in $\Gamma$ are invalidated. This could happen one of two ways: either a field map in $\Gamma$ for an alias of $x$ duplicates

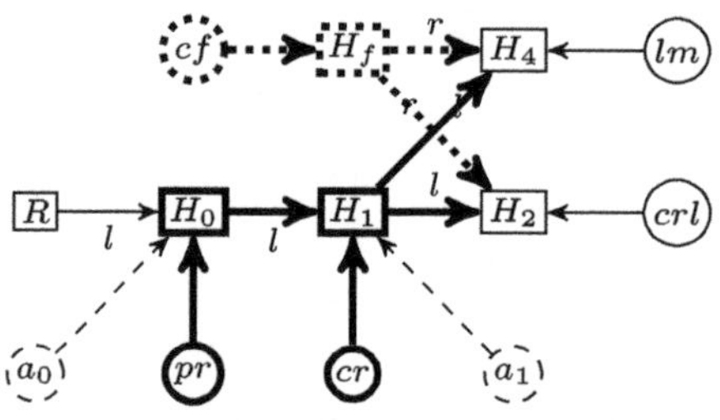


(a) *Freshly* allocated heap node referenced by $cf$

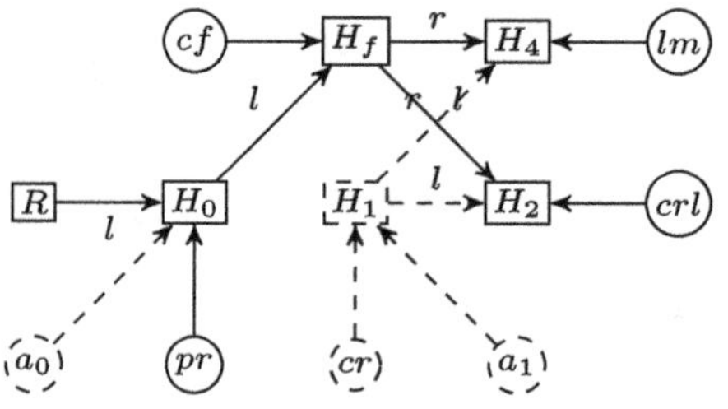


(b) Safe replacement of the heap node referenced by *cr* with the *fresh* heap node referenced by $cf$.

**Fig. 7.** Replacing *existing* heap nodes with *fresh* ones. Type rule T-REPLACE.

the assumption that $x.f_1 == z$ (which is changed by this write), or $\Gamma$ contains a descendant of $r$, whose path from the root will change when its ancestor is modified. The final assumption of T-UNLINKH (the implication) checks that for every rcultr reference $n$ in $\Gamma$, it is not a path alias of $x$, $z$, or $r$; no entry of its field map ($m$) refers to $r$ or $z$ (which would imply $n$ aliased $x$ or $z$ initially); and its path is not an extension of $r$ (i.e., it is not a descendant). MayAlias is a predicate on two paths (or a path and set of paths) which is true if it is possible that any concrete paths the arguments may abstract (e.g., via adding non-determinism through|or abstracting iteration with indexing) *could* be the same. The negation of a MayAlias use is true only when the paths are guaranteed to refer to different locations in the heap.

**Replacing with a Fresh Node.** Replacing with a rcuFresh reference faces the same aliasing complications as direct unlinking. We illustrate these challenges in Figs. 7a and b. Our technical report [20] also includes Figures 32a and 32b in Appendix D to illustrate complexities in unlinking. The square $R$ nodes are root nodes, and $H$ nodes are general heap nodes. All resources in thick straight lines and dotted lines form the memory foot print of a node replacement. The hollow thick circular nodes – *pr* and *cr* – point to the nodes involved in replacing $H_1$ (referenced by cr) with $H_f$ (referenced by $cf$) in the structure. We may have $a_0$ and $a_1$ which are aliases with *pr* and *cr* respectively. They are *path-aliases* as they share the same path from root to the node that they reference. Edge labels $l$ and $r$ are abbreviations for the $Left$ and *Right* fields of a binary search tree. The thick dotted $H_f$ denotes the freshly allocated heap node referenced by thick dotted $cf$. The thick dotted field $l$ is set to point to the referent of *cl* and the thick dotted field $r$ is set to point to the referent of the heap node referenced by $lm$.

$H_f$ initially (Fig. 7a) is not part of the shared structure. If it was, it would violate the tree shape requirement imposed by the type system. This is why we highlight it separately in thick dots—its static type would be rcuFresh. Note that we cannot duplicate a rcuFresh variable, nor read a field of an object it points to. This restriction localizes our reasoning about the effects of replacing with a fresh node to just one fresh reference and the object it points to. Otherwise another mechanism would be required to ensure that once a fresh reference was linked into the heap, there were no aliases still typed as fresh—since that would have risked linking the same reference into the heap in two locations.

The transition from the Fig. 7a to b illustrates the effects of the heap mutation (replacing with a fresh node). The reasoning in the type system for replacing with a fresh node is nearly the same as for unlinking an existing node, with one exception. In replacing with a fresh node, there is no need to consider the paths of nodes deeper in the tree than the point of mutation. In the unlinking case, those nodes' static paths would become invalid. In the case of replacing with a fresh node, those descendants' paths are preserved. Our type rule for ensuring safe replacement (T-REPLACE) prevents path aliasing (representing the nonexistence of $a_0$ and $a_1$ via dashed lines and circles) by negating a MayAlias query and prevents field mapping aliasing (nonexistence of any object field from any other context pointing to $cr$) via asserting $(y \neq o)$. It is important to note that objects $(H_4, H_2)$ in the field mappings of the $cr$ whose referent is to be unlinked captured by the heap node's field mappings referenced by $cf$ in rcuFresh. This is part of enforcing locality on the heap mutation and captured by assertion $\mathcal{N} = \mathcal{N}'$ in the type rule (T-REPLACE).

**Inserting a Fresh Node.** T-INSERT type checks heap updates that link a fresh node into a linked data structure. Inserting a rcuFresh reference also faces some of the aliasing complications that we have already discussed for direct unlinking and replacing a node. Unlike the replacement case, the path to the last heap node (the referent of $o$) from the root is *extended* by $f$, which risks falsifying the paths for aliases and descendants of $o$. The final assumption (the implication) of T-INSERT checks for this inconsistency.

There is also another rule, T-LINKF-NULL, not shown in Fig. 6, which handles the case where the fields of the fresh node are not object references, but instead all contain null (e.g., for appending to the end of a linked list or inserting a leaf node in a tree).

**Critical Sections (*Referencing inside RCU Blocks*).** We introduce the *syntactic sugaring* RCUWrite $x.f$ as $y$ in $\{C\}$ for write-side critical sections where the analogous syntactic sugaring can be found for read-side critical sections in Appendix E of the technical report [20].

The type system ensures unlinked and freeable references are handled linearly, as they cannot be dropped – coerced to undef. The top-level rule ToRCUWRITE in Fig. 6 ensures unlinked references have been freed by forbidding them in the critical section's post-type environment. Our technical report [20] also includes the analogous rule ToRCUREAD for the read critical section in Figure 33 of Appendix E.

Preventing the reuse of rcuItr references across critical sections is subtler: the non-critical section system is not flow-sensitive, and does not include rcuItr. Therefore, the initial environment lacks rcuItr references, and trailing rcuItr references may not escape.

# 5 Evaluation

We have used our type system to check correct use of RCU primitives in two RCU data structures representative of the broader space.

Figure 1 gives the type-annotated code for `add` and `remove` operations on a linked list implementation of a bag data structure, following McKenney's example [25]. Our technical report [20] contains code for membership checking.

We have also type checked the most challenging part of an RCU binary search tree, the deletion (which also contains the code for a lookup). Our implementation is a slightly simplified version of the Citrus BST [3]: their code supports fine-grained locking for multiple writers, while ours supports only one writer by virtue of using our single-writer primitives. For lack of space the annotated code is only in Appendix B of the technical report [20], but here we emphasise the important aspects our type system via showing its capabilities of typing BST delete method, which also includes looking up for the node to be deleted.

In Fig. 8, we show the steps for deleting the heap node $H_1$. To locate the node $H_1$, as shown in Fig. 8a, we first traverse the subtree $T_0$ with references *pr* and *cr*, where *pr* is the parent of *cr* during traversal:

$$pr : rcuItr(l|r)^k\{l|r \rightarrow cr\},\ cr : rcuItr(l|r)^k.(l|r)\{\}$$

Traversal of $T_0$ is summarized as $(l|k)^k$. The most subtle aspect of the deletion is the final step in the case the node $H_1$ to remove has both children; as shown in Fig. 8b, the code must traverse the subtree $T_4$ to locate the next element in collection order: the node $H_s$, the left-most node of $H_1$'s right child ($sc$) and its parent ($lp$):

$$lp : (l|r)^k.(l|r).r.(l|r)^m\{l|r \rightarrow sc\},\ sc : (l|r)^k.(l|r).r.l.(l)^m.l\{\}$$

where the traversal of $T_4$ is summarized as $(l|m)^m$.

Then $H_s$ is copied into a new *freshly-allocated* node as shown in Fig. 8b, which is then used to *replace* node $H_1$ as shown in Fig. 8c: the replacement's fields exactly match $H_1$'s except for the data (T-Replace via $\mathcal{N}_1 = \mathcal{N}_2$) as shown in Fig. 8b, and the parent is updated to reference the replacement, unlinking $H_1$.

At this point, as shown in Figs. 8c and d, there are two nodes with the same value in the tree (the *weak* BST property of the Citrus BST [3]): the replacement node, and what was the left-most node under $H_1$'s right child. This latter (original) node $H_s$ must be unlinked as shown in Fig. 8e, which is simpler because by being left-most the left child is null, avoiding another round of replacement (T-UnlinkH via $\forall_{f \in dom(\mathcal{N}_1)}. f \neq f_2 \implies (\mathcal{N}_1(f) = \mathsf{null})$.

Traversing $T_4$ to find successor complicates the reasoning in an interesting way. After the successor node $H_s$ is found in Fig. 8b, there are *two* local unlinking operations as shown in Figs. 8c and e, at different depths of the tree. This is why the type system must keep separate abstract iteration counts, e.g., $k$ of $(l|r)^k$ or $m$ of $(l|r)^m$, for traversals in loops—these indices act like multiple cursors into the data structure, and allow the types to carry enough information to keep those changes separate and ensure neither introduces a cycle.

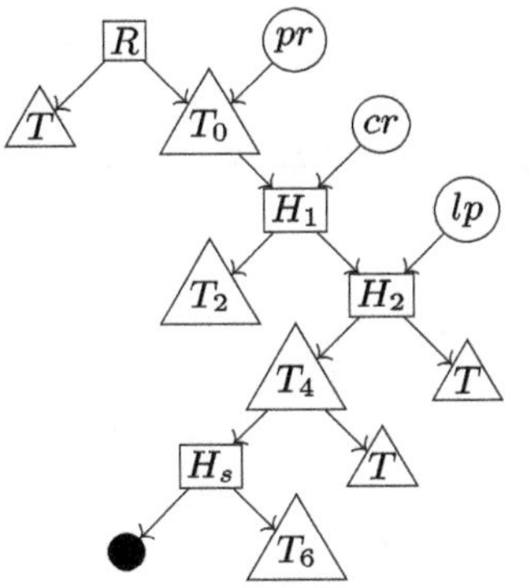


(a) The writer traverses subtree $T_0$ to find the heap node $H_1$ with local references *pr* and *cr*. Black-filled node representing the null node.

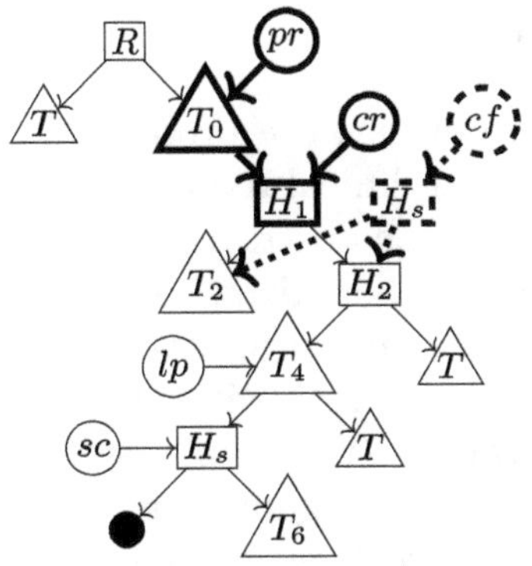


(b) Traverse subtree $T_4$ starting from $H_2$ with references *lp* and *sc* to find successor $H_s$ of $H_1$. Duplicating $H_s$ as a fresh heap node before replacing $H_1$ with the fresh one.

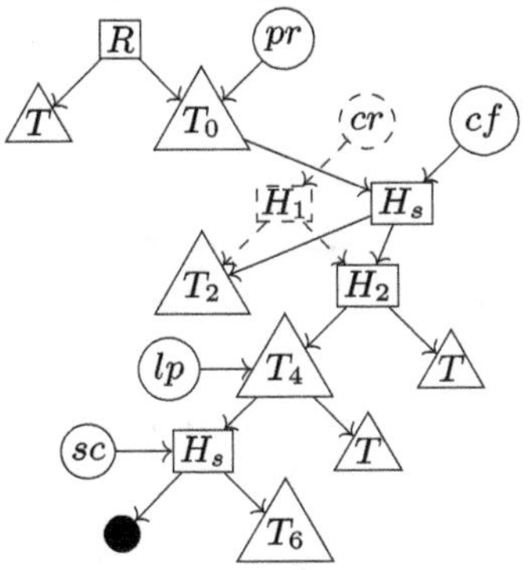


(c) Replace $H_1$ with fresh successor and synchronize with the readers.

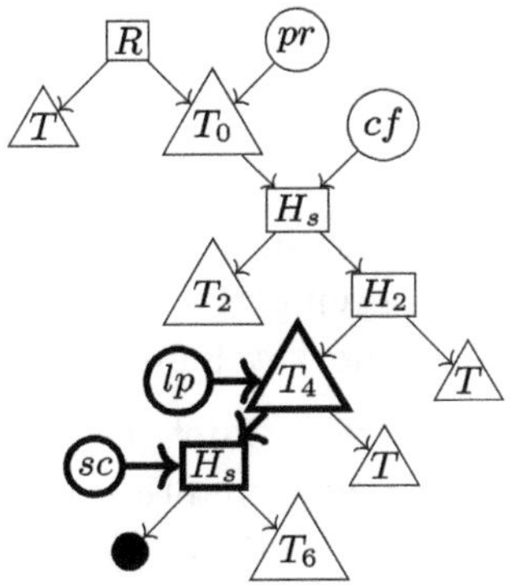


(d) Unlinks old successor referenced by *sc*.

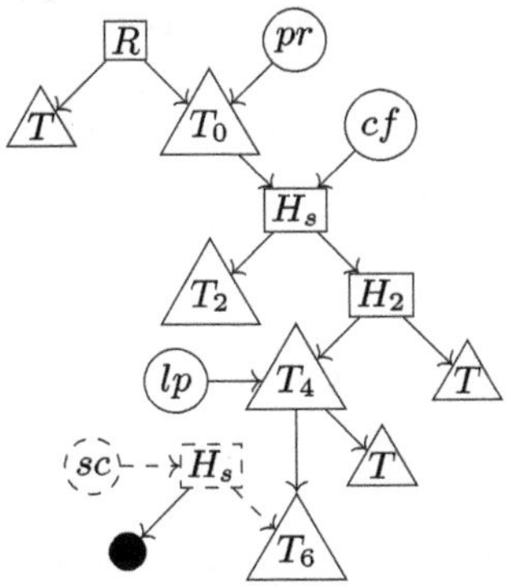


(e) Safe unlinking of the old successor whose left subtree is null.

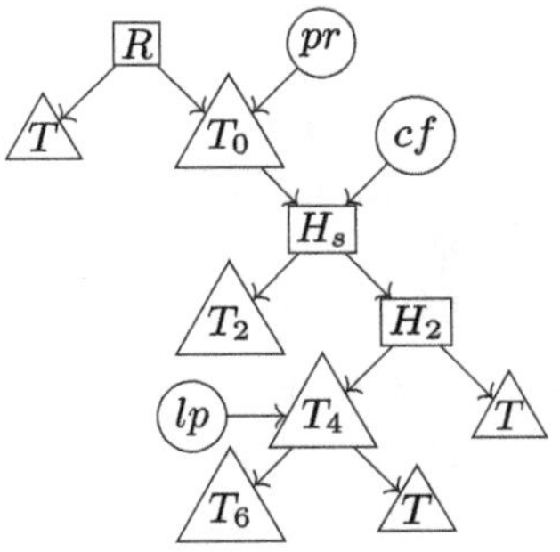


(f) Reclamation of the old successor.

**Fig. 8.** Delete of a heap node with two children in BST [3].

To the best of our knowledge, we are the first to check such code for memory-safe use of RCU primitives modularly, without appeal to the specific implementation of RCU primitives.

# 6 Soundness

This section outlines the proof of type soundness – our full proof appears the accompanying technical report [20]. We prove type soundness by embedding the type system into an abstract concurrent separation logic called the Views Framework [9], which when given certain information about proofs for a specific language (primitives and primitive typing) gives back a full program logic including choice and iteration. As with other work taking this approach [13, 14], this consists of several key steps explained in the following subsections, but a high-level informal soundness argument is twofold. First, because the parameters given to the Views framework ensure the Views logic's Hoare triples $\{-\}C\{-\}$ are sound, this proves soundness of the type rules with respect to type denotations. Second, as our denotation of types encodes the property that the post-environment of any type rule accurately characterizes which memory is linked vs. unlinked, etc., and the global invariants ensure all allocated heap memory is reachable from the root or from some thread's stack, this entails that our type system prevents memory leaks.

## 6.1 Proof

This section provides more details on how the Views Framework [9] is used to prove soundness, giving the major parameters to the framework and outlining global invariants and key lemmas.

**Logical State.** Section 3 defined what Views calls *atomic actions* (the primitive operations) and their semantics on runtime *machine states*. The Views Framework uses a separate notion of instrumented (logical) state over which the logic is built, related by a concretization function $\lfloor - \rfloor$ taking an instrumented state to the machine states of Sect. 3. Most often—including in our proof—the logical state adds useful auxiliary state to the machine state, and the concretization is simply projection. Thus we define our logical states $\mathsf{LState}$ as:

- A machine state, $\sigma = (s, h, l, rt, R, B)$
- An observation map, O, of type $\mathsf{Loc} \rightarrow \mathcal{P}(\mathsf{obs})$
- Undefined variable map, $U$, of type $\mathcal{P}(\mathsf{Var} \times \mathsf{TID})$
- Set of threads, $T$, of type $\mathcal{P}(\mathsf{TIDS})$
- A to-free map (or free list), $F$, of type $\mathsf{Loc} \rightharpoonup \mathcal{P}(\mathsf{TID})$

The thread ID set $T$ includes the thread ID of all running threads. The free map $F$ tracks which reader threads may hold references to each location. It is not required for execution of code, and for validating an implementation could be ignored, but we use it later with our type system to help prove that memory deallocation is safe. The (per-thread) variables in the undefined variable map $U$ are those that should not be accessed (e.g., dangling pointers).

The remaining component, the observation map $O$, requires some further explanation. Each memory allocation/object can be *observed* in one of the following states by a variety of threads, depending on how it was used.

$$\mathsf{obs} := \texttt{iterator}\ \mathsf{tid} \mid \texttt{unlinked} \mid \texttt{fresh} \mid \texttt{freeable} \mid \texttt{root}$$

An object can be observed as part of the structure (`iterator`), removed but possibly accessible to other threads, freshly allocated, safe to deallocate, or the root of the structure.

**Invariants of RCU Views and Denotations of Types.** Next, we aim to convey the intuition behind the predicate WellFormed which enforces global invariants on logical states, and how it interacts with the denotations of types (Fig. 9) in key ways.

WellFormed is the conjunction of a number of more specific invariants, which we outline here. For full details, see Appendix A.2 of the technical report [20].

*The Invariant for Read Traversal.* Reader threads access valid heap locations even during the grace period. The validity of their heap accesses ensured by the observations they make over the heap locations—which can only be iterator as they can only use local rcultr references. To this end, a Readers-Iterators-Only invariant asserts that reader threads can only observe a heap location as iterator.

*Invariants on Grace-Period.* Our logical state includes a "free list" auxiliary state tracking which readers are still accessing *each* unlinked node during grace periods. This must be consistent with the bounding thread set $B$ in the machine state, and this consistency is asserted by the Readers-In-Free-List invariant. This is essentially tracking which readers are being "shown grace" for each location. The Iterators-Free-List invariant complements this by asserting all readers with such observations on unlinked nodes are in the bounding thread set.

The writer thread can refer to a heap location in the free list with a local reference either in type freeable or unlinked. Once the writer unlinks a heap node, it first observes the heap node as unlinked then freeable. The denotation of freeable is only valid following a grace period: it asserts no readers hold aliases of the freeable reference. The denotation of unlinked permits the either the same (perhaps no readers overlapped) or that it is in the to-free list.

*Invariants on Safe Traversal Against Unlinking.* The write-side critical section must guarantee that no updates to the heap cause invalid memory accesses. The Writer-Unlink invariant asserts that a heap location observed as iterator by the writer thread cannot be observed differently by other threads. The denotation of the writer thread's rcultr reference, $[\![\mathsf{rcultr}\,\rho\,\mathcal{N}]\!]_{tid}$, asserts that following a path from the root compatible with $\rho$ reaches the referent, and all are observed as iterator.

The denotation of a reader thread's rcultr reference, $[\![\mathsf{rcultr}]\!]_{tid}$ and the invariants Readers-Iterator-Only, Iterators-Free-List and Readers-In-Free-List all together assert that a reader thread (which can also be a bounding thread) can view an unlinked heap location (which can be in the free list) only as iterator. At the same time, it is essential that reader threads arriving after a node is unlinked cannot access it. The invariants Unlinked-Reachability and Free-List-Reachability ensure that any unlinked nodes are reachable only from other unlinked nodes, and never from the root.

$$
\begin{aligned}
[\![ x : \mathsf{rcultr}\,\rho\,\mathcal{N} ]\!]_{tid} &= \left\{ m \in \mathcal{M} \,\middle|\, \begin{array}{l} (\mathsf{iterator}\,tid \in O(s(x,tid))) \wedge (x \notin U) \\ \wedge(\forall_{f_i \in dom(\mathcal{N}) x_i \in codom(\mathcal{N})} . \left\{ \begin{array}{l} s(x_i,tid) = h(s(x,tid),f_i) \\ \wedge \mathsf{iterator} \in O(s(x_i,tid))) \end{array} \right. \\ \wedge(\forall_{\rho',\rho''} . \rho'.\rho'' = \rho \implies \mathsf{iterator}\,tid \in O(h^*(rt,\rho'))) \\ \wedge h^*(rt,\rho) = s(x,tid) \wedge (l = tid \wedge s(x,\_) \notin dom(F))) \end{array} \right\} \\
[\![ x : \mathsf{rcultr} ]\!]_{tid} &= \left\{ m \in \mathcal{M} \,\middle|\, \begin{array}{l} (\mathsf{iterator}\,tid \in O(s(x,tid))) \wedge (x \notin U) \wedge \\ (tid \in B) \implies \left\{ \begin{array}{l} (\exists_{T' \subseteq B} . \{s(x,tid) \mapsto T'\} \cap F \neq \emptyset) \wedge \\ \wedge (tid \in T') \end{array} \right. \end{array} \right\} \\
[\![ x : \mathsf{unlinked} ]\!]_{tid} &= \left\{ m \in \mathcal{M} \,\middle|\, \begin{array}{l} (\mathsf{unlinked} \in O(.s(x,tid)) \wedge l = tid \wedge x \notin U) \wedge \\ (\exists_{T' \subseteq T} . s(x,tid) \mapsto T' \in F \implies T' \subseteq B \wedge tid \notin T') \end{array} \right\} \\
[\![ x : \mathsf{freeable} ]\!]_{tid} &= \left\{ m \in \mathcal{M} \,\middle|\, \begin{array}{l} \mathsf{freeable} \in O(s(x,tid)) \wedge l = tid \wedge x \notin U \wedge \\ s(x,tid) \mapsto \{\emptyset\} \in F \end{array} \right\} \\
[\![ x : \mathsf{rcuFresh}\,\mathcal{N} ]\!]_{tid} &= \left\{ m \in \mathcal{M} \,\middle|\, \begin{array}{l} (\mathsf{fresh} \in O(s(x,tid)) \wedge x \notin U \wedge s(x,tid) \notin dom(F)) \\ (\forall_{f_i \in dom(\mathcal{N}), x_i \in codom(\mathcal{N})} . s(x_i,tid) = h(s(x,tid),f_i) \\ \wedge \mathsf{iterator}\,tid \in O(s(x_i,tid)) \wedge s(x_i,tid) \notin dom(F)) \end{array} \right\} \\
[\![ x : \mathsf{undef} ]\!]_{tid} &= \left\{ m \in \mathcal{M} \,\middle|\, (x,tid) \in U \wedge s(x,tid) \notin dom(F) \right\} \\
[\![ x : \mathsf{rcuRoot} ]\!]_{tid} &= \left\{ m \in \mathcal{M} \,\middle|\, \begin{array}{l} ((rt \notin U \wedge s(x,tid) = rt \wedge rt \in dom(h) \wedge \\ O(rt) \in \mathsf{root} \wedge s(x,tid) \notin dom(F)) \end{array} \right\}
\end{aligned}
$$

$$\text{provided } h^* : (\mathsf{Loc} \times \mathsf{Path}) \rightharpoonup \mathsf{Val}$$

**Fig. 9.** Type environments

*Invariants on Safe Traversal Against Inserting/Replacing.* A writer replacing an existing node with a fresh one or inserting a single fresh node assumes the fresh (before insertion) node is unreachable to readers before it is published/linked. The Fresh-Writes invariant asserts that a fresh heap location can only be allocated and referenced by the writer thread. The relation between a freshly allocated heap and the rest of the heap is established by the Fresh-Reachable invariant, which requires that there exists no heap node pointing to the freshly allocated one. This invariant supports the preservation of the tree structure. The Fresh-Not-Reader invariant supports the safe traversal of the reader threads via asserting that they cannot observe a heap location as fresh. Moreover, the denotation of the rcuFresh type, $[\![\mathsf{rcuFresh}\,\mathcal{N}]\!]_{tid}$, enforces that fields in $\mathcal{N}$ point to valid heap locations (observed as iterator by the writer thread).

*Invariants on Tree Structure.* Our invariants enforce the *tree* structure heap layouts for data structures. The Unique-Reachable invariant asserts that every heap location reachable from root can only be reached with following an unique path. To preserve the tree structure, Unique-Root enforces unreachability of the root from any heap location that is reachable from root itself.

**Type Environments.** Assertions in the Views logic are (almost) sets of the logical states that satisfy a validity predicate WellFormed, outlined above:

$$\mathcal{M} \stackrel{def}{=} \{m \in (\mathsf{MState} \times O \times U \times T \times F) \mid \mathsf{WellFormed}(m)\}$$

Every type environment represents a set of possible views (WellFormed logical states) consistent with the types in the environment. We make this precise with a denotation function

$$[\![-]\!]\_ : \mathsf{TypeEnv} \to \mathsf{TID} \to \mathcal{P}(\mathcal{M})$$

$$\bullet \stackrel{\text{def}}{=} (\bullet_\sigma, \bullet_O, \cup, \cup) \quad (F_1 \bullet_F F_2) \stackrel{\text{def}}{=} F_1 \cup F_2 \texttt{ when } dom(F_1) \cap dom(F_2) = \emptyset$$

$$O_1 \bullet_O O_2(loc) \stackrel{\text{def}}{=} O_1(loc) \cup O_2(loc) \quad (s_1 \bullet_s s_2) \stackrel{\text{def}}{=} s_1 \cup s_2 \texttt{ when } dom(s_1) \cap dom(s_2) = \emptyset$$

$$(h_1 \bullet_h h_2)(o, f) \stackrel{\text{def}}{=} \begin{cases} \text{undef if } h_1(o,f) = v \wedge h_2(o,f) = v' \wedge v' \neq v \\ v \quad\quad \text{if } h_1(o,f) = v \wedge h_2(o,f) = v \\ v \quad\quad \text{if } h_1(o,f) = \text{undef} \wedge h_2(o,f) = v \\ v \quad\quad \text{if } h_1(o,f) = v \wedge h_2(o,f) = \text{undef} \\ \text{undef if } h_1(o,f) = \text{undef} \wedge h_2(o,f) = \text{undef} \end{cases}$$

$$((s,h,l,rt,R,B),O,U,T,F)\mathcal{R}_0((s',h',l',rt',R',B'),O',U',T',F') \stackrel{\text{def}}{=}$$
$$\bigwedge \begin{Bmatrix} l \in T \to (h = h' \wedge l = l') \\ l \in T \to F = F' \\ \forall tid, o.\, \mathsf{iterator}\ tid \in O(o) \to o \in dom(h) \\ \forall tid, o.\, \mathsf{iterator}\ tid \in O(o) \to o \in dom(h') \\ \forall tid, o.\, \mathsf{root}\ tid \in O(o) \to o \in dom(h) \\ \forall tid, o.\, \mathsf{root}\ tid \in O(o) \to o \in dom(h') \\ O = O' \wedge U = U' \wedge T = T' \wedge R = R' \wedge rt = rt' \\ \forall x, t \in T.\, s(x,t) = s'(x,t) \end{Bmatrix}$$

**Fig. 10.** Composition ($\bullet$) and Thread Interference Relation ($\mathcal{R}_0$)

that yields the set of states corresponding to a given type environment. This is defined as the intersection of individual variables' types as in Fig. 9.

Individual variables' denotations are extended to context denotations slightly differently depending on whether the environment is a reader or writer thread context: writer threads own the global lock, while readers do not:

- For read-side as $[\![x_1 : T_1, \ldots x_n : T_n]\!]_{tid,\mathsf{R}} = [\![x_1 : T_1]\!]_{tid} \cap \ldots \cap [\![x_n : T_n]\!]_{tid} \cap [\![\mathsf{R}]\!]_{tid}$ where $[\![\mathsf{R}]\!]_{tid} = \{(s,h,l,rt,R,B),O,U,T,F \mid tid \in R\}$
- For write-side as $[\![x_1 : T_1, \ldots x_n : T_n]\!]_{tid,\mathsf{M}} = [\![x_1 : T_1]\!]_{tid} \cap \ldots \cap [\![x_n : T_n]\!]_{tid} \cap [\![\mathsf{M}]\!]_{tid}$ where $[\![\mathsf{M}]\!]_{tid} = \{(s,h,l,rt,R,B),O,U,T,F \mid tid = l\}$

**Composition and Interference.** To support framing (weakening), the Views Framework requires that views form a partial commutative monoid under an operation $\bullet : \mathcal{M} \longrightarrow \mathcal{M} \longrightarrow \mathcal{M}$, provided as a parameter to the framework. The framework also requires an interference relation $\mathcal{R} \subseteq \mathcal{M} \times \mathcal{M}$ between views to reason about local updates to one view preserving validity of adjacent views (akin to the small-footprint property of separation logic). Figure 10 defines our composition operator and the core interference relation $\mathcal{R}_0$—the actual interference between views (between threads, or between a local action and framed-away state) is the reflexive transitive closure of $\mathcal{R}_0$. Composition is mostly straightforward point-wise union (threads' views may overlap) of each component. Interference bounds the interference writers and readers may inflict on each other. Notably, if a view contains the writer thread, other threads may not modify the shared portion of the heap, or release the writer lock. Other aspects of interference are natural restrictions like that threads may not modify each others' local variables. WellFormed states are closed under both composition (with another WellFormed state) and interference ($\mathcal{R}$ relates WellFormed states only to other WellFormed states).

$$\downarrow \mathsf{if}\ (x.f == y)\ C_1\ C_2 \downarrow tid \stackrel{\text{def}}{=} z = x.f; ((\mathsf{assume}(z = y); C_1) + (\mathsf{assume}(z \neq y); C_2))$$

$$[\![\mathtt{assume}(\mathcal{S})]\!](s) \stackrel{\text{def}}{=} \begin{cases} \{s\} & \text{if } s \in \mathcal{S} \\ \emptyset & \text{Otherwise} \end{cases} \quad \downarrow \mathsf{while}\ (e)\ C \downarrow \stackrel{\text{def}}{=} (\mathsf{assume}(e); C)^* ; (\mathsf{assume}(\neg e));$$

$$\frac{\{P\} \cap \{\lceil \mathcal{S} \rceil\} \sqsubseteq \{Q\}}{\{P\}\mathtt{assume}\,(\mathcal{S})\,\{Q\}} \quad \text{where } \lceil \mathcal{S} \rceil = \{m | \lfloor m \rfloor \cap \mathcal{S} \neq \emptyset\}$$

**Fig. 11.** Encoding branch conditions with assume(b)

**Stable Environment and Views Shift.** The framing/weakening type rule will be translated to a use of the frame rule in the Views Framework's logic. There separating conjunction is simply the existence of two composable instrumented states:

$$m \in P * Q \stackrel{def}{=} \exists m'. \exists m''. m' \in P \wedge m'' \in Q \wedge m \in m' \bullet m''$$

In order to validate the frame rule in the Views Framework's logic, the assertions in its logic—sets of well-formed instrumented states—must be restricted to sets of logical states that are *stable* with respect to expected interference from other threads or contexts, and interference must be compatible in some way with separating conjunction. Thus a View—the actual base assertions in the Views logic—are then:

$$\mathsf{View}_{\mathcal{M}} \stackrel{def}{=} \{M \in \mathcal{P}(\mathcal{M}) | \mathcal{R}(M) \subseteq M\}$$

Additionally, interference must distribute over composition:

$$\forall m_1, m_2, m. (m_1 \bullet m_2)\mathcal{R}m \implies \exists m_1' m_2'. m_1 \mathcal{R} m_1' \wedge m_2 \mathcal{R} m_2' \wedge m \in m_1' \bullet m_2'$$

Because we use this induced Views logic to prove soundness of our type system by translation, we must ensure any type environment denotes a valid view:

**Lemma 1 (Stable Environment Denotation-M).** *For any* closed *environment $\Gamma$ (i.e., $\forall x \in \mathsf{dom}(\Gamma).,\mathsf{FV}(\Gamma(x)) \subseteq \mathsf{dom}(\Gamma)$): $\mathcal{R}([\![\Gamma]\!]_{\mathsf{M},tid}) \subseteq [\![\Gamma]\!]_{\mathsf{M},tid}$. Alternatively, we say that environment denotation is* stable *(closed under $\mathcal{R}$).*

*Proof.* In Appendix A.1 Lemma 7 of the technical report [20].

We elide the statement of the analogous result for the read-side critical section, available in Appendix A.1 of the technical report.

With this setup done, we can state the connection between the Views Framework logic induced by earlier parameters, and the type system from Sect. 4. The induced Views logic has a familiar notion of Hoare triple—$\{p\}C\{q\}$ where $p$ and $q$ are elements of $\mathsf{View}_{\mathcal{M}}$—with the usual rules for non-deterministic choice, non-deterministic iteration, sequential composition, and parallel composition, sound given the proof obligations just described above. It is parameterized by a rule for atomic commands that requires a specification of the triples for primitive operations, and their soundness (an obligation we must prove). This can then be used to prove that every typing derivation embeds to a valid derivation in the

Views Logic, roughly $\forall \Gamma, C, \Gamma', tid.\, \Gamma \vdash C \dashv \Gamma' \Rightarrow \{[\![\Gamma]\!]_{tid}\}[\![C]\!]_{tid}\{[\![\Gamma']\!]_{tid}\}$ once for the writer type system, once for the readers.

There are two remaining subtleties to address. First, commands $C$ also require translation: the Views Framework has only non-deterministic branches and loops, so the standard versions from our core language must be encoded. The approach to this is based on a standard idea in verification, which we show here for conditionals as shown in Fig. 11. assume($b$) is a standard idea in verification semantics [4,30], which "does nothing" (freezes) if the condition $b$ is false, so its postcondition in the Views logic can reflect the truth of $b$. assume in Fig. 11 adapts this for the Views Framework as in other Views-based proofs [13,14], specifying sets of machine states as a predicate. We write boolean expressions as shorthand for the set of machine states making that expression true. With this setup done, the top-level soundness claim then requires proving – once for the reader type system, once for the writer type system – that every valid source typing derivation corresponds to a valid derivation in the Views logic: $\forall \Gamma, C, \Gamma', \Gamma \vdash_M C \dashv \Gamma' \Rightarrow \{[\![\Gamma]\!]\} \downarrow C \downarrow \{[\![\Gamma']\!]\}$.

Second, we have not addressed a way to encode subtyping. One might hope this corresponds to a kind of implication, and therefore subtyping corresponds to consequence. Indeed, this is how we (and prior work [13,14]) address subtyping in a Views-based proof. Views defines the notion of *view shift*[2] ($\sqsubseteq$) as a way to reinterpret a set of instrumented states as a new (compatible) set of instrumented states, offering a kind of logical consequence, used in a rule of consequence in the Views logic:

$$p \sqsubseteq q \stackrel{def}{=} \forall m \in \mathcal{M}.\, \lfloor p * \{m\} \rfloor \subseteq \lfloor q * \mathcal{R}(\{m\}) \rfloor$$

We are now finally ready to prove the key lemmas of the soundness proof, relating subtying to view shifts, proving soundness of the primitive actions, and finally for the full type system. These proofs occur once for the writer type system, and once for the reader; we show here only the (more complex) writer obligations:

**Lemma 2 (Axiom of Soundness for Atomic Commands).** *For each axiom,* $\Gamma_1 \vdash_M \alpha \dashv \Gamma_2$, *we show* $\forall m.\, [\![\alpha]\!](\lfloor [\![\Gamma_1]\!]_{tid} * \{m\} \rfloor) \subseteq \lfloor [\![\Gamma_2]\!]_{tid} * \mathcal{R}(\{m\}) \rfloor$

*Proof.* By case analysis on $\alpha$. Details in Appendix A.1 of the technical report [20].

**Lemma 3 (Context-SubTyping-M).** $\Gamma \prec: \Gamma' \implies [\![\Gamma]\!]_{M,tid} \sqsubseteq [\![\Gamma']\!]_{M,tid}$

*Proof.* Induction on the subtyping derivation, then inducting on the single-type subtype relation for the first variable in the non-empty context case.

**Lemma 4 (Views Embedding for Write-Side).**

$$\forall \Gamma, C, \Gamma', t.\, \Gamma \vdash_M C \dashv \Gamma' \Rightarrow [\![\Gamma]\!]_t \cap [\![M]\!]_t \vdash [\![C]\!]_t \dashv [\![\Gamma']\!]_t \cap [\![M]\!]_t$$

[2] This is the same notion present in later program logics like Iris [18], though more recent variants are more powerful.

*Proof.* By induction on the typing derivation, appealing to Lemma 2 for primitives, Lemma 3 and consequence for subtyping, and otherwise appealing to structural rules of the Views logic and inductive hypotheses. Full details in Appendix A.1 of the technical report [20].

The corresponding obligations and proofs for the read-side critical section type system are similar in statement and proof approach, just for the read-side type judgments and environment denotations.

## 7 Discussion and Related Work

Our type system builds on a great deal of related work on RCU implementations and models; and general concurrent program verification. Due to space limit, this section captures only discussions on program logics, modeling RCU and memory models, but our technical report [20] includes detailed discussions on model-checking [8, 17, 21], language oriented approaches [6, 16, 16] and realization of our semantics in an implementation as well.

**Modeling RCU and Memory Models.** Alglave et al. [2] propose a memory model to be assumed by the platform-independent parts of the Linux kernel, regardless of the underlying hardware's memory model. As part of this, they give the first formalization of what it means for an RCU implementation to be correct (previously this was difficult to state, as the guarantees in principle could vary by underlying CPU architecture). Essentially, reader critical sections must not span grace periods. They prove by hand that the Linux kernel RCU implementation [1] satisfies this property. McKenney has defined fundamental requirements of RCU implementations [26]; our model in Sect. 3 is a valid RCU implementation according to those requirements (assuming sequential consistency) aside from one performance optimization, *Read-to-Write Upgrade*, which is important in practice but not memory-safety centric – see the technical report [20] for detailed discussion on satisfying RCU requirements. To the best of our knowledge, ours is the first abstract *operational* model for a Linux kernel-style RCU implementation – others are implementation-specific [22] or axiomatic like Alglave et al.'s.

Tassarotti et al. model a well-known way of implementing RCU synchronization without hurting readers' performance—Quiescent State Based Reclamation (QSBR) [8]—where synchronization between the writer thread and reader threads occurs via per-thread counters. Tassarotti et al. [32] uses a protocol based program logic based on separation and ghost variables called GPS [34] to verify a user-level implementation of RCU with a singly linked list client under *release-acquire* semantics, which is a weaker memory model than sequential-consistency. Despite the weaker model, the protocol that they enforce on their RCU primitives is nearly the same what our type system requires. The reads and writes to per thread QSBR structures are similar to our more abstract updates to reader and bounding sets. Therefore, we anticipate it would be possible to extend our type system in the future for similar weak memory models.

**Program Logics.** Fu et al. [12] extend Rely-Guarantee and Separation-Logic [10,11,35] with the *past-tense* temporal operator to eliminate the need for using a history variable and lift the standard separation conjunction to assert over on execution histories. Gotsman et al. [15] take assertions from temporal logic to separation logic [35] to capture the essence of epoch-based memory reclamation algorithms and have a simpler proof than what Fu et al. have [12] for Michael's non-blocking stack [29] implementation under a sequentially consistent memory model.

Tassarotti et al. [32] use *abstract-predicates* – e.g. WriterSafe – that are specialized to the singly-linked structure in their evaluation. This means reusing their ideas for another structure, such as a binary search tree, would require revising many of their invariants. By contrast, our types carry similar information (our denotations are similar to their definitions), but are reusable across at least singly-linked and tree data structures (Sect. 5). Their proofs of a linked list also require managing assertions about RCU implementation resources, while these are effectively hidden in the type denotations in our system. On the other hand, their proofs ensure full functional correctness. Meyer and Wolff [28] make a compelling argument that separating memory safety from correctness if profitable, and we provide such a decoupled memory safety argument.

## 8 Conclusions

We presented the first type system that ensures code uses RCU memory management safely, and which is significantly simpler than full-blown verification logics. To this end, we gave the first general operational model for RCU-based memory management. Based on our suitable abstractions for RCU in the operational semantics we are the first showing that decoupling the *memory-safety* proofs of RCU clients from the underlying reclamation model is possible. Meyer et al. [28] took similar approach for decoupling the *correctness* verification of the data structures from the underlying reclamation model under the assumption of the *memory-safety* for the data structures. We demonstrated the applicability/reusability of our types on two examples: a linked-list based bag [25] and a binary search tree [3]. To our best knowledge, we are the first presenting the *memory-safety* proof for a tree client of RCU. We managed to prove type soundness by embedding the type system into an abstract concurrent separation logic called the Views Framework [9] and encode many RCU properties as either type-denotations or global invariants over abstract RCU state. By doing this, we managed to discharge these invariants once as a part of soundness proof and did not need to prove them for each different client.

**Acknowledgements.** We are grateful to Matthew Parkinson for guidance and productive discussions on the early phase of this project. We also thank to Nik Sultana and Klaus V. Gleissenthall for their helpful comments and suggestions for improving the paper.

## References


1. Alglave, J., Kroening, D., Tautschnig, M.: Partial orders for efficient bounded model checking of concurrent software. In: Sharygina, N., Veith, H. (eds.) CAV 2013. LNCS, vol. 8044, pp. 141–157. Springer, Heidelberg (2013). https://doi.org/10.1007/978-3-642-39799-8_9
2. Alglave, J., Maranget, L., McKenney, P.E., Parri, A., Stern, A.: Frightening small children and disconcerting grown-ups: concurrency in the Linux kernel. In: Proceedings of the Twenty-Third International Conference on Architectural Support for Programming Languages and Operating Systems, ASPLOS 2018, pp. 405–418. ACM, New York (2018). https://doi.org/10.1145/3173162.3177156. http://doi.acm.org/10.1145/3173162.3177156
3. Arbel, M., Attiya, H.: Concurrent updates with RCU: search tree as an example. In: Proceedings of the 2014 ACM Symposium on Principles of Distributed Computing, PODC 2014, pp. 196–205. ACM, New York (2014). https://doi.org/10.1145/2611462.2611471. http://doi.acm.org/10.1145/2611462.2611471
4. Barnett, M., Chang, B.-Y.E., DeLine, R., Jacobs, B., Leino, K.R.M.: Boogie: a modular reusable verifier for object-oriented programs. In: de Boer, F.S., Bonsangue, M.M., Graf, S., de Roever, W.-P. (eds.) FMCO 2005. LNCS, vol. 4111, pp. 364–387. Springer, Heidelberg (2006). https://doi.org/10.1007/11804192_17
5. Clements, A.T., Kaashoek, M.F., Zeldovich, N.: Scalable address spaces using RCU balanced trees. In: Proceedings of the 17th International Conference on Architectural Support for Programming Languages and Operating Systems, ASPLOS 2012, London, UK, 3–7 March 2012, pp. 199–210 (2012). https://doi.org/10.1145/2150976.2150998. http://doi.acm.org/10.1145/2150976.2150998
6. Cooper, T., Walpole, J.: Relativistic programming in Haskell using types to enforce a critical section discipline (2015). http://web.cecs.pdx.edu/~walpole/papers/haskell2015.pdf
7. Desnoyers, M., McKenney, P.E., Dagenais, M.R.: Multi-core systems modeling forformal verification of parallel algorithms. SIGOPS Oper. Syst. Rev. **47**(2), 51–65 (2013). https://doi.org/10.1145/2506164.2506174. http://doi.acm.org/10.1145/2506164.2506174
8. Desnoyers, M., McKenney, P.E., Stern, A., Walpole, J.: User-level implementations of read-copy update. IEEE Trans. Parallel Distrib. Syst. (2009). /static/publications/desnoyers-ieee-urcu-submitted.pdf
9. Dinsdale-Young, T., Birkedal, L., Gardner, P., Parkinson, M.J., Yang, H.: Views: compositional reasoning for concurrent programs. In: The 40th Annual ACM SIGPLAN-SIGACT Symposium on Principles of Programming Languages, POPL 2013, Rome, Italy, 23–25 January, 2013, pp. 287–300 (2013). https://doi.org/10.1145/2429069.2429104. http://doi.acm.org/10.1145/2429069.2429104
10. Feng, X.: Local rely-guarantee reasoning. In: Proceedings of the 36th Annual ACM SIGPLAN-SIGACT Symposium on Principles of Programming Languages, POPL 2009, pp. 315–327. ACM, New York (2009). https://doi.org/10.1145/1480881.1480922. http://doi.acm.org/10.1145/1480881.1480922
11. Feng, X., Ferreira, R., Shao, Z.: On the relationship between concurrent separation logic and assume-guarantee reasoning. In: De Nicola, R. (ed.) ESOP 2007. LNCS, vol. 4421, pp. 173–188. Springer, Heidelberg (2007). https://doi.org/10.1007/978-3-540-71316-6_13
12. Fu, M., Li, Y., Feng, X., Shao, Z., Zhang, Y.: Reasoning about optimistic concurrency using a program logic for history. In: Gastin, P., Laroussinie, F. (eds.) CON-

CUR 2010. LNCS, vol. 6269, pp. 388–402. Springer, Heidelberg (2010). https://doi.org/10.1007/978-3-642-15375-4_27
13. Gordon, C.S., Ernst, M.D., Grossman, D., Parkinson, M.J.: Verifying invariants of lock-free data structures with rely-guarantee and refinement types. ACM Trans. Program. Lang. Syst. (TOPLAS) **39**(3) (2017). https://doi.org/10.1145/3064850. http://doi.acm.org/10.1145/3064850
14. Gordon, C.S., Parkinson, M.J., Parsons, J., Bromfield, A., Duffy, J.: Uniqueness and reference immutability for safe parallelism. In: Proceedings of the 2012 ACM International Conference on Object Oriented Programming, Systems, Languages, and Applications (OOPSLA 2012), Tucson, AZ, USA, October 2012. https://doi.org/10.1145/2384616.2384619. http://dl.acm.org/citation.cfm?id=2384619
15. Gotsman, A., Rinetzky, N., Yang, H.: Verifying concurrent memory reclamation algorithms with grace. In: Felleisen, M., Gardner, P. (eds.) ESOP 2013. LNCS, vol. 7792, pp. 249–269. Springer, Heidelberg (2013). https://doi.org/10.1007/978-3-642-37036-6_15
16. Howard, P.W., Walpole, J.: A relativistic enhancement to software transactional memory. In: Proceedings of the 3rd USENIX Conference on Hot Topic in Parallelism, HotPar 2011, p. 15. USENIX Association, Berkeley (2011). http://dl.acm.org/citation.cfm?id=2001252.2001267
17. Kokologiannakis, M., Sagonas, K.: Stateless model checking of the Linux kernel's hierarchical read-copy-update (tree RCU). In: Proceedings of the 24th ACM SIGSOFT International SPIN Symposium on Model Checking of Software, SPIN 2017, pp. 172–181. ACM, New York (2017). https://doi.org/10.1145/3092282.3092287. http://doi.acm.org/10.1145/3092282.3092287
18. Krebbers, R., Jung, R., Bizjak, A., Jourdan, J.-H., Dreyer, D., Birkedal, L.: The essence of higher-order concurrent separation logic. In: Yang, H. (ed.) ESOP 2017. LNCS, vol. 10201, pp. 696–723. Springer, Heidelberg (2017). https://doi.org/10.1007/978-3-662-54434-1_26
19. Kung, H.T., Lehman, P.L.: Concurrent manipulation of binary search trees. ACMTrans. Database Syst. **5**(3), 354–382 (1980). https://doi.org/10.1145/320613.320619. http://doi.acm.org/10.1145/320613.320619
20. Kuru, I., Gordon, C.S.: Safe deferred memory reclamation with types. CoRR **abs/1811.11853** (2018). http://arxiv.org/abs/1811.11853
21. Liang, L., McKenney, P.E., Kroening, D., Melham, T.: Verification of the tree-based hierarchical read-copy update in the Linux kernel. CoRR **abs/1610.03052** (2016). http://arxiv.org/abs/1610.03052
22. Mandrykin, M.U., Khoroshilov, A.V.: Towards deductive verification of C programs with shared data. Program. Comput. Softw. **42**(5), 324–332 (2016). https://doi.org/10.1134/S0361768816050054
23. Mckenney, P.E.: Exploiting deferred destruction: an analysis of read-copy-update techniques in operating system kernels. Ph.D. thesis, Oregon Health & Science University (2004). aAI3139819
24. McKenney, P.E.: N4037: non-transactional implementation of atomic tree move, May 2014. http://www.open-std.org/jtc1/sc22/wg21/docs/papers/2014/n4037.pdf
25. McKenney, P.E.: Some examples of kernel-hacker informal correctness reasoning. Technical report paulmck.2015.06.17a (2015). http://www2.rdrop.com/users/paulmck/techreports/IntroRCU.2015.06.17a.pdf
26. Mckenney, P.E.: A tour through RCU's requirements (2017). https://www.kernel.org/doc/Documentation/RCU/Design/Requirements/Requirements.html

27. Mckenney, P.E., et al.: Read-copy update. In: Ottawa Linux Symposium, pp. 338–367 (2001)
28. Meyer, R., Wolff, S.: Decoupling lock-free data structures from memory reclamation for static analysis. PACMPL **3**(POPL), 58:1–58:31 (2019). https://dl.acm.org/citation.cfm?id=3290371
29. Michael, M.M.: Hazard pointers: safe memory reclamation for lock-free objects. IEEE Trans. Parallel Distrib. Syst. **15**(6), 491–504 (2004). https://doi.org/10.1109/TPDS.2004.8
30. Müller, P., Schwerhoff, M., Summers, A.J.: Viper: a verification infrastructure for permission-based reasoning. In: Jobstmann, B., Leino, K.R.M. (eds.) VMCAI 2016. LNCS, vol. 9583, pp. 41–62. Springer, Heidelberg (2016). https://doi.org/10.1007/978-3-662-49122-5_2
31. McKenney, P.E., Mathieu Desnoyers, L.J., Triplett, J.: The RCU-barrier menagerie, November 2016. https://lwn.net/Articles/573497/
32. Tassarotti, J., Dreyer, D., Vafeiadis, V.: Verifying read-copy-update in a logic for weak memory. In: Proceedings of the 36th ACM SIGPLAN Conference on Programming Language Design and Implementation, PLDI 2015, pp. 110–120. ACM, New York (2015). https://doi.org/10.1145/2737924.2737992. http://doi.acm.org/10.1145/2737924.2737992
33. Triplett, J., McKenney, P.E., Walpole, J.: Resizable, scalable, concurrent hash tables via relativistic programming. In: Proceedings of the 2011 USENIX Conference on USENIX Annual Technical Conference, USENIXATC 2011, p. 11. USENIX Association, Berkeley (2011). http://dl.acm.org/citation.cfm?id=2002181.2002192
34. Turon, A., Vafeiadis, V., Dreyer, D.: Gps: Navigating weak memory with ghosts, protocols, and separation. In: Proceedings of the 2014 ACM International Conference on Object Oriented Programming Systems Languages and Applications, OOPSLA 2014, pp. 691–707. ACM, New York (2014). https://doi.org/10.1145/2660193.2660243. http://doi.acm.org/10.1145/2660193.2660243
35. Vafeiadis, V., Parkinson, M.: A marriage of rely/guarantee and separation logic. In: Caires, L., Vasconcelos, V.T. (eds.) CONCUR 2007. LNCS, vol. 4703, pp. 256–271. Springer, Heidelberg (2007). https://doi.org/10.1007/978-3-540-74407-8_18

# 4

# Manifest Deadlock-Freedom for Shared Session Types

Stephanie Balzer[1(✉)], Bernardo Toninho[2(✉)], and Frank Pfenning[1]

[1] Carnegie Mellon University, Pittsburgh, USA
balzers@cs.cmu.edu
[2] NOVA LINCS, Universidade Nova de Lisboa, Lisbon, Portugal
btoninho@fct.unl.pt

**Abstract.** Shared session types generalize the Curry-Howard correspondence between intuitionistic linear logic and the session-typed $\pi$-calculus with adjoint modalities that mediate between linear and shared session types, giving rise to a programming model where shared channels must be used according to a locking discipline of acquire-release. While this generalization greatly increases the range of programs that can be written, the gain in expressiveness comes at the cost of deadlock-freedom, a property which holds for many linear session type systems. In this paper, we develop a type system for logically-shared sessions in which types capture not only the interactive behavior of processes but also constrain the order of resources (i.e., shared processes) they may acquire. This type-level information is then used to rule out cyclic dependencies among acquires and synchronization points, resulting in a system that ensures *deadlock-free communication* for well-typed processes in the presence of shared sessions, higher-order channel passing, and recursive processes. We illustrate our approach on a series of examples, showing that it rules out deadlocks in circular networks of both shared and linear recursive processes, while still being permissive enough to type concurrent implementations of shared imperative data structures as processes.

**Keywords:** Linear and shared session types · Deadlock-freedom

## 1 Introduction

*Session types* [25–27] naturally describe the interaction protocols that arise amongst concurrent processes that communicate via message-passing. This typing discipline has been integrated (with varying static safety guarantees) into several mainstream language such as Java [28,29], F# [43], Scala [49,50], Go [11] and Rust [33]. Session types moreover enjoy a logical correspondence between *linear logic* and the *session-typed $\pi$-calculus* [8,9,51,55]. Languages building on this correspondence [24,52,55] not only guarantee *session* *fidelity* (i.e., type preservation) but also *deadlock-freedom* (i.e., global progress). The latter is guaranteed even in the presence of interleaved sessions, which are often excluded from the deadlock-free fragments of traditional session-typed frameworks [20, 26, 27, 53]. These logical session types, however, exclude programming scenarios that demand *sharing* of mutable resources (e.g., shared databases or shared output devices) instead of functional resource replication.

To increase their practicality, logical session types have been extended with *manifest sharing* [2]. In the resulting language, linear and shared sessions coexist, but the type system enforces that clients of shared sessions run in mutual exclusion of each other. This separation is achieved by enforcing an *acquire-release* policy, where a client of a shared session must first acquire the session before it can participate in it along a private linear channel. Conversely, when a client releases a session, it gives up its linear channel and only retains a shared reference to the session. Thus, sessions in the presence of manifest sharing can change, or *shift*, between shared and linear execution modes. At the type-level, the acquire-release policy manifests in a stratification of session types into linear and shared with adjoint modalities [5, 47, 48], connecting the two strata. Operationally, the modality shifting *up* from the linear to the shared layer translates into an *acquire* and the one shifting *down* from shared to linear into a *release*.

Manifest sharing greatly increases the range of programs that can be written because it recovers the expressiveness of the untyped asynchronous $\pi$-calculus [3] while maintaining session fidelity. As in the $\pi$-calculus, however, the gain in expressiveness comes at the cost of *deadlock-freedom*. An illustrative example is an implementation of the classical dining philosophers problem, shown in Fig. 1, using the language $\mathsf{SILL_S}$ [2] that supports manifest sharing (in this setting we often equate a process with the session it offers along a distinguished channel). The code shows the process *fork_proc*, implementing a session of type sfork, and the processes *thinking* and *eating*, implementing sessions of type philosopher. We defer the details of the typing and the definition of the session types sfork and philosopher to Sect. 2 and focus on the programmatic working of the processes for now. For ease of reading, we typeset shared session types and variables denoting shared channel references in red.

A *fork_proc* process represents a fork that can be perpetually acquired and released. The actions accept and detach are the duals of acquire and release, respectively, allowing a process to accept an acquire by a client and to initiate a release by a client, respectively. Process thinking has two shared channel references as arguments, for the forks to the left and right of the philosopher, which the process tries to acquire. If the acquire succeeds, the process recurs as an eating philosopher with two (now) linear channel references of type lfork. Once a philosopher is done eating, it releases both forks and recurs as a thinking philosopher. Let's set a table for three philosopher that share three forks, all spawned as processes executing in parallel:

$$f_0 \leftarrow \mathit{fork\_proc}\ ;\ f_1 \leftarrow \mathit{fork\_proc}\ ;\ f_2 \leftarrow \mathit{fork\_proc}\ ;$$
$$p_0 \leftarrow \mathit{thinking} \leftarrow f_0, f_1\ ;\ p_1 \leftarrow \mathit{thinking} \leftarrow f_1, f_2\ ;\ p_2 \leftarrow \mathit{thinking} \leftarrow f_2, f_0\ ;$$

$$
\begin{array}{lll}
\mathit{fork\_proc} : \{\mathsf{sfork}\} & \mathit{thinking} : \{\mathsf{phil} \leftarrow \mathsf{sfork}, \mathsf{sfork}\} & \mathit{eating} : \{\mathsf{phil} \leftarrow \mathsf{lfork}, \mathsf{lfork}\} \\
c \leftarrow \mathit{fork\_proc} = & c \leftarrow \mathit{thinking} \leftarrow \mathit{left}, \mathit{right} = & c \leftarrow \mathit{eating} \leftarrow \mathit{left}', \mathit{right}' = \\
\quad c' \leftarrow \mathsf{accept}\ c\ ; & \quad \mathit{left}' \leftarrow \mathsf{acquire}\ \mathit{left}\ ; & \quad \mathit{right} \leftarrow \mathsf{release}\ \mathit{right}'\ ; \\
\quad c \leftarrow \mathsf{detach}\ c'\ ; & \quad \mathit{right}' \leftarrow \mathsf{acquire}\ \mathit{right}\ ; & \quad \mathit{left} \leftarrow \mathsf{release}\ \mathit{left}'\ ; \\
\quad c \leftarrow \mathit{fork\_proc} & \quad c \leftarrow \mathit{eating} \leftarrow \mathit{left}', \mathit{right}'\ ; & \quad c \leftarrow \mathit{thinking} \leftarrow \mathit{left}, \mathit{right}
\end{array}
$$

**Fig. 1.** Dining philosophers in $\mathsf{SILL_S}$ [2].

Infamously, this configuration may deadlock because of the *circular* dependency between the acquires. We can break this cycle by changing the last line to $p_2 \leftarrow \mathit{thinking} \leftarrow f_0, f_2$, ensuring that forks are acquired in increasing order.

Perhaps surprisingly, cyclic dependencies between acquire requests are not the only source of deadlocks. Fig. 2 gives an example, defining the processes *owner* and *contester*, which both have a shared channel reference to a common resource that can be perpetually acquired and released. Both processes acquire the shared resource, but additionally exchange the message ping. More precisely, process *owner* spawns the process *contester*, acquires the shared resource, and only releases the resource after having received the message ping from the *contester*. Process *contester*, on the other hand, first attempts to acquire the resource and then sends the message *ping* to the owner. The program deadlocks if process *owner* acquires the resource first. In that case, process *owner* waits for process *contester* to send the message ping while process *contester* waits to acquire the resource held by process *owner*. We note that this deadlock arises in both synchronous and asynchronous semantics.

$$
\begin{array}{ll}
\mathit{owner} : \{\mathbf{1} \leftarrow \mathsf{sres}\} & \mathit{contester} : \{\oplus\{\mathsf{ping} : \mathbf{1}\} \leftarrow \mathsf{sres}\} \\
o \leftarrow \mathit{owner} \leftarrow \mathit{sr} = & c \leftarrow \mathit{contester} \leftarrow \mathit{sr} = \\
\quad c \leftarrow \mathit{contester} \leftarrow \mathit{sr}\ ; & \quad \mathit{lr} \leftarrow \mathsf{acquire}\ \mathit{sr}\ ; \\
\quad \mathit{lr} \leftarrow \mathsf{acquire}\ \mathit{sr}\ ; & \quad c.\mathsf{ping}\ ; \\
\quad \mathsf{case}\ c\ \mathsf{of} & \quad \mathit{sr} \leftarrow \mathsf{release}\ \mathit{lr}\ ; \\
\quad \mid \mathsf{ping} \rightarrow \mathsf{wait}\ c\ ; & \quad \mathsf{close}\ c \\
\qquad\qquad \mathit{sr} \leftarrow \mathsf{release}\ \mathit{lr}\ ; \mathsf{close}\ o &
\end{array}
$$

**Fig. 2.** Circular dependencies among acquire and synchronization actions.

In this paper, we develop a type system for manifest sharing that rules out cycles between acquire requests and interdependencies between acquire requests and synchronization actions, detecting the two kinds of deadlocks explained above. In our type system, session types not only prescribe *when* resources must be acquired and released, but also the *range* of resources that may be acquired. To this end, we equip the type system with the notion of a *world*, an abstract value at which a process resides, and type processes relative to an acyclic *ordering* on worlds, akin to the partial-order based approaches of [34,37]. The contributions of this paper are:

- a characterization of the possible forms of deadlocks that can arise in shared session types;
- the introduction of manifest deadlock-freedom, where resource dependencies are manifest in the type structure via world modalities;
- its elaboration in the programming language $\mathsf{SILL}_{\mathsf{S}^+}$, resulting in a type system, a synchronous operational semantics, and proofs of session fidelity (preservation) and a strong form of progress that excludes all deadlocks;
- the novel abstraction of green and red arrows to reason about the interdependencies between processes;
- an illustration of the concepts on various examples, including an extensive comparison with related work.

This paper is structured as follows: Sect. 2 provides a short introduction to manifest sharing. Sect. 3 develops the type system and dynamics of the language $\mathsf{SILL}_{\mathsf{S}^+}$. Sect. 4 illustrates the introduced concepts on an extended example. Sect. 5 discusses the meta-theoretical properties of $\mathsf{SILL}_{\mathsf{S}^+}$, emphasizing progress. Sect. 6 compares with examples of related work and identifies future work. Sect. 7 discusses related work, and Sect. 8 concludes this paper.

## 2 Manifest Sharing

In the previous section, we have already explored the programmatic workings of *manifest sharing* [2], which enforces an *acquire-release* policy on shared channel references. In this section, we clarify the typing of shared processes.

A key contribution of manifest sharing is not only to support acquire-release as a programming primitive but also to make it *manifest* in the type system. Generalizing the idea of type *stratification* [5,47,48], session types are partitioned into a linear and shared layer with two *adjoint modalities* connecting the layers:

$$\begin{array}{ll} A_{\mathsf{S}} & \triangleq \uparrow_{\mathsf{L}}^{\mathsf{S}} A_{\mathsf{L}} \\ A_{\mathsf{L}}, B_{\mathsf{L}} & \triangleq A_{\mathsf{L}} \otimes B_{\mathsf{L}} \mid \oplus\{\overline{l : A_{\mathsf{L}}}\} \mid \&\{\overline{l : A_{\mathsf{L}}}\} \mid A_{\mathsf{L}} \multimap B_{\mathsf{L}} \mid \exists x{:}A_{\mathsf{S}}.B_{\mathsf{L}} \mid \Pi x{:}A_{\mathsf{S}}.B_{\mathsf{L}} \mid \mathbf{1} \mid \downarrow_{\mathsf{L}}^{\mathsf{S}} A_{\mathsf{S}} \end{array}$$

In the linear layer, we get the standard connectives of intuitionistic linear logic ($A_{\mathsf{L}} \otimes B_{\mathsf{L}}$, $A_{\mathsf{L}} \multimap B_{\mathsf{L}}$, $\oplus\{\overline{l : A_{\mathsf{L}}}\}$, $\&\{\overline{l : A_{\mathsf{L}}}\}$, and $\mathbf{1}$). These connectives are extended with the modal operator $\downarrow_{\mathsf{L}}^{\mathsf{S}} A_{\mathsf{S}}$, shifting *down* from the shared to the linear layer. Similarly, in the shared layer, we have the operator $\uparrow_{\mathsf{L}}^{\mathsf{S}} A_{\mathsf{L}}$, shifting *up* from the linear to the shared layer. The former translates into a *release* (and, dually, detach), the latter into an *acquire* (and, dually, accept). As a result, we obtain a system in which session types prescribe all forms of communication, including the acquisition and release of shared processes.

Table 1 provides an overview of $\mathsf{SILL}_{\mathsf{S}}$'s session types and their operational reading. Since $\mathsf{SILL}_{\mathsf{S}}$ is based on an intuitionistic interpretation of linear logic session types [8], types are expressed from the point of view of the *providing process* with the channel along which the process provides the session behavior being characterized by its session type. This choice avoids the explicit duality operation present in original presentations of session types [25,26] and in those based

**Table 1.** Session types in $\mathsf{SILL_S}$ and their operational meaning.

| Session type current | cont | Process term current | cont | Description |
|---|---|---|---|---|
| $c_L : \oplus\{\overline{l : A_L}\}$ | $c_L : A_{L_h}$ | $c_L.l_h\ ; P$ | $P$ | sends label $l_h$ along $c_L$ |
| | | $\mathsf{case}\ c_L\ \mathsf{of}\ \overline{l \Rightarrow Q}$ | $Q_h$ | receives label $l_h$ along $c_L$ |
| $c_L : \&\{\overline{l : A_L}\}$ | $c_L : A_{L_h}$ | $\mathsf{case}\ c_L\ \mathsf{of}\ \overline{l \Rightarrow P}$ | $P_h$ | receives label $l_h$ along $c$ |
| | | $c_L.l_h\ ; Q$ | $Q$ | sends label $l_h$ along $c_L$ |
| $c_L : A_L \otimes B_L$ | $c_L : B_L$ | $\mathsf{send}\ c_L\ d_L\ ; P$ | $P$ | sends channel $d_L : A_L$ along $c_L$ |
| | | $y_L \leftarrow \mathsf{recv}\ c_L\ ; Q_{y_L}$ | $[d_L/y_L]\,Q_{y_L}$ | receives channel $d_L : A_L$ along $c_L$ |
| $c_L : A_L \multimap B_L$ | $c_L : B_L$ | $y_L \leftarrow \mathsf{recv}\ c_L\ ; P_{y_L}$ | $[d_L/y_L]\,P_{y_L}$ | receives channel $d_L : A_L$ along $c_L$ |
| | | $\mathsf{send}\ c_L\ d_L\ ; Q$ | $Q$ | sends channel $d_L : A_L$ along $c_L$ |
| $c_L : \Pi x{:}A_S.B_L$ | $c_L : B_L$ | $\mathsf{send}\ c_L\ d_S\ ; P$ | $P$ | sends channel $d_S : A_S$ along $c_L$ |
| | | $y_S \leftarrow \mathsf{recv}\ c_L\ ; Q_{y_S}$ | $[d_S/y_S]\,Q_{y_S}$ | receives channel $d_S : A_S$ along $c_L$ |
| $c_L : \exists x{:}A_S.B_L$ | $c_L : B_L$ | $y_S \leftarrow \mathsf{recv}\ c_L\ ; P_{y_S}$ | $[d_S/y_S]\,P_{y_S}$ | receives channel $d_S : A_S$ along $c_L$ |
| | | $\mathsf{send}\ c_L\ d_S\ ; Q$ | $Q$ | sends channel $d_S : A_S$ along $c_L$ |
| $c_L : \mathbf{1}$ | - | $\mathsf{close}\ c_L$ | - | sends "end" along $c_L$ |
| | | $\mathsf{wait}\ c_L\ ; Q$ | $Q$ | receives "end" along $c_L$ |
| $c_L : \downarrow_L^S A_S$ | $c_S : A_S$ | $c_S \leftarrow \mathsf{detach}\ c_L\ ; P_{x_S}$ | $[c_S/x_S]\,P_{x_S}$ | sends "detach $c_S$" along $c_L$ |
| | | $x_S \leftarrow \mathsf{release}\ c_L\ ; Q_{x_S}$ | $[c_S/x_S]\,Q_{x_S}$ | receives "detach $c_S$" along $c_L$ |
| $c_S : \uparrow_L^S A_L$ | $c_L : A_L$ | $c_L \leftarrow \mathsf{acquire}\ c_S\ ; Q_{x_L}$ | $[c_L/x_L]\,Q_{x_L}$ | sends "acquire $c_L$" along $c_S$ |
| | | $x_L \leftarrow \mathsf{accept}\ c_S\ ; P_{x_L}$ | $[c_L/x_L]\,P_{x_L}$ | receives "acquire $c_L$" along $c_S$ |

on classical linear logic [55]. Table 1 lists the points of view of the *provider* and *client* of a given connective in the first and second lines, respectively. Moreover, Table 1 gives for each connective its session type before and after the message exchange, along with their respective process terms. We can see that the process terms of a provider and a client for a given connective come in matching pairs, indicating that the participants' views of the session change consistently. We use the subscripts L and S to distinguish between linear and shared channels, respectively.

We are now able to give the session types of the processes *fork_proc*, *thinking*, and *eating* defined in the previous section:

$\mathsf{lfork} = \downarrow_L^S \mathsf{sfork}$
$\mathsf{sfork} = \uparrow_L^S \mathsf{lfork}$
$\mathsf{phil} = \mathbf{1}$

The mutually recursive session types lfork and sfork represent a fork that can perpetually be acquired and released. We adopt an *equi-recursive* [14] interpretation for recursive session types, silently equating a recursive type with its unfolding and requiring types to be *contractive* [19].

We briefly discuss the typing and the dynamics of acquire-release. The typing and the dynamics of the residual linear connectives are standard, and we detail them in the context of $\mathsf{SILL_{S+}}$ (see Sect. 3). As is usual for an intuitionistic interpretation, each connective gives rise to a left and a right rule, denoting the use and provision, respectively, of a session of the given type:

$$(\text{T-}{\uparrow}^{\mathsf{S}}_{\mathsf{L}}\text{R})\quad \frac{\Gamma; \cdot \vdash P_{x_{\mathsf{L}}} :: (x_{\mathsf{L}} : A_{\mathsf{L}})}{\Gamma \vdash x_{\mathsf{L}} \leftarrow \mathsf{accept}\, x_{\mathsf{S}}; P_{x_{\mathsf{L}}} :: (x_{\mathsf{S}} : {\uparrow}^{\mathsf{S}}_{\mathsf{L}} A_{\mathsf{L}})}$$

$$(\text{T-}{\uparrow}^{\mathsf{S}}_{\mathsf{L}}\text{L})\quad \frac{\Gamma, x_{\mathsf{S}} : {\uparrow}^{\mathsf{S}}_{\mathsf{L}} A_{\mathsf{L}}; \Delta, x_{\mathsf{L}} : A_{\mathsf{L}} \vdash Q_{x_{\mathsf{L}}} :: (z_{\mathsf{L}} : C_{\mathsf{L}})}{\Gamma, x_{\mathsf{S}} : {\uparrow}^{\mathsf{S}}_{\mathsf{L}} A_{\mathsf{L}}; \Delta \vdash x_{\mathsf{L}} \leftarrow \mathsf{acquire}\, x_{\mathsf{S}}; Q_{x_{\mathsf{L}}} :: (z_{\mathsf{L}} : C_{\mathsf{L}})}$$

$$(\text{T-}{\downarrow}^{\mathsf{S}}_{\mathsf{L}}\text{R})\quad \frac{\Gamma \vdash P_{x_{\mathsf{S}}} :: (x_{\mathsf{S}} : A_{\mathsf{S}})}{\Gamma; \cdot \vdash x_{\mathsf{S}} \leftarrow \mathsf{detach}\, x_{\mathsf{L}}; P_{x_{\mathsf{S}}} :: (x_{\mathsf{L}} : {\downarrow}^{\mathsf{S}}_{\mathsf{L}} A_{\mathsf{S}})}$$

$$(\text{T-}{\downarrow}^{\mathsf{S}}_{\mathsf{L}}\text{L})\quad \frac{\Gamma, x_{\mathsf{S}} : A_{\mathsf{S}}; \Delta \vdash Q_{x_{\mathsf{S}}} :: (z_{\mathsf{L}} : C_{\mathsf{L}})}{\Gamma; \Delta, x_{\mathsf{L}} : {\downarrow}^{\mathsf{S}}_{\mathsf{L}} A_{\mathsf{S}} \vdash x_{\mathsf{S}} \leftarrow \mathsf{release}\, x_{\mathsf{L}}; Q_{x_{\mathsf{S}}} :: (z_{\mathsf{L}} : C_{\mathsf{L}})}$$

The typing judgments $\Gamma \vdash P :: (x_{\mathsf{S}} : A_{\mathsf{S}})$ and $\Gamma; \Delta \vdash P :: (x_{\mathsf{L}} : A_{\mathsf{L}})$ indicate that process $P$ provides a session of type $A$ along channel $x$, given the typing of the channels specified in typing contexts $\Gamma$ (and $\Delta$). $\Gamma$ and $\Delta$ consist of hypotheses on the typing of shared and linear channels, respectively, where $\Gamma$ is a structural and $\Delta$ a linear context. To allow for recursive process definitions, the typing judgment depends on a signature $\Sigma$ that is populated with all process definitions prior to type-checking. The adjoint formulation precludes shared processes from depending on linear channel references [2,47], a restriction motivated from logic referred to as the independence principle [47]. Thus, when a shared session accepts an acquire and shifts to linear, it starts with an empty linear context.

Operationally, the dynamics of $\mathsf{SILL_S}$ is captured by *multiset rewriting rules* [12], which denote computation in terms of state transitions between configurations of processes. Multiset rewriting rules are local in that they only mention the parts of a configuration they rewrite. For acquire-release we have the following:

$$(\text{D-}{\uparrow}^{\mathsf{S}}_{\mathsf{L}})$$
$$\mathsf{proc}(a_{\mathsf{S}},\, x_{\mathsf{L}} \leftarrow \mathsf{accept}\; a_{\mathsf{S}}\,;\, P_{x_{\mathsf{L}}}),\ \mathsf{proc}(c_{\mathsf{L}},\, x_{\mathsf{L}} \leftarrow \mathsf{acquire}\; a_{\mathsf{S}}\,;\, Q_{x_{\mathsf{L}}})$$
$$\longrightarrow \mathsf{proc}(a_{\mathsf{L}},\, [a_{\mathsf{L}}/x_{\mathsf{L}}]\, P_{x_{\mathsf{L}}}),\ \mathsf{proc}(c_{\mathsf{L}},\, [a_{\mathsf{L}}/x_{\mathsf{L}}]\, Q_{x_{\mathsf{L}}}),\ \mathsf{unavail}(a_{\mathsf{S}})$$

$$(\text{D-}{\downarrow}^{\mathsf{S}}_{\mathsf{L}})$$
$$\mathsf{proc}(a_{\mathsf{L}},\, x_{\mathsf{S}} \leftarrow \mathsf{detach}\; a_{\mathsf{L}}\,;\, P_{x_{\mathsf{S}}}),\ \mathsf{proc}(c_{\mathsf{L}},\, x_{\mathsf{S}} \leftarrow \mathsf{release}\; a_{\mathsf{L}}\,;\, Q_{x_{\mathsf{S}}}),\ \mathsf{unavail}(a_{\mathsf{S}})$$
$$\longrightarrow \mathsf{proc}(a_{\mathsf{S}},\, [a_{\mathsf{S}}/x_{\mathsf{S}}]\, P_{x_{\mathsf{S}}}),\ \mathsf{proc}(c_{\mathsf{L}},\, [a_{\mathsf{S}}/x_{\mathsf{S}}]\, Q_{x_{\mathsf{S}}})$$

Configuration states are defined by the predicates $\mathsf{proc}(c_m,\, P)$ and $\mathsf{unavail}(a_{\mathsf{S}})$. The former denotes a running process with process term $P$ providing along channel $c_m$, the latter acts as a placeholder for a shared process providing along channel $a_{\mathsf{S}}$ that is currently not available. The above rule exploits the invariant that a process' providing channel $a$ can appear at one of two modes, a linear one, $a_{\mathsf{L}}$, and a shared one, $a_{\mathsf{S}}$. While the process (i.e. the session) is linear, it provides along $a_{\mathsf{L}}$, while it is shared, along $a_{\mathsf{S}}$. When a process shifts between modes, it switches between the two modes of its offering channel. The channel at the appropriate mode is substituted for the variables occurring in process terms.

## 3 Manifest Deadlock-Freedom

In this section, we introduce our language $\mathsf{SILL_{S^+}}$, a session-typed language that supports sharing without deadlock. We focus on $\mathsf{SILL_{S^+}}$'s type system and dynamics in this section and discuss its meta-theoretical properties in Sect. 5.

### 3.1 Competition and Collaboration

The introduction of acquire-release, to ensure that the multiple clients of a shared process interact with the process in mutual exclusion from each other, gives rise to an obvious source of deadlocks, as acquire-release effectively amounts to a locking discipline. The typical approach to prevent deadlocks in that case is to impose a partial order on the resources and to *"lock-up"*, i.e., to lock the resources in ascending order. We adopted this strategy in Sect. 1 (Fig. 1) to break the cyclic dependencies among the acquires in the dining philosophers.

In Sect. 1, however, we also considered another example (Fig. 2) and discovered that *cyclic acquisitions* are not the only source of deadlocks, but deadlocks can also arise from *interdependent acquisitions and synchronizations*. In that example, we can prevent the deadlock by moving the acquire past the synchronization, in either of the two processes. Whereas in a purely linear session-typed system the sequencing of actions within a process do not affect other processes, the relative placement of acquire requests and synchronizations become relevant in a shared session-typed system.

Based on this observation, we can divide the processes in a shared-session discipline into *competitors* and *collaborators*. The former compete for a set of resources, whereas the latter do not overlap in the set of resources they acquire. For example, in the dining philosophers (Fig. 1), the philosophers $p_0$, $p_1$, and $p_2$ compete with each other for the set of forks $f_0$, $f_1$, and $f_2$, whereas the process that spawns the philosophers and the forks collaborates with either of them.

Transferring this idea to the process graph that emerges at run-time, we note that competitors are siblings whereas collaborators stand in a parent-descendant relationship. We illustrate this outcome on Fig. 3 that shows a possible run-time process graph for the dining philosophers. Linear processes are depicted as solid black circles with a white identifier and shared processes are depicted as dotted filled violet circles with a black identifier. Linear channels are depicted as black lines, shared channel references as dotted violet lines with the arrow head pointing to the shared process being acquired[1]. The identifiers $P_0$, $P_1$, and $P_2$ stand for the three philosophers, $F_0$, $F_1$, and $F_2$ for the three forks, and $T$ for the process that sets the table. The current run-time graph depicts the scenario in which $P_1$ is eating, while the other two philosophers are still thinking.

Embedded in the graph is a *tree* that arises from the linear processes and the linear channels connecting them. For any two nodes in this tree, the *parent* node denotes the *client* process and the *child* node the *providing* process. We note that the *independence principle* (see Sect. 2), which precludes shared processes from depending on linear channel references, guarantees that there exists exactly one tree in the process graph, with the linear main process as its root. The shape of the tree changes when new processes are spawned, linear channels exchanged (through $\otimes$ and $\multimap$), or shared processes acquired. For example, process $P_2$ could acquire the shared fork $F_0$, which then becomes a linear child process of $P_2$, should the acquire succeed. As indicated by the shared channel references, the

[1] We have made sure to make the different concepts distinguishable in greyscale mode.

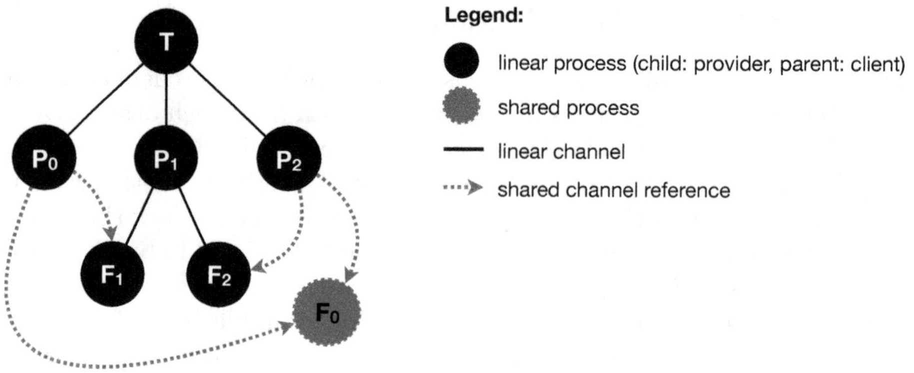


**Fig. 3.** Run-time process graph for dining philosophers (see Fig. 1).

sibling nodes $P_0$, $P_1$, and $P_2$ compete with each other for the nodes $F_0$, $F_1$, and $F_2$, whereas the node $T$ does not compete for any of the resources acquired by its *descendants* (including $F_1$ and $F_2$). Our type system enforces this paradigm, as we discuss in the next section.

## 3.2 Type System

**Invariants.** Having identified the notions of *collaborators* and *competitors*, our type system must guarantee: *(i)* that collaborators acquire mutually disjoint sets of resources; *(ii)* that competitors employ a locking-up strategy for the resources they share; and, *(iii)* that competitors have released all acquired resources when synchronizing with other competitors. Invariant *(ii)* rules out cyclic acquisitions and invariants *(i)* and *(iii)* combined rule out interdependent acquisitions and synchronizations.

To express the high-level invariants above in our type system, we introduce the notion of a *world* – an abstract value that is equipped with a partial order – and associate such a world with every process. Programmers can *create* worlds, indicate the world at which a process resides at spawn time, and define an *order* on worlds. Moreover, we associate with each process a *range of worlds* that indicates the worlds of resources that the process may acquire. As a result, we obtain the following typing judgments:

$$\Psi; \Gamma \vdash P :: (x_{\mathsf{S}} : A_{\mathsf{S}}[\omega_k \updownarrow^{\omega_n}_{\omega_l}]) \quad \text{(where } \Psi^+ \text{ irreflexive)}$$

$$\Psi; \Gamma; \Phi; \Delta \vdash P :: (x_{\mathsf{L}} : A_{\mathsf{L}}[\omega_k \updownarrow^{\omega_n}_{\omega_l}]) \quad \text{(where } \Psi^+ \text{ irreflexive)}$$

The typing judgments reveal that we impose worlds at the *judgmental level*, resulting in a *hybrid system*, in which the adjoint modalities for acquire-release are complemented with world modalities that occur as *syntactic objects* in propositions [7]. We use the notation $x_m : A_m[\omega_k \updownarrow^{\omega_n}_{\omega_l}]$ (where $m$ stands for $\mathsf{S}$ or $\mathsf{L}$) to associate worlds $\omega_k$, $\omega_l$, and $\omega_n$ with a process that offers a session of type $A_m$ along channel $x$. World $\omega_k$ denotes the world at which the process resides.

We refer to this world as the *self* world. Worlds $\omega_l$ and $\omega_n$ indicate the range of worlds of resources that the process may acquire, with $\omega_l$ denoting the *minimal (min)* world in this range and $\omega_n$ the *maximal (max)* one.

Process terms are typed relative to the order specified in $\Psi$ and the contexts $\Gamma$, $\Phi$, and $\Delta$. As in Sect. 2, $\Gamma$ is a structural context consisting of hypotheses on the typing of variables bound to shared channel references, augmented with world annotations. We find it necessary to split the linear context "$\Delta$" from Sect. 2 into the two disjoint contexts $\Phi$ and $\Delta$, allowing us to separate channels that are possibly aliased (due to sharing) from those that are not, respectively. Both $\Phi$ and $\Delta$ consist of hypotheses on the typing of variables that are bound to linear channels, augmented with world annotations. $\Psi$ is presupposed to be *acyclic* and defined as: $\Psi \triangleq \cdot \mid \Psi', \omega_k < \omega_l \mid \Psi', \omega_o$, where $\omega$ stands for a concrete *world* $\mathsf{w}$ or a *world variable* $\delta$. We allow $\Psi$ to contain single worlds, to support singletons as well as to accommodate world creation prior to order declaration. We define the transitive closure $\Psi^+$, yielding a *strict partial order*, and the reflexive transitive closure $\Psi^*$, yielding a *partial order*.

The high-level invariants *(i)*, *(ii)*, and *(iii)* identified earlier naturally transcribe into the following invariants, which we impose on the typing judgments above. We use the notation $\_\langle x_m \rangle; P$ to denote a process term that currently executes an action along channel $x_m$.

1. $\mathsf{min(parent)} \leq \mathsf{self(acquired\_child)} \leq \mathsf{max(parent)}$:
   $\forall y_{\mathsf{L}} : B_{\mathsf{L}}[\omega_o \updownarrow^{\omega_r}_{\omega_p}] \in \Phi : \Psi^* \vdash \omega_l \leq \omega_o \leq \omega_n$
2. $\mathsf{max(parent)} < \mathsf{min(child)}$:
   $\forall y_{\mathsf{L}} : B_{\mathsf{L}}[\omega_o \updownarrow^{\omega_r}_{\omega_p}] \in \Delta \cup \Phi : \Psi^+ \vdash \omega_n < \omega_p$
3. If $\Psi;\, \Gamma, x_{\mathsf{S}} : \hat{A}[\omega_t \updownarrow^{\omega_v}_{\omega_u}];\, \Phi;\, \Delta \vdash x_{\mathsf{L}} \leftarrow \mathsf{acquire}\ x_{\mathsf{S}};\, Q_{x_{\mathsf{S}}} :: (z_{\mathsf{L}} : C_{\mathsf{L}}[\omega_k \updownarrow^{\omega_n}_{\omega_l}])$, then
   $\forall y_{\mathsf{L}} : B_{\mathsf{L}}[\omega_o \updownarrow^{\omega_r}_{\omega_p}] \in \Phi : \Psi^+ \vdash \omega_o < \omega_t$.
4. If $\Psi;\, \Gamma;\, \Phi;\, \Delta \vdash \_\langle x_m \rangle; P :: (x_{\mathsf{L}} : A_{\mathsf{L}}[\omega_k \updownarrow^{\omega_n}_{\omega_l}])$, then $\Phi = (\cdot)$.

Invariants 1 and 2 ensure that, for any node in the tree, the acquired resources reside at smaller worlds than those acquired by any descendant. As a result, the two invariants guarantee high-level invariant *(i)*. Invariant 3, on the other hand, imposes a lock-up strategy on acquires and thus guarantees high-level invariant *(ii)*. To guarantee high-level invariant *(iii)*, we impose Invariant 4, which forces a process to release any acquired resources before communicating along its offering channel. Since sibling nodes cannot be directly connected by a linear channel, the only way for them to synchronize is through a common parent. Finally, to guarantee that world annotations are internally consistent, we require for each annotation $[\omega_k \updownarrow^{\omega_n}_{\omega_l}]$ that $\omega_k < \omega_l \leq \omega_n$.

**Rules.** We now present select process typing rules, a complete listing is provided in the companion technical report [4]. The only new rules with respect to the language $\mathsf{SILL_S}$ [2] are those pertaining to world creation and order determination. These are extra-logical judgmental rules. We allow both linear and shared processes to create and relate worlds. Rules (T-NEW$_{\mathsf{L}}$) and (T-NEW$_{\mathsf{S}}$) create a new world $\mathsf{w}$ and make it available to the continuation $Q_{\mathsf{w}}$. Rules (T-ORD$_{\mathsf{L}}$) and (T-ORD$_{\mathsf{S}}$) relate two existing worlds, while preserving acyclicity of the order.

$$\frac{\Psi, \mathsf{w};\ \Gamma;\ \Phi;\ \Delta \vdash Q_{\mathsf{w}} :: (x_{\mathsf{L}} : A_{\mathsf{L}}[\omega_m \updownarrow^{\omega_v}_{\omega_u}])}{\Psi;\ \Gamma;\ \Phi;\ \Delta \vdash \mathsf{w} \leftarrow \mathsf{new\_world};\ Q_{\mathsf{w}} :: (x_{\mathsf{L}} : A_{\mathsf{L}}[\omega_m \updownarrow^{\omega_v}_{\omega_u}])}\ (\text{T-New}_{\mathsf{L}})$$

$$\frac{\Psi, \mathsf{w};\ \Gamma \vdash Q_{\mathsf{w}} :: (x_{\mathsf{S}} : A_{\mathsf{S}}[\omega_m \updownarrow^{\omega_v}_{\omega_u}])}{\Psi;\ \Gamma \vdash \mathsf{w} \leftarrow \mathsf{new\_world};\ Q_{\mathsf{w}} :: (x_{\mathsf{S}} : A_{\mathsf{S}}[\omega_m \updownarrow^{\omega_v}_{\omega_u}])}\ (\text{T-New}_{\mathsf{S}})$$

$$\frac{\omega_p, \omega_r \in \Psi \qquad (\Psi, \omega_p < \omega_r)^+ \text{ irreflexive} \qquad \Psi, \omega_p < \omega_r;\ \Gamma;\ \Phi;\ \Delta \vdash Q :: (x_{\mathsf{L}} : A_{\mathsf{L}}[\omega_m \updownarrow^{\omega_v}_{\omega_u}])}{\Psi;\ \Gamma;\ \Phi;\ \Delta \vdash \omega_p < \omega_r;\ Q :: (x_{\mathsf{L}} : A_{\mathsf{L}}[\omega_m \updownarrow^{\omega_v}_{\omega_u}])}\ (\text{T-Ord}_{\mathsf{L}})$$

$$\frac{\omega_p, \omega_r \in \Psi \qquad (\Psi, \omega_p < \omega_r)^+ \text{ irreflexive} \qquad \Psi, \omega_p < \omega_r;\ \Gamma \vdash Q :: (x_{\mathsf{S}} : A_{\mathsf{S}}[\omega_m \updownarrow^{\omega_v}_{\omega_u}])}{\Psi;\ \Gamma \vdash \omega_p < \omega_r;\ Q :: (x_{\mathsf{S}} : A_{\mathsf{S}}[\omega_m \updownarrow^{\omega_v}_{\omega_u}])}\ (\text{T-Ord}_{\mathsf{S}})$$

We now consider the typing rule for acquire, which must explicitly enforce the various low-level invariants above. Since an acquire results in the addition of a new child node to the executing process, the rule can interfere with Invariants 1 and 2. The first two premises of the rule ensure that the two invariants are preserved. Moreover, the rule has to ensure that the acquiring process is locking-up (Invariant 3), which is achieved by the third premise.

$$\frac{\Psi^* \vdash \omega_k \leq \omega_m \leq \omega_n \qquad \Psi^+ \vdash \omega_n < \omega_u \qquad \forall y_{\mathsf{L}} : B_{\mathsf{L}}[\omega_l \updownarrow^{\omega_r}_{\omega_p}] \in \Phi : \omega_l < \omega_m \qquad \Psi;\ \Gamma, x_{\mathsf{S}} : \uparrow^{\mathsf{S}}_{\mathsf{L}} A_{\mathsf{L}}[\omega_m \updownarrow^{\omega_v}_{\omega_u}];\ \Phi, x_{\mathsf{L}} : A_{\mathsf{L}}[\omega_m \updownarrow^{\omega_v}_{\omega_u}];\ \Delta \vdash Q_{x_{\mathsf{L}}} :: (z_{\mathsf{L}} : C_{\mathsf{L}}[\omega_j \updownarrow^{\omega_n}_{\omega_k}])}{\Psi;\ \Gamma, x_{\mathsf{S}} : \uparrow^{\mathsf{S}}_{\mathsf{L}} A_{\mathsf{L}}[\omega_m \updownarrow^{\omega_v}_{\omega_u}];\ \Phi;\ \Delta \vdash x_{\mathsf{L}} \leftarrow \mathsf{acquire}\, x_{\mathsf{S}}\,;\ Q_{x_{\mathsf{L}}} :: (z_{\mathsf{L}} : C_{\mathsf{L}}[\omega_j \updownarrow^{\omega_n}_{\omega_k}])}\ (\text{T-}\uparrow^{\mathsf{S}}_{\mathsf{L}}\text{L})$$

The remaining shift rules are actually *unchanged* with respect to $\mathsf{SILL_S}$, modulo the world annotations. In particular, low-level Invariant 4 is already satisfied because the conclusion of rule (T-$\uparrow^{\mathsf{S}}_{\mathsf{L}}$R) does not have a context $\Phi$ and because the independence principle forces $\Phi$ to be empty in rule (T-$\downarrow^{\mathsf{S}}_{\mathsf{L}}$R).

$$\frac{\Psi;\ \Gamma;\ \cdot;\ \cdot \vdash P_{x_{\mathsf{L}}} :: (x_{\mathsf{L}} : A_{\mathsf{L}}[\omega_m \updownarrow^{\omega_v}_{\omega_u}])}{\Psi;\ \Gamma \vdash x_{\mathsf{L}} \leftarrow \mathsf{accept}\, x_{\mathsf{S}}\,;\ P_{x_{\mathsf{L}}} :: (x_{\mathsf{S}} : \uparrow^{\mathsf{S}}_{\mathsf{L}} A_{\mathsf{L}}[\omega_m \updownarrow^{\omega_v}_{\omega_u}])}\ (\text{T-}\uparrow^{\mathsf{S}}_{\mathsf{L}}\text{R})$$

$$\frac{\Psi;\ \Gamma, x_{\mathsf{S}} : A_{\mathsf{S}}[\omega_m \updownarrow^{\omega_v}_{\omega_u}];\ \Phi;\ \Delta \vdash Q_{x_{\mathsf{S}}} :: (z_{\mathsf{L}} : C_{\mathsf{L}}[\omega_j \updownarrow^{\omega_n}_{\omega_k}])}{\Psi;\ \Gamma;\ \Phi, x_{\mathsf{L}} : \downarrow^{\mathsf{S}}_{\mathsf{L}} A_{\mathsf{S}}[\omega_m \updownarrow^{\omega_v}_{\omega_u}];\ \Delta \vdash x_{\mathsf{S}} \leftarrow \mathsf{release}\, x_{\mathsf{L}}\,;\ Q_{x_{\mathsf{S}}} :: (z_{\mathsf{L}} : C_{\mathsf{L}}[\omega_j \updownarrow^{\omega_n}_{\omega_k}])}\ (\text{T-}\downarrow^{\mathsf{S}}_{\mathsf{L}}\text{L})$$

$$\frac{\Psi;\ \Gamma \vdash P_{x_{\mathsf{S}}} :: (x_{\mathsf{S}} : A_{\mathsf{S}}[\omega_m \updownarrow^{\omega_v}_{\omega_u}])}{\Psi;\ \Gamma;\ \cdot;\ \cdot \vdash x_{\mathsf{S}} \leftarrow \mathsf{detach}\, x_{\mathsf{L}}\,;\ P_{x_{\mathsf{S}}} :: (x_{\mathsf{L}} : \downarrow^{\mathsf{S}}_{\mathsf{L}} A_{\mathsf{S}}[\omega_m \updownarrow^{\omega_v}_{\omega_u}])}\ (\text{T-}\downarrow^{\mathsf{S}}_{\mathsf{L}}\text{R})$$

We now consider the linear connectives, starting with **1**. Rule (T-$\mathbf{1}_{\mathrm{L}}$) reveals that only processes that have never been acquired may be terminated. This restriction is important to guarantee progress because existing clients of a shared process may wait indefinitely otherwise. We impose the restriction as a well-formedness condition on a session type, giving rise to a *strictly equi-synchronizing* session type. The notion of an *equi-synchronizing* session type [2] has been defined for $\mathsf{SILL_S}$ and guarantees that a process that has been acquired at a type $A_{\mathsf{S}}$ is released back to the type $A_{\mathsf{S}}$, should it ever be released. A *strictly* equi-synchronizing session type additionally requires that an acquired resource *must* be released. The corresponding rules can be found in [4]. Linearity enforces Invariant 4 in rule (T-$\mathbf{1}_{\mathrm{R}}$), making sure that no linear channels are left behind.

$$\frac{\Psi;\ \Gamma;\ \Phi;\ \Delta \vdash Q :: (z_{\mathsf{L}} : C_{\mathsf{L}}[\omega_j \updownarrow_{\omega_k}^{\omega_n}])}{\Psi;\ \Gamma;\ \Phi;\ \Delta, x_{\mathsf{L}} : \mathbf{1}[\omega_m \updownarrow_{\omega_u}^{\omega_v}] \vdash \mathsf{wait}\, x_{\mathsf{L}}\,; Q :: (z_{\mathsf{L}} : C_{\mathsf{L}}[\omega_j \updownarrow_{\omega_k}^{\omega_n}])}\ (\text{T-}\mathbf{1}_{\text{L}})$$

$$\frac{}{\Psi;\ \Gamma;\ \cdot\,;\ \cdot \vdash \mathsf{close}\, x_{\mathsf{L}} :: (x_{\mathsf{L}} : \mathbf{1}[\omega_m \updownarrow_{\omega_u}^{\omega_v}])}\ (\text{T-}\mathbf{1}_{\text{R}})$$

Next, we consider internal and external choice. Since internal and external choice cannot alter the linear process tree of a process graph, the rules are very similar to the ones in $\mathsf{SILL_S}$. The only differences are that we get two left rules for each connective and that the $\Phi$-context of each right rule must be empty to satisfy Invariant 4. The former is merely due to the tracking of possibly aliased sessions in the $\Phi$ context. We only list rules for internal choice, those for external choice are dual and can be found in [4].

$$\frac{(\forall i)\ \ \Psi;\ \Gamma;\ \Phi;\ \Delta, x_{\mathsf{L}} : A_{\mathsf{L}_i}[\omega_m \updownarrow_{\omega_u}^{\omega_v}] \vdash Q_i :: (z_{\mathsf{L}} : C_{\mathsf{L}}[\omega_j \updownarrow_{\omega_k}^{\omega_n}])}{\Psi;\ \Gamma;\ \Phi;\ \Delta, x_{\mathsf{L}} : \oplus\{\overline{l : A_{\mathsf{L}}}\}[\omega_m \updownarrow_{\omega_u}^{\omega_v}] \vdash \mathsf{case}\, x_{\mathsf{L}}\ \mathsf{of}\ \overline{l \Rightarrow Q} :: (z_{\mathsf{L}} : C_{\mathsf{L}}[\omega_j \updownarrow_{\omega_k}^{\omega_n}])}\ (\text{T-}\oplus_{\text{L}_1})$$

$$\frac{(\forall i)\ \ \Psi;\ \Gamma;\ \Phi, x_{\mathsf{L}} : A_{\mathsf{L}_i}[\omega_m \updownarrow_{\omega_u}^{\omega_v}];\ \Delta \vdash Q_i :: (z_{\mathsf{L}} : C_{\mathsf{L}}[\omega_j \updownarrow_{\omega_k}^{\omega_n}])}{\Psi;\ \Gamma;\ \Phi, x_{\mathsf{L}} : \oplus\{\overline{l : A_{\mathsf{L}}}\}[\omega_m \updownarrow_{\omega_u}^{\omega_v}];\ \Delta \vdash \mathsf{case}\, x_{\mathsf{L}}\ \mathsf{of}\ \overline{l \Rightarrow Q} :: (z_{\mathsf{L}} : C_{\mathsf{L}}[\omega_j \updownarrow_{\omega_k}^{\omega_n}])}\ (\text{T-}\oplus_{\text{L}_2})$$

$$\frac{\Psi;\ \Gamma;\ \cdot\,;\ \Delta \vdash P :: (x_{\mathsf{L}} : A_{\mathsf{L}\,h}[\omega_m \updownarrow_{\omega_u}^{\omega_v}])}{\Psi;\ \Gamma;\ \cdot\,;\ \Delta \vdash x_{\mathsf{L}}.l_h\,; P :: (x_{\mathsf{L}} : \oplus\{\overline{l : A_{\mathsf{L}}}\}[\omega_m \updownarrow_{\omega_u}^{\omega_v}])}\ (\text{T-}\oplus_{\text{R}})$$

More interesting are linear channel output and input, since these alter the linear process tree of a process graph. Moreover, additional world annotations are needed to indicate the worlds of the channel that is exchanged. For the latter we use the notation $@\omega_l \updownarrow_{\omega_p}^{\omega_r}$, indicating that the exchanged channel has the worlds $\omega_l$, $\omega_p$, and $\omega_r$ for self, min, and max, respectively. To account for induced changes in the process graph, the rules that type an input of a linear channel must guard against any disturbance of Invariants 1 and 2. Because the two invariants guarantee that parents do not overlap with their descendants in terms of acquired resources, they prevent any exchange of acquired channels. We thus restrict $\otimes$ and $\multimap$ to the exchange of channels that have not yet been acquired. This is not a limitation since, as we will see below, shared channel output and input are unrestricted.

Even with the above restriction in place, we still have to make sure that a received channel satisfies Invariant 2. If we were to state a corresponding premise on the receiving rules, invertibility of the rules would be disturbed. To uphold invertibility, we impose a well-formedness condition on session types that ensures for a session of type $A_{\mathsf{L}}@\omega_l \updownarrow_{\omega_p}^{\omega_r} \otimes B_{\mathsf{L}}[\omega_m \updownarrow_{\omega_u}^{\omega_v}]$ that $\omega_v < \omega_p$ and, analogously, for a session of type $A_{\mathsf{L}}@\omega_l \updownarrow_{\omega_p}^{\omega_r} \multimap B_{\mathsf{L}}[\omega_m \updownarrow_{\omega_u}^{\omega_v}]$ that $\omega_v < \omega_p$. Session types are checked to be well-formed upon process definition. Given type well-formedness, we obtain the following rules for $\multimap$, noting that the right rule enforces Invariant 4 by requiring an empty $\Phi$-context. The rules for $\otimes$ are dual.

$$\frac{\Psi;\ \Gamma;\ \Phi;\ \Delta, x_{\mathsf{L}} : B_{\mathsf{L}}[\omega_m \updownarrow_{\omega_u}^{\omega_v}] \vdash Q :: (z_{\mathsf{L}} : C_{\mathsf{L}}[\omega_j \updownarrow_{\omega_k}^{\omega_n}])}{\Psi;\ \Gamma;\ \Phi;\ \Delta, x_{\mathsf{L}} : A_{\mathsf{L}} @ \omega_l \updownarrow_{\omega_p}^{\omega_r} \multimap B_{\mathsf{L}}[\omega_m \updownarrow_{\omega_u}^{\omega_v}], y_{\mathsf{L}} : A_{\mathsf{L}}[\omega_l \updownarrow_{\omega_p}^{\omega_r}] \vdash \mathsf{send}\ x_{\mathsf{L}}\ y_{\mathsf{L}}\ ; Q :: (z_{\mathsf{L}} : C_{\mathsf{L}}[\omega_j \updownarrow_{\omega_k}^{\omega_n}])}\ (\text{T-}{\multimap}\text{L}_1)$$

$$\frac{\Psi;\ \Gamma;\ \Phi, x_{\mathsf{L}} : B_{\mathsf{L}}[\omega_m \updownarrow_{\omega_u}^{\omega_v}];\ \Delta \vdash Q :: (z_{\mathsf{L}} : C_{\mathsf{L}}[\omega_j \updownarrow_{\omega_k}^{\omega_n}])}{\Psi;\ \Gamma;\ \Phi, x_{\mathsf{L}} : A_{\mathsf{L}} @ \omega_l \updownarrow_{\omega_p}^{\omega_r} \multimap B_{\mathsf{L}}[\omega_m \updownarrow_{\omega_u}^{\omega_v}];\ \Delta, y_{\mathsf{L}} : A_{\mathsf{L}}[\omega_l \updownarrow_{\omega_p}^{\omega_r}] \vdash \mathsf{send}\ x_{\mathsf{L}}\ y_{\mathsf{L}}\ ; Q :: (z_{\mathsf{L}} : C_{\mathsf{L}}[\omega_j \updownarrow_{\omega_k}^{\omega_n}])}\ (\text{T-}{\multimap}\text{L}_2)$$

$$\frac{\Psi;\ \Gamma;\ \cdot\ ;\ \Delta, y_{\mathsf{L}} : A_{\mathsf{L}}[\omega_l \updownarrow_{\omega_p}^{\omega_r}] \vdash P_{y_{\mathsf{L}}} :: (x_{\mathsf{L}} : B_{\mathsf{L}}[\omega_m \updownarrow_{\omega_u}^{\omega_v}])}{\Psi;\ \Gamma;\ \cdot\ ;\ \Delta \vdash y_{\mathsf{L}} \leftarrow \mathsf{recv}\ x_{\mathsf{L}}\ ; P_{y_{\mathsf{L}}} :: (x_{\mathsf{L}} : A_{\mathsf{L}} @ \omega_l \updownarrow_{\omega_p}^{\omega_r} \multimap B_{\mathsf{L}}[\omega_m \updownarrow_{\omega_u}^{\omega_v}])}\ (\text{T-}{\multimap}\text{R})$$

Since there are no invariants imposed on the shared context $\Gamma$, the rules for shared channel output and input are identical to those in $\mathsf{SILL_S}$. The only differences are that we have two left rules and that the $\Phi$-context of the right rule must be empty to satisfy Invariant 4. The former is merely due to the tracking of possibly aliased sessions in the $\Phi$ context.

$$\frac{\Psi;\ \Gamma, y_{\mathsf{S}} : A_{\mathsf{S}}[\omega_l \updownarrow_{\omega_p}^{\omega_r}];\Phi;\ \Delta, x_{\mathsf{L}} : B_{\mathsf{L}}[\omega_m \updownarrow_{\omega_u}^{\omega_v}] \vdash Q_{y_{\mathsf{S}}} :: (z_{\mathsf{L}} : C_{\mathsf{L}}[\omega_j \updownarrow_{\omega_k}^{\omega_n}])}{\Psi;\ \Gamma;\Phi;\ \Delta, x_{\mathsf{L}} : \exists x{:}A_{\mathsf{S}} @ \omega_l \updownarrow_{\omega_p}^{\omega_r} . B_{\mathsf{L}}[\omega_m \updownarrow_{\omega_u}^{\omega_v}] \vdash y_{\mathsf{S}} \leftarrow \mathsf{recv}\ x_{\mathsf{L}}\ ; Q_{y_{\mathsf{S}}} :: (z_{\mathsf{L}} : C_{\mathsf{L}}[\omega_j \updownarrow_{\omega_k}^{\omega_n}])}\ (\text{T-}\exists\text{L}_1)$$

$$\frac{\Psi;\ \Gamma, y_{\mathsf{S}} : A_{\mathsf{S}}[\omega_l \updownarrow_{\omega_p}^{\omega_r}];\Phi, x_{\mathsf{L}} : B_{\mathsf{L}}[\omega_m \updownarrow_{\omega_u}^{\omega_v}];\ \Delta \vdash Q_{y_{\mathsf{S}}} :: (z_{\mathsf{L}} : C_{\mathsf{L}}[\omega_j \updownarrow_{\omega_k}^{\omega_n}])}{\Psi;\ \Gamma;\Phi, x_{\mathsf{L}} : \exists x{:}A_{\mathsf{S}} @ \omega_l \updownarrow_{\omega_p}^{\omega_r} . B_{\mathsf{L}}[\omega_m \updownarrow_{\omega_u}^{\omega_v}];\ \Delta \vdash y_{\mathsf{S}} \leftarrow \mathsf{recv}\ x_{\mathsf{L}}\ ; Q_{y_{\mathsf{S}}} :: (z_{\mathsf{L}} : C_{\mathsf{L}}[\omega_j \updownarrow_{\omega_k}^{\omega_n}])}\ (\text{T-}\exists\text{L}_2)$$

$$\frac{\Psi;\ \Gamma, y_{\mathsf{S}} : A_{\mathsf{S}}[\omega_l \updownarrow_{\omega_p}^{\omega_r}];\cdot\ ;\ \Delta \vdash P :: (x_{\mathsf{L}} : B_{\mathsf{L}}[\omega_m \updownarrow_{\omega_u}^{\omega_v}])}{\Psi;\ \Gamma, y_{\mathsf{S}} : A_{\mathsf{S}}[\omega_l \updownarrow_{\omega_p}^{\omega_r}];\cdot\ ;\ \Delta \vdash \mathsf{send}\ x_{\mathsf{L}}\ y_{\mathsf{S}}\ ; P :: (x_{\mathsf{L}} : \exists x{:}A_{\mathsf{S}} @ \omega_l \updownarrow_{\omega_p}^{\omega_r} . B_{\mathsf{L}}[\omega_m \updownarrow_{\omega_u}^{\omega_v}])}\ (\text{T-}\exists\text{R})$$

We finally consider the rules for forwarding and spawning. We allow a shared forward between processes that offer the same session at the same worlds. Because forwards have to be *world-invariant*, however, no well-typed program could ever have a linear forward. The process being forwarded to must be in either of the contexts $\Phi$ or $\Delta$, and thus satisfies Invariant 2, making it impossible for the world annotations of the forwarder and forwardee to match. We omit linear forwarding and discuss possible future extensions in Sect. 6.

$$\frac{}{\Psi;\ \Gamma, y_{\mathsf{S}} : A_{\mathsf{S}}[\omega_j \updownarrow_{\omega_k}^{\omega_n}] \vdash \mathsf{fwd}\ x_{\mathsf{S}}\ y_{\mathsf{S}} :: (x_{\mathsf{S}} : A_{\mathsf{S}}[\omega_j \updownarrow_{\omega_k}^{\omega_n}])}\ (\text{T-ID}_{\mathsf{S}})$$

The rules for spawning depend on the possible modes of the spawning and spawned processes: (T-SPAWN$_{\mathsf{LL}}$) specifies how a linear process can spawn another linear process; (T-SPAWN$_{\mathsf{SS}}$) specifies how a shared processes can spawn another shared process. The rules are checked relative to a process definition found in the signature $\Sigma$ and to a world substitution mapping $\gamma : |\Psi| \rightarrow |\Psi'|$, such that for each $\delta \in \Psi'$ we have $\Psi \vdash \gamma(\delta)$, where $|\Psi|$ denotes the *field* of $\Psi$ (i.e., the union of its domain and range). As usual, we lift substitution to types $\hat{\gamma}(A_m)$, contexts $\hat{\gamma}(\Gamma)$, and orders $\hat{\gamma}(\Psi)$. Both rules ensure that, given the mapping $\gamma$, the order $\Psi$ of the spawning process entails the one of the process definition ($\Psi \vdash \hat{\gamma}(\Psi')$). The linear spawn rule (T-SPAWN$_{\mathsf{LL}}$) further enforces Invariant 2 for the spawned child. We note that the spawned child enters the linear context $\Delta$ in the spawning process' continuation since no aliases to such a process can exist at this point.

$$\dfrac{\begin{array}{c}\Delta_1 = \overline{y_{\mathsf{L}} : B_{\mathsf{L}}[\omega_m \updownarrow^{\omega_v}_{\omega_u}]} \qquad \Phi_1 = \overline{\tilde{y}_{\mathsf{L}} : \tilde{B}_{\mathsf{L}}[\tilde{\omega}_m \updownarrow^{\tilde{\omega}_v}_{\tilde{\omega}_u}]} \qquad \Gamma_1 = \overline{z_{\mathsf{S}} : C_{\mathsf{S}}[\omega_l \updownarrow^{\omega_r}_{\omega_p}]} \\ (\Psi' \vdash x'_{\mathsf{L}} : A'_{\mathsf{L}}[\delta_j \updownarrow^{\delta_n}_{\delta_k}] \leftarrow X_{\mathsf{L}} \leftarrow \Delta', \Phi', \Gamma' = P_{x'_{\mathsf{L}}, \mathsf{dom}(\Delta'), \mathsf{dom}(\Phi'), \mathsf{dom}(\Gamma'), \Psi''}) \in \Sigma \\ \hat{\gamma}(A'_{\mathsf{L}}[\delta_j \updownarrow^{\delta_n}_{\delta_k}]) = A_{\mathsf{L}}[\omega_j \updownarrow^{\omega_n}_{\omega_k}] \qquad \hat{\gamma}(\Delta') = \Delta_1 \qquad \hat{\gamma}(\Phi') = \Phi_1 \qquad \hat{\gamma}(\Gamma') = \Gamma_1 \qquad \Psi \vdash \hat{\gamma}(\Psi') \\ \Psi^+ \vdash \omega_t < \omega_k \\ \Psi;\ \Gamma_1, \Gamma_2;\ \Phi_2;\ \Delta_2, x_{\mathsf{L}} : A_{\mathsf{L}}[\omega_j \updownarrow^{\omega_n}_{\omega_k}] \vdash Q_{x_{\mathsf{L}}} :: (z''_{\mathsf{L}} : D_{\mathsf{L}}[\omega_i \updownarrow^{\omega_t}_{\omega_q}])\end{array}}{\Psi;\ \Gamma_1, \Gamma_2;\ \Phi_1, \Phi_2;\ \Delta_1, \Delta_2 \vdash x_{\mathsf{L}} : A_{\mathsf{L}}[\omega_j \updownarrow^{\omega_n}_{\omega_k}] \leftarrow X_{\mathsf{L}} \leftarrow \overline{y_{\mathsf{L}}}, \overline{\tilde{y}_{\mathsf{L}}}, \overline{z_{\mathsf{S}}};\ Q_{x_{\mathsf{L}}} :: (z''_{\mathsf{L}} : D_{\mathsf{L}}[\omega_i \updownarrow^{\omega_t}_{\omega_q}])} \ (\text{T-S}\text{PAWN}_{\mathsf{LL}})$$

$$\dfrac{\begin{array}{c}\Gamma_1 = \overline{z_{\mathsf{S}} : C_{\mathsf{S}}[\omega_l \updownarrow^{\omega_r}_{\omega_p}]} \qquad (\Psi' \vdash x'_{\mathsf{S}} : A'_{\mathsf{S}}[\delta_j \updownarrow^{\delta_n}_{\delta_k}] \leftarrow X_{\mathsf{S}} \leftarrow \Gamma' = P_{x'_{\mathsf{S}}, \mathsf{dom}(\Gamma'), \Psi''}) \in \Sigma \\ \hat{\gamma}(A'_{\mathsf{S}}[\delta_j \updownarrow^{\delta_n}_{\delta_k}]) = A_{\mathsf{S}}[\omega_j \updownarrow^{\omega_n}_{\omega_k}] \qquad \hat{\gamma}(\Gamma') = \Gamma_1 \qquad \Psi \vdash \hat{\gamma}(\Psi') \\ \Psi;\ \Gamma_1, \Gamma_2, x_{\mathsf{S}} : A_{\mathsf{S}}[\omega_j \updownarrow^{\omega_n}_{\omega_k}] \vdash Q_{x_{\mathsf{S}}} :: (z''_{\mathsf{S}} : D_{\mathsf{S}}[\omega_i \updownarrow^{\omega_t}_{\omega_q}])\end{array}}{\Psi;\ \Gamma_1, \Gamma_2 \vdash x_{\mathsf{S}} : A_{\mathsf{S}}[\omega_j \updownarrow^{\omega_n}_{\omega_k}] \leftarrow X_{\mathsf{S}} \leftarrow \overline{z_{\mathsf{S}}};\ Q_{x_{\mathsf{S}}} :: (z''_{\mathsf{S}} : D_{\mathsf{S}}[\omega_i \updownarrow^{\omega_t}_{\omega_q}])} \ (\text{T-S}\text{PAWN}_{\mathsf{SS}})$$

In the companion technical report [4], we provide a variant of rule (T-SPAWN$_{\mathsf{LL}}$) for the case of a linear recursive tail call. Without linear forwarding, a linear tail call can no longer be implicitly "de-sugared" into a spawn and a linear forward [2,22,52], but must be accounted for explicitly. In the report, we also provide the rules for checking process definitions. Those rules make sure that the process' world order is acyclic, that the types of the providing session and argument sessions are well-formed, and that the process satisfies Invariants 1 and 2.

### 3.3 Dining Philosophers in $\mathsf{SILL}_{\mathsf{S}^+}$

Having introduced our type system, we revisit the dining philosophers from Sect. 1 and show how to program the example in $\mathsf{SILL}_{\mathsf{S}^+}$, ensuring that the program will run without deadlocks. The code is given in Fig. 4. We note the world annotations in the signature of the process definitions. For instance,

$$\textit{thinking} : \{\delta_0 < \delta_1, \delta_1 < \delta_2, \delta_2 < \delta_3 \vdash \mathsf{phil}[\delta_0 \updownarrow^{\delta_2}_{\delta_1}] \leftarrow \mathsf{sfork}[\delta_1 \updownarrow^{\delta_3}_{\delta_3}], \mathsf{sfork}[\delta_2 \updownarrow^{\delta_3}_{\delta_3}]; \cdot; \cdot\}$$

indicates that, given the order $\delta_0 < \delta_1 < \delta_2 < \delta_3$, process *thinking* provides a session of type $\mathsf{phil}[\delta_0 \updownarrow^{\delta_2}_{\delta_1}]$ and uses two shared channel references of type $\mathsf{sfork}[\delta_1 \updownarrow^{\delta_3}_{\delta_3}]$ and $\mathsf{sfork}[\delta_2 \updownarrow^{\delta_3}_{\delta_3}]$. The two $\cdot$ signify that neither acquired nor linear channel references are given as arguments. The signature indicates that the two shared fork references reside at different worlds, such that the world of the first one is smaller than the one of the second.

Let's briefly convince ourselves that the two acquires in process *thinking* in Fig. 4 are type-correct. For each acquire we have to show that: the world of the resource to be acquired is within the acquiring process' range; the max of the acquiring process is smaller than the min of the acquired resource; and, that the self of the acquired resource is larger than those of all already acquired resources. We can convince ourselves that all those conditions are readily met.

$$\begin{array}{l}
\mathit{thinking} : \{\delta_0 < \delta_1, \delta_1 < \delta_2, \delta_2 < \delta_3 \vdash \\
\quad \mathsf{phil}[\delta_0 \updownarrow^{\delta_2}_{\delta_1}] \leftarrow \mathsf{sfork}[\delta_1 \updownarrow^{\delta_3}_{\delta_3}], \mathsf{sfork}[\delta_2 \updownarrow^{\delta_3}_{\delta_3}]; \cdot; \cdot\} \\
c[\delta_0 \updownarrow^{\delta_2}_{\delta_1}] \leftarrow \mathit{thinking} \leftarrow \mathit{left}[\delta_1 \updownarrow^{\delta_3}_{\delta_3}], \mathit{right}[\delta_2 \updownarrow^{\delta_3}_{\delta_3}] = \\
\quad \mathit{left}' \leftarrow \mathsf{acquire}\ \mathit{left} ; \\
\quad \mathit{right}' \leftarrow \mathsf{acquire}\ \mathit{right} ; \\
\quad c \leftarrow \mathit{eating} \leftarrow \mathit{left}', \mathit{right}' ; \\
\mathit{eating} : \{\delta_0 < \delta_1, \delta_1 < \delta_2, \delta_2 < \delta_3 \vdash \\
\quad \mathsf{phil}[\delta_0 \updownarrow^{\delta_2}_{\delta_1}] \leftarrow \cdot; \mathsf{lfork}[\delta_1 \updownarrow^{\delta_3}_{\delta_3}], \mathsf{lfork}[\delta_2 \updownarrow^{\delta_3}_{\delta_3}]; \cdot\} \\
c[\delta_0 \updownarrow^{\delta_2}_{\delta_1}] \leftarrow \mathit{eating} \leftarrow \mathit{left}'[\delta_1 \updownarrow^{\delta_3}_{\delta_3}], \mathit{right}'[\delta_2 \updownarrow^{\delta_3}_{\delta_3}] = \\
\quad \mathit{right} \leftarrow \mathsf{release}\ \mathit{right}' ; \\
\quad \mathit{left} \leftarrow \mathsf{release}\ \mathit{left}' ; \\
\quad c \leftarrow \mathit{thinking} \leftarrow \mathit{left}, \mathit{right}
\end{array}$$

$$\begin{array}{l}
\mathsf{lfork} = \downarrow^{\mathsf{S}}_{\mathsf{L}} \mathsf{sfork} \\
\mathsf{sfork} = \uparrow^{\mathsf{S}}_{\mathsf{L}} \mathsf{lfork} \\
\mathsf{phil} = \mathbf{1}
\end{array}$$

$$\begin{array}{l}
\mathit{fork_proc} : \{\delta_0 < \delta_1 \vdash \mathsf{sfork}[\delta_0 \updownarrow^{\delta_1}_{\delta_1}]\} \\
c[\delta_0 \updownarrow^{\delta_1}_{\delta_1}] \leftarrow \mathit{fork_proc} = \\
\quad c' \leftarrow \mathsf{accept}\ c ; \\
\quad c \leftarrow \mathsf{detach}\ c' ; \\
\quad c'' : \mathsf{sfork}[\delta_0 \updownarrow^{\delta_1}_{\delta_1}] \leftarrow \mathit{fork_proc} ; \\
\quad \mathsf{fwd}\ c\ c''
\end{array}$$

**Fig. 4.** Deadlock-free version of dining philosophers in $\mathsf{SILL}_{\mathsf{S}+}$.

We note, however, that if we were to swap the two acquires, the program would not type-check.

Let us once more set the table for three philosophers and three forks. We execute this code in a process with world annotations $[\delta_a \updownarrow^{\delta_b}_{\delta_b}]$ such that $\delta_a < \delta_b$. We first create new worlds and define their order:

$$\begin{array}{l}
\mathsf{w}_1 \leftarrow \mathsf{new_world}; \mathsf{w}_2 \leftarrow \mathsf{new_world}; \mathsf{w}_3 \leftarrow \mathsf{new_world}; \mathsf{w}_4 \leftarrow \mathsf{new_world}; \\
\delta_a < \mathsf{w}_1; \delta_a < \mathsf{w}_2; \delta_b < \mathsf{w}_1; \mathsf{w}_1 < \mathsf{w}_2; \mathsf{w}_1 < \mathsf{w}_3; \mathsf{w}_1 < \mathsf{w}_4; \mathsf{w}_2 < \mathsf{w}_3; \mathsf{w}_2 < \mathsf{w}_4; \mathsf{w}_3 < \mathsf{w}_4;
\end{array}$$

We then spawn the forks, each residing at a different world, such that the max world of a fork is higher than the self of the highest fork, ensuring Invariant 2 for the philosopher processes that we spawn afterwards:

$$\begin{array}{l}
f_1 : \mathsf{sfork}[\mathsf{w}_1 \updownarrow^{\mathsf{w}_4}_{\mathsf{w}_4}] \leftarrow \mathit{fork_proc} ; f_2 : \mathsf{sfork}[\mathsf{w}_2 \updownarrow^{\mathsf{w}_4}_{\mathsf{w}_4}] \leftarrow \mathit{fork_proc} ; \\
f_3 : \mathsf{sfork}[\mathsf{w}_3 \updownarrow^{\mathsf{w}_4}_{\mathsf{w}_4}] \leftarrow \mathit{fork_proc} ;
\end{array}$$

When we spawn the philosophers, we ensure that $P_0$ is going to pick up fork $F_1$ and then $F_2$, $P_1$ is going to pick up $F_2$ and then $F_3$, and $P_2$ is going to pick up $F_1$ and then $F_3$.

$$\begin{array}{l}
p_0 : \mathsf{phil}[\delta_a \updownarrow^{\mathsf{w}_2}_{\mathsf{w}_1}] \leftarrow \mathit{thinking} \leftarrow \cdot; \cdot; f_1, f_2 ; p_1 : \mathsf{phil}[\delta_a \updownarrow^{\mathsf{w}_3}_{\mathsf{w}_2}] \leftarrow \mathit{thinking} \leftarrow \cdot; \cdot; f_2, f_3 ; \\
p_2 : \mathsf{phil}[\delta_a \updownarrow^{\mathsf{w}_3}_{\mathsf{w}_1}] \leftarrow \mathit{thinking} \leftarrow \cdot; \cdot; f_1, f_3 ;
\end{array}$$

We note that the deadlocking spawn

$$p_2 : \mathsf{phil}[\delta_a \updownarrow^{\mathsf{w}_3}_{\mathsf{w}_1}] \leftarrow \mathit{thinking} \leftarrow \cdot; \cdot; f_3, f_1 ;$$

is type-incorrect since we would substitute both $\mathsf{w}_1$ and $\mathsf{w}_3$ for $\delta_1$ and $\mathsf{w}_3$ and $\mathsf{w}_1$ for $\delta_2$, which violates the ordering constraints put in place by typing.

### 3.4 Dynamics

We now give the *dynamics* of $\mathsf{SILL}_{\mathsf{S+}}$. Our current system is based on a *synchronous* dynamics. While this choice is more conservative, it allows us to narrow the complexity of the problem at hand.

As in $\mathsf{SILL}_{\mathsf{S}}$, we use *multiset rewriting rules* [12] to capture the dynamics of $\mathsf{SILL}_{\mathsf{S+}}$ (see Sect. 2). Multiset rewriting rules represent computation in terms of local state transitions between configurations of processes, only mentioning the parts of a configuration they rewrite. We use the predicates $\mathsf{proc}(a_m, \mathsf{w}_{\mathsf{a}_1} \updownarrow^{\mathsf{w}_{\mathsf{a}_3}}_{\mathsf{w}_{\mathsf{a}_2}}, P_{a_m})$ and $\mathsf{unavail}(a_{\mathsf{S}}, \mathsf{w}_{\mathsf{a}_1} \updownarrow^{\mathsf{w}_{\mathsf{a}_3}}_{\mathsf{w}_{\mathsf{a}_2}})$ to define the states of a configuration (see Sect. 5.1). The former denotes a process executing term $P$ that provides along channel $a_m$ at mode $m$ with worlds $\mathsf{w}_{\mathsf{a}_1}$, $\mathsf{w}_{\mathsf{a}_2}$, and $\mathsf{w}_{\mathsf{a}_3}$ for $\mathsf{self}$, $\mathsf{min}$, and $\mathsf{max}$, respectively. The latter acts as a placeholder for a shared process providing along channel $a_{\mathsf{S}}$ with worlds $\mathsf{w}_{\mathsf{a}_1}$, $\mathsf{w}_{\mathsf{a}_2}$, and $\mathsf{w}_{\mathsf{a}_3}$ for $\mathsf{self}$, $\mathsf{min}$, and $\mathsf{max}$, respectively, that is currently unavailable. We note that since worlds are also run-time artifacts, they must occur as part of the state-defining predicates.

Fig. 5 lists selected rules of the dynamics. Since the rules remain largely the same as those of $\mathsf{SILL}_{\mathsf{S}}$, apart from the world annotations that are "threaded through" unchanged, we only discuss the rules that actually differ from the $\mathsf{SILL}_{\mathsf{S}}$ rules. The interested reader can find the remaining rules in the companion technical report [4].

(D-SPAWN$_{\mathsf{LL}}$)

$$\mathsf{proc}(a_{\mathsf{L}}, \mathsf{w}_{\mathsf{a}_1} \updownarrow^{\mathsf{w}_{\mathsf{a}_3}}_{\mathsf{w}_{\mathsf{a}_2}}, x_{\mathsf{L}} : A_{\mathsf{L}}[\mathsf{w}_{\mathsf{b}_1} \updownarrow^{\mathsf{w}_{\mathsf{b}_3}}_{\mathsf{w}_{\mathsf{b}_2}}] \leftarrow X_{\mathsf{L}} \leftarrow \overline{c_{\mathsf{L}}}, \overline{\tilde{c}_{\mathsf{L}}}, \overline{d_{\mathsf{S}}}\,;\ Q_{x_{\mathsf{L}}}),$$
$$!\mathsf{def}(\Psi' \vdash x'_{\mathsf{L}} : A'_{\mathsf{L}}[\delta_j \updownarrow^{\delta_n}_{\delta_k}] \leftarrow X_{\mathsf{L}} \leftarrow \Delta', \Phi', \Gamma' = P_{x'_{\mathsf{L}},\mathsf{dom}(\Delta'),\mathsf{dom}(\Phi'),\mathsf{dom}(\Gamma'),\Psi''})$$
$$\longrightarrow \mathsf{proc}(b_{\mathsf{L}}, \mathsf{w}_{\mathsf{b}_1} \updownarrow^{\mathsf{w}_{\mathsf{b}_3}}_{\mathsf{w}_{\mathsf{b}_2}}, [b_{\mathsf{L}}/x'_{\mathsf{L}}, \overline{c_{\mathsf{L}}}/\mathsf{dom}(\Delta'), \overline{\tilde{c}_{\mathsf{L}}}/\mathsf{dom}(\Phi'), \overline{d_{\mathsf{S}}}/\mathsf{dom}(\Gamma')]\hat{\gamma}(P_{x'_{\mathsf{L}},\mathsf{dom}(\Delta'),\mathsf{dom}(\Phi'),\mathsf{dom}(\Gamma'),\Psi''})),$$
$$\mathsf{proc}(a_{\mathsf{L}}, \mathsf{w}_{\mathsf{a}_1} \updownarrow^{\mathsf{w}_{\mathsf{a}_3}}_{\mathsf{w}_{\mathsf{a}_2}}, [b_{\mathsf{L}}/x_{\mathsf{L}}]\, Q_{x_{\mathsf{L}}}),$$
$$\mathsf{unavail}(b_{\mathsf{S}}, \mathsf{w}_{\mathsf{b}_1} \updownarrow^{\mathsf{w}_{\mathsf{b}_3}}_{\mathsf{w}_{\mathsf{b}_2}}) \quad (b \textit{ fresh})$$

(D-NEW)

$$\mathsf{proc}(a, \mathsf{w}_{\mathsf{a}_1} \updownarrow^{\mathsf{w}_{\mathsf{a}_3}}_{\mathsf{w}_{\mathsf{a}_2}}, \mathsf{w} \leftarrow \mathsf{new\_world};\ Q_{\mathsf{w}}) \longrightarrow \mathsf{proc}(a, \mathsf{w}_{\mathsf{a}_1} \updownarrow^{\mathsf{w}_{\mathsf{a}_3}}_{\mathsf{w}_{\mathsf{a}_2}}, Q_{\mathsf{w}}) \quad (\mathsf{w} \textit{ fresh})$$

(D-ORD)

$$\mathsf{proc}(a, \mathsf{w}_{\mathsf{a}_1} \updownarrow^{\mathsf{w}_{\mathsf{a}_3}}_{\mathsf{w}_{\mathsf{a}_2}}, \mathsf{w} < \mathsf{w}';\ Q) \longrightarrow \mathsf{proc}(a, \mathsf{w}_{\mathsf{a}_1} \updownarrow^{\mathsf{w}_{\mathsf{a}_3}}_{\mathsf{w}_{\mathsf{a}_2}}, Q)$$

**Fig. 5.** Selected multiset rewriting rules of $\mathsf{SILL}_{\mathsf{S+}}$.

Noteworthy are the rules D-NEW and D-ORD for creating and relating worlds, respectively. Rule D-NEW creates a fresh world, which will be globally available in the configuration. Rule D-ORD, on the other hand, updates the configuration's order with the pair $\mathsf{w} < \mathsf{w}'$. Rule D-SPAWN$_{\mathsf{LL}}$, lastly, substitutes actual worlds for world variables in the body of the spawned process, using the substitution mapping $\gamma$ defined earlier. It relies on the existence of a corresponding definition predicate for each process definition contained in the signature $\Sigma$. We note that the substitution $\gamma$ in rule D-SPAWN$_{\mathsf{LL}}$ instantiates the appropriate world variables in the spawned process $P$.

# 4 Extended Example: An Imperative Shared Queue

We now develop a typical imperative-style implementation of a queue that uses a list data structure internally to store the queue's elements and has shared references to the front and the back of the list for concurrent dequeueing and enqueueing, respectively. The session types for the queue and the list are[2]

$$\begin{aligned}\mathsf{queue}\ A_{\mathsf{S}} = {\uparrow}^{\mathsf{S}}_{\mathsf{L}}\&\{&\mathsf{enq} : \Pi x{:}A_{\mathsf{S}}.\ {\downarrow}^{\mathsf{S}}_{\mathsf{L}}\mathsf{queue}\ A_{\mathsf{S}},\\ &\mathsf{deq} : \oplus\{\mathsf{none} : {\downarrow}^{\mathsf{S}}_{\mathsf{L}}\mathsf{queue}\ A_{\mathsf{S}}, \mathsf{some} : \exists x{:}A_{\mathsf{S}}.\ {\downarrow}^{\mathsf{S}}_{\mathsf{L}}\mathsf{queue}\ A_{\mathsf{S}}\}\}\end{aligned}$$

$$\begin{aligned}\mathsf{list}\ A_{\mathsf{S}} = {\uparrow}^{\mathsf{S}}_{\mathsf{L}}\&\{&\mathsf{ins} : \Pi x{:}A_{\mathsf{S}}.\exists y{:}\mathsf{list}\ A_{\mathsf{S}}.\ {\downarrow}^{\mathsf{S}}_{\mathsf{L}}\mathsf{list}\ A_{\mathsf{S}},\\ &\mathsf{del} : \oplus\{\mathsf{none} : {\downarrow}^{\mathsf{S}}_{\mathsf{L}}\mathsf{list}\ A_{\mathsf{S}}, \mathsf{some} : \exists x{:}A_{\mathsf{S}}.\ {\downarrow}^{\mathsf{S}}_{\mathsf{L}}\mathsf{list}\ A_{\mathsf{S}}\}\end{aligned}$$

The list is implemented in terms of processes *empty* and *elem*, denoting the empty list and a cons cell, respectively. We show the more interesting case of a cons cell (Fig. 6). The queue is defined by processes *head* (Fig. 7) and *queue_proc* (Fig. 8), the latter being the queue's interface to its clients.

$$\begin{array}{l}
elem : \{\delta_1 < \delta_2, \delta_2 < \delta_3, \delta_3 < \delta_4 \vdash \mathsf{list}[\delta_1 \updownarrow^{\delta_2}_{\delta_2}]A_{\mathsf{S}}[\delta_3 \updownarrow^{\delta_4}_{\delta_4}] \leftarrow A_{\mathsf{S}}[\delta_3 \updownarrow^{\delta_4}_{\delta_4}], \mathsf{list}[\delta_1 \updownarrow^{\delta_2}_{\delta_2}]A_{\mathsf{S}}[\delta_3 \updownarrow^{\delta_4}_{\delta_4}]\}\\
c[\delta_1 \updownarrow^{\delta_2}_{\delta_2}][\delta_3 \updownarrow^{\delta_4}_{\delta_4}] \leftarrow elem \leftarrow x[\delta_3 \updownarrow^{\delta_4}_{\delta_4}], next[\delta_1 \updownarrow^{\delta_2}_{\delta_2}][\delta_3 \updownarrow^{\delta_4}_{\delta_4}] =\\
\quad c' \leftarrow \mathsf{accept}\ c\ ;\\
\quad \mathsf{case}\ c'\ \mathsf{of}\\
\quad \mid \mathsf{ins} \rightarrow y \leftarrow \mathsf{recv}\ c'\ ;\ n \leftarrow elem \leftarrow y,\ next\ ;\ \mathsf{send}\ c'\ n\ ;\\
\qquad\qquad c \leftarrow \mathsf{detach}\ c'\ ;\\
\qquad\qquad c'' : \mathsf{list}[\delta_1 \updownarrow^{\delta_2}_{\delta_2}]A_{\mathsf{S}}[\delta_3 \updownarrow^{\delta_4}_{\delta_4}] \leftarrow elem \leftarrow x,\ n\ ;\ \mathsf{fwd}\ c\ c''\\
\quad \mid \mathsf{del} \rightarrow c'.\mathsf{some}\ ;\ \mathsf{send}\ c'\ x\ ;\\
\qquad\qquad c \leftarrow \mathsf{detach}\ c'\ ;\ \mathsf{fwd}\ c\ next
\end{array}$$

**Fig. 6.** Imperative queue – *elem* process.

We can now define a client (Fig. 8) for the queue, assuming existence of a corresponding shared session type item and a process *item_proc* offering a session of type $\mathsf{item}[\delta_3 \updownarrow^{\delta_4}_{\delta_4}]$. The client instantiates the queue at world $\delta_b$, allowing it to acquire resources at world $\mathsf{w}_1$, which is exactly the world at which process *queue_proc* instantiates the list. Given that the client itself resides at world $\delta_a$, which is smaller than the queue's world $\delta_b$, the client is allowed to acquire the queue, which in turn will acquire the list to satisfy any requests by the client.

The example showcases a paradigmatic use of several collaborators, where collaborators can hold resources while they "talk down" in the tree. In particular, as illustrated in Fig. 9, the clients $C_1$, $C_2$, and $C_3$ compete for resources at

[2] We adopt polymorphism for the example without formal treatment since it is orthogonal and has been studied for session types in [23, 46].

$$\mathit{head} : \{\delta_0 < \delta_1, \delta_1 < \delta_2, \delta_2 < \delta_3, \delta_3 < \delta_4 \vdash \mathsf{queue}[\delta_0 \updownarrow^{\delta_1}_{\delta_1}] A_{\mathsf{S}}[\delta_3 \updownarrow^{\delta_4}_{\delta_4}] \leftarrow \mathsf{list}[\delta_1 \updownarrow^{\delta_2}_{\delta_2}] A_{\mathsf{S}}[\delta_3 \updownarrow^{\delta_4}_{\delta_4}], \mathsf{list}[\delta_1 \updownarrow^{\delta_2}_{\delta_2}] A_{\mathsf{S}}[\delta_3 \updownarrow^{\delta_4}_{\delta_4}]\}$$

$c[\delta_0 \updownarrow^{\delta_1}_{\delta_1}][\delta_3 \updownarrow^{\delta_4}_{\delta_4}] \leftarrow \mathit{head} \leftarrow \mathit{front}[\delta_1 \updownarrow^{\delta_2}_{\delta_2}][\delta_3 \updownarrow^{\delta_4}_{\delta_4}],\ \mathit{back}[\delta_1 \updownarrow^{\delta_2}_{\delta_2}][\delta_3 \updownarrow^{\delta_4}_{\delta_4}] =$
  $c' \leftarrow$ accept $c$ ;
  case $c'$ of
  | enq $\rightarrow x \leftarrow$ recv $c'$ ;
      $\mathit{back}' \leftarrow$ acquire $\mathit{back}$ ;
      $\mathit{back}'$.ins ; send $\mathit{back}'\ x$ ; $e \leftarrow$ recv $\mathit{back}'$ ;
      $\mathit{back} \leftarrow$ release $\mathit{back}'$ ;
      $c \leftarrow$ detach $c'$ ; $c''$ : $\mathsf{queue}[\delta_0 \updownarrow^{\delta_1}_{\delta_1}] A_{\mathsf{S}}[\delta_3 \updownarrow^{\delta_4}_{\delta_4}] \leftarrow \mathit{head} \leftarrow \mathit{front},\ e$ ; fwd $c\ c''$
  | deq $\rightarrow \mathit{front}' \leftarrow$ acquire $\mathit{front}$ ;
      $\mathit{front}'$.del ;
      (case $\mathit{front}'$ of
      | none $\rightarrow \mathit{front} \leftarrow$ release $\mathit{front}'$ ; $c'$.none ; $c \leftarrow$ detach $c'$ ;
          $c''$ : $\mathsf{queue}[\delta_0 \updownarrow^{\delta_1}_{\delta_1}] A_{\mathsf{S}}[\delta_3 \updownarrow^{\delta_4}_{\delta_4}] \leftarrow \mathit{head} \leftarrow \mathit{front},\ \mathit{back}$ ; fwd $c\ c''$
      | some $\rightarrow x \leftarrow$ recv $\mathit{front}'$ ;
          $\mathit{front} \leftarrow$ release $\mathit{front}'$ ;
          $c'$.some ; send $c'\ x$ ; $c \leftarrow$ detach $c'$ ;
          $c''$ : $\mathsf{queue}[\delta_0 \updownarrow^{\delta_1}_{\delta_1}] A_{\mathsf{S}}[\delta_3 \updownarrow^{\delta_4}_{\delta_4}] \leftarrow \mathit{head} \leftarrow \mathit{front},\ \mathit{back}$ ; fwd $c\ c''$)

**Fig. 7.** Imperative queue – *head* process.

$\mathit{queue\_proc} : \{\delta_0 < \delta_1, \delta_1 < \delta_3, \delta_3 < \delta_4$
  $\vdash \mathsf{queue}[\delta_0 \updownarrow^{\delta_1}_{\delta_1}] A_{\mathsf{S}}[\delta_3 \updownarrow^{\delta_4}_{\delta_4}]\}$

$c[\delta_0 \updownarrow^{\delta_1}_{\delta_1}][\delta_3 \updownarrow^{\delta_4}_{\delta_4}] \leftarrow \mathit{queue\_proc} =$
  $\mathsf{w}_2 \leftarrow$ new_world ;
  $\delta_1 < \mathsf{w}_2$ ; $\mathsf{w}_2 < \delta_3$ ;
  $e$ : $\mathsf{list}[\delta_1 \updownarrow^{\mathsf{w}_2}_{\mathsf{w}_2}] A_{\mathsf{S}}[\delta_3 \updownarrow^{\delta_4}_{\delta_4}] \leftarrow \mathit{empty}$ ;
  $c''$ : $\mathsf{queue}[\delta_0 \updownarrow^{\delta_1}_{\delta_1}] A_{\mathsf{S}}[\delta_3 \updownarrow^{\delta_4}_{\delta_4}] \leftarrow \mathit{head}$
    $\leftarrow e, e$ ;
  fwd $c\ c''$

$\mathit{client} : \{\delta_a < \delta_b \vdash \mathbf{1}[\delta_a \updownarrow^{\delta_b}_{\delta_b}]\}$

$c[\delta_a \updownarrow^{\delta_b}_{\delta_b}] \leftarrow \mathit{client} =$
  $\mathsf{w}_1 \leftarrow$ new_world ; $\mathsf{w}_3 \leftarrow$ new_world ;
  $\mathsf{w}_4 \leftarrow$ new_world ;
  $\delta_b < \mathsf{w}_1$ ; $\mathsf{w}_1 < \mathsf{w}_3$ ; $\mathsf{w}_3 < \mathsf{w}_4$ ;
  $i_0$ : $\mathsf{item}[\mathsf{w}_3 \updownarrow^{\mathsf{w}_4}_{\mathsf{w}_4}] \leftarrow \mathit{item\_proc}$ ;
  $q$ : $\mathsf{queue}[\delta_b \updownarrow^{\mathsf{w}_1}_{\mathsf{w}_1}] A_{\mathsf{S}}[\mathsf{w}_3 \updownarrow^{\mathsf{w}_4}_{\mathsf{w}_4}] \leftarrow \mathit{queue\_proc}$ ;
  $q' \leftarrow$ acquire $q$ ; $q'$.enq ; send $q'\ i_0$ ;
  $q \leftarrow$ release $q'$ ; close $c$

**Fig. 8.** Imperative queue – *queue_proc* process and *client* process.

world $\delta_b$, i.e., the queue $Q$. On the other hand, a client $C_i$ collaborates with the queue $Q$, the list elements $L_i$, and the items $I_i$, since they do not overlap in the set of resources they may acquire: a client acquires resources at $\delta_b$, a queue resources at $\mathsf{w}_1$, a list resources at $\mathsf{w}_2$, and an item resources at $\mathsf{w}_4$, and we have $\delta_a < \delta_b < \mathsf{w}_1 < \mathsf{w}_2 < \mathsf{w}_3 < \mathsf{w}_4$. We note in particular that the setup prevents a list element from acquiring its successor, forcing linear access through the queue.

## 5 Semantics

In this section, we discuss the meta-theoretical properties of $\mathsf{SILL}_{\mathsf{S}^+}$, focusing on deadlock-freedom. The companion technical report [4] provides further details.

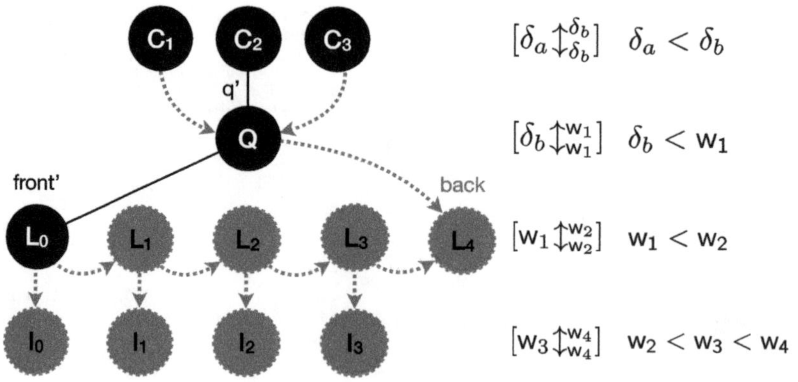


**Fig. 9.** Run-time process graph for imperative queue (see Fig. 3 for legend).

### 5.1 Configuration Typing and Preservation

Given the hierarchy between mode $\mathsf{S}$ and $\mathsf{L}$ and the fact that shared processes cannot depend on linear processes, we divide a configuration into a *shared* part $\Lambda$ and a linear part $\Theta$. We use the typing judgment $\Psi; \Gamma \vDash \Lambda; \Theta :: \Gamma; \Phi, \Delta$ to type configurations. The judgment expresses that a well-formed configuration $\Lambda; \Theta$ provides the shared channels in $\Gamma$ and the linear channels in $\Phi$ and $\Delta$. A configuration is type-checked relative to all shared channel references and a global order $\Psi$. While type-checking is compositional insofar as each process definition can be type-checked separately, solely relying on the process' local $\Psi$ (and $\Gamma$), at run-time, the entire order that a configuration relies upon is considered. We give the configuration typing rules in Fig. 10.

Our progress theorem crucially depends on the guarantee that the Invariants 1 and 2 from Sect. 3 hold for every linear process in a configuration's tree. This is expressed by the premises $\mathsf{Inv}_1(\mathsf{proc}(a_{\mathsf{L}}, \mathsf{w}_{a_1} \updownarrow^{\mathsf{w}_{a_3}}_{\mathsf{w}_{a_2}}, P_{a_{\mathsf{L}}}))$ and $\mathsf{Inv}_2(\mathsf{proc}(a_{\mathsf{L}}, \mathsf{w}_{a_1} \updownarrow^{\mathsf{w}_{a_3}}_{\mathsf{w}_{a_2}}, P_{a_{\mathsf{L}}}))$ in rule (T-$\Theta_2$), based on the Definitions 1 and 2 below that restate Invariants 1 and 2 for an entire configuration. We note that Invariant 2 is based on the set of all transitive children (i.e., *descendants*) of a process. We formally define the notion of a descendant inductively over a well-typed linear configuration. The interested reader can find the definition in the companion technical report [4].

**Invariant 1** ($\mathsf{min(parent)} \leq \mathsf{self(acquired\_child)} \leq \mathsf{max(parent)}$). *If* $\Psi; \Gamma \vDash \Theta :: \Phi, \Delta$ *and for any* $\mathsf{proc}(a_{\mathsf{L}}, \mathsf{w}_{a_1} \updownarrow^{\mathsf{w}_{a_3}}_{\mathsf{w}_{a_2}}, P_{a_{\mathsf{L}}}) \in \Theta$ *such that* $\Psi; \Gamma; \Phi_1; \Delta_1 \vdash P_{a_{\mathsf{L}}} :: (a_{\mathsf{L}} : A_{\mathsf{L}}[\mathsf{w}_{a_1} \updownarrow^{\mathsf{w}_{a_3}}_{\mathsf{w}_{a_2}}])$, $\mathsf{Inv}_1(\mathsf{proc}(a_{\mathsf{L}}, \mathsf{w}_{a_1} \updownarrow^{\mathsf{w}_{a_3}}_{\mathsf{w}_{a_2}}, P_{a_{\mathsf{L}}}))$ *holds if an only if for every acquired resource* $b_{\mathsf{L}} : B_{\mathsf{L}}[\mathsf{w}_{b_1} \updownarrow^{\mathsf{w}_{b_3}}_{\mathsf{w}_{b_2}}] \in \Phi_1$ *it holds that* $\Psi^* \vdash \mathsf{w}_{a_2} \leq \mathsf{w}_{b_1} \leq \mathsf{w}_{a_3}$. *Moreover, if* $P_{a_{\mathsf{L}}} = x_{\mathsf{L}} \leftarrow \mathsf{acquire}\, c_{\mathsf{S}}\, ; Q_{x_{\mathsf{L}}}$, *for a* $(c_{\mathsf{S}} : \uparrow^{\mathsf{S}}_{\mathsf{L}} C_{\mathsf{L}}[\mathsf{w}_{c_1} \updownarrow^{\mathsf{w}_{c_3}}_{\mathsf{w}_{c_2}}]) \in \Gamma$, *then, for every acquired resource* $b_{\mathsf{L}} : B_{\mathsf{L}}[\mathsf{w}_{b_1} \updownarrow^{\mathsf{w}_{b_3}}_{\mathsf{w}_{b_2}}] \in \Phi_1$, *it holds that* $\Psi^+ \vdash \mathsf{w}_{b_1} < \mathsf{w}_{c_1}$ *and that* $\Psi^* \vdash \mathsf{w}_{a_2} \leq \mathsf{w}_{c_1} \leq \mathsf{w}_{a_3}$.

$$\frac{}{\Psi; \Gamma \vDash (\cdot) :: (\cdot)}\ (\text{T-}\Theta_1)$$

$$\frac{\begin{array}{c}(a_{\mathsf{S}} : \hat{B}[\mathsf{w}_{a_1} \updownarrow^{\mathsf{w}_{a_3}}_{\mathsf{w}_{a_2}}]) \in \Gamma \qquad \vdash (A_{\mathsf{L}}, \hat{B})\ \mathsf{sesync} \qquad \Psi \vdash A_{\mathsf{L}}[\mathsf{w}_{a_1} \updownarrow^{\mathsf{w}_{a_3}}_{\mathsf{w}_{a_2}}]\ \mathsf{type} \\ \Psi^* \vdash \mathsf{w}_{a_2} \leq \mathsf{w}_{a_3} \qquad \mathsf{Inv}_1(\mathsf{proc}(a_{\mathsf{L}}, \mathsf{w}_{a_1} \updownarrow^{\mathsf{w}_{a_3}}_{\mathsf{w}_{a_2}}, P_{a_{\mathsf{L}}})) \qquad \mathsf{Inv}_2(\mathsf{proc}(a_{\mathsf{L}}, \mathsf{w}_{a_1} \updownarrow^{\mathsf{w}_{a_3}}_{\mathsf{w}_{a_2}}, P_{a_{\mathsf{L}}})) \\ \Psi; \Gamma \vDash \Theta :: \Phi, \Phi_1, \Delta, \Delta_1 \qquad \Psi; \Gamma; \Phi_1; \Delta_1 \vdash P_{a_{\mathsf{L}}} :: (a_{\mathsf{L}} : A_{\mathsf{L}}[\mathsf{w}_{a_1} \updownarrow^{\mathsf{w}_{a_3}}_{\mathsf{w}_{a_2}}])\end{array}}{\Psi; \Gamma \vDash \Theta, \mathsf{proc}(a_{\mathsf{L}}, \mathsf{w}_{a_1} \updownarrow^{\mathsf{w}_{a_3}}_{\mathsf{w}_{a_2}}, P_{a_{\mathsf{L}}}) :: (\Phi, \Delta, a_{\mathsf{L}} : A_{\mathsf{L}}[\mathsf{w}_{a_1} \updownarrow^{\mathsf{w}_{a_3}}_{\mathsf{w}_{a_2}}])}\ (\text{T-}\Theta_2)$$

$$\frac{}{\Psi; \Gamma \vDash (\cdot) :: (\cdot)}\ (\text{T-}\Lambda_1) \qquad \frac{\begin{array}{c}\vdash (\uparrow_{\mathsf{L}}^{\mathsf{S}} A_{\mathsf{L}}, \uparrow_{\mathsf{L}}^{\mathsf{S}} A_{\mathsf{L}})\ \mathsf{sesync} \qquad \Psi \vdash \uparrow_{\mathsf{L}}^{\mathsf{S}} A_{\mathsf{L}}[\mathsf{w}_{a_1} \updownarrow^{\mathsf{w}_{a_3}}_{\mathsf{w}_{a_2}}]\ \mathsf{type} \\ \Psi^* \vdash \mathsf{w}_{a_2} \leq \mathsf{w}_{a_3} \qquad \Psi; \Gamma \vdash P_{a_{\mathsf{S}}} :: (a_{\mathsf{S}} : \uparrow_{\mathsf{L}}^{\mathsf{S}} A_{\mathsf{L}}[\mathsf{w}_{a_1} \updownarrow^{\mathsf{w}_{a_3}}_{\mathsf{w}_{a_2}}])\end{array}}{\Psi; \Gamma \vDash \mathsf{proc}(a_{\mathsf{S}}, \mathsf{w}_{a_1} \updownarrow^{\mathsf{w}_{a_3}}_{\mathsf{w}_{a_2}}, P_{a_{\mathsf{S}}}) :: (a_{\mathsf{S}} : \uparrow_{\mathsf{L}}^{\mathsf{S}} A_{\mathsf{L}}[\mathsf{w}_{a_1} \updownarrow^{\mathsf{w}_{a_3}}_{\mathsf{w}_{a_2}}])}\ (\text{T-}\Lambda_2)$$

$$\frac{}{\Psi; \Gamma \vDash \mathsf{unavail}(a_{\mathsf{S}}, \mathsf{w}_{a_1} \updownarrow^{\mathsf{w}_{a_3}}_{\mathsf{w}_{a_2}}) :: (a_{\mathsf{S}} : \hat{A}[\mathsf{w}_{a_1} \updownarrow^{\mathsf{w}_{a_3}}_{\mathsf{w}_{a_2}}])}\ (\text{T-}\Lambda_3) \qquad \frac{\Psi; \Gamma \vDash \Lambda :: \Gamma_1 \qquad \Psi; \Gamma \vDash \Lambda' :: \Gamma_2}{\Psi; \Gamma \vDash \Lambda, \Lambda' :: \Gamma_1, \Gamma_2}\ (\text{T-}\Lambda_4)$$

$$\frac{\Psi; \Gamma \vDash \Lambda :: \Gamma \qquad \Psi; \Gamma \vDash \Theta :: \Phi, \Delta}{\Psi; \Gamma \vDash \Lambda; \Theta :: \Gamma; \Phi, \Delta}\ (\text{T-}\Omega)$$

**Fig. 10.** Configuration typing

**Invariant 2 (max(parent) < minima(descendants)).** *If* $\Psi; \Gamma \vDash \Theta :: \Phi, \Delta$ *and for any* $\mathsf{proc}(a_{\mathsf{L}}, \mathsf{w}_{a_1} \updownarrow^{\mathsf{w}_{a_3}}_{\mathsf{w}_{a_2}}, P_{a_{\mathsf{L}}}) \in \Theta$ *and that process' descendants* $(\Psi; \Gamma \vDash \Theta :: \Phi, \Delta) \rhd a_{\mathsf{L}} = (\Phi', \Delta')$, $\mathsf{Inv}_2(\mathsf{proc}(a_{\mathsf{L}}, \mathsf{w}_{a_1} \updownarrow^{\mathsf{w}_{a_3}}_{\mathsf{w}_{a_2}}, P_{a_{\mathsf{L}}}))$ *holds iff for every descendant* $b_{\mathsf{L}} : B_{\mathsf{L}}[\mathsf{w}_{b_1} \updownarrow^{\mathsf{w}_{b_3}}_{\mathsf{w}_{b_2}}] \in (\Phi', \Delta')$ *it holds that* $\Psi^+ \vdash \mathsf{w}_{a_3} < \mathsf{w}_{b_2}$.

Our preservation theorem states that Invariants 1 and 2 are preserved for every linear process in the configuration along transitions. Moreover, the theorem expresses that the types of the providing linear channels $\Phi$ and $\Delta$ are maintained along transitions and that new shared channels and worlds may be allocated. The proof relies, in particular, on session types being strictly equi-synchronizing, on a process' type well-formedness and assurance that the process' min world is less than or equal to its max world.

**Theorem 5.1 (Preservation).** *If* $\Psi; \Gamma \vDash \Lambda; \Theta :: \Gamma; \Phi, \Delta$ *and* $\Lambda; \Theta \longrightarrow \Lambda'; \Theta'$, *then* $\Psi'; \Gamma' \vDash \Lambda'; \Theta' :: \Gamma'; \Phi, \Delta$, *for some* $\Lambda'$, $\Theta'$, $\Psi'$, *and* $\Gamma'$.

## 5.2 Progress

In our development so far we have distilled the two scenarios of interdependencies between processes that can lead to deadlocks: *cyclic acquisitions* and *interdependent acquisitions and synchronizations*. This has lead to the development of a type system that ingrains the notions of *competitors* and *collaborators*, such that the former compete for a set of resources whereas the latter do not overlap in the set of resources they acquire. Our type system then ties these notions to a configuration's linear process tree such that collaborators stand in a parent-descendant relationship to each other and competitors in a sibling/cousin relationship. In this section, we prove that this orchestration is sufficient to rule out any of the aforementioned interdependencies.

To this end we introduce the notions of *red* and *green arrows* that allow us to reason about process interdependencies in a configuration's tree. A red arrow points from a linear $\mathsf{proc}(a_{\mathsf{L}},\, \mathsf{w}_{\mathsf{a}_1} \updownarrow^{\mathsf{w}_{\mathsf{a}_3}}_{\mathsf{w}_{\mathsf{a}_2}},\, Q)$ to a linear $\mathsf{proc}(b_{\mathsf{L}},\, \mathsf{w}_{\mathsf{b}_1} \updownarrow^{\mathsf{w}_{\mathsf{b}_3}}_{\mathsf{w}_{\mathsf{b}_2}},\, P)$, if the former is attempting to acquire a resource held by the latter and, consequently, is waiting for the latter to release that resource. A green arrow points from a linear $\mathsf{proc}(a_{\mathsf{L}},\, \mathsf{w}_{\mathsf{a}_1} \updownarrow^{\mathsf{w}_{\mathsf{a}_3}}_{\mathsf{w}_{\mathsf{a}_2}},\, Q)$ to a linear $\mathsf{proc}(b_{\mathsf{L}},\, \mathsf{w}_{\mathsf{b}_1} \updownarrow^{\mathsf{w}_{\mathsf{b}_3}}_{\mathsf{w}_{\mathsf{b}_2}},\, P)$, if the former is waiting to synchronize with the latter. We define these arrows formally as follows:

**Definition 5.2 (Acquire Dependency — "Red Arrow").** *Given a well-formed and well-typed configuration* $\Psi; \Gamma \vDash \Lambda; \Theta :: \Gamma; \Phi, \Delta$*, there exists a waiting-due-to-acquire relation* $\mathcal{A}(\Theta)$ *among linear processes in* $\Theta$ *at run-time such that*

$$\mathsf{proc}(a_{\mathsf{L}},\, \mathsf{w}_{\mathsf{a}_1} \updownarrow^{\mathsf{w}_{\mathsf{a}_3}}_{\mathsf{w}_{\mathsf{a}_2}},\, x_{\mathsf{L}} \leftarrow \mathsf{acquire}\ c_{\mathsf{S}};\ Q_{x_{\mathsf{L}}}) <_{\mathcal{A}} \mathsf{proc}(b_{\mathsf{L}},\, \mathsf{w}_{\mathsf{b}_1} \updownarrow^{\mathsf{w}_{\mathsf{b}_3}}_{\mathsf{w}_{\mathsf{b}_2}},\, P\langle c_{\mathsf{L}}\rangle)$$

*where* $P\langle c_{\mathsf{L}}\rangle$ *denotes a process term with an occurrence of channel* $c_{\mathsf{L}}$*.*

**Definition 5.3 (Synchronization Dependency — "Green Arrow").** *Given a well-formed and well-typed configuration* $\Psi; \Gamma \vDash \Lambda; \Theta :: \Gamma; \Phi, \Delta$*, there exists a waiting-due-to-synchronization relation* $\mathcal{S}(\Theta)$ *among linear processes in* $\Theta$ *at run-time such that*

$$\mathsf{proc}(a_{\mathsf{L}},\, \mathsf{w}_{\mathsf{a}_1} \updownarrow^{\mathsf{w}_{\mathsf{a}_3}}_{\mathsf{w}_{\mathsf{a}_2}},\, \_\langle b_{\mathsf{L}}\rangle; Q) <_{\mathcal{S}} \mathsf{proc}(b_{\mathsf{L}},\, \mathsf{w}_{\mathsf{b}_1} \updownarrow^{\mathsf{w}_{\mathsf{b}_3}}_{\mathsf{w}_{\mathsf{b}_2}},\, \_\langle \neg b_{\mathsf{L}}\rangle; P)$$
$$\mathsf{proc}(b_{\mathsf{L}},\, \mathsf{w}_{\mathsf{b}_1} \updownarrow^{\mathsf{w}_{\mathsf{b}_3}}_{\mathsf{w}_{\mathsf{b}_2}},\, \_\langle b_{\mathsf{L}}\rangle; P) <_{\mathcal{S}} \mathsf{proc}(a_{\mathsf{L}},\, \mathsf{w}_{\mathsf{a}_1} \updownarrow^{\mathsf{w}_{\mathsf{a}_3}}_{\mathsf{w}_{\mathsf{a}_2}},\, \_\langle \neg b_{\mathsf{L}}\rangle; Q\langle b_{\mathsf{L}}\rangle)$$

*where* $P\langle a_{\mathsf{L}}\rangle$ *denotes a process term with an occurrence of channel* $b_{\mathsf{L}}$*,* $\_\langle a\rangle; P$ *a process term that currently executes an action along channel* $a$*, and* $\_\langle \neg a\rangle; P$ *a process term whose currently executing action does not involve the channel* $a$*.*

It may be helpful to consult Fig. 3 at this point and note the semantic difference between the violet arrows in that figure and the red arrows discussed here. Whereas violet arrows point from the acquiring process to the resource being acquired, red arrows point from the acquiring process to the process that is holding the resource. Thus, violet arrows can go out of the tree, while red arrows stay within. Given the definitions of red and green arrows, we can define the relation $\mathcal{W}(\Theta)$ on the configuration's tree, which contains all process pairs that are in some way waiting for each other:

**Definition 5.4 (Waiting Dependency).** *Given a well-formed and well-typed configuration* $\Psi; \Gamma \vDash \Lambda; \Theta :: \Gamma; \Phi, \Delta$*, there exists a waiting relation* $\mathcal{W}(\Theta)$ *among processes in* $\Theta$ *at run-time such that* $\mathsf{proc}(a_{\mathsf{L}},\, \mathsf{w}_{\mathsf{a}_1} \updownarrow^{\mathsf{w}_{\mathsf{a}_3}}_{\mathsf{w}_{\mathsf{a}_2}},\, P) <_{\mathcal{W}} \mathsf{proc}(b_{\mathsf{L}},\, \mathsf{w}_{\mathsf{b}_1} \updownarrow^{\mathsf{w}_{\mathsf{b}_3}}_{\mathsf{w}_{\mathsf{b}_2}},\, Q)$,

- *if* $\mathsf{proc}(a_{\mathsf{L}},\, \mathsf{w}_{\mathsf{a}_1} \updownarrow^{\mathsf{w}_{\mathsf{a}_3}}_{\mathsf{w}_{\mathsf{a}_2}},\, P) <_{\mathcal{A}} \mathsf{proc}(b_{\mathsf{L}},\, \mathsf{w}_{\mathsf{b}_1} \updownarrow^{\mathsf{w}_{\mathsf{b}_3}}_{\mathsf{w}_{\mathsf{b}_2}},\, Q)$*, or*
- *if* $\mathsf{proc}(a_{\mathsf{L}},\, \mathsf{w}_{\mathsf{a}_1} \updownarrow^{\mathsf{w}_{\mathsf{a}_3}}_{\mathsf{w}_{\mathsf{a}_2}},\, P) <_{\mathcal{S}} \mathsf{proc}(b_{\mathsf{L}},\, \mathsf{w}_{\mathsf{b}_1} \updownarrow^{\mathsf{w}_{\mathsf{b}_3}}_{\mathsf{w}_{\mathsf{b}_2}},\, Q)$.

Having defined the relation $\mathcal{W}(\Theta)$, we can now state the key lemma underlying our progress theorem, indicating that $\mathcal{W}(\Theta)$ is acyclic in a well-formed and well-typed configuration.

**Lemma 5.5 (Acyclicity of $\mathcal{W}(\Theta)$).** *If $\Psi; \Gamma \models \Lambda; \Theta :: \Gamma; \Phi, \Delta$, then $\mathcal{W}(\Theta)$ is acyclic.*

We focus on explaining the main idea of the proof here. The proof proceeds by induction on $\Psi; \Gamma \models \Theta :: \Phi, \Delta$, assuming for the non-empty case $\Psi; \Gamma \models \Theta, \mathsf{proc}(a_{\mathsf{L}}, \mathsf{w}_{a_1} \updownarrow^{\mathsf{w}_{a_3}}_{\mathsf{w}_{a_2}}, P_{a_{\mathsf{L}}}) :: (\Phi, \Delta, a_{\mathsf{L}} : A_{\mathsf{L}}[\mathsf{w}_{a_1} \updownarrow^{\mathsf{w}_{a_3}}_{\mathsf{w}_{a_2}}])$ that $\mathcal{W}(\Theta)$ is acyclic, by the inductive hypothesis. We then know that there cannot exist any paths of green and red arrows in $\Theta$ that form a cycle, and we have to show that there is no way of introducing such a cyclic path by adding node $\mathsf{proc}(a_{\mathsf{L}}, \mathsf{w}_{a_1} \updownarrow^{\mathsf{w}_{a_3}}_{\mathsf{w}_{a_2}}, P_{a_{\mathsf{L}}})$ to the configuration $\Theta$. In particular, the proof considers all possible new arrows that may be introduced by adding the node and that are necessary for creating a cycle, showing that such arrows cannot come about in a well-typed configuration.

We illustrate the reasoning for the two selected cases shown in Fig. 11. Case **(a)** represents a case in which process $P_{a_{\mathsf{L}}}$ is waiting to synchronize with its child $P_{b_{\mathsf{L}}}$ while holding a resource a descendant of $P_{b_{\mathsf{L}}}$ or $P_{b_{\mathsf{L}}}$ itself wants to acquire. However, this scenario cannot come about in a well-typed configuration because $P_{a_{\mathsf{L}}}$ and $P_{b_{\mathsf{L}}}$ are collaborators and thus cannot overlap in resources they acquire. Case **(b)** represents a case in which process $P_{a_{\mathsf{L}}}$ is waiting to synchronize with its child $P_{b_{\mathsf{L}}}$ while another child, process $P_{c_{\mathsf{L}}}$, is waiting to synchronize with $P_{a_{\mathsf{L}}}$. Given acyclicity of $\mathcal{W}(\Theta)$, a necessary condition for a cycle to form is that there already must exist a red arrow **C** in the configuration that connects the subtrees in which the siblings $P_{b_{\mathsf{L}}}$ and $P_{c_{\mathsf{L}}}$ reside. However, this scenario cannot come about in a well-typed configuration because $P_{b_{\mathsf{L}}}$ and $P_{c_{\mathsf{L}}}$ are competitors, forcing $P_{c_{\mathsf{L}}}$ or any of its descendant to release a resource before synchronizing with $P_{a_{\mathsf{L}}}$. These arguments are made precise in various lemmas in [4].

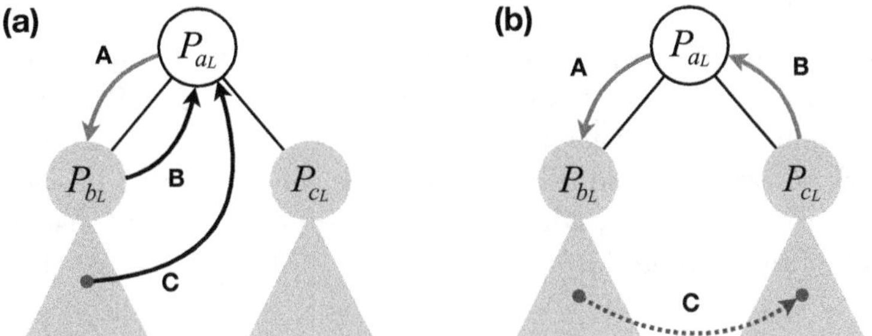


**Fig. 11.** Two prototypical cases in proof of acyclicty of $\mathcal{W}(\Theta)$.

Given acyclicity of $\mathcal{W}(\Theta)$, we can state and prove the following strong progress theorem. The theorem relies on the notion of a *poised* process, a process currently executing an action along its offering channel, and distinguishes a configuration only consisting of the top-level, linear "main" process from one that consists of several linear processes. We use $|\Theta|$ to denote the cardinality of $\Theta$:

**Theorem 5.6 (Progress).** *If* $\Psi; \Gamma \vDash \Lambda; \Theta :: (\Gamma; c_{\mathsf{L}} : \mathbf{1}[\mathsf{w}_{c_1} \updownarrow^{\mathsf{w}_{c_3}}_{\mathsf{w}_{c_2}}])$*, then either*

- $\Lambda \longrightarrow \Lambda'$*, for some* $\Lambda'$*, or*
- $\Lambda$ *is poised and*
  - *if* $|\Theta| = 1$*, then either* $\Lambda; \Theta \longrightarrow \Lambda'; \Theta'$*, for some* $\Lambda'$ *and* $\Theta'$*, or* $\Theta$ *is poised, or*
  - *if* $|\Theta| > 1$*, then* $\Lambda; \Theta \longrightarrow \Lambda'; \Theta'$*, for some* $\Lambda'$ *and* $\Theta'$*.*

The theorem indicates that, as long as there exist at least two linear processes in the configuration, the configuration can always step. If the configuration only consists of the main process, then this process will become poised (i.e., ready to close), once all sub-computations are finished. The proof of the theorem relies on the acyclicity of $\mathcal{W}(\Theta)$ and the fact that all sessions must be strictly equi-synchronizing.

## 6 Additional Discussion

**Linear Forwarding.** Our current formalization does not include linear forwarding because a forward changes the process tree and thus endangers the invariants imposed on it. This means that certain programs from the purely linear fragment may not type-check in our system. However, the correspondingly $\eta$-expanded versions of these programs should be expressible and type-checkable in $\mathsf{SILL}_{\mathsf{S}^+}$. As part of future work, we want to explore the addition of the linear forward

$$\frac{\Psi^+ \vdash \omega_n < \omega_u}{\Psi;\ \Gamma;\ \cdot;\ y_{\mathsf{L}} : A_{\mathsf{L}}[\omega_m \updownarrow^{\omega_v}_{\omega_u}] \vdash \mathsf{fwd}\ x_{\mathsf{L}}\ y_{\mathsf{L}} :: (x_{\mathsf{L}} : A_{\mathsf{L}}[\omega_j \updownarrow^{\omega_n}_{\omega_k}])}\ (\text{T-ID}_{\mathsf{L}})$$

which allows forwarding to processes that are known to not yet be aliased and whose world annotations meet the premise $\Psi^+ \vdash \omega_n < \omega_u$. Restricting to processes in $\Delta$ should uphold Invariant 1, while the premise of the rule should uphold Invariant 2. However, this change will affect the inner working of the proofs, the use of inversion in particular, which might have far-reaching consequences that need to be carefully explored.

**Unbounded Process Networks and World Polymorphism.** The typing discipline presented in the previous sections, while rich enough to account for a wide range of interesting programs, cannot type programs that spawn a statically undetermined number of shared sessions that are then to be used. For instance, while we can easily type a configuration of any given number of dining philosophers (Sect. 3.3), we cannot type a recursive process in which the number of philosophers (and forks) is potentially unbounded (as done in [21,38]), due to the way worlds are created and propagated across processes.

The general issue lies in implementing a statically unbounded network of processes that interact with each other. These interactions require the processes to be spawned at different worlds which must be generated dynamically as needed.

To interact with such a statically unknown number of processes uniformly, their offering channels must be stored in a list-like structure for later use. However, in our system, recursive types have to be invariant with respect to worlds. For instance, in a recursive type such as $T = A_{\mathsf{L}}@\omega_l \updownarrow^{\omega_r}_{\omega_p} \otimes T$, the worlds $\omega_l$, $\omega_p$, $\omega_r$ are fixed in the unfoldings of $T$. Thus, we cannot type a world-heterogeneous list and cannot form such process networks.

Given that the issues preventing us from typing such unbounded networks lie in problems of world invariance, the natural solution is to explore some form of *world polymorphism*, where types can be parameterized by worlds which are instantiated at a later stage. Such techniques have been studied in the context of hybrid logical processes in [7] by considering session types of the form $\forall\delta.A$ and $\exists\delta.A$, sessions that are parametric in the world variable $\delta$, that is instantiated by a concrete reachable world at runtime. While their development cannot be mapped directly to our setting, it is a promising avenue of future work.

## 7 Related Work

**Behavioral Type Analysis of Deadlocks.** The addition of channel usage information to types in a concurrent, message-passing setting was pioneered by Kobayashi and Igarashi [30,34], who applied the idea to deadlock prevention in the $\pi$-calculus and later to more general properties [31,32], giving rise to a generic system that can be instantiated to produce a variety of concrete typing disciplines for the $\pi$-calculus (e.g., race detection, deadlock detection, etc.).

This line of work types $\pi$-calculus processes with a simplified form of *process* (akin to CCS [42] terms without name restriction) that characterizes the input/output behavior of processes. These types are augmented with abstract data that pertain to the relative ordering of channel actions, with the type system ensuring that the transitive closure of such orderings forms a strict partial order, ensuring deadlock-freedom (i.e., communication succeeds unless a process diverges). Building on this, Kobayashi et al. proposed type systems that ensure a stronger property dubbed lock-freedom [35] (i.e., communication always succeeds), and variants that are amenable to type inference [36,39]. Kobayashi [37] extended this latter system to more accurately account for recursive processes while preserving the existence of a type inference algorithm.

Our system draws significant inspiration from this line of work, insofar as we also equip types with abstract ordering data on certain communication actions, which is then statically enforced to form a strict partial order. We note that our $\mathsf{SILL}_{\mathsf{S+}}$ language differs sufficiently from the pure $\pi$-calculus in terms of its constructs and semantics to make the formulation of a direct comparison or an immediate application of their work unclear (e.g., [37] uses replication to encode recursive processes). Moreover, we integrate this style of order-based reasoning with both linear and shared session typing, which interact in non-trivial ways (especially in the presence of recursive types and recursive process definitions).

In terms of typability, enforcing session fidelity can be a double-edged sword: some examples of the works above can be transposed to $\mathsf{SILL}_{\mathsf{S+}}$ with mostly cosmetic changes and without making use of shared sessions (e.g., a parallel implementation of factorial that recurses via replication but always answers on a private channel); others are incompatible with linear sessions and require the use of shared sessions via the acquire-release discipline, which entails a more indirect but still arguably faithful modelling of the original $\pi$-calculus behavior; some examples, however, cannot be easily adapted to the shared session discipline (e.g., $*c?(x, y).x?(z).y?(z) \mid *c?(x, y).y?(z).x?(z)$ is typable in [37], where $x?(z)$ denotes input on $x$ and $*c?(x, y)$ denotes replicated input) and their transcription, while possible, would be too far removed from the original term to be deemed a faithful representation. Recursive processes are known to produce patterns that can be challenging to analyze using such order-based techniques. The work of [21,38] specializes Kobayashi's system to account for potentially unbounded process networks with non-trivial forms of sharing. Such systems are not typable in our work (see Sect. 6 for additional discussion on this topic).

The work of Padovani [44] develops techniques inspired by [35,37] to develop a typing system for deadlock (and lock) freedom for the linear $\pi$-calculus where (linear) channels must be used exactly once. By enforcing this form of linearity, the resulting system uses only one piece of ordering data per channel usage and can easily integrate a form of channel polymorphism that accounts for intricate cyclic interleavings of recursive processes. The combination of manifest sharing and linear session typing does not seem possible without the use of additional ordering data, and the lack of single-use linear channels make the robust channel polymorphism of [44] not feasible in our setting.

Dardha and Gay [15] recently integrated a system of Kobayashi-style orderings in a logical session $\pi$-calculus based on classical linear logic, extended with the ability to form *cyclic dependencies* of actions on *linear* session channels (Atkey et al. [1] study similar cycles but do not consider deadlock-freedom), without the need for new process constructs or an acquire-release discipline. Their work considers only a restricted form of replication common in linear logic-based works, not including recursive types nor recursive process definitions. This reduces the complexity of their system, at the cost of expressiveness. We also note that the cycles enabled by their system are produced by processes sharing multiple *linear* names. Since linearity is still enforced, they cannot represent the more general form of cycles that exploit shared channels, as we do.

A comparative study of session typing and Kobayashi-style systems in terms of sharing was developed by Dardha and Pérez [16], showing that such order-based techniques can account for sharing in ways that are out of reach of both classical session typing and pure logic-based session typing. Our system (and that of [15]) aims to combine the heightened power of Kobayashi-style systems with the benefits of session typing, which seems to be better suited as a typing discipline for a high-level programming language [18].

**Progress and Session Typing.** To address limitations of classical binary session types, Honda et al. [27] introduced *multiparty* session types, where sessions are described by so-called global types that capture the interactions between an arbitrary number of session participants. Under some well-formedness constraints, global types can be used to ensure that a collection of processes correctly implements the global behavior in a deadlock-free way. However, these global type-based approaches do not ensure deadlock freedom in the presence of higher-order channel passing or interleaved multiparty sessions. Coppo et al. [13] and Bettini et al. [6] develop systems that track usage orders among interleaved multiparty sessions, ruling out cyclic dependencies that can lead to deadlocks. The resulting system is quite intricate, since it combines the full multiparty session theory with the order tracking mechanism, interacts negatively with recursion (essentially disallowing interleaving with recursion) and, by tracking order at the multiparty session-level, ends up rejecting various benign configurations that can be accounted for by our more fine-grained analysis. We also highlight the analyses of Vieira and Vasconcelos [54] and Padovani et al. [45] that are more powerful than the approaches above, at the cost of a more complex analysis based on conversation types [10] (themselves a partial-order based technique).

**Static Analysis of Concurrent Programs.** Lange et al. [40,41] develop a deadlock detection framework applied to the Go programming language. Their work distills CCS processes from programs which are then checked for deadlocks by a form of symbolic execution [40] and *model-checked* against modal $\mu$-calculus formulae [41] which encode deadlock-freedom of the abstracted process (among other properties of interest). Their abstraction introduces some distance between the original program and the analysed process and so the analysis is sound only for certain restricted program fragments, excluding any combination of recursion and process spawning. Our direct approach does not suffer from this limitation.

de'Liguoro and Padovani [17] develop a typing discipline for deadlock-freedom in a setting where processes exchange messages via unordered mailboxes. Their calculus subsumes the actor model and their analysis combines both so-called mailbox types and specialized dependency graphs to track potential cycles between mailboxes in actor-based systems. The unordered nature of actor-based communication introduces significant differences wrt our work, which crucially exploits the ordering of exchanged messages.

## 8 Concluding Remarks

In this paper we have developed the concept of manifest deadlock-freedom in the context of the language $\mathsf{SILL}_{\mathsf{S}^+}$, a shared session-typed language, showcasing both the programming methodology and the expressiveness of our framework with a series of examples. Deadlock-freedom of well-typed programs is established by a novel abstraction of so-called green and red arrows to reason about the interdependencies between processes in terms of linear and shared channel references.

In future work, we plan to address some of the limitations of the interactions of deadlock-free shared sessions with recursion, by considering promising notions of world polymorphism and world communication. We also plan to study the problem of world inference and the inclusion of a linear forwarding construct.

## References


1. Atkey, R., Lindley, S., Morris, J.G.: Conflation confers concurrency. In: Lindley, S., McBride, C., Trinder, P., Sannella, D. (eds.) A List of Successes That Can Change the World. LNCS, vol. 9600, pp. 32–55. Springer, Cham (2016). https://doi.org/10.1007/978-3-319-30936-1_2
2. Balzer, S., Pfenning, F.: Manifest sharing with session types. Proc. ACM Program. Lang. (PACMPL) **1**(ICEP), 37:1–37:29 (2017)
3. Balzer, S., Pfenning, F., Toninho, B.: A universal session type for untyped asynchronous communication. In: 29th International Conference on Concurrency Theory (CONCUR). LIPIcs, pp. 30:1–30:18. Schloss Dagstuhl - Leibniz-Zentrum fuer Informatik (2018)
4. Balzer, S., Toninho, B., Pfenning, F.: Manifest deadlock-freedom for shared session types. Technical report CMU-CS-19-102, Carnegie Mellon University (2019)
5. Benton, P.N.: A mixed linear and non-linear logic: proofs, terms and models. In: Pacholski, L., Tiuryn, J. (eds.) CSL 1994. LNCS, vol. 933, pp. 121–135. Springer, Heidelberg (1995). https://doi.org/10.1007/BFb0022251
6. Bettini, L., Coppo, M., D'Antoni, L., Luca, M.D., Dezani-Ciancaglini, M., Yoshida, N.: Global progress in dynamically interleaved multiparty sessions. In: van Breugel, F., Chechik, M. (eds.) CONCUR 2008. LNCS, vol. 5201, pp. 418–433. Springer, Heidelberg (2008). https://doi.org/10.1007/978-3-540-85361-9_33
7. Caires, L., Pérez, J.A., Pfenning, F., Toninho, B.: Logic-based domain-aware session types, unpublished draft
8. Caires, L., Pfenning, F.: Session types as intuitionistic linear propositions. In: Gastin, P., Laroussinie, F. (eds.) CONCUR 2010. LNCS, vol. 6269, pp. 222–236. Springer, Heidelberg (2010). https://doi.org/10.1007/978-3-642-15375-4_16
9. Caires, L., Pfenning, F., Toninho, B.: Linear logic propositions as session types. Math. Struct. Comput. Sci. **26**(3), 367–423 (2016)
10. Caires, L., Vieira, H.T.: Conversation types. Theor. Comput. Sci. **411**(51–52), 4399–4440 (2010)
11. Castro, D., Hu, R., Jongmans, S., Ng, N., Yoshida, N.: Distributed programming using role-parametric session types in go: statically-typed endpoint APIs for dynamically-instantiated communication structures. PACMPL **3**(POPL), 29:1–29:30 (2019)
12. Cervesato, I., Scedrov, A.: Relating state-based and process-based concurrency through linear logic. Inf. Comput. **207**(10), 1044–1077 (2009)
13. Coppo, M., Dezani-Ciancaglini, M., Yoshida, N., Padovani, L.: Global progress for dynamically interleaved multiparty sessions. Math. Struct. Comput. Sci. **26**(2), 238–302 (2016)
14. Crary, K., Harper, R., Puri, S.: What is a recursive module? In: ACM SIGPLAN Conference on Programming Language Design and Implementation (PLDI), pp. 50–63 (1999)
15. Dardha, O., Gay, S.J.: A new linear logic for deadlock-free session-typed processes. In: Baier, C., Dal Lago, U. (eds.) FoSSaCS 2018. LNCS, vol. 10803, pp. 91–109. Springer, Cham (2018). https://doi.org/10.1007/978-3-319-89366-2_5
16. Dardha, O., Pérez, J.A.: Comparing deadlock-free session typed processes. In: EXPRESS/SOS, pp. 1–15 (2015)
17. de'Liguoro, U., Padovani, L.: Mailbox types for unordered interactions. In: 32nd European Conference on Object-Oriented Programming, ECOOP 2018, pp. 15:1–15:28 (2018)

18. Gay, S.J., Gesbert, N., Ravara, A.: Session types as generic process types. In: 21st International Workshop on Expressiveness in Concurrency and 11th Workshop on Structural Operational Semantics, EXPRESS/SOS 2014, pp. 94–110 (2014)
19. Gay, S.J., Hole, M.: Subtyping for session types in the $\pi$-calculus. Acta Informatica **42**(2–3), 191–225 (2005)
20. Gay, S.J., Vasconcelos, V.T., Ravara, A., Gesbert, N., Caldeira, A.Z.: Modular session types for distributed object-oriented programming. In: 37th ACM SIGPLAN-SIGACT Symposium on Principles of Programming Languages (POPL), pp. 299–312 (2010)
21. Giachino, E., Kobayashi, N., Laneve, C.: Deadlock analysis of unbounded process networks. In: Baldan, P., Gorla, D. (eds.) CONCUR 2014. LNCS, vol. 8704, pp. 63–77. Springer, Heidelberg (2014). https://doi.org/10.1007/978-3-662-44584-6_6
22. Gommerstadt, H., Jia, L., Pfenning, F.: Session-typed concurrent contracts. In: Ahmed, A. (ed.) ESOP 2018. LNCS, vol. 10801, pp. 771–798. Springer, Cham (2018). https://doi.org/10.1007/978-3-319-89884-1_27
23. Griffith, D.: Polarized substructural session types. Ph.D. thesis, University of Illinois at Urbana-Champaign (2016)
24. Griffith, D., Pfenning, F.: SILL (2015). https://github.com/ISANobody/sill
25. Honda, K.: Types for dyadic interaction. In: Best, E. (ed.) CONCUR 1993. LNCS, vol. 715, pp. 509–523. Springer, Heidelberg (1993). https://doi.org/10.1007/3-540-57208-2_35
26. Honda, K., Vasconcelos, V.T., Kubo, M.: Language primitives and type discipline for structured communication-based programming. In: Hankin, C. (ed.) ESOP 1998. LNCS, vol. 1381, pp. 122–138. Springer, Heidelberg (1998). https://doi.org/10.1007/BFb0053567
27. Honda, K., Yoshida, N., Carbone, M.: Multiparty asynchronous session types. In: 35th ACM SIGPLAN-SIGACT Symposium on Principles of Programming Languages (POPL), pp. 273–284. ACM (2008)
28. Hu, R., Yoshida, N.: Hybrid session verification through endpoint API generation. In: Stevens, P., Wąsowski, A. (eds.) FASE 2016. LNCS, vol. 9633, pp. 401–418. Springer, Heidelberg (2016). https://doi.org/10.1007/978-3-662-49665-7_24
29. Hu, R., Yoshida, N.: Explicit connection actions in multiparty session types. In: Huisman, M., Rubin, J. (eds.) FASE 2017. LNCS, vol. 10202, pp. 116–133. Springer, Heidelberg (2017). https://doi.org/10.1007/978-3-662-54494-5_7
30. Igarashi, A., Kobayashi, N.: Type-based analysis of communication for concurrent programming languages. In: Van Hentenryck, P. (ed.) SAS 1997. LNCS, vol. 1302, pp. 187–201. Springer, Heidelberg (1997). https://doi.org/10.1007/BFb0032742
31. Igarashi, A., Kobayashi, N.: A generic type system for the Pi-calculus. In: Conference Record of POPL 2001: The 28th ACM SIGPLAN-SIGACT Symposium on Principles of Programming Languages, pp. 128–141 (2001)
32. Igarashi, A., Kobayashi, N.: A generic type system for the Pi-calculus. Theor. Comput. Sci. **311**(1–3), 121–163 (2004)
33. Jespersen, T.B.L., Munksgaard, P., Larsen, K.F.: Session types for rust. In: 11th ACM SIGPLAN Workshop on Generic Programming, WGP 2015, pp. 13–22 (2015)
34. Kobayashi, N.: A partially deadlock-free typed process calculus. In: Proceedings of the 12th Annual IEEE Symposium on Logic in Computer Science, pp. 128–139 (1997)
35. Kobayashi, N.: A type system for lock-free processes. Inf. Comput. **177**(2), 122–159 (2002)
36. Kobayashi, N.: Type-based information flow analysis for the $\pi$-calculus. Acta Inf. **42**(4–5), 291–347 (2005)

37. Kobayashi, N.: A new type system for deadlock-free processes. In: Baier, C., Hermanns, H. (eds.) CONCUR 2006. LNCS, vol. 4137, pp. 233–247. Springer, Heidelberg (2006). https://doi.org/10.1007/11817949_16
38. Kobayashi, N., Laneve, C.: Deadlock analysis of unbounded process networks. Inf. Comput. **252**, 48–70 (2017)
39. Kobayashi, N., Saito, S., Sumii, E.: An implicitly-typed deadlock-free process calculus. In: Palamidessi, C. (ed.) CONCUR 2000. LNCS, vol. 1877, pp. 489–504. Springer, Heidelberg (2000). https://doi.org/10.1007/3-540-44618-4_35
40. Lange, J., Ng, N., Toninho, B., Yoshida, N.: Fencing off go: liveness and safety for channel-based programming. In: 44th ACM SIGPLAN-SIGACT Symposium on Principles of Programming Languages (POPL), pp. 748–761. ACM (2017)
41. Lange, J., Ng, N., Toninho, B., Yoshida, N.: A static verification framework for message passing in go using behavioural types. In: Proceedings of the 40th International Conference on Software Engineering, ICSE 2018, Gothenburg, Sweden, 27 May–03 June 2018, pp. 1137–1148 (2018)
42. Milner, R.: A Calculus of Communicating Systems. LNCS, vol. 92. Springer, Heidelberg (1980). https://doi.org/10.1007/3-540-10235-3
43. Neykova, R., Hu, R., Yoshida, N., Abdeljallal, F.: A session type provider: compile-time API generation of distributed protocols with refinements in F#. In: Proceedings of the 27th International Conference on Compiler Construction, CC 2018, pp. 128–138 (2018)
44. Padovani, L.: Deadlock and lock freedom in the linear $\pi$-calculus. In: Computer Science Logic - Logic in Computer Science (CSL-LICS), pp. 72:1–72:10 (2014)
45. Padovani, L., Vasconcelos, V.T., Vieira, H.T.: Typing liveness in multiparty communicating systems. In: Kühn, E., Pugliese, R. (eds.) COORDINATION 2014. LNCS, vol. 8459, pp. 147–162. Springer, Heidelberg (2014). https://doi.org/10.1007/978-3-662-43376-8_10
46. Pérez, J.A., Caires, L., Pfenning, F., Toninho, B.: Linear logical relations and observational equivalences for session-based concurrency. Inf. Comput. **239**, 254–302 (2014)
47. Pfenning, F., Griffith, D.: Polarized substructural session types. In: Pitts, A. (ed.) FoSSaCS 2015. LNCS, vol. 9034, pp. 3–22. Springer, Heidelberg (2015). https://doi.org/10.1007/978-3-662-46678-0_1
48. Reed, J.: A judgmental deconstruction of modal logic, January 2009. http://www.cs.cmu.edu/~jcreed/papers/jdml.pdf, unpublished manuscript
49. Scalas, A., Dardha, O., Hu, R., Yoshida, N.: A linear decomposition of multiparty sessions for safe distributed programming. In: 31st European Conference on Object-Oriented Programming, ECOOP 2017, pp. 24:1–24:31 (2017)
50. Scalas, A., Yoshida, N.: Lightweight session programming in scala. In: 30th European Conference on Object-Oriented Programming, ECOOP 2016, pp. 21:1–21:28 (2016)
51. Toninho, B.: A logical foundation for session-based concurrent computation. Ph.D. thesis, Carnegie Mellon University and New University of Lisbon (2015)
52. Toninho, B., Caires, L., Pfenning, F.: Higher-order processes, functions, and sessions: a monadic integration. In: Felleisen, M., Gardner, P. (eds.) ESOP 2013. LNCS, vol. 7792, pp. 350–369. Springer, Heidelberg (2013). https://doi.org/10.1007/978-3-642-37036-6_20
53. Vasconcelos, V.T.: Fundamentals of session types. Inf. Comput. **217**, 52–70 (2012)
54. Vieira, H.T., Vasconcelos, V.T.: Typing progress in communication-centred sys-

tems. In: De Nicola, R., Julien, C. (eds.) COORDINATION 2013. LNCS, vol. 7890, pp. 236–250. Springer, Heidelberg (2013). https://doi.org/10.1007/978-3-642-38493-6_17
55. Wadler, P.: Propositions as sessions. In: 17th ACM SIGPLAN International Conference on Functional Programming (ICFP), pp. 273–286. ACM (2012)

# 5

# On the Multi-Language Construction

Samuele Buro(✉) and Isabella Mastroeni(✉)

Department of Computer Science, University of Verona,
Strada le Grazie 15, 37134 Verona, Italy
{samuele.buro,isabella.mastroeni}@univr.it

**Abstract.** Modern software is no more developed in a single programming language. Instead, programmers tend to exploit *cross-language interoperability mechanisms* to combine code stemming from different languages, and thus yielding fully-fledged *multi-language programs*. Whilst this approach enables developers to benefit from the strengths of each single-language, on the other hand it complicates the semantics of such programs. Indeed, the resulting multi-language does not meet any of the semantics of the combined languages. In this paper, we broaden the *boundary functions*-based approach à la Matthews and Findler to propose an algebraic framework that provides a constructive mathematical notion of *multi-language* able to determine its *semantics*. The aim of this work is to overcome the lack of a formal method (resp., model) to design (resp., represent) a multi-language, regardless of the inherent nature of the underlying languages. We show that our construction ensures the uniqueness of the *semantic function* (i.e., the multi-language semantics induced by the combined languages) by proving the *initiality* of the term model (i.e., the abstract syntax of the multi-language) in its category.

**Keywords:** Multi-language design · Program semantics · Interoperability

## 1 Introduction

Two elementary arguments lie at the heart of the *multi-language paradigm*: the large availability of existing programming languages, along with a very high number of already written libraries, and software that, in general, needs to *interoperate*. Although there is consensus in claiming that there is no best programming language regardless of the context [4,8], it is equally true that many of them are conceived and designed in order to excel for specific tasks. Such examples are R for statistical and graphical computation, Perl for data wrangling, Assembly and C for low-level memory management, etc. *"Interoperability between languages has been a problem since the second programming language was invented"* [8], so it is hardly surprising that developers have focused on the design of *cross-language interoperability mechanisms*, enabling programmers to combine code written in different languages. In this sense, we speak of *multi-languages*.

The field of cross-language interoperability has been driven more by practical concerns than by theoretical questions. The current scenario sees several engines and frameworks [13,28,29,44,47] (among others) to mix programming languages but only [30] discusses the semantic issues related to the multi-language design from a theoretical perspective. Moreover, the existing interoperability mechanisms differ considerably not only from the viewpoint of the combined languages, but also in terms of the approach used to provide the interoperation. For instance, Nashorn [47] is a JavaScript interpreter written in Java to allow embedding JavaScript in Java applications. Such engineering design works in a similar fashion of *embedded interpreters* [40,41].[1] On the contrary, Java Native Interface (JNI) framework [29] enables the interoperation of Java with native code written in C, C++, or Assembly through external procedure calls between languages, mirroring the widespread mechanism of *foreign function interfaces (FFI)* [14], whereas theoretical papers follow the more elegant approach of *boundary functions* (or, for short, *boundaries*) in the style of Matthews and Findler's multi-language semantics [30]. Simply put, boundaries act as a gate between single-languages. When a value needs to flow on the other language, they perform a conversion so that it complies to the other language specifications.

The major issue concerning this new paradigm is that multi-language programs do not obey any of the semantics of the combined languages. As a consequence, any method of formal reasoning (such as static program analysis or verification) is neutralized by the absence of a semantics specification. In this paper, we propose an algebraic framework based on the mechanism of boundary functions [30] that unambiguously yields the syntax and the semantics of the multi-language regardless the combined languages.

*The Lack of a Multi-Language Framework.* The notion of *multi-language* is employed naively in several works in literature [2,14,21,30,35–37,49] to indicate the embedding of two programming languages into a new one, with its own syntax and semantics.

The most recurring way to design a multi-language is to exploit a mechanism (like embedded interpreters, FFI, or boundary functions) able to regulate both control flow and value conversion between the underlying languages [30], thus adequate to provide *cross-language interoperability* [8]. The full construction is usually carried out manually by language designers, which define the multi-language by reusing the formal specifications of the single-languages [2,30,36,37] and by applying the selected mechanism for achieving the interoperation. Inevitably, therefore, all these resulting multi-languages notably differ one from another.

These different ways to achieve a cross-language interoperation are all attributable to the lack of a formal description of multi-language that does not provide neither a method for language designers to conceive new multi-languages nor any guarantee on the correctness of such constructions.

[1] Other popular engines that obey the embedded interpreters paradigm are Jython [28], JScript [44], and Rhino [13].

*The Proposed Framework: Roadmap and Contributions.* Matthews and Findler [30] propose *boundary functions* as a way to regulate the flow of values between languages. They show their approach on different variants of the same multi-language obtained by mixing ML [33] and Scheme [9], representing two "syntactically sugared" versions of the simply-typed and untyped lambda calculi, respectively.

Rather than showing the embedding of two fixed languages, we extend their approach to the much broader class of *order-sorted algebras* [19] with the aim of providing a framework that works regardless of the inherent nature of the combined languages. There are a number of reasons to choose order-sorted algebras as the underlying framework for generalizing the multi-language construction. From the first formulation of *initial algebra semantics* [17], the algebraic approach to program semantics [16] has become a cornerstone in the theory of programming languages [27]. Order-sorted algebras provide a mathematical tool for representing formal systems as algebraic structures through a systematic use of the notion of *sort* and *subsort* to model different forms of polymorphism [18,19], a key aspect when dealing with multi-languages sharing operators among the single-languages. They were initially proposed to ensure a rigorous model-theoretic semantics for error handling, multiple inheritance, retracts, selectors for multiple constructors, polymorphism, and overloading. In the years, several uses [3,6,11,24,25,38,39,52] and different variants [38,43,45, 51] have been proposed for order-sorted algebras, making them a solid starting point for the development of a new framework. In particular, results on *rewriting logic* [32] extend easily to the order-sorted case [31], thus facilitating a future extension of this paper towards the *operational semantics* world. Improvements of the order-sorted algebra framework have also been proposed to model languages together with their type systems [10] and to extend order-sorted specification with high-order functions [38] (see [48] and [18] for detailed surveys).

In this paper, we propose three different multi-language constructions according to the semantic properties of boundary functions. The first one models a general notion of multi-language that do not require any constraints on boundaries (Sect. 3). We argue that when such generality is superfluous, we can achieve a neater approach where boundary functions do not need to be annotated with sorts. Indeed, we show that when the cross-language conversion of a term does not depend on the sort at which the term is considered (i.e., when boundaries are *subsort polymorphic*) the framework is powerful enough to apply the correct conversion (Sect. 4.1). This last construction is an improvement of the original notion of boundaries in [30]. From a practical point of view, it allows programmers to avoid to explicitly deal with sorts when writing code, a non-trivial task that could introduce type cast bugs in real world languages. Finally, we provide a very specific notion of multi-language where no extra operator is added to the syntax (Sect. 4.2). This approach is particularly useful to extend a language in a modular fashion and ensuring the backward compatibility with "old" programs. For each one of these variants we prove an *initiality theorem*, which in turn ensures the uniqueness of the multi-language semantics and thereby legitimating the proposed framework. Moreover, we show that the framework guarantees a fundamental closure property on the construction: The resulting multi-language admits an order-sorted representation, i.e., it falls within the same formal model of the combined languages. Finally, we model the multi-language designed in [30] in order to show an instantiation of the framework (Sect. 6).

## 2 Background

All the algebraic background of the paper is firstly stated in [15,17,19]. We briefly introduce here the main definitions and results, and we illustrate them on a simple running example.

Given a *set of sorts* $S$, an *$S$-sorted set* $A$ is a family of sets indexed by $S$, i.e., $A = \{ A_s \mid s \in S \}$. Similarly, an *$S$-sorted function* $f\colon A \to B$ is a family of functions $f = \{ f_s\colon A_s \to B_s \mid s \in S \}$. We stick to the convention of using $s$ and $w$ as metavariables for sorts in $S$ and $S^*$, respectively, and we use the blackboard bold typeface to indicate a specific sort in $S$. In addition, if $A$ is an $S$-sorted set and $w = s_1 \dots s_n \in S^+$, we denote by $A_w$ the cartesian product $A_{s_1} \times \cdots \times A_{s_n}$. Likewise, if $f$ is an $S$-sorted function and $a_i \in A_{s_i}$ for $i = 1, \dots, n$, then the function $f_w\colon A_w \to B_w$ is such that $f_w(a_1, \dots, a_n) = (f_{s_1}(a_1), \dots, f_{s_n}(a_n))$. Given $P \subseteq S$, the restriction of an $S$-sorted function $f$ to $P$ is denoted by $f|_P$ and it is the $P$-sorted function $f|_P = \{ f_s \mid s \in P \}$. Finally, if $g\colon A \to B$ is a function, we still use the symbol $g$ to denote the *direct image map of $g$* (also called the *additive lift* of $g$), i.e., the function $g\colon \wp(A) \to \wp(B)$ such that $g(X) = \{ g(a) \in B \mid a \in X \}$. Analogously, if $\leq$ is a binary relation on a set $A$ (with elements $a \in A$), we use the same relation symbol to denote its *pointwise extension*, i.e., we write $a_1 \dots a_n \leq a'_1 \dots a'_n$ for $a_1 \leq a'_1, \dots, a_n \leq a'_n$.

The basic notions underpinning the order-sorted algebra framework are the definitions of *signature*, that models symbols forming terms of the language, and *algebra*, that provides an algebraic meaning to symbols.

**Definition 1 (Order-Sorted Signature).** *An* order-sorted signature *is a triple $\langle S, \leq, \Sigma \rangle$, where $S$ is a set of sorts, $\leq$ is a binary relation on $S$, and $\Sigma$ is an $S^* \times S$-sorted set $\Sigma = \{ \Sigma_{w,s} \mid w \in S^* \wedge s \in S \}$, satisfying the following conditions:*

*(1os) $\langle S, \leq \rangle$ is a poset; and*
*(2os) $\sigma \in \Sigma_{w_1,s_1} \cap \Sigma_{w_2,s_2}$ and $w_1 \leq w_2$ imply $s_1 \leq s_2$.*

If $\sigma \in \Sigma_{w,s}$ (or, $\sigma\colon w \to s$ and $\sigma\colon s$ when $w = \varepsilon$, as shorthands), we call $\sigma$ an *operator* (*symbol*) or *function symbol*, $w$ the *arity*, $s$ the *sort*, and $(w, s)$ the *rank* of $\sigma$; if $w = \varepsilon$, we say that $\sigma$ is a *constant* (*symbol*). We name $\leq$ the *subsort relation* and $\Sigma$ a *signature* when $\langle S, \leq \rangle$ is clear from the context. We abuse notation and write $\sigma \in \Sigma$ when $\sigma \in \bigcup_{w,s} \Sigma_{w,s}$.

**Definition 2 (Order-Sorted Algebra).** *An* order-sorted $\langle S, \leq, \Sigma \rangle$-algebra $\mathcal{A}$ *over an order-sorted signature* $\langle S, \leq, \Sigma \rangle$ *is an S-sorted set A of* interpretation domains *(or,* carrier sets *or* semantic domains*)* $A = \{ A_s \mid s \in S \}$, *together with* interpretation functions $[\![\sigma]\!]_{\mathcal{A}}^{w,s} \colon A_w \to A_s$ *(or, if* $w = \varepsilon$, $[\![\sigma]\!]_{\mathcal{A}}^{\varepsilon,s} \in A_s$*)*[2] *for each* $\sigma \in \Sigma_{w,s}$, *such that:*

*(1oa)* $s \leq s'$ *implies* $A_s \subseteq A_{s'}$*; and*
*(2oa)* $\sigma \in \Sigma_{w_1,s_1} \cap \Sigma_{w_2,s_2}$ *and* $w_1 \leq w_2$ *imply that* $[\![\sigma]\!]_{\mathcal{A}}^{w_1,s_1}(a) = [\![\sigma]\!]_{\mathcal{A}}^{w_2,s_2}(a)$ *for each* $a \in A_{w_1}$.

An important property of signatures, related to polymorphism, is *regularity.* Its relevance lies in the possibility of linking each term to a unique least sort (see Proposition 2.10 in [19]).

**Definition 3 (Regularity of an Order-Sorted Signature).** *An order-sorted signature* $\langle S, \leq, \Sigma \rangle$ *is* regular *if for each* $\sigma \in \Sigma_{\tilde{w},\tilde{s}}$ *and for each* lower bound $w_0 \leq \tilde{w}$ *the set* $\{ (w, s) \mid \sigma \in \Sigma_{w,s} \wedge w_0 \leq w \}$ *has minimum. This minimum is called least rank of* $\sigma$ *with respect to* $w_0$.

The freely generated algebra $\mathcal{T}_\Sigma$ over a given signature $\mathfrak{S} = \langle S, \leq, \Sigma \rangle$ provides the notion of *term* with respect to $\mathfrak{S}$.

**Definition 4 (Order-Sorted Term Algebra).** *Let* $\langle S, \leq, \Sigma \rangle$ *be an order-sorted signature. The* order-sorted term $\langle S, \leq, \Sigma \rangle$-algebra $\mathcal{T}_\Sigma$ *is an order-sorted algebra such that:*

- *The S-sorted set* $T_\Sigma = \{ T_{\Sigma,s} \mid s \in S \}$ *is inductively defined as the least family satisfying:*

*(1ot)* $\Sigma_{\varepsilon,s} \subseteq T_{\Sigma,s}$;
*(2ot)* $s \leq s'$ *implies* $T_{\Sigma,s} \subseteq T_{\Sigma,s'}$*; and*
*(3ot)* $\sigma \in \Sigma_{w,s}$, $w = s_1 \ldots s_n \in S^+$, *and* $t_i \in T_{\Sigma,s_i}$ *for* $i = 1, \ldots, n$ *imply* $\sigma(t_1 \ldots t_n) \in T_{\Sigma,s}$.

- *For each* $\sigma \in \Sigma_{w,s}$ *the interpretation function* $[\![\sigma]\!]_{\mathcal{T}_\Sigma}^{w,s} \colon T_{\Sigma,w} \to T_{\Sigma,s}$ *is defined as*

*(4ot)* $[\![\sigma]\!]_{\mathcal{T}_\Sigma}^{\varepsilon,s} = \sigma$ *if* $\sigma \in \Sigma_{\varepsilon,s}$*; and*
*(5ot)* $[\![\sigma]\!]_{\mathcal{T}_\Sigma}^{w,s}(t_1, \ldots, t_n) = \sigma(t_1 \ldots t_n)$ *if* $\sigma \in \Sigma_{w,s}$, $w = s_1 \ldots s_n \in S^+$, *and* $t_i \in T_{\Sigma,s_i}$ *for* $i = 1, \ldots, n$.

Homomorphisms between algebras capture the *compositionality* nature of semantics: The meaning of a term is determined by the meanings of its constituents. They are defined as order-sorted functions that preserve the interpretation of operators.

[2] To be pedantic, we should introduce the *one-point domain* $A_\varepsilon = \{ \bullet \}$ and then define $[\![\sigma]\!]_{\mathcal{A}}^{\varepsilon,s}(\bullet) \in A_s$.

$e ::= n \mid e + e \quad \text{where } n \in \mathbb{N}$

(a) The BNF grammar of $L_1$.

$s ::= \texttt{-} \mid a \mid s + s \quad \text{where } a \in \mathbb{A}$

(b) The BNF grammar of $L_2$.

**Fig. 1.** The BNF grammars of the running example languages.

$$\begin{cases} [\![n]\!] = n \\ [\![e + e']\!] = [\![e]\!] + [\![e']\!] \end{cases}$$

(a) The formal semantics of $L_1$.

$$\begin{cases} [\![\texttt{-}]\!] = \varepsilon \\ [\![a]\!] = a \\ [\![s + \texttt{-}]\!] = [\![\texttt{-} + s]\!] = [\![s]\!] \\ [\![s + \texttt{-} + s']\!] = [\![s + s']\!] \\ [\![a_0 + \ldots + a_n]\!] = a_0 \ldots a_n \quad n > 0 \end{cases}$$

(b) The formal semantics of $L_2$.

**Fig. 2.** The two formal semantics of the running example languages.

**Definition 5 (Order-Sorted Homomorphism).** *Let $\mathcal{A}$ and $\mathcal{B}$ be $\langle S, \leq, \Sigma\rangle$-algebras. An* order-sorted $\langle S, \leq, \Sigma\rangle$-homomorphism *from $\mathcal{A}$ to $\mathcal{B}$, denoted by $h\colon \mathcal{A} \to \mathcal{B}$, is an $S$-sorted function $h\colon A \to B = \{ h_s\colon A_s \to B_s \mid s \in S \}$ such that:*

*(1oh) $h_s([\![\sigma]\!]^{w,s}_{\mathcal{A}}(a)) = [\![\sigma]\!]^{w,s}_{\mathcal{B}}(h_w(a))$ for each $\sigma \in \Sigma_{w,s}$ and $a \in A_w$; and*
*(2oh) $s \leq s'$ implies $h_s(a) = h_{s'}(a)$ for each $a \in A_s$.*

The class of all the order-sorted $\langle S, \leq, \Sigma\rangle$-algebras and the class of all order-sorted $\langle S, \leq, \Sigma\rangle$-homomorphisms form a category denote by $\mathbf{OSAlg}(S, \leq, \Sigma)$. Furthermore, the homomorphism definition determines the property of the term algebra $\mathcal{T}_\Sigma$ of being an *initial object* in its category whenever the signature is *regular*. Since *initiality* is preserved by isomorphisms, it allows to identify $\mathcal{T}_\Sigma$ with the *abstract syntax* of the language. If $\mathcal{T}_\Sigma$ is initial, the homomorphism leaving $\mathcal{T}_\Sigma$ and going to an algebra $\mathcal{A}$ is called the *semantic function* (with respect to $\mathcal{A}$).

**Example.** Let $L_1$ and $L_2$ be two formal languages (see Fig. 1). The former is a language to construct simple mathematical expressions: $n \in \mathbb{N}$ is the metavariable for natural numbers, while $e$ inductively generates all the possible additions (Fig. 1a). The latter is a language to build strings over a finite alphabet of symbols $\mathbb{A} = \{ \mathsf{a}, \mathsf{b}, \ldots, \mathsf{z} \}$: $a \in \mathbb{A}$ is the metavariable for atoms (or, characters), whereas $s$ concatenates them into strings (Fig. 1b). A term in $L_1$ and $L_2$ denotes an element in the sets $\mathbb{N}$ and $\mathbb{A}^*$, accordingly to equations in Fig. 2a and b, respectively.

The syntax of the language $L_1$ can be modeled by an order-sorted signature $\mathfrak{S}_1 = \langle S_1, \leq_1, \Sigma_1\rangle$ defined as follows: $S_1 = \{ \mathbb{e}, \mathbb{n} \}$, a set with sorts $\mathbb{e}$ (stands for *expressions*) and $\mathbb{n}$ (stands for *natural numbers*); $\leq_1$ is the reflexive relation on $S_1$ plus $\mathbb{n} \leq_1 \mathbb{e}$ (natural numbers are expressions); and the operators in $\Sigma_1$ are $0, 1, 2, \ldots : \mathbb{n}$ and $+\colon \mathbb{e}\,\mathbb{e} \to \mathbb{e}$. Similarly, the signature $\mathfrak{S}_2 = \langle S_2, \leq_2, \Sigma_2\rangle$ models the syntax of the language $L_2$: the set $S_2 = \{ \mathbb{s}, \mathbb{a} \}$ carries the sort for *strings*

$\mathbb{s}$ and the sort for *atomic symbols* (or, characters) $\mathbb{a}$; the subsort relation $\leq_2$ is the reflexive relation on $S_2$ plus $\mathbb{a} \leq_2 \mathbb{s}$ (characters are one-symbol strings); and the operator symbols in $\Sigma_2$ are $\mathtt{a}, \ldots, \mathtt{z} \colon \mathbb{a}$, $\mathtt{-} \colon \mathbb{s}$, and $\mathtt{+} \colon \mathbb{s}\,\mathbb{s} \to \mathbb{s}$. Semantics of $L_1$ and $L_2$ can be embodied by algebras $\mathcal{A}_1$ and $\mathcal{A}_2$ over the signatures $\mathfrak{S}_1$ and $\mathfrak{S}_2$, respectively. We set the interpretation domains of $\mathcal{A}_1$ to $A^1_{\mathbb{n}} = A^1_{\mathbb{e}} = \mathbb{N}$ and those of $\mathcal{A}_2$ to $A^2_{\mathbb{a}} = \mathbb{A} \subseteq \mathbb{A}^* = A^2_{\mathbb{s}}$. Moreover, we define the interpretation functions as follows (the juxtaposition of two or more strings denotes their concatenation, and we use $\hat{a}$ as metavariable ranging over $\mathbb{A}^*$):

$$\begin{cases} [\![n]\!]^{\varepsilon,\mathbb{n}}_{\mathcal{A}_1} = n \\ [\![\mathtt{+}]\!]^{\mathbb{e}\,\mathbb{e},\mathbb{e}}_{\mathcal{A}_1}(n_1, n_2) = n_1 + n_2 \end{cases} \qquad \begin{cases} [\![\mathtt{-}]\!]^{\varepsilon,\mathbb{s}}_{\mathcal{A}_2} = \varepsilon \\ [\![a]\!]^{\varepsilon,\mathbb{a}}_{\mathcal{A}_2} = a \\ [\![\mathtt{+}]\!]^{\mathbb{s}\,\mathbb{s},\mathbb{s}}_{\mathcal{A}_2}(\hat{a}_1, \hat{a}_2) = \hat{a}_1\hat{a}_2 \end{cases}$$

Since $\mathfrak{S}_1$ and $\mathfrak{S}_2$ are regular, then $\mathcal{A}_1$ and $\mathcal{A}_2$ induce the semantic functions $h_1 \colon \mathcal{T}_{\Sigma_1} \to \mathcal{A}_1$ and $h_2 \colon \mathcal{T}_{\Sigma_2} \to \mathcal{A}_2$, providing semantics to the languages.

## 3 Combining Order-Sorted Theories

The first step towards a multi-language specification is the choice of which terms of one language can be employed in the others [30, 35, 36]. For instance, a multi-language requirement could demand to use ML expressions in place of Scheme expressions and, possibly, but not necessarily, vice versa (such a multi-language is designed in [30]). A *multi-language signature* is an amenable formalism to specify the compatibility relation between syntactic categories across two languages.

**Definition 6 (Multi-Language Signature).** *A* multi-language signature *is a triple $\langle \mathfrak{S}_1, \mathfrak{S}_2, \leq \rangle$, where $\mathfrak{S}_1 = \langle S_1, \leq_1, \Sigma_1 \rangle$ and $\mathfrak{S}_2 = \langle S_2, \leq_2, \Sigma_2 \rangle$ are order-sorted signatures, and $\leq$ is a binary relation on $S = S_1 \cup S_2$, such that satisfies the following condition:*

*(1s) $s, s' \in S_i$ implies $s \leq s'$ if and only if $s \leq_i s'$, for $i = 1, 2$.*

*To make the notation lighter, we introduce the following binary relations on $S$: $s \ltimes s'$ if $s \leq s'$ but neither $s \leq_1 s'$ nor $s \leq_2 s'$, and $s \preccurlyeq s'$ if $s \leq s'$ but not $s \ltimes s'$.*

In the following, we always assume that the sets of sorts $S_1$ and $S_2$ of the order-sorted signatures $\mathfrak{S}_1$ and $\mathfrak{S}_2$ are disjoint.[3] Condition (1s) requires the *multi-language subsort relation* $\leq$ to *preserve* the original subsort relations $\leq_1$ and $\leq_2$ (i.e., $\leq \cap\, S_i \times S_i = \leq_i$). The *join relation* $\ltimes$ provides a compatibility relation between sorts[4] in $\mathfrak{S}_1$ and $\mathfrak{S}_2$. More precisely, $S_i \ni s \ltimes s' \in S_j$ suggests that we want to use terms in $\mathcal{T}_{\Sigma_i,s}$ in place of terms in $\mathcal{T}_{\Sigma_j,s'}$, whereas the *intra-language*

[3] This hypothesis is non-restrictive: We can always perform a renaming of the sorts.

[4] Sorts may be understood as syntactic categories, in the sense of formal grammars. Given a context-free grammar $G$, it is possible to define a many-sorted signature $\Sigma_G$ where non-terminals become sorts and such that each term $t$ in the term algebra $\mathcal{T}_{\Sigma_G}$ is isomorphic to the parse tree of $t$ with respect to $G$ (see [15] for details).

*subsort relation* $\preccurlyeq$ shifts the standard notion of subsort from the order-sorted to the multi-language world. In a nutshell, the relation $\leq\, = \,\preccurlyeq \cup \ltimes$ can only join (through $\ltimes$) the underlying languages without introducing distortions (indeed, $\preccurlyeq\, = \,\leq_1 \cup \leq_2$).

The role of an algebra is to provide an interpretation domain for each sort, as well as the meaning of every operator symbol in a given signature. When moving towards the multi-language context, the join relation $\ltimes$ may add subsort constraints between sorts belonging to different signatures. Consequently, if $s \ltimes s'$, a multi-language algebra has to specify how values of sort $s$ may be interpreted as values of sort $s'$. These specifications are called *boundary functions* [30] and provide an algebraic meaning to the subsort constraints added by $\ltimes$. Henceforth, we define $S = S_1 \cup S_2$, $\Sigma = \Sigma_1 \cup \Sigma_2$, and, given $(w, s) \in S_i^* \times S_i$, we denote by $\Sigma^i_{w,s}$ the $(w, s)$-sorted component in $\Sigma_i$.

**Definition 7 (Multi-Language Algebra).** *Let $\langle \mathfrak{S}_1, \mathfrak{S}_2, \leq\rangle$ be a multi-language signature. A* multi-language $\langle \mathfrak{S}_1, \mathfrak{S}_2, \leq\rangle$-algebra $\mathcal{A}$ *is an $S$-sorted set $A$ of* interpretation domains *(or,* carrier sets *or* semantic domains*) $A = \{ A_s \mid s \in S \}$, together with* interpretation functions $[\![\sigma]\!]^{w,s}_{\mathcal{A}} \colon A_w \to A_s$ *for each $\sigma \in \Sigma_{w,s}$, and with a $\ltimes$-sorted set $\alpha$ of* boundary functions $\alpha = \{ \alpha_{s,s'} \colon A_s \to A_{s'} \mid s \ltimes s' \}$, *such that the following constraint holds:*

*(1a) the* projected algebra *$\mathcal{A}_i$, where $i = 1, 2$, specified by the carrier set $A_i = \{ A^i_s = A_s \mid s \in S_i \}$ and interpretation functions $[\![\sigma]\!]^{w,s}_{\mathcal{A}_i} = [\![\sigma]\!]^{w,s}_{\mathcal{A}}$ for each $\sigma \in \Sigma^i_{w,s}$, must be an order-sorted $\mathfrak{S}_i$-algebra.*

If $\mathcal{M}$ is an algebra, we adopt the convention of denoting by $M$ (standard math font) its carrier set and by $\mu$ (Greek math font) its boundary functions whenever possible. Condition (1a) is the semantic counterpart of condition (1s): It requires the multi-language to carry (i.e., preserve) the underlying languages order-sorted algebras, whereas the boundary functions model how values can flow between languages.

Given two multi-language $\langle \mathfrak{S}_1, \mathfrak{S}_2, \leq\rangle$-algebras $\mathcal{A}$ and $\mathcal{B}$ we can define morphisms between them that preserve the sorted structure of the underlying projected algebras.

**Definition 8 (Multi-Language Homomorphism).** *Let $\mathcal{A}$ and $\mathcal{B}$ be multi-language $\langle \mathfrak{S}_1, \mathfrak{S}_2, \leq\rangle$-algebras with sets of boundary functions $\alpha$ and $\beta$, respectively. A* multi-language $\langle \mathfrak{S}_1, \mathfrak{S}_2, \leq\rangle$-homomorphism *$h \colon \mathcal{A} \to \mathcal{B}$ is an $S$-sorted function $h \colon A \to B$ such that:*

*(1h) the restriction $h|_{S_i}$ is an order-sorted $\mathfrak{S}_i$-homomorphism $h|_{S_i} \colon \mathcal{A}_i \to \mathcal{B}_i$, for $i = 1, 2$; and*
*(2h) $s \ltimes s'$ implies $h_{s'} \circ \alpha_{s,s'} = \beta_{s,s'} \circ h_s$.*

Conditions (1h) and (2h) are easily intelligible when the domain algebra is the abstract syntax of the language [15]: Simply put, both conditions require the semantics of a term to be a function of the meaning of its subterms, in the sense of [15,46]. In particular, the second condition demands that boundary functions act as operators.[5]

The identity homomorphism on a multi-language algebra $\mathcal{A}$ is denoted by $\mathrm{id}_{\mathcal{A}}$ and it is the set-theoretic identity on the carrier set $A$ of the algebra $\mathcal{A}$. The composition of two homomorphisms $f\colon \mathcal{A} \to \mathcal{B}$ and $g\colon \mathcal{B} \to \mathcal{C}$ is defined as the sorted function composition $g \circ f\colon A \to C$, thus $\mathrm{id}_{\mathcal{A}} \circ f = f = f \circ \mathrm{id}_{\mathcal{B}}$ and associativity follows easily by the definition of $\circ$.

**Proposition 1.** *Multi-language homomorphisms are closed under composition.*

Hence, as in the many-sorted and order-sorted case [15,19], we have immediately the category of all the multi-language algebras over a multi-language signature:

**Theorem 1.** *Let $\langle \mathfrak{S}_1, \mathfrak{S}_2, \leq \rangle$ be a multi-language signature. The class of all $\langle \mathfrak{S}_1, \mathfrak{S}_2, \leq \rangle$-algebras and the class of all $\langle \mathfrak{S}_1, \mathfrak{S}_2, \leq \rangle$-homomorphisms form a category denoted by $\mathbf{Alg}(\mathfrak{S}_1, \mathfrak{S}_2, \leq)$.*

### 3.1 The Initial Term Model

In this section, we introduce the concepts of *(multi-language) term* and *(multi-language) semantics* in order to show how a multi-language algebra yields a unique interpretation for any *regular* (see Definition 11) multi-language specification.

Multi-language terms should comprise all of the underlying languages terms, plus those obtained by the merging of the two languages according to the join relation $\ltimes$. In particular, we aim for a construction where subterms of sort $s'$ may have been replaced by terms of sort $s$, whenever $s \ltimes s'$ (we recall that $s$ and $s'$ are two syntactic categories of different languages due to Definition 6). Nonetheless, we must be careful not to add ambiguities during this process: A term $t$ may belong to both $\mathfrak{S}_1$ and $\mathfrak{S}_2$ term algebras but with different meanings $[\![t]\!]_{\mathcal{A}_1}$ and $[\![t]\!]_{\mathcal{A}_2}$ (assuming that $\mathcal{A}_1$ and $\mathcal{A}_2$ are algebras over $\mathfrak{S}_1$ and $\mathfrak{S}_2$, respectively). When $t$ is included in the multi-language, we lose the information to determine which one of the two interpretations choose, thus making the (multi-language) semantics of $t$ ambiguous. The same problem arises whenever an operator $\sigma$ belongs to both languages with different interpretation functions. The simplest solution to avoid such issues is to add syntactical notations to make explicit the context of the language in which we are operating.

**Definition 9 (Associated Signature).** *The* associated signature *to the multi-language signature $\langle \mathfrak{S}_1, \mathfrak{S}_2, \leq \rangle$ is the ordered triple $\langle S, \preccurlyeq, \Pi \rangle$, where $S = S_1 \cup S_2$, $\preccurlyeq = \leq_1 \cup \leq_2$, and*

$$\begin{aligned} \Pi = &\{\, \sigma_1\colon w \to s \mid \sigma\colon w \to s \in \Sigma_1 \,\} \\ \cup &\{\, \sigma_2\colon w \to s \mid \sigma\colon w \to s \in \Sigma_2 \,\} \\ \cup &\{\, \hookrightarrow_{s,s'}\colon s \to s' \mid s \ltimes s' \,\} \end{aligned}$$

[5] This is essential in order to generalize the concept of syntactical boundary functions of [30] to semantic-only functions in Sect. 4.2.

It is trivial to prove that an associated signature is indeed an order-sorted signature, thus admitting a term algebra $\mathcal{T}_\Pi$. All the symbols forming terms in $\mathcal{T}_\Pi$ carry the source language information as a subscript, and all the new operators $\hookrightarrow_{s,s'}$ specify when a term of sort $s$ is used in place of a term of sort $s'$. Although $\mathcal{T}_\Pi$ seems a suitable definition for multi-language terms, it is not a multi-language algebra according to Definition 7. However, we can exploit the construction of $\mathcal{T}_\Pi$ in order to provide a fully-fledged multi-language algebra able to generate multi-language terms.

**Definition 10 (Multi-Language Term Algebra).** *The* multi-language term algebra $\mathcal{T}$ *over a multi-language signature* $\langle \mathfrak{S}_1, \mathfrak{S}_2, \leq \rangle$ *with boundary functions* $\tau$ *is defined as follows:*

*(1t)* $s \in S$ *implies* $T_s = T_{\Pi,s}$*;*
*(2t)* $\sigma \in \Sigma^i_{w,s}$ *implies* $[\![\sigma]\!]^{w,s}_{\mathcal{T}} = [\![\sigma_i]\!]^{w,s}_{\mathcal{T}_\Pi}$ *for* $i = 1, 2$*; and*
*(3t)* $s \ltimes s'$ *implies* $\tau_{s,s'} = [\![\hookrightarrow_{s,s'}]\!]^{s,s'}_{\mathcal{T}_\Pi}$.

Proving that $\mathcal{T}$ satisfies Definition 7 is easy and omitted. $\mathcal{T}$ and $\mathcal{T}_\Pi$ share the same carrier sets (condition (1t)), and each single-language operator $\sigma \in \Sigma^i_{w,s}$ is interpreted as its annotated version $\sigma_i$ in $\mathcal{T}_\Pi$ (condition (2t)). Furthermore, the multi-language operators $\hookrightarrow_{s,s'}$ no longer belong to the signature (they do not belong neither to $\mathfrak{S}_1$ nor to $\mathfrak{S}_2$) but their semantics is inherited by the boundary functions $\tau$ (condition (3t)), while their syntactic values are still in the carrier sets of the algebra (this construction is highly technical and very similar to the freely generated $\Sigma(X)$-algebra over a set of variables $X$, see [15]).

Note that this is exactly the formalization of the ad hoc multi-language specifications in [2,30,36,37]: [2,36,37] exploit distinct colors to disambiguate the source language of the operators, whereas [30] use different font styles for different languages. Moreover, boundary functions in [30] conceptually match the introduced operators $\hookrightarrow_{s,s'}$.

The last step in order to finalize the framework is to provide semantics for each term in $\mathcal{T}$. As with the order-sorted case, we need a notion of *regularity* for proving the initiality of the term algebra in its category, which in turn ensures a single eligible *(initial algebra) semantics.*

**Definition 11 (Regularity).** *A multi-language signature* $\langle \mathfrak{S}_1, \mathfrak{S}_2, \leq \rangle$ *is* regular *if its associated signature* $\langle S, \preccurlyeq, \Pi \rangle$ *is regular.*

**Proposition 2.** *The associated signature* $\langle S, \preccurlyeq, \Pi \rangle$ *of a multi-language signature* $\langle \mathfrak{S}_1, \mathfrak{S}_2, \leq \rangle$ *is regular if and only if* $\mathfrak{S}_1$ *and* $\mathfrak{S}_2$ *are regular.*

The last proposition enables to avoid checking the multi-language regularity whenever the regularity of the order-sorted signatures is known.

**Theorem 2 (Initiality of $\mathcal{T}$).** *The multi-language term algebra* $\mathcal{T}$ *over a regular multi-language signature* $\langle \mathfrak{S}_1, \mathfrak{S}_2, \leq \rangle$ *is initial in the category* $\mathbf{Alg}(\mathfrak{S}_1, \mathfrak{S}_2, \leq)$.

Initiality of $\mathcal{T}$ is essential to assign a unique mathematical meaning to each term, as in the order-sorted case: Given a multi-language algebra $\mathcal{A}$, there is only one way of interpreting each term $t \in \mathcal{T}$ in $\mathcal{A}$ (satisfying the homomorphism conditions).

**Definition 12 ((Multi-Language) Semantics).** *Let $\mathcal{A}$ be a multi-language algebra over a regular multi-language signature $\langle \mathfrak{S}_1, \mathfrak{S}_2, \leq \rangle$. The* (multi-language) semantics *of a (multi-language) term $t \in \mathcal{T}$ induced by $\mathcal{A}$ is defined as*

$$[\![t]\!]_{\mathcal{A}} = h_{\mathrm{ls}(t)}(t)$$

The last equation is well-defined since $h$ is the unique multi-language homomorphism $h \colon \mathcal{T} \to \mathcal{A}$ and for each $t \in \mathcal{T}$ there exists a least sort $\mathrm{ls}(t) \in S$ such that $t \in T_{\Pi,\mathrm{ls}(t)}$ (see Prop. 2.10 in [19]).

**Example.** Suppose we are interested in a multi-language over the signatures $\mathfrak{S}_1$ and $\mathfrak{S}_2$ specified in the example given in the background section such that satisfies the following properties:

- Terms denoting natural numbers can be used in place of characters $a \in \mathbb{A}$ according to the function $\mathrm{chr} \colon \mathbb{N} \to \mathbb{A}$ that maps the natural number $n$ to the character symbol $a^{(n \mod |\mathbb{A}|)}$ (we are assuming a total lexicographical order $a^{(0)}, a^{(1)}, \ldots, a^{(|A|-1)}$ on $\mathbb{A}$);
- Terms denoting strings can be used in place of natural numbers $n \in \mathbb{N}$ according to the function $\mathrm{ord} \colon \mathbb{A} \to \mathbb{N}$, which is the inverse of chr restricted the initial segment on natural numbers $\mathbb{N}_{<|A|}$.

In order to achieve such a multi-language specification, we can simply provide a join relation $\ltimes$ on $S$ and a boundary function $\alpha_{s,s'}$ for each extra-language subsort relation $s \ltimes s'$ introduced by $\ltimes$. We define the join relation and the boundary functions as follows:

$$\mathbb{e} \ltimes \mathbb{a} \quad \wedge \quad \mathbb{n} \ltimes \mathbb{a} \quad \longrightarrow \quad \alpha_{\mathbb{e},\mathbb{a}}(n) = \alpha_{\mathbb{n},\mathbb{a}}(n) = \mathrm{chr}(n)$$

$$\mathbb{s} \ltimes \mathbb{n} \quad \wedge \quad \mathbb{a} \ltimes \mathbb{n} \quad \longrightarrow \quad \begin{cases} \alpha_{\mathbb{a},\mathbb{n}}(a) = \mathrm{ord}(a) \\ \alpha_{\mathbb{s},\mathbb{n}}(a_0 \ldots a_n) = \displaystyle\sum_{k=0}^{n} \alpha_{\mathbb{a},\mathbb{n}}(a_k) \cdot 10^k \end{cases}$$

The multi-language $\langle \mathfrak{S}_1, \mathfrak{S}_2, \leq \rangle$-algebra $\mathcal{A}$ can now be obtained by joining the projected algebras $\mathcal{A}_1$ and $\mathcal{A}_2$ with the set of boundary functions $\alpha$. The term algebra $\mathcal{T}$ over $\langle \mathfrak{S}_1, \mathfrak{S}_2, \leq \rangle$ provides all the multi-language terms, and Theorem 2 ensures a unique denotation of each $t \in \mathcal{T}$ in $\mathcal{A}$. For instance, the term

$$t = \hookrightarrow_{\mathbb{s},\mathbb{n}}(\underbrace{+_2(\mathtt{f}_2, \overbrace{+_2(\mathtt{o}_2, \underbrace{\hookrightarrow_{\mathbb{e},\mathbb{a}}(\overbrace{+_1(10_1, 5_1)}^{t_4})}_{t_3})}^{t_2})}_{t_1}) \tag{1}$$

is syntactically equivalent to the following but with a less pedantic notation, where language subscripts are replaced by colors (red for one, and blue for two) and prefix notation is replaced by infix notation

$$\hookrightarrow_{\mathbb{s},\mathbb{n}}(\texttt{f} + \texttt{o} + \hookrightarrow_{\mathbb{e},\mathbb{a}}(10 + 5))$$

and it denotes the natural numbers 765:

$$\begin{aligned}
[\![t_4]\!]_{\mathcal{A}} &= h_{\mathrm{ls}(t_4)}(t_4) = h_{\mathbb{e}}(t_4) = [\![+]\!]_{\mathcal{A}}^{\mathbb{e}\,\mathbb{e},\mathbb{e}}([\![10]\!]_{\mathcal{A}}, [\![5]\!]_{\mathcal{A}}) = [\![+]\!]_{\mathcal{A}}^{\mathbb{e}\,\mathbb{e},\mathbb{e}}(10, 5) = 15 \\
[\![t_3]\!]_{\mathcal{A}} &= h_{\mathrm{ls}(t_3)}(t_3) = h_{\mathbb{a}}(t_3) = [\![\hookrightarrow_{\mathbb{e},\mathbb{a}}]\!]_{\mathcal{A}}^{\mathbb{e},\mathbb{a}}([\![t_4]\!]_{\mathcal{A}}) = [\![\hookrightarrow_{\mathbb{e},\mathbb{a}}]\!]_{\mathcal{A}}^{\mathbb{e},\mathbb{a}}(15) = \texttt{o} \\
[\![t_2]\!]_{\mathcal{A}} &= h_{\mathrm{ls}(t_2)}(t_2) = h_{\mathbb{s}}(t_2) = [\![+]\!]_{\mathcal{A}}^{\mathbb{s}\,\mathbb{s},\mathbb{s}}([\![\texttt{o}]\!]_{\mathcal{A}}, [\![t_3]\!]_{\mathcal{A}}) = [\![+]\!]_{\mathcal{A}}^{\mathbb{s}\,\mathbb{s},\mathbb{s}}(\texttt{o}, \texttt{o}) = \texttt{oo} \\
[\![t_1]\!]_{\mathcal{A}} &= h_{\mathrm{ls}(t_1)}(t_1) = h_{\mathbb{s}}(t_1) = [\![+]\!]_{\mathcal{A}}^{\mathbb{s}\,\mathbb{s},\mathbb{s}}([\![\texttt{f}]\!]_{\mathcal{A}}, [\![t_2]\!]_{\mathcal{A}}) = [\![+]\!]_{\mathcal{A}}^{\mathbb{s}\,\mathbb{s},\mathbb{s}}(\texttt{f}, \texttt{oo}) = \texttt{foo} \\
[\![t]\!]_{\mathcal{A}} &= h_{\mathrm{ls}(t)}(t) = h_{\mathbb{n}}(t) = [\![\hookrightarrow_{\mathbb{s},\mathbb{n}}]\!]_{\mathcal{A}}^{\mathbb{s},\mathbb{n}}([\![t_1]\!]_{\mathcal{A}}) = [\![\hookrightarrow_{\mathbb{s},\mathbb{n}}]\!]_{\mathcal{A}}^{\mathbb{s},\mathbb{n}}(\texttt{foo}) = 765
\end{aligned}$$

(see the proof of Prop. 2.10 in [19] to check how to compute the least sort of a term).

# 4 Refining the Construction

The construction in Sect. 3 does not set any constraint on boundary functions, thus giving a great deal of flexibility to language designers. For instance, they can provide boundary functions that act differently with respect to the intra-language subsort relation $\preccurlyeq$: According to the previous example, it would have been possible to define $\alpha_{\mathbb{n},\mathbb{a}} \neq \alpha_{\mathbb{e},\mathbb{a}}$ to employ different value conversion specifications for terms in $T_{\mathbb{n}}$, based on whether they are used as natural numbers ($\mathbb{n}$) or as expressions ($\mathbb{e}$). However, when this amount of flexibility is not needed, we can refine the previous construction by reducing the amount of syntax introduced by the associated signature. In this section we examine

- the case where boundary functions satisfy the monotonicity conditions of order-sorted algebra operators (Sect. 4.1); and
- the case where boundary functions commutes with the semantics of operator symbols (Sect. 4.2).

In both cases, we prove that the introduced refinements do not affect the initiality of the term algebra, thereby providing unambiguous semantics to the multi-language.

## 4.1 Subsort Polymorphic Boundary Functions

In Sect. 3, the join relation constraints $s \ltimes s'$ are turned in syntactical operators $\hookrightarrow_{s,s'}$ in the associated signature $\langle S, \preccurlyeq, \Pi\rangle$. We now show how to handle all the syntactical overhead introduced by $\ltimes$ with a single polymorphic operator $\hookrightarrow$ whenever the boundary functions satisfy the monotonicity conditions of the order-sorted algebras [19]. Such conditions require a subsort relation $s_1 \leq s_2$ between the sorts of a polymorphic operator $\sigma \in \Sigma_{w_1,s_1} \cap \Sigma_{w_2,s_2}$, assuming that

$w_1 \leq w_2$. In our case, $\sigma = \hookrightarrow$, and thus we extend Definition 6 with the following ad hoc constraint (2s*):

**Definition 6* (SP Multi-Language Signature).** *A* subsort polymorphic (SP) multi-language signature *is a multi-language signature* $\langle \mathfrak{S}_1, \mathfrak{S}_2, \leq \rangle$ *such that*

*(2s*)* $s_1 \ltimes s_1'$, $s_2 \ltimes s_2'$, *and* $s_1 \preccurlyeq s_2$ imply $s_1' \preccurlyeq s_2'$.

Furthermore, order-sorted algebras demand consistency of the interpretation functions of a subsort polymorphic operator on the smaller domain, which results in the following condition (2a*) on boundary functions (that extends Definition 7):

**Definition 7* (SP Multi-Language Algebra).** *Let* $\langle \mathfrak{S}_1, \mathfrak{S}_2, \leq \rangle$ *be a SP multi-language signature. A* subsort polymorphic (SP) multi-language $\langle \mathfrak{S}_1, \mathfrak{S}_2, \leq \rangle$-algebra *is a multi-language* $\langle \mathfrak{S}_1, \mathfrak{S}_2, \leq \rangle$*-algebra* $\mathcal{A}$ *such that*

*(2a*)* $s_1 \ltimes s_1'$, $s_2 \ltimes s_2'$, *and* $s_1 \preccurlyeq s_2$ *imply that* $\alpha_{s_1,s_1'}(a) = \alpha_{s_2,s_2'}(a)$ *for each* $a \in A_{s_1}$.

The notion of homomorphism in this new context does not change (an homomorphism between two SP algebras is still an $S$-sorted function decomposable in two order-sorted homomorphisms that commutes with boundaries), whereas the associated signature to an SP multi-language signature merely differs from Definition 9 for having a unique polymorphic operator $\hookrightarrow$ instead of a family of parametrized symbols $\{ \hookrightarrow_{s,s'} : s \to s' \mid s \ltimes s' \}$.

**Definition 9* (SP Associated Signature).** *The* subsort polymorphic (SP) associated signature *to the SP multi-language signature* $\langle \mathfrak{S}_1, \mathfrak{S}_2, \leq \rangle$ *is the ordered triple* $\langle S, \preccurlyeq, \Pi \rangle$, *where* $S = S_1 \cup S_2$, $\preccurlyeq = \leq_1 \cup \leq_2$, *and*

$$\begin{aligned} \Pi = &\{ \sigma_1 \colon w \to s \mid \sigma \colon w \to s \in \Sigma_1 \} \\ \cup &\{ \sigma_2 \colon w \to s \mid \sigma \colon w \to s \in \Sigma_2 \} \\ \cup &\{ \hookrightarrow \colon s \to s' \mid s \ltimes s' \} \end{aligned}$$

Since the associated signature is the basis for the term algebra, we need to modify the condition (3t) in Definition 9:

**Definition 10* (SP Multi-Language Term Algebra).** *The* subsort polymorphic (SP) multi-language term algebra $\mathcal{T}$ *over a SP multi-language signature* $\langle \mathfrak{S}_1, \mathfrak{S}_2, \leq \rangle$ *with boundary functions* $\tau$ *is defined as follows:*

*(1t)* $s \in S$ *implies* $T_s = T_{\Pi,s}$;
*(2t)* $\sigma \in \Sigma^i_{w,s}$ *implies* $[\![\sigma]\!]^{w,s}_{\mathcal{T}} = [\![\sigma_i]\!]^{w,s}_{\mathcal{T}_\Pi}$ for $i = 1, 2$; *and*
*(3t*)* $s \ltimes s'$ *implies* $\tau_{s,s'} = [\![\hookrightarrow]\!]^{s,s'}_{\mathcal{T}_\Pi}$.

Signature regularity is still defined as in Definition 11 and Proposition 2 still holds for the extended version developed in this section. As a result, the SP multi-language term $\langle \mathfrak{S}_1, \mathfrak{S}_2, \leq \rangle$-algebra $\mathcal{T}$ is still initial in the category $\mathbf{Alg}^*(\mathfrak{S}_1, \mathfrak{S}_2, \leq)$ of SP multi-language algebras over the SP multi-language signature $\langle \mathfrak{S}_1, \mathfrak{S}_2, \leq \rangle$.

**Theorem 3.** *Let $\langle \mathfrak{S}_1, \mathfrak{S}_2, \leq \rangle$ be a SP multi-language signature. The class of all SP $\langle \mathfrak{S}_1, \mathfrak{S}_2, \leq \rangle$-algebras and the class of all $\langle \mathfrak{S}_1, \mathfrak{S}_2, \leq \rangle$-homomorphisms form a category denoted by $\mathbf{Alg}^*(\mathfrak{S}_1, \mathfrak{S}_2, \leq)$.*

**Theorem 4 (Initiality of $\mathcal{T}$).** *The SP multi-language term algebra $\mathcal{T}$ over a regular SP multi-language signature $\langle \mathfrak{S}_1, \mathfrak{S}_2, \leq \rangle$ is initial in the category $\mathbf{Alg}^*(\mathfrak{S}_1, \mathfrak{S}_2, \leq)$.*

The semantics of a term $t$ induced by a SP multi-language algebra $\mathcal{A}$ is defined in the same way of Definition 12, thanks to the initiality result: $[\![t]\!]_{\mathcal{A}} = h_{\mathrm{ls}(t)}(t)$. The main advantage of dealing with SP multi-language terms is that the framework is able to determine the correct interpretation function of the operator $\hookrightarrow$, making the subscript notation developed in the previous section superfluous. This also means that programmers are exempted from explicitly annotating multi-language programs with sorts, a non-trivial task in the general case that could introduce type cast bugs.

**Example.** The boundary functions of the previous example are subsort polymorphic: $\alpha_{\mathbb{c},\mathbb{n}}(a) = \mathrm{ord}(a) = \alpha_{\mathbb{s},\mathbb{n}}(a)$ for each character $a \in \mathbb{A}$, and $\alpha_{\mathbb{n},\mathbb{c}} = \alpha_{\mathbb{e},\mathbb{c}}$ by definition. Thus, the equivalent of the term $t$ (see Eq. 1) in the SP term algebra is

$$\dot{t} = \hookrightarrow(\texttt{+}_2(\texttt{f}_2, \texttt{+}_2(\texttt{o}_2, \hookrightarrow(\texttt{+}_1(10_1, 5_1))))) \tag{2}$$

or, according to the previous notation,

$$\hookrightarrow(\texttt{f + o + } \hookrightarrow(10 \texttt{ + } 5))$$

and denoting the same natural number 765.

### 4.2 Semantic-Only Boundary Functions

In the previous section, we have shown how to handle the flow of values across different languages with a single polymorphic operator. Now, we present a new multi-language construction where neither extra operators are added to the associated signature, nor single-language operators have to be annotated with subscripts indicating their original language. Thus, the resulting multi-language syntax comprises only symbols in $\Sigma_1 \cup \Sigma_2$. Such a construction is achieved by:

- Imposing commutativity conditions on algebras, making homomorphisms transparently inherit the semantics of boundary functions. The framework is therefore able to apply the correct value conversion function whenever is necessary, without the need for an explicit syntactical operator $\hookrightarrow$.
- Requiring a new form of *cross-language polymorphism* able to cope with shared operators among languages. The initiality of term algebras is preserved by modifying the notion of signature in a way that every operator admits a least sort.

The variant of the framework presented in this section is particularly useful when designing the extension of a language in a modular fashion. For instance, if the signature $\mathfrak{S}_1$ models the syntax of a simple functional language (for an example, see [15, p. 77]) without an explicit encoding for string values, and $\mathfrak{S}_2$ is a language for manipulating strings (similar to the language $L_2$ of the running example of this paper), we can exploit the construction presented below in order to embed $\mathfrak{S}_2$ into $\mathfrak{S}_1$.

**Signature.** The main issue that can arise at this stage of multi-language signature is the presence of shared operators in $\Sigma_1$ and $\Sigma_2$. Contrary to the previous cases where such ambiguity is solved by adding subscripts in the associated signature, the trade off here is requiring ad hoc or subsort polymorphism across signatures.

**Definition 6$^\star$ (SO Multi-Language Signature).** *A* semantic-only (SO) multi-language signature *is a multi-language signature* $\langle \mathfrak{S}_1, \mathfrak{S}_2, \leq \rangle$ *such that*

*(2s$^\star$)* $\langle S, \leq \rangle$ *is a poset; and*
*(3s$^\star$)* $\sigma \in \Sigma^i_{w_1,s_1} \cap \Sigma^j_{w_2,s_2}$ *and* $w_1 \ltimes w_2$ *imply* $s_1 \ltimes s_2$ *with* $i, j = 1, 2$ *and* $i \neq j$.

Condition (2s$^\star$) forces the subsort relation to be directed, avoiding symmetricity of syntactic categories (this is typical when modeling language extensions), while condition (3s$^\star$) shifts the monotonicity condition of order-sorted signature to syntactically equal operators in $\Sigma_1 \cap \Sigma_2$.
The associated signature is defined without adding extra symbols in the signature, i.e., $\Pi = \Sigma_1 \cup \Sigma_2$, and deliberately confounding the relations $\ltimes$ and $\preccurlyeq$ in $\leq$:

**Definition 9$^\star$ (SO Associated Signature).** *The* SO associated signature *to the SO multi-language signature* $\langle \mathfrak{S}_1, \mathfrak{S}_2, \leq \rangle$ *is the ordered triple* $\langle S, \leq, \Pi \rangle$, *where* $S = S_1 \cup S_2$, $\leq \; = \; \preccurlyeq \cup \ltimes$, and $\Pi = \Sigma_1 \cup \Sigma_2$.

The embedding of $\ltimes$ in $\leq$ (i.e., $\ltimes \subseteq \leq$) in the associated signature enables the order-sorted term algebra construction to automatically build multi-language terms, without the need for an explicit operator $\hookrightarrow$ that acts as a bridge between syntactic categories. It is easy to see that the term algebra over the associated signature is precisely the symbols-free version of multi-language described at the beginning.

Unfortunately, multi-language regularity does not follow anymore from single-languages regularity and vice versa (see Figs. 3 and 4)[6]. More formally, Proposition 2 does not hold in this new context:

6 An (horizontal) arrow from an arity symbol $w$ to a sort $s$ labelled with an operator symbol $\sigma$ is an alternative shorthand for $\sigma\colon w \to s$. A (vertical) single line between two sorts $s$ below $s'$ labelled with a binary relation $\leq$ means that $s \leq s'$ (if the binary relation is the join relation $\ltimes$ the line is doubled). A dotted rectangle around operators is a graphical representation of the set of ranks $(w, s)$ that must have a minimum element (red arrows) in order for the signature to be regular.

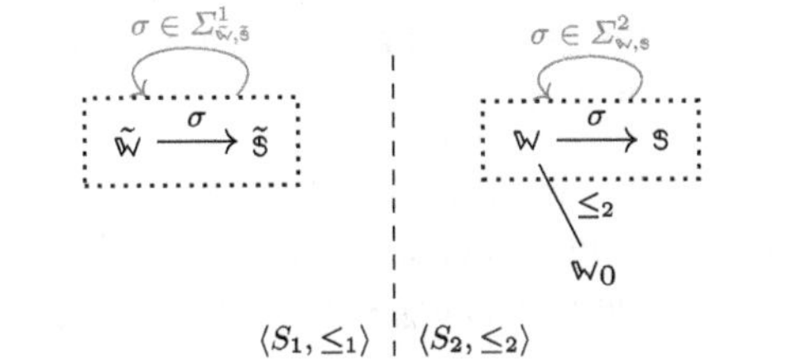

(a) The Hasse-like diagrams of regular signatures $\mathfrak{S}_1$ (left) and $\mathfrak{S}_2$ (right).

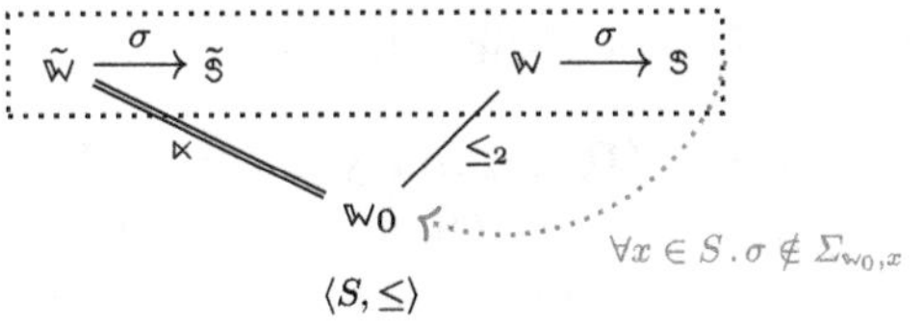

(b) The Hasse-like diagram of the non-regular multi-language signature $\langle \mathfrak{S}_1, \mathfrak{S}_2, \leq \rangle$.

**Fig. 3.** A non-regular multi-language signature comprising two regular order-sorted signatures.

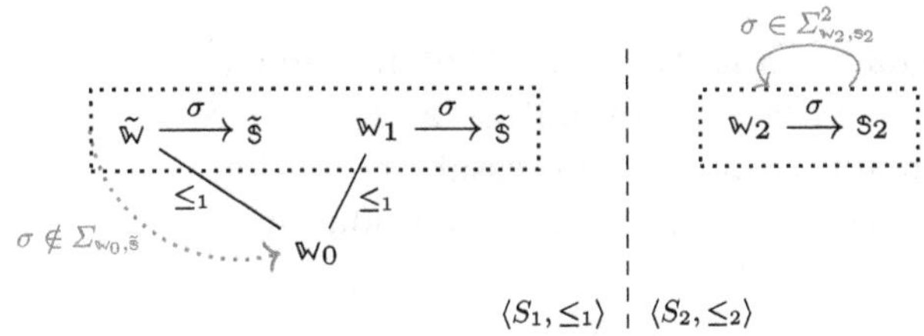

(a) The Hasse-like diagrams of signatures $\mathfrak{S}_1$ (non-regular, left) and $\mathfrak{S}_2$ (regular, right).

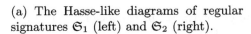

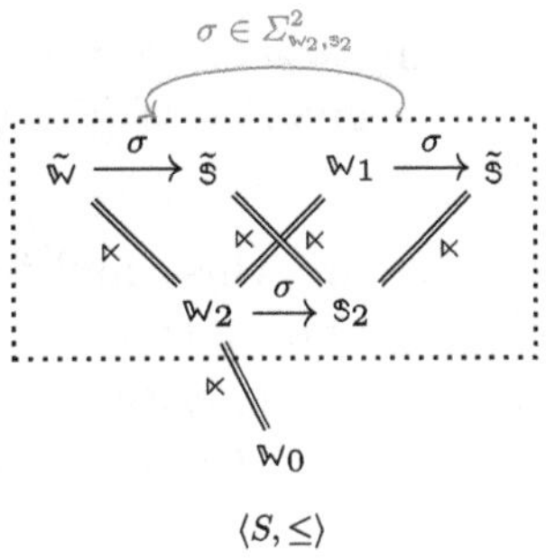

(b) The Hasse-like diagram of the regular multi-language signature $\langle \mathfrak{S}_1, \mathfrak{S}_2, \leq \rangle$.

**Fig. 4.** A regular multi-language signature comprising a non-regular order-sorted signature.

- Suppose $S_1 = \{\tilde{\mathtt{w}}, \tilde{\mathtt{s}}\}$, $S_2 = \{\mathtt{w}_0, \mathtt{w}, \mathtt{s}\}$, $\leq_1$ and $\leq_2$ to be the reflexive relations on $S_1$ and $S_2$, respectively, plus $\mathtt{w}_0 \leq_2 \mathtt{w}$, and $\sigma \in \Sigma^1_{\tilde{\mathtt{w}},\tilde{\mathtt{s}}} \cap \Sigma^2_{\mathtt{w},\mathtt{s}}$. If the join relation $\ltimes$ is defined as $\mathtt{w}_0 \ltimes \tilde{\mathtt{w}}$ and $\mathtt{s} \ltimes \tilde{\mathtt{s}}$, the resulting associated signature is no longer regular, although $\mathfrak{S}_1$ and $\mathfrak{S}_2$ are regular (Fig. 3a). In Fig. 3b, it is easy to see that $\sigma \in \Sigma_{\tilde{\mathtt{w}},\tilde{\mathtt{s}}}$ and $\mathtt{w}_0 \leq \mathtt{w}$, but the set $\{(\mathtt{w}, \mathtt{s}) \mid \sigma \in \Sigma_{\mathtt{w},\mathtt{s}} \wedge \mathtt{w}_0 \leq \mathtt{w}\} = \{(\tilde{\mathtt{w}}, \tilde{\mathtt{s}}), (\mathtt{w}, \mathtt{s})\}$ does not have a least element w.r.t. $\mathtt{w}_0$.
- On the other hand, let $S_1 = \{\tilde{\mathtt{w}}, \mathtt{w}_0, \mathtt{w}_1, \tilde{\mathtt{s}}\}$, $S_2 = \{\mathtt{w}_2, \mathtt{s}_2\}$, $\leq_1$ and $\leq_2$ be the reflexive relations on $S_1$ and $S_2$, respectively, plus $\mathtt{w}_0 \leq_1 \tilde{\mathtt{w}}$ and $\mathtt{w}_0 \leq_1 \mathtt{w}_1$, and $\sigma \in \Sigma^1_{\tilde{\mathtt{w}},\tilde{\mathtt{s}}} \cap \Sigma^1_{\mathtt{w}_1,\tilde{\mathtt{s}}} \cap \Sigma^2_{\mathtt{w}_2,\mathtt{s}_2}$. If the join relation $\ltimes$ is defined as $\mathtt{w}_2 \ltimes \tilde{\mathtt{w}}$, $\mathtt{w}_2 \ltimes \mathtt{w}_1$, $\mathtt{w}_0 \ltimes \mathtt{w}_2$, and $\mathtt{s}_2 \ltimes \tilde{\mathtt{s}}$, the resulting associated signature is regular (Fig. 4a), although $\mathfrak{S}_1$ is not: given $\sigma \in \Sigma_{\tilde{\mathtt{w}},\tilde{\mathtt{s}}}$ and $\mathtt{w}_0 \leq \tilde{\mathtt{w}}$, the set $\{(\mathtt{w}, \mathtt{s}) \mid \sigma \in \Sigma_{\mathtt{w},\mathtt{s}} \wedge \mathtt{w}_0 \leq \mathtt{w}\} = \{(\tilde{\mathtt{w}}, \tilde{\mathtt{s}}), (\mathtt{w}_1, \tilde{\mathtt{s}}), (\mathtt{w}_2, \mathtt{s}_2)\}$ has least element $(\mathtt{w}_2, \mathtt{s}_2)$ w.r.t. $\mathtt{w}_0$ (Fig. 4b).

A positive result can be obtained by recalling that regularity is easier to check when $\langle S, \leq \rangle$ satisfies the descending chain condition (DCC):

**Lemma 1 (Regularity over DCC poset [19]).** *An order-sorted signature $\Sigma$ over a DCC poset $\langle S, \leq \rangle$ is regular if and only if whenever $\sigma \in \Sigma_{w_1,s_1} \cap \Sigma_{w_2,s_2}$ and there is some $w_0 \leq w_1, w_2$, then there is some $w \leq w_1, w_2$ such that $\sigma \in \Sigma_{w,s}$ and $w_0 \leq w$.*

At this point, we can relate the DCC of the poset $\langle S, \leq \rangle$ in the associated signature of $\langle \mathfrak{S}_1, \mathfrak{S}_2, \leq \rangle$ to the DCC of $\langle S_1, \leq_1 \rangle$ and $\langle S_2, \leq_2 \rangle$:

**Proposition 3.** *Let $\langle S, \leq, \Sigma \rangle$ be the associated signature of $\langle \mathfrak{S}_1, \mathfrak{S}_2, \leq \rangle$. Then, $\langle S, \leq \rangle$ is DCC if and only if $\langle S_1, \leq_1 \rangle$ and $\langle S_2, \leq_2 \rangle$ are DCC.*

As a result, whenever we know that $\langle S_1, \leq_1 \rangle$ and $\langle S_2, \leq_2 \rangle$ are DCC, we can check the regularity of $\langle \mathfrak{S}_1, \mathfrak{S}_2, \leq \rangle$ by employing the Lemma 1 without checking whether $\langle S, \leq \rangle$ is DCC.

**Algebra.** In this multi-language construction, the boundary functions behaviour is no more bounded to syntactical operators as in the previous sections, but it is inherited by homomorphisms. A necessary condition to accomplish this aim is the commutativity of interpretation functions with boundary functions:

**Definition 7* (SO Multi-Language Algebra).** *Let $\langle \mathfrak{S}_1, \mathfrak{S}_2, \leq \rangle$ be an SO multi-language signature. A* semantic-only (SO) multi-language $\langle \mathfrak{S}_1, \mathfrak{S}_2, \leq \rangle$-algebra *is an SP multi-language $\langle \mathfrak{S}_1, \mathfrak{S}_2, \leq \rangle$-algebra $\mathcal{A}$ such that*

*(3a*)* $\sigma \in \Sigma_{w_1,s_1} \cap \Sigma_{w_2,s_2}$ and $w_1 \ltimes w_2$ imply that $\alpha_{s_1,s_2}(\llbracket \sigma \rrbracket_{\mathcal{A}}^{w_1,s_1}(a)) = \llbracket \sigma \rrbracket_{\mathcal{A}}^{w_2,s_2}(\alpha_{w_1,w_2}(a))$ for each $a \in A_{w_1}$.

Note that $\sigma \in \Sigma_{w_1,s_1} \cap \Sigma_{w_2,s_2}$ and $w_1 \ltimes w_2$ imply $s_1 \ltimes s_2$ by condition (3s*). The notion of homomorphism remains unchanged from Definition 8 (to understand how the homomorphisms inherit the boundary functions behaviour, see the proof of Theorem 6).

The term algebra is defined similarly to Definition 10, except for boundary functions:

**Definition 10* (SO Multi-Language Term Algebra).** *The* semantic-only (SO) multi-language term algebra $\mathcal{T}$ *over an SO multi-language signature $\langle \mathfrak{S}_1, \mathfrak{S}_2, \leq \rangle$ with boundary functions $\tau$ is defined as follows:*

*(1t*) $s \in S$ implies $T_s = T_{\Pi,s}$;*
*(2t*) $\sigma \in \Sigma_{w,s}$ implies $\llbracket \sigma \rrbracket_{\mathcal{T}}^{w,s} = \llbracket \sigma \rrbracket_{\mathcal{T}_\Pi}^{w,s}$; and*
*(3t*) $s \ltimes s'$ implies $\tau_{s,s'} = \mathrm{id}_{T_s}$.*

Since the subsort relation $\leq$ includes the join relation $\ltimes$, $s \ltimes s'$ implies $T_{\Pi,s} = T_s \subseteq T_{s'} = T_{\Pi,s'}$. Thus, the boundary function $\tau_{s,s'}$ can be defined as the identity on the smaller domain (note that it trivially satisfies the commutativity condition (3a*)).

**Proposition 4.** *Let $\langle \mathfrak{S}_1, \mathfrak{S}_2, \leq \rangle$ be an SO multi-language signature. Then, the SO multi-language term $\langle \mathfrak{S}_1, \mathfrak{S}_2, \leq \rangle$-algebra is a proper SO multi-language algebra.*

**Theorem 5.** *Let $\langle \mathfrak{S}_1, \mathfrak{S}_2, \leq \rangle$ be a SO multi-language signature. The class of all SO $\langle \mathfrak{S}_1, \mathfrak{S}_2, \leq \rangle$-algebras and the class of all $\langle \mathfrak{S}_1, \mathfrak{S}_2, \leq \rangle$-homomorphisms form a category denoted by $\mathbf{Alg}^{\star}(\mathfrak{S}_1, \mathfrak{S}_2, \leq)$.*

We can now prove the initiality of $\mathcal{T}$ in its category.

**Theorem 6 (Initiality of $\mathcal{T}$).** *Let $\langle \mathfrak{S}_1, \mathfrak{S}_2, \leq \rangle$ be a regular multi-language signature. Then, the term algebra $\mathcal{T}$ is an initial object in the category $\mathbf{Alg}(\mathfrak{S}_1, \mathfrak{S}_2, \leq)$.*

Thanks to the initiality of the term algebra, the definition of term semantics is the same of Definition 12.

**Example.** Let $\mathcal{A}_1$ and $\mathcal{A}_2$ be two order-sorted algebras over the signatures $\mathfrak{S}_1$ and $\mathfrak{S}_2$, respectively, as formalized in the example in Sect. 3. Suppose we are interested in a new multi-language $\mathcal{A}$ over $\mathfrak{S}_1$ and $\mathfrak{S}_2$ such that any string expressions $t$ of sort $\mathbb{s}$ in $\mathfrak{S}_2$ can denote the natural number $\text{length}([\![t]\!]_{\mathcal{A}_2})$ when embedded in $\mathfrak{S}_1$ terms. For instance, we require that $[\![\texttt{10 + 5}]\!]_{\mathcal{A}} = [\![\texttt{10 + 5}]\!]_{\mathcal{A}_1} = 15$ and $[\![\texttt{f + o}]\!]_{\mathcal{A}} = [\![\texttt{f + o}]\!]_{\mathcal{A}_2} = \texttt{fo}$, but $[\![\texttt{(f + o) + (10 + 5)}]\!]_{\mathcal{A}} = [\![\texttt{fo + 15}]\!]_{L} = 17$ (parentheses in the last term have only been used to disambiguate the parsing result).

Since the requirements demand to use string expressions in place of natural numbers, the join relation $\ltimes$ shall define $\mathbb{s} \ltimes \mathbb{n}$ and ensure transitivity, hence $\mathbb{s} \ltimes \mathbb{e}$, $\mathbb{a} \ltimes \mathbb{n}$, and $\mathbb{a} \ltimes \mathbb{e}$.

The signatures $\mathfrak{S}_1$ and $\mathfrak{S}_2$ are trivially regular. However, by merging $\mathfrak{S}_1$ and $\mathfrak{S}_2$, we are causing subsort polymorphism on the symbol +, which is used as sum operator in $\mathcal{A}_1$ and as concatenation operator in $\mathcal{A}_2$, and therefore we have to check the regularity: Let $w_1 = \mathbb{e}\mathbb{e}$, $w_2 = \mathbb{s}\mathbb{s}$, $s_1 = \mathbb{e}$, and $s_2 = \mathbb{s}$. Given $+ \in \Sigma_{w_1,s_1} \cap \Sigma_{w_2,s_2}$ and the lower bound $w_0 = \mathbb{a}\mathbb{a} \leq w_1, w_2$, then there exists $w = \mathbb{s}\mathbb{s}$ such that $w \leq w_1, w_2$ and $+ \in \Sigma_{w,s}$, where $s = \mathbb{s} \leq s_1, s_2$ (we have employed Lemma 1 thanks to Proposition 3). Analogously, when $w_0 = w_1, w_2$ the relative least rank is $(\mathbb{s}\mathbb{s}, \mathbb{s})$.

The multi-language $\langle \mathfrak{S}_1, \mathfrak{S}_2, \leq \rangle$-algebra $\mathcal{A}$ is now defined by joining the projected algebras $\mathcal{A}_1$ and $\mathcal{A}_2$ and by defining boundary functions $a_{s,s'}$ for each $s \ltimes s'$ such that convert strings in naturals (their length) when strings are used in place of naturals:

$$a_{\mathbb{a},\mathbb{n}}(a) = a_{\mathbb{a},\mathbb{e}}(a) = 1 \qquad\qquad a_{\mathbb{s},\mathbb{n}}(\hat{a}) = a_{\mathbb{s},\mathbb{e}}(\hat{a}) = \text{length}(\hat{a})$$

The above definition of boundary functions satisfy both conditions (2a*) and (3a*).

The initiality theorem yields the semantic homomorphism from $\mathcal{T}$ to $\mathcal{A}$. For instance, suppose we want to compute the semantics of the term

$$t = \texttt{+}(\underbrace{\texttt{+}(\texttt{f}, \texttt{o})}_{t_1}, \overbrace{\texttt{+}(10, 5)}^{t_2})$$

The least sorts of $t$, $t_1$, and $t_2$ are $\mathbb{e}$, $\mathbb{s}$, and $\mathbb{e}$, respectively. The operator + belongs to both $\Sigma_{\mathbb{e}\,\mathbb{e},\mathbb{e}}$ and $\Sigma_{\mathbb{s}\,\mathbb{s},\mathbb{s}}$, and its least rank w.r.t. the lower bound $\text{ls}(t_1)\,\text{ls}(t_2) = \mathbb{s}\,\mathbb{e}$ is $(\mathbb{e}\,\mathbb{e}, \mathbb{e})$. By Definition 12 we have

$$[\![t]\!]_{\mathcal{A}} = h_{\mathbb{e}}(t) = [\![\texttt{+}]\!]_{\mathcal{A}}^{\mathbb{e}\,\mathbb{e},\mathbb{e}}(h_{\mathbb{e}}(t_1), h_{\mathbb{e}}(t_2))$$

At this point, since $\text{ls}(t_1) = \mathbb{s}$ and $\text{ls}(\texttt{f}) = \text{ls}(\texttt{o}) = \mathbb{c}$, then the least rank of the root symbol + of $t_1$ w.r.t. the lower bound $\text{ls}(\texttt{f})\,\text{ls}(\texttt{o}) = \mathbb{c}\,\mathbb{c}$ is $(\mathbb{s}\,\mathbb{s}, \mathbb{s})$, thus

$$h_{\mathbb{e}}(t_1) = a_{\mathbb{s},\mathbb{e}}(h_{\mathbb{s}}(t_1)) = a_{\mathbb{s},\mathbb{e}}([\![\texttt{+}]\!]_{\mathcal{A}}^{\mathbb{s}\,\mathbb{s},\mathbb{s}}(h_{\mathbb{s}}(\texttt{f}), h_{\mathbb{s}}(\texttt{o}))) = a_{\mathbb{s},\mathbb{e}}([\![\texttt{+}]\!]_{\mathcal{A}}^{\mathbb{s}\,\mathbb{s},\mathbb{s}}(\texttt{f}, \texttt{o})) = a_{\mathbb{s},\mathbb{e}}(\texttt{fo}) = 2$$

Similarly, $\text{ls}(t_2) = \mathbb{e}$ and $\text{ls}(10) = \text{ls}(5) = \mathbb{n}$. Then, the least rank of the root symbol + of $t_2$ w.r.t. the lower bound $(\mathbb{n}, \mathbb{n})$ is $(\mathbb{e}\,\mathbb{e}, \mathbb{e})$ and therefore we have

$$h_{\mathbb{e}}(t_2) = [\![\texttt{+}]\!]_{\mathcal{A}}^{\mathbb{e}\,\mathbb{e},\mathbb{e}}(h_{\mathbb{n}}(10), h_{\mathbb{n}}(5)) = [\![\texttt{+}]\!]_{\mathcal{A}}^{\mathbb{e}\,\mathbb{e},\mathbb{e}}(10, 5) = 15$$

Finally,

$$[\![t]\!]_{\mathcal{A}} = h_{\mathbb{e}}(t) = [\![\texttt{+}]\!]_{\mathcal{A}}^{\mathbb{e}\,\mathbb{e},\mathbb{e}}(h_{\mathbb{e}}(t_1), h_{\mathbb{e}}(t_2)) = [\![\texttt{+}]\!]_{\mathcal{A}}^{\mathbb{e}\,\mathbb{e},\mathbb{e}}(2, 15) = 17$$

as desired.

We can observe that without any syntactical operator the framework is still able to apply the correct boundary functions to move values across languages.

## 5 Reduction to Order-Sorted Algebra

The constructions in the previous sections beg the question whether a multi-language algebra admits an equivalent order-sorted representation. Conceptually, it would mean that being a multi-language is essentially a matter of perspective: By forgetting how the multi-language has been constructed, what is left is simply an ordinary language. Mathematically speaking, it requires us to exhibit a *reduction functor* $F$ from the multi-language category to an order-sorted one, such that there is an isomorphism $\phi$ between the carrier sets of the multi-language term $\langle \mathfrak{S}_1, \mathfrak{S}_2, \leq \rangle$-algebra $\mathcal{T}$ and $F(\mathcal{T})$, and such that $[\![t]\!]_{\mathcal{A}} = [\![\phi(t)]\!]_{F(\mathcal{A})}$ for each $t \in \mathcal{T}$ and for each multi-language $\langle \mathfrak{S}_1, \mathfrak{S}_2, \leq \rangle$-algebra $\mathcal{A}$.

In the following, we denote the reduction functor by $F$, $F^*$, and $F^\star$ accordingly whether its domain is the category $\mathbf{Alg}(\mathfrak{S}_1, \mathfrak{S}_2, \leq)$, $\mathbf{Alg}^*(\mathfrak{S}_1, \mathfrak{S}_2, \leq)$, and $\mathbf{Alg}^\star(\mathfrak{S}_1, \mathfrak{S}_2, \leq)$, respectively.

In the case of $\mathbf{Alg}(\mathfrak{S}_1, \mathfrak{S}_2, \leq)$ and $\mathbf{Alg}^*(\mathfrak{S}_1, \mathfrak{S}_2, \leq)$ categories, the construction of $F$ and $F^*$ is very simple, and we illustrate it only for the plain multi-language algebras of Sect. 3: Let $\mathcal{A}$ be a multi-language $\langle \mathfrak{S}_1, \mathfrak{S}_2, \leq \rangle$-algebra. Then, we define the order-sorted $\langle S, \preccurlyeq, \Pi \rangle$-algebra $\mathcal{A}_\Pi$ (called the *associated order-sorted algebra* of $\mathcal{A}$) by setting

(1π) $A_{\Pi,s} = A_s$ for each $s \in S$;
(2π) $[\![\sigma_i]\!]^{w,s}_{\mathcal{A}_\Pi} = [\![\sigma]\!]^{w,s}_{\mathcal{A}}$ for each $\sigma \in \Sigma^i_{w,s}$ and $i = 1, 2$; and
(3π) $[\![\hookrightarrow_{s,s'}]\!]^{s,s'}_{\mathcal{A}_\Pi} = \alpha_{s,s'}$ for each $s \ltimes s'$.

If $\mathcal{A}$ and $\mathcal{B}$ are multi-language $\langle \mathfrak{S}_1, \mathfrak{S}_2, \leq \rangle$-algebras, and $h$ is a multi-language $\langle \mathfrak{S}_1, \mathfrak{S}_2, \leq \rangle$-homomorphism from $\mathcal{A}$ to $\mathcal{B}$, the functor $F$ maps $\mathcal{A}$ and $\mathcal{B}$ to their associated order-sorted algebras $\mathcal{A}_\Pi$ and $\mathcal{B}_\Pi$ and the homomorphism $h$ to itself. Since $A_\Pi = A$, the isomorphism $\phi$ is the identity function.

**Theorem 7.** *$F\colon \mathbf{Alg}(\mathfrak{S}_1, \mathfrak{S}_2, \leq) \to \mathbf{OSAlg}(\mathfrak{S}_1, \mathfrak{S}_2, \leq)$ is a functor for every multi-language signature $\langle \mathfrak{S}_1, \mathfrak{S}_2, \leq \rangle$. Moreover, $[\![t]\!]_{\mathcal{A}} = [\![t]\!]_{F(\mathcal{A})}$ for each $t \in \mathcal{T}$ and for each multi-language $\langle \mathfrak{S}_1, \mathfrak{S}_2, \leq \rangle$-algebra $\mathcal{A}$.*

If $\mathcal{A}$ is an SP multi-language $\langle \mathfrak{S}_1, \mathfrak{S}_2, \leq \rangle$-algebra, the construction of the reduction functor $F^*$ is similar to the definition of $F$. The only difference is the equation in the condition (3π) that turns into

(3π*) $[\![\hookrightarrow]\!]^{s,s'}_{\mathcal{A}_\Pi} = \alpha_{s,s'}$ for each $s \ltimes s'$.

Finally, the definition of $F^\star$ starting from the category $\mathbf{Alg}^\star(\mathfrak{S}_1, \mathfrak{S}_2, \leq)$ of SO multi-language algebras is slightly different. We define $F^\star$ as a map from the multi-language category $\mathbf{Alg}^\star(\mathfrak{S}_1, \mathfrak{S}_2, \leq)$ to the order-sorted category $\mathbf{OSAlg}(S, \preccurlyeq, \Sigma)$. We denote the reduction of a multi-language algebra $\mathcal{A}$ and a homomorphism $h\colon \mathcal{A} \to \mathcal{B}$ as $F(\mathcal{A}) = \mathcal{A}_\downarrow$ and $F(h) = h_\downarrow\colon \mathcal{A}_\downarrow \to \mathcal{B}_\downarrow$. The order-sorted algebra $\mathcal{A}_\downarrow$ has the same carrier sets of the multi-language algebra $\mathcal{A}$, i.e., $A_\downarrow = A$, and interpretation functions $[\![\sigma]\!]^{w,s}_{\mathcal{A}_\downarrow} = [\![\sigma]\!]^{w,s}_{\mathcal{A}}$. Furthermore, we define $h_\downarrow = h$. Intuitively, the algebra $\mathcal{A}_\downarrow$ is formally defined simply by forgetting about the boundary functions, while the homomorphism $h_\downarrow\colon \mathcal{A}_\downarrow \to \mathcal{B}_\downarrow$ inherits their semantics from $h$. Again, the isomorphism $\phi$ is the identity.

**Theorem 8.** *$F^\star\colon \mathbf{Alg}^\star(\mathfrak{S}_1, \mathfrak{S}_2, \leq) \to \mathbf{OSAlg}(S, \preccurlyeq, \Sigma)$ is a functor for every SO multi-language signature $\langle \mathfrak{S}_1, \mathfrak{S}_2, \leq \rangle$. Moreover, $[\![t]\!]_{\mathcal{A}} = [\![t]\!]_{F^\star(\mathcal{A})}$ for each $t \in \mathcal{T}$ and for each SO multi-language $\langle \mathfrak{S}_1, \mathfrak{S}_2, \leq \rangle$-algebra $\mathcal{A}$.*

Unfortunately, even though $\mathcal{T}$ is an initial algebra in its category, $F^\star(\mathcal{T}) = \mathcal{T}_\downarrow$ is not: Given two multi-language algebras $\mathcal{A}$ and $\mathcal{A}'$ that differ only in the boundary functions (we denote by $\alpha$ and $\alpha'$ the families of boundary functions of $\mathcal{A}$ and $\mathcal{A}'$, respectively) they both get mapped by $F^\star$ to the same order-sorted algebra $\mathcal{A}_\downarrow$. Thus, if $h\colon \mathcal{T} \to \mathcal{A}$ and $h'\colon \mathcal{T} \to \mathcal{A}'$ are the unique homomorphisms going from $\mathcal{T}$ to $\mathcal{A}$ and $\mathcal{A}'$, the functor $F$ maps them to two different order-sorted homomorphisms $h_\downarrow\colon \mathcal{T}_\downarrow \to \mathcal{A}_\downarrow$ and $h'_\downarrow\colon \mathcal{T}_\downarrow \to \mathcal{A}_\downarrow$ both leaving $\mathcal{T}_\downarrow$ and going to $\mathcal{A}_\downarrow$, hence losing the uniqueness property. However, this does not pose a problem once fixed a family of boundary functions:

**Theorem 9.** *Let $\mathcal{T}$ be the multi-language term $\langle \mathfrak{S}_1, \mathfrak{S}_2, \leq \rangle$-algebra and $\mathcal{A}$ be an order-sorted $\langle S, \preccurlyeq, \Sigma \rangle$-algebra. Given a family of boundary functions $\alpha = \{ \alpha_{s,s'} \mid s \ltimes s' \}$ such that satisfies condition (3a*), there exists a unique order-sorted $\langle S, \preccurlyeq, \Sigma \rangle$-homomorphism $h^\alpha\colon \mathcal{T}_\downarrow \to \mathcal{A}$ commuting with $\alpha$, i.e., if $s \ltimes s'$, then $h^\alpha_{s'}(t) = \alpha_{s,s'}(h^\alpha_s(t))$ for each $t \in T_s$.*

The reduction theorems presented in this section have a strong consequence: all the already known results for the order-sorted algebras can be lifted to the multi-language world.

## 6 An Example of Multi-Language Construction

The first theoretical paper addressing the problem of multi-language construction is [30]. The authors study the so-called *natural embedding* (a more realistic improvement of the *lump embedding* [7,30,34,40]), in which Scheme terms can be converted to equivalent ML terms, and vice versa.[7] The novelty in their approach is how they succeed to define boundaries in order to translate values from Scheme to ML. Indeed, the latter does not admit an equivalent representation for each Scheme function. Their solution is to *"represent a Scheme procedure in ML at type $\tau_1 \rightarrow \tau_2$ by a new procedure that takes an argument of type $\tau_1$, converts it to a Scheme equivalent, runs the original Scheme procedure on that value, and then converts the result back to ML at type $\tau_2$"*.

Our goal here is not to discuss a fully explained presentation of ML and Scheme languages in the form of order-sorted algebras, but rather to show how we can model the natural embedding construction in our framework. Doing so, we provide a sketchy formalization of Scheme and ML syntax and semantics, and we redirect the reader to [30] for all the languages details.

To provide the semantics of Scheme, we follow the same approach of Goguen et al. [15] where the denotational semantics of the *simple applicative language* (SAL) introduced by Reynolds [42] is given by means of an algebra, exploiting the initiality theorem. Such a language is a "syntactically sugared" version of the untyped lambda calculus with the fixpoint operator, which in turn is very similar to Scheme.

Let $X = \{\mathrm{x}_1, \mathrm{x}_2, \ldots\}$ be a set of variables and $\mathbb{N}^\diamond$ be the naturals lattice with $\top$ and $\bot$ adjoined. From [46], there exists a complete lattice $V$ such that satisfies the isomorphism $\phi \colon V \cong \mathbb{N}^\diamond + V \diamond\!\!\rightarrow V$, where $+$ is the disjoint union with minimum and maximum elements identified, and $V \diamond\!\!\rightarrow V$ is the complete lattice of Scott-continuous functions from $V$ to $V$. Given $\xi \in \{\mathbb{N}^\diamond, V \diamond\!\!\rightarrow V\}$, we define the injections $j_\xi \colon \xi \rightarrow \mathbb{N}^\diamond + V \diamond\!\!\rightarrow V$ and $i_\xi = \phi^{-1} \circ j_\xi$, and the projection $\pi_\xi \colon V \rightarrow \xi$ such that $\pi_\xi(v) = (\!| \phi(v) \in \xi \ ?\ \phi(v) \ ⸬\ \bot |\!)$. The set of all Scheme environments is the lattice of all total functions $\mathrm{P} = X \rightarrow V$ with componentwise ordering $\rho \sqsubseteq \rho'$ if and only if $\rho(x) \sqsubseteq \rho'(x)$ in $V$ for all $x \in X$. Furthermore, we define auxiliary functions (see [15] for a more detailed explanation) in order to provide the semantics of the language (in the following, $x \in X$ and $n \in \mathbb{N}^\diamond$):

- $get_x \colon \mathrm{P} \rightarrow V$, $get_x(\rho) = \rho(x)$ (evaluation function);
- $val_n \colon \mathrm{P} \rightarrow V$, $val_n(\rho) = n$ ($n$-constant function);

[7] To be specific, the authors combine *"an extended model of the untyped call-by-value lambda calculus, which is used as a stand-in for Scheme, and an extended model of the simply-typed lambda calculus, which is used as a stand-in for ML"*.

- $put_x \colon \mathrm{P} \times V \to \mathrm{P}$, $put_x(\rho, v) = \rho[v/x]$, where $\rho[v/x](x') = (\!| x = x' \ ?\ v \ \text{\textfrac{}}\ \rho(x') |\!)$ (environment updating);
- $app : V^2 \to V$, $app(v_1, v_2) = (\pi_{V \circ\!\!\to V}(v_1))(v_2)$ (function application);
- $nat? : V \to V$, $nat?(v) = (\!| v \in \mathbb{N}^{\diamond}\ ?\ val_0 \ ;\ val_1 |\!)$ (natural predicate);
- $proc? : V \to V$, $proc?(v) = (\!| v \in V \circ\!\!\to V\ ?\ val_0 \ ;\ val_1 |\!)$ (function predicate);
- given $\hat{e}_i \colon \mathrm{P} \to V$ for $1 \leq i \leq k$, then $\langle\!| \hat{e}_1, \ldots, \hat{e}_k |\!\rangle \colon \mathrm{P} \to V^k$ is defined by $\langle\!| \hat{e}_1, \ldots, \hat{e}_k |\!\rangle(\rho) = (\hat{e}_1(\rho), \ldots, \hat{e}_k(\rho))$ (target-tupling); and
- given $D$, $D'$ and $D''$, then $abs$: $((D \times D') \circ\!\!\to D'') \to (D \circ\!\!\to (D' \circ\!\!\to D''))$ is defined by $((abs(f))(x))(y) = f(x, y)$ (abstraction); and
- $choice : V^3 \to V$ (conditional function), $add$: $V^2 \to V$ (addition), and $sub$: $V^2 \to V$ (subtraction)

$$choice(v_1, v_2, v_3) = \begin{cases} \top & \text{if } v_1 = \top \\ v_2 & \text{if } v_1 = 0 \\ v_3 & \text{if } v_1 \neq 0 \\ \bot & \text{otherwise} \end{cases} \qquad add(v_1, v_2) = \begin{cases} \top & \text{if } v_1, v_2 = \top \\ v_1 + v_2 & \text{if } v_1, v_2 \in \mathbb{N} \\ \bot & \text{otherwise} \end{cases}$$

The definition of $sub$ is analogous to the function $add$, with the only difference that, in the second case, $sub(v_1, v_2) = v_1 -_{\mathbb{N}} v_2$, where $v_1 -_{\mathbb{N}} v_2 = \max\{ v_1 - v_2, 0 \}$ for each $v_1, v_2 \in \mathbb{N}$.

The semantics of the language is obtained by defining an algebra $\mathcal{H}$ over a signature $\mathfrak{H}$,[8] then the initiality yields the unique homomorphism from the term algebra. A Scheme term denotes a continuous function in the semantic domain $H_{\mathbb{e}} = \mathrm{P} \circ\!\!\to V$. The interpretation functions of the operators are defined by the following equations:

$$\begin{aligned} &[\![x]\!]^{\varepsilon,\mathbb{e}}_{\mathcal{H}} = get_x && [\![\lambda x]\!]^{\mathbb{e},\mathbb{e}}_{\mathcal{H}}(\hat{e}) = i_{V \circ\!\to V} \circ abs_{\mathrm{P},V,V}(\hat{e} \circ put_x) \\ &[\![\blacksquare]\!]^{\mathbb{e}\mathbb{e},\mathbb{e}}_{\mathcal{H}}(\hat{e}_1, \hat{e}_2) = app \circ \langle\!| \hat{e}_1, \hat{e}_2 |\!\rangle && [\![\texttt{proc?}]\!]^{\mathbb{e},\mathbb{e}}_{\mathcal{H}}(\hat{e}) = proc? \circ \hat{e} \\ &[\![\overline{n}]\!]^{\varepsilon,\mathbb{e}}_{\mathcal{H}} = val_n && [\![\texttt{if0}]\!]^{\mathbb{e}\mathbb{e}\mathbb{e},\mathbb{e}}_{\mathcal{H}}(\hat{e}_1, \hat{e}_2, \hat{e}_3) = choice \circ \langle\!| \hat{e}_1, \hat{e}_2, \hat{e}_3 |\!\rangle \\ &[\![\texttt{+}]\!]^{\mathbb{e}\mathbb{e},\mathbb{e}}_{\mathcal{H}}(\hat{e}_1, \hat{e}_2) = add \circ \langle\!| \hat{e}_1, \hat{e}_2 |\!\rangle && [\![\texttt{nat?}]\!]^{\mathbb{e},\mathbb{e}}_{\mathcal{H}}(\hat{e}) = nat? \circ \hat{e} \\ &[\![\texttt{-}]\!]^{\mathbb{e}\mathbb{e},\mathbb{e}}_{\mathcal{H}}(\hat{e}_1, \hat{e}_2) = sub \circ \langle\!| \hat{e}_1, \hat{e}_2 |\!\rangle \end{aligned}$$

For the sake of simplicity, we made a minor change to the language presented in [30]. They have an extra operator `wrong` to print an error message in case of an illegal operation, due to the lack of a type system. For instance, the sum of two functions produces the error `wrong "non-number"`. To avoid to add cases almost everywhere in the definition of the interpretation functions, we let ill-typed terms to denote the value $\bot$ without an explicit encoding of the error message. Furthermore, we denote by $\blacksquare$ the function application.

[8] We do not define $\mathfrak{H}$ explicitly since it can be inferred by the algebra equations below.

The ML-like language defined in [30] is an extended version of the simply-typed lambda calculus. As before, we provide its semantics by defining an algebra $\mathcal{M}$ over an order-sorted signature $\mathfrak{M} = \langle S_2, \leq_2, \Sigma_2 \rangle$.

Let I (should read 'iota') be a set of *base types* and $K$ a I-sorted set of *base values* $K = \{ K_\iota \mid \iota \in \mathrm{I} \}$. We inductively define the set of *simple types* T: If $\iota$ is a base type, then it is a simple type; If $\tau, \tau'$ are simple types, then $(\tau) \to (\tau')$ is a simple type (henceforth we omit the parentheses). We abuse notation and extend $K$ to the T-sorted set of *simple values* $K = \{ K_\tau \mid \tau \in \mathrm{T} \}$ where $K_{\tau \to \tau'} = K_\tau \to K_{\tau'}$.

The set of all ML environments is defined as the set of all total functions $\Delta = Y \to K$, where $Y = \{\mathtt{y}_1, \mathtt{y}_2, \ldots\}$ is a set of variables disjoint from $X$ (this assumption comes from [30]) and $K = \bigcup_{\tau \in \mathrm{T}} K_\tau$. We instantiate $\mathrm{I} = \{ \mathbb{n} \}$ and $K_{\mathbb{n}} = \mathbb{N}$. The poset $\langle S_2, \leq_2 \rangle$ carries all the simple types (i.e., $\mathrm{T} \subseteq S_2$) and the sort $\mathbb{t}$; $\leq_2$ is the reflexive relation on $S_2$ plus $\tau \leq_2 \mathbb{t}$ for each $\tau \in \mathrm{T}$. An ML term of type $\tau$ denotes a total function in $M_\tau = \Delta \to K_\tau$, and we define $M_{\mathbb{t}} = \Delta \to K$. Due to the Turing-incompleteness of such a language, we do not need all the mathematical machinery of [15,46] to formalize its semantics.

$$[\![y]\!]^{\varepsilon,\mathbb{t}}_{\mathcal{M}} = \delta \mapsto \delta(y) \qquad [\![\lambda y^\tau]\!]^{\tau',\tau\to\tau'}_{\mathcal{M}}(\hat{t}) = \delta \mapsto k_\tau \mapsto \hat{t}(\delta[k_\tau/y])$$

$$[\![\overline{n}]\!]^{\varepsilon,\mathbb{n}}_{\mathcal{M}} = \delta \mapsto n \qquad [\![\blacksquare]\!]^{\tau\to\tau'\,\tau,\tau'}_{\mathcal{M}}(\hat{t}_1, \hat{t}_2) = \delta \mapsto (\hat{t}_1(\delta))(\hat{t}_2(\delta))$$

$$[\![+]\!]^{\mathbb{n}\,\mathbb{n},\mathbb{n}}_{\mathcal{M}}(\hat{n}_1, \hat{n}_2) = \delta \mapsto \hat{n}_1(\delta) + \hat{n}_2(\delta) \qquad [\![-]\!]^{\mathbb{n}\,\mathbb{n},\mathbb{n}}_{\mathcal{M}}(\hat{n}_1, \hat{n}_2) = \delta \mapsto \hat{n}_1(\delta) -_{\mathbb{N}} \hat{n}_2(\delta)$$

$$[\![\mathtt{if0}]\!]^{\mathbb{n}\,\tau\,\tau,\tau}_{\mathcal{M}}(\hat{n}, \hat{t}_1, \hat{t}_2) = \delta \mapsto \\ (\!| \hat{n}(\delta) = 0 \; ? \; \hat{t}_1(\delta) \; : \; \hat{t}_2(\delta) |\!)$$

Until now, we have just formalized the single-languages. The multi-language $\mathcal{A}$ that combines Scheme and ML is obtained by requiring $\mathbb{e} \ltimes \tau$ and $\tau \ltimes \mathbb{e}$ in order to use ML terms in place of Scheme terms and vice versa. However, in the simplest version of the natural embedding, *"the system has stuck states, since a boundary might receive a value of an inappropriate shape"* [30]. They restore the type-soundness by first employing dynamic checks, and then by decoupling error-handling from the value conversion through the use of higher-order contracts [12]. We limit ourselves here to describe the first version; the subsequent refinements can be embodied by further complicating the semantics of the boundary functions (we do not have forced any constraints on them).

Since we need a value representing the notion of *stuck state* in ML, we have to extend the algebra $\mathcal{M}$. This is particularly easy by exploiting the underlying framework: We make $\mathcal{M}^\perp$ into an order-sorted $\mathfrak{M}$-algebra by defining $M^\perp_\tau = \Delta^\perp \to K^\perp_\tau$, where $\Delta^\perp = Y \to K^\perp$, $K^\perp = \bigcup_{\tau \in \mathrm{T}} K^\perp_\tau$, and $K^\perp_\tau = K_\tau \cup \{ \perp \}$, and the T-sorted injection $\phi$ from $M_\tau$ to $M^\perp_\tau$ such that $\varphi(\hat{t}) = \hat{t}$. Now, $\mathcal{M}^\perp$ becomes an algebra by letting $\varphi$ to be an order-sorted $\mathfrak{M}$-homomorphism (this in turn forces $[\![-]\!]^{w,s}_{\mathcal{M}^\perp} = [\![-]\!]^{w,s}_{\mathcal{M}}$) and letting the interpretation functions to denote the value $\perp$ in the remaining non-yet defined cases (namely, they compute the value $\perp$ whenever one of their arguments is $\perp$).

The boundary function $\alpha_{\mathbb{e},\tau}(\hat{e})$ moves the Scheme value $\hat{e}\colon \mathrm{P} \diamond\!\!\rightarrow V$ in $M_\tau$:

$$\alpha_{\mathbb{e},\tau}(\hat{e}) = \begin{cases} \alpha^{\mathbb{N}^\diamond}_{\mathbb{e},\tau}(\hat{e}) & \text{if } \hat{e} = val_n \text{ for some } n \in \mathbb{N}^\diamond \\ \alpha^{V \diamond\!\!\rightarrow V}_{\mathbb{e},\tau}(\hat{e}) & \text{otherwise} \end{cases}$$

where $\alpha^{\mathbb{N}^\diamond}_{\mathbb{e},\tau}(val_n) = (\!| \tau = \mathbb{n} \wedge n \in \mathbb{N} \mathrel{?} \delta \mapsto n \mathrel{:} \bot |\!)$ and

$$\alpha^{V \diamond\!\!\rightarrow V}_{\mathbb{e},\tau}(\hat{e}) = \begin{cases} \delta \mapsto k'_\tau \mapsto [\![\lambda y^{\tau'}]\!]^{\tau'',\tau' \to \tau''}_{\mathcal{M}^\perp} (\alpha_{\mathbb{e},\tau''}(\hat{e}' \circ put_x(\bot, \alpha_{\tau',\mathbb{e}}(k_{\tau'})))) \\ \qquad \text{if } \tau = \tau' \to \tau'' \text{ and } \hat{e} = i_{V \diamond\!\!\rightarrow V} \circ abs_{\mathrm{P},V,V}(\hat{e}' \circ put_x) \\ \qquad\quad \text{for some } x \in X \text{ and } \hat{e}' \in V \diamond\!\!\rightarrow V \\ \bot \\ \qquad \text{otherwise} \end{cases}$$

Vice versa, $\alpha_{\tau,\mathbb{e}}(\hat{t})$ moves values from ML to Scheme. Its definition is analogous to the previous case: $\alpha_{\mathbb{n},\mathbb{e}}(\hat{n}) = val_n$ where $\hat{n} = \delta \mapsto n$, and

$$\alpha_{\tau \to \tau',\mathbb{e}} = \rho \mapsto v \mapsto [\![\lambda x]\!]^{\mathbb{e},\mathbb{e}}_{\mathcal{H}} (\alpha_{\tau',\mathbb{e}}(\hat{t}(\bot[\alpha_{\mathbb{e},\tau}(v)/y])))$$

These definitions adhere the conversion approach of the natural embedding in [30]: If $\hat{e}$ is the value denoted by a natural number in Scheme, then it is converted—aside from cases deriving from ill-typed terms—by $\alpha^{\mathbb{N}^\diamond}_{\mathbb{e},\mathbb{n}}$ to the corresponding constant function denoting the same natural value in ML. Otherwise, if $\hat{e}$ is the value denoted by a Scheme function, then it is mapped by $\alpha^{V \diamond\!\!\rightarrow V}_{\mathbb{e},\tau \to \tau'}$ to the ML function with variable $x$ at type $\tau \to \tau'$ such that converts its argument of type $\tau$ to the Scheme equivalent by its conversion through $\alpha_{\tau,\mathbb{e}}$ to $x$. Then it runs the original procedure $\hat{e}$ on it and convert back the result by $\alpha_{\mathbb{e},\tau'}$.

Since the given boundary functions are subsort polymorphic, we can improve the construction and handle all the value conversions with a single polymorphic operator as explained in Sect. 4.1.

## 7 Concluding Remarks

In this paper, we have addressed the problem of providing a formal semantics to the combination of programming languages, the so-called *multi-languages*. We have introduced a new algebraic framework for modeling this new paradigm, and we have constructively shown how to attain a multi-language specification by only stipulate (1) how the syntactic categories of the single-languages have to be combined and (2) how the values may flow from one language to the other. We have proved the suitability of the framework to unambiguously yield the algebraic semantics of each multi-language term, while simultaneously preserving the single-languages semantics. We have also proved that combining languages is a close operation, i.e., that every multi-language admits an equivalent order-sorted representation. In particular, we have focused our study on the semantic properties of boundary functions in order to provide three different notions of multi-language designed to suit both general and specific cases.

To the best of our knowledge, this is the first attempt to provide a formal semantics of a multi-language independently from the combined languages.

*Related Works.* Cross-language interoperability is a well-researched area both from theoretical and practical points of view. The most related work to our approach is undoubtedly [30], which provides operational semantics to a combined language obtained by embedding a Scheme-like language into an ML-like language. Such an outcome is achieved by introducing *boundaries*, syntactic constructs that model the flow of values from one language to the other. Ours *boundary functions* draw heavily from their work. Nonetheless, we shift them to a semantic level, in order to several variants of multi-language constructions.

[7,21,36,40,53] take a similar line and combine typed and untyped languages (Lua and ML [40], Java and PLT Scheme [21], or Assembly and a typed functional language [36]), focusing on typing issues and values exchanging techniques. Instead of focusing on a particular problem, we adopt a rather general framework to model languages. This choice abstracts away many low-level details, allowing us to reason on semantic concerns in more general terms, without having to fix any particular pair of languages.

A lot of work has been done on multi-language runtime mechanisms: [20] provides a type system for a fragment of Microsoft Intermediate Language (IL) used by the .NET framework, that allows programmers to write components in several languages (C#, Visual Basic, VBScript, ...) which are then translated to IL. [22] proposes a virtual machine that can execute the composition of dynamically typed programming languages (Ruby and JavaScript) and statically typed one (C). [4,5] describes a multi-language runtime mechanism achieved by combining single-language interpreters of (different versions of) Python and Prolog.

*Future Works.* From our perspective, the research presented in this paper opens up on three directions. Firstly, future works should aim to provide an operational semantics to the formalization of multi-languages. Rewriting logic seems the most reasonable approach to unifying the denotational world, presented in this paper, to the operational one [31]. This line of research is particularly useful in order to move towards an implementation of an automatic tool able to combine languages such that the resulting multi-language guarantees the results proved in the paper.

Secondly, future research applies to use the multi-language model in order to study the problem of analyzing multi-language programs. In particular, we aim at investigating how it is possible to obtain analyses of multi-language programs by merging already existing analyses of the single combined languages.

Finally, further studies should investigate the problem of compiling multi-languages. Current compilers are closed tools, non-parametric on language constructs (for instance, we cannot compile a single `if-then-else` term of a standard language like C or Java unless it is plugged into a valid program). Several works on typing [1,20,26], compiling [2,37], and running [23,50] multi-language programs already exist, but without providing a formal notion of multi-language. It would be beneficial to study how their approaches can be applied to the formal framework developed in this paper.

## References


1. Abadi, M., Cardelli, L., Pierce, B.C., Plotkin, G.D.: Dynamic typing in a statically typed language. ACM Trans. Program. Lang. Syst. **13**(2), 237–268 (1991)
2. Ahmed, A., Blume, M.: An equivalence-preserving CPS translation via multi-language semantics. SIGPLAN Not. **46**(9), 431–444 (2011)
3. Alencar, A.J., Goguen, J.A.: Object-oriented specification case studies. In: Lano, K., Haughton, H. (eds.) Specification in OOZE with Examples, pp. 158–183. Prentice Hall International (UK) Ltd., Hertfordshire (1994)
4. Barrett, E., Bolz, C.F., Tratt, L.: Unipycation: a case study in cross-language tracing. In: Proceedings of the 7th ACM Workshop on Virtual Machines and Intermediate Languages, pp. 31–40. ACM, New York (2013)
5. Barrett, E., Bolz, C.F., Tratt, L.: Approaches to interpreter composition. Comput. Lang. Syst. Struct. **44**, 199–217 (2015)
6. Beierle, C., Meyer, G.: Run-time type computations in the Warren abstract machine. J. Log. Program. **18**(2), 123–148 (1994)
7. Benton, N.: Embedded interpreters. J. Funct. Program. **15**(4), 503–542 (2005)
8. Chisnall, D.: The challenge of cross-language interoperability. Commun. ACM **56**(12), 50–56 (2013)
9. Dybvig, R.K.: The Scheme Programming Language, 4th edn. The MIT Press, Cambridge (2009)
10. Erwig, M.: Specifying type systems with multi-level order-sorted algebra. In: Nivat, M., Rattray, C., Rus, T., Scollo, G. (eds.) Algebraic Methodology and Software Technology (AMAST 1993). WORKSHOPS COMP., pp. 177–184. Springer, London (1994). https://doi.org/10.1007/978-1-4471-3227-1_17
11. Erwig, M., Güting, R.H.: Explicit graphs in a functional model for spatial databases. IEEE Trans. Knowl. Data Eng. **6**(5), 787–804 (1994)
12. Findler, R.B., Felleisen, M.: Contracts for higher-order functions. In: Proceedings of the Seventh ACM SIGPLAN International Conference on Functional Programming, ICFP 2002, pp. 48–59. ACM, New York (2002)
13. Flanagan, D.: JavaScript: The Definitive Guide. O'Reilly Media Inc., Sebastopol (2006)
14. Furr, M., Foster, J.S.: Checking type safety of foreign function calls. SIGPLAN Not. **40**(6), 62–72 (2005)
15. Goguen, J.A., Thatcher, J.W., Wagner, E.G., Wright, J.B.: Initial algebra semantics and continuous algebras. J. ACM **24**(1), 68–95 (1977)
16. Goguen, J.: Tossing algebraic flowers down the great divide (1999)
17. Goguen, J.A.: Semantics of computation. In: Manes, E.G. (ed.) Category Theory Applied to Computation and Control. LNCS, vol. 25, pp. 151–163. Springer, Heidelberg (1975). https://doi.org/10.1007/3-540-07142-3_75
18. Goguen, J.A., Diaconescu, R.: An oxford survey of order sorted algebra. Math. Struct. Comput. Sci. **4**(3), 363–392 (1994)
19. Goguen, J.A., Meseguer, J.: Order-sorted algebra I: equational deduction for multiple inheritance, overloading, exceptions and partial operations. Theor. Comput. Sci. **105**(2), 217–273 (1992)

20. Gordon, A.D., Syme, D.: Typing a multi-language intermediate code. In: Conference Record of POPL 2001: The 28th ACM SIGPLAN-SIGACT Symposium on Principles of Programming Languages, London, UK, 17–19 January 2001, pp. 248–260. ACM, New York (2001)
21. Gray, K.E.: Safe cross-language inheritance. In: Vitek, J. (ed.) ECOOP 2008. LNCS, vol. 5142, pp. 52–75. Springer, Heidelberg (2008). https://doi.org/10.1007/978-3-540-70592-5_4
22. Grimmer, M., Schatz, R., Seaton, C., Würthinger, T., Luján, M.: Cross-language interoperability in a multi-language runtime. ACM Trans. Program. Lang. Syst. **40**(2), 8:1–8:43 (2018)
23. Grimmer, M., Seaton, C., Schatz, R., Würthinger, T., Mössenböck, H.: High-performance cross-language interoperability in a multi-language runtime. In: Proceedings of the 11th Symposium on Dynamic Languages, DLS 2015, Part of SPLASH 2015, Pittsburgh, PA, USA, 25–30 October 2015, pp. 78–90. ACM, New York (2015)
24. Haxthausen, A.E.: Order-sorted algebraic specifications with higher-order functions. Theor. Comput. Sci. **183**(2), 157–185 (1997)
25. Hearn, A.C., Schrüfer, E.: A computer algebra system based on order-sorted algebra. J. Symb. Comput. **19**(1), 65–77 (1995)
26. Henglein, F., Rehof, J.: Safe polymorphic type inference for scheme: translating scheme to ML. In: Proceedings of the Seventh International Conference on Functional Programming Languages and Computer Architecture, FPCA 1995, La Jolla, California, USA, 25–28 June 1995, pp. 192–203. ACM, New York (1995)
27. Johann, P., Ghani, N.: Initial algebra semantics is enough!. In: Della Rocca, S.R. (ed.) TLCA 2007. LNCS, vol. 4583, pp. 207–222. Springer, Heidelberg (2007). https://doi.org/10.1007/978-3-540-73228-0_16
28. Juneau, J., Baker, J., Wierzbicki, F., Soto, L., Ng, V.: The Definitive Guide to Jython: Python for the Java Platform, 1st edn. Apress, Berkely (2010)
29. Liang, S.: Java Native Interface: Programmer's Guide and Reference, 1st edn. Addison-Wesley Longman Publishing Co., Inc., Boston (1999)
30. Matthews, J., Findler, R.B.: Operational semantics for multi-language programs. SIGPLAN Not. **42**(1), 3–10 (2007)
31. Meseguer, J., Rosu, G.: The rewriting logic semantics project. Electr. Notes Theor. Comput. Sci. **156**(1), 27–56 (2006)
32. Meseguer, J.: Conditional rewriting logic as a unified model of concurrency. Theor. Comput. Sci. **96**(1), 73–155 (1992)
33. Milner, R., Tofte, M., Macqueen, D.: The Definition of Standard ML. MIT Press, Cambridge (1997)
34. Ohori, A., Kato, K.: Semantics for communication primitives in a polymorphic language. In: Proceedings of the 20th ACM SIGPLAN-SIGACT Symposium on Principles of Programming Languages, POPL 1993, pp. 99–112. ACM, New York (1993)
35. Osera, P.M., Sjöberg, V., Zdancewic, S.: Dependent interoperability. In: Proceedings of the Sixth Workshop on Programming Languages Meets Program Verification, PLPV 2012, pp. 3–14. ACM, New York (2012)
36. Patterson, D., Perconti, J., Dimoulas, C., Ahmed, A.: FunTAL: reasonably mixing a functional language with assembly. SIGPLAN Not. **52**(6), 495–509 (2017)
37. Perconti, J.T., Ahmed, A.: Verifying an open compiler using multi-language semantics. In: Shao, Z. (ed.) ESOP 2014. LNCS, vol. 8410, pp. 128–148. Springer, Heidelberg (2014). https://doi.org/10.1007/978-3-642-54833-8_8

38. Poigné, A.: Parametrization for order-sorted algebraic specification. J. Comput. Syst. Sci. **40**(2), 229–268 (1990)
39. Qian, Z.: Another look at parameterization for order-sorted algebraic specifications. J. Comput. Syst. Sci. **49**(3), 620–666 (1994)
40. Ramsey, N.: Embedding an interpreted language using higher-order functions and types. In: Proceedings of the 2003 Workshop on Interpreters, Virtual Machines and Emulators, IVME 2003, pp. 6–14. ACM, New York (2003)
41. Ramsey, N.: ML module mania: a type-safe, separately compiled, extensible interpreter. Electron. Notes Theor. Comput. Sci. **148**(2), 181–209 (2006)
42. Reynolds, J.C.: Definitional interpreters for higher-order programming languages. In: Proceedings of the ACM Annual Conference - Volume 2, ACM 1972, pp. 717–740. ACM, New York (1972)
43. Robinson, E.: Variations on algebra: monadicity and generalisations of equational therories. Form. Asp. Comput. **13**(3), 308–326 (2002)
44. Rogers, J.: Microsoft JScript.Net Programming. Sams, Indianapolis (2001)
45. Schmidt-Schauß, M. (ed.): Computational Aspects of an Order-Sorted Logic with Term Declarations. LNCS, vol. 395. Springer, Heidelberg (1989). https://doi.org/10.1007/BFb0024065
46. Scott, D.S., Strachey, C.: Toward a Mathematical Semantics for Computer Languages, vol. 1. Oxford University Computing Laboratory, Programming Research Group, Oxford (1971)
47. Sharan, K.: Scripting in Java: Integrating with Groovy and JavaScript, 1st edn. Apress, Berkely (2014)
48. Stell, J.G.: A framework for order-sorted algebra. In: Kirchner, H., Ringeissen, C. (eds.) AMAST 2002. LNCS, vol. 2422, pp. 396–411. Springer, Heidelberg (2002). https://doi.org/10.1007/3-540-45719-4_27
49. Tan, G., Morrisett, G.: Ilea: Inter-language analysis across Java and C. SIGPLAN Not. **42**(10), 39–56 (2007)
50. Trifonov, V., Shao, Z.: Safe and principled language interoperation. In: Swierstra, S.D. (ed.) ESOP 1999. LNCS, vol. 1576, pp. 128–146. Springer, Heidelberg (2002). https://doi.org/10.1007/3-540-49099-X_9
51. Waldmann, U.: Semantics of order-sorted specifications. Theor. Comput. Sci. **94**(1), 1–35 (1992)
52. Wieringa, R.J.: A formalization of objects using equational dynamic logic. In: Delobel, C., Kifer, M., Masunaga, Y. (eds.) DOOD 1991. LNCS, vol. 566, pp. 431–452. Springer, Heidelberg (1991). https://doi.org/10.1007/3-540-55015-1_23
53. Wrigstad, T., Nardelli, F.Z., Lebresne, S., Östlund, J., Vitek, J.: Integrating typed and untyped code in a scripting language. In: Hermenegildo, M.V., Palsberg, J. (eds.) Proceedings of the 37th ACM SIGPLAN-SIGACT Symposium on Principles of Programming Languages, POPL 2010, Madrid, Spain, 17–23 January 2010, pp. 377–388. ACM (2010)

# 6

# Meta-F★: Proof Automation with SMT, Tactics and Metaprograms

Guido Martínez[1,2(✉)], Danel Ahman[3], Victor Dumitrescu[4], Nick Giannarakis[5], Chris Hawblitzel[6], Cătălin Hriţcu[2], Monal Narasimhamurthy[8], Zoe Paraskevopoulou[5], Clément Pit-Claudel[9], Jonathan Protzenko[6], Tahina Ramananandro[6], Aseem Rastogi[7], and Nikhil Swamy[6]

[1] CIFASIS-CONICET, Rosario, Argentina
martinez@cifasis-conicet.gov.ar
[2] Inria, Paris, France
[3] University of Ljubljana, Ljubljana, Slovenia
[4] MSR-Inria Joint Centre, Paris, France
[5] Princeton University, Princeton, USA
[6] Microsoft Research, Redmond, USA
[7] Microsoft Research, Bangalore, India
[8] University of Colorado Boulder, Boulder, USA
[9] MIT CSAIL, Cambridge, USA

**Abstract.** We introduce Meta-F*, a tactics and metaprogramming framework for the F* program verifier. The main novelty of Meta-F* is allowing the use of tactics and metaprogramming to discharge assertions not solvable by SMT, or to just simplify them into well-behaved SMT fragments. Plus, Meta-F* can be used to generate verified code automatically.

Meta-F* is implemented as an F* *effect*, which, given the powerful effect system of F*, heavily increases code reuse and even enables the lightweight verification of metaprograms. Metaprograms can be either interpreted, or compiled to efficient native code that can be dynamically loaded into the F* type-checker and can interoperate with interpreted code. Evaluation on realistic case studies shows that Meta-F* provides substantial gains in proof development, efficiency, and robustness.

**Keywords:** Tactics · Metaprogramming · Program verification · Verification conditions · SMT solvers · Proof assistants

## 1 Introduction

Scripting proofs using tactics and metaprogramming has a long tradition in interactive theorem provers (ITPs), starting with Milner's Edinburgh LCF [37]. In this lineage, properties of *pure* programs are specified in expressive higher-order (and often dependently typed) logics, and proofs are conducted using various imperative programming languages, starting originally with ML.

Along a different axis, program verifiers like Dafny [47], VCC [23], Why3 [33], and Liquid Haskell [59] target both pure *and effectful* programs, with side-effects ranging from divergence to concurrency, but provide relatively weak logics for specification (e.g., first-order logic with a few selected theories like linear arithmetic). They work primarily by computing verification conditions (VCs) from programs, usually relying on annotations such as pre- and postconditions, and encoding them to automated theorem provers (ATPs) such as satisfiability modulo theories (SMT) solvers, often providing excellent automation.

These two sub-fields have influenced one another, though the situation is somewhat asymmetric. On the one hand, most interactive provers have gained support for exploiting SMT solvers or other ATPs, providing push-button automation for certain kinds of assertions [26, 31, 43, 44, 54]. On the other hand, recognizing the importance of interactive proofs, Why3 [33] interfaces with ITPs like Coq. However, working over proof obligations translated from Why3 requires users to be familiar not only with both these systems, but also with the specifics of the translation. And beyond Why3 and the tools based on it [25], no other SMT-based program verifiers have full-fledged support for interactive proving, leading to several downsides:

**Limits to expressiveness.** The expressiveness of program verifiers can be limited by the ATP used. When dealing with theories that are undecidable and difficult to automate (e.g., non-linear arithmetic or separation logic), proofs in ATP-based systems may become impossible or, at best, extremely tedious.

**Boilerplate.** To work around this lack of automation, programmers have to construct detailed proofs by hand, often repeating many tedious yet error-prone steps, so as to provide hints to the underlying solver to discover the proof. In contrast, ITPs with metaprogramming facilities excel at expressing domain-specific automation to complete such tedious proofs.

**Implicit proof context.** In most program verifiers, the logical context of a proof is implicit in the program text and depends on the control flow and the pre- and postconditions of preceding computations. Unlike in interactive proof assistants, programmers have no explicit access, neither visual nor programmatic, to this context, making proof structuring and exploration extremely difficult.

In direct response to these drawbacks, we seek a system that successfully combines the convenience of an automated program verifier for the common case, while seamlessly transitioning to an interactive proving experience for those parts of a proof that are hard to automate. Towards this end, we propose Meta-F*, a tactics and metaprogramming framework for the F* [1, 58] program verifier.

## Highlights and Contributions of Meta-F*

F* has historically been more deeply rooted as an SMT-based program verifier. Until now, F* discharged VCs exclusively by calling an SMT solver (usually Z3 [28]), providing good automation for many common program verification tasks, but also exhibiting the drawbacks discussed above.

Meta-F* is a framework that allows F* users to manipulate VCs using *tactics*. More generally, it supports *metaprogramming*, allowing programmers to script the construction of programs, by manipulating their syntax and customizing the way they are type-checked. This allows programmers to (1) implement custom procedures for manipulating VCs; (2) eliminate boilerplate in proofs and programs; and (3) to inspect the proof state visually and to manipulate it programmatically, addressing the drawbacks discussed above. SMT still plays a central role in Meta-F$^\star$: a typical usage involves implementing tactics to transform VCs, so as to bring them into theories well-supported by SMT, without needing to (re)implement full decision procedures. Further, the generality of Meta-F$^\star$ allows implementing non-trivial language extensions (e.g., typeclass resolution) entirely as metaprogramming libraries, without changes to the F$^\star$ type-checker.

The technical **contributions** of our work include the following:

**"Meta-" is just an effect (Sect. 3.1).** Meta-F$^\star$ is implemented using F$^\star$'s extensible effect system, which keeps programs and metaprograms properly isolated. Being first-class F$^\star$ programs, metaprograms are typed, call-by-value, direct-style, higher-order functional programs, much like the original ML. Further, metaprograms can be themselves verified (to a degree, see Sect. 3.4) and metaprogrammed.

**Reconciling tactics with VC generation (Sect. 4.2).** In program verifiers the programmer often guides the solver towards the proof by supplying intermediate assertions. Meta-F$^\star$ retains this style, but additionally allows assertions to be solved by tactics. To this end, a contribution of our work is extracting, from a VC, a proof state encompassing all relevant hypotheses, including those implicit in the program text.

**Executing metaprograms efficiently (Sect. 5).** Metaprograms are executed during type-checking. As a baseline, they can be interpreted using F$^\star$'s existing (but slow) abstract machine for term normalization, or a faster normalizer based on normalization by evaluation (NbE) [10, 16]. For much faster execution speed, metaprograms can also be run natively. This is achieved by combining the existing extraction mechanism of F$^\star$ to OCaml with a new framework for safely extending the F$^\star$ type-checker with such native code.

**Examples (Sect. 2) and evaluation (Sect. 6).** We evaluate Meta-F$^\star$ on several case studies. First, we present a functional correctness proof for the Poly1305 message authentication code (MAC) [11], using a novel combination of proofs by reflection for dealing with non-linear arithmetic and SMT solving for linear arithmetic. We measure a clear gain in proof robustness: SMT-only proofs succeed only rarely (for reasonable timeouts), whereas our tactic+SMT proof is concise, never fails, and is faster. Next, we demonstrate an improvement in expressiveness, by developing a small library for proofs of heap-manipulating programs in separation logic, which was previously out-of-scope for F$^\star$. Finally, we illustrate the ability to automatically construct verified effectful programs, by introducing a library for metaprogramming verified low-level parsers and serializers with applications to network programming, where verification is accelerated by processing the VC with tactics, and by programmatically tweaking the SMT context.

We conclude that tactics and metaprogramming can be prosperously combined with VC generation and SMT solving to build verified programs with better, more scalable, and more robust automation.

The full version of this paper, including appendices, can be found online in https://www.fstar-lang.org/papers/metafstar.

## 2 Meta-F⋆ by Example

F⋆ is a general-purpose programming language aimed at program verification. It puts together the automation of an SMT-backed deductive verification tool with the expressive power of a language with full-spectrum dependent types. Briefly, it is a functional, higher-order, effectful, dependently typed language, with syntax loosely based on OCaml. F⋆ supports refinement types and Hoare-style specifications, computing VCs of computations via a type-level weakest precondition (WP) calculus packed within *Dijkstra monads* [57]. F⋆'s effect system is also user-extensible [1]. Using it, one can model or embed imperative programming in styles ranging from ML to C [55] and assembly [35]. After verification, F⋆ programs can be extracted to efficient OCaml or F# code. A first-order fragment of F⋆, called Low⋆, can also be extracted to C via the KreMLin compiler [55].

This paper introduces Meta-F⋆, a metaprogramming framework for F⋆ that allows users to safely customize and extend F⋆ in many ways. For instance, Meta-F⋆ can be used to preprocess or solve proof obligations; synthesize F⋆ expressions; generate top-level definitions; and resolve implicit arguments in user-defined ways, enabling non-trivial extensions. This paper primarily discusses the first two features. Technically, none of these features deeply increase the expressive power of F⋆, since one could manually program in F⋆ terms that can now be metaprogrammed. However, as we will see shortly, manually programming terms and their proofs can be so prohibitively costly as to be practically infeasible.

Meta-F⋆ is similar to other tactic frameworks, such as Coq's [29] or Lean's [30], in presenting a set of goals to the programmer, providing commands to break them down, allowing to inspect and build abstract syntax, etc. In this paper, we mostly detail the characteristics where Meta-F⋆ *differs* from other engines.

This section presents Meta-F⋆ informally, displaying its usage through case studies. We present any necessary F⋆ background as needed.

### 2.1 Tactics for Individual Assertions and Partial Canonicalization

Non-linear arithmetic reasoning is crucially needed for the verification of optimized, low-level cryptographic primitives [18,64], an important use case for F⋆ [13] and other verification frameworks, including those that rely on SMT solving alone (e.g., Dafny [47]) as well as those that rely exclusively on tactic-based proofs (e.g., FiatCrypto [32]). While both styles have demonstrated significant successes, we make a case for a middle ground, leveraging the SMT solver for the parts of a VC where it is effective, and using tactics only where it is not.

We focus on Poly1305 [11], a widely-used cryptographic MAC that computes a series of integer multiplications and additions modulo a large prime number $p = 2^{130} - 5$. Implementations of the Poly1305 multiplication and mod operations are carefully hand-optimized to represent 130-bit numbers in terms of smaller 32-bit or 64-bit registers, using clever tricks; proving their correctness requires reasoning about long sequences of additions and multiplications.

**Previously: Guiding SMT Solvers by Manually Applying Lemmas.** Prior proofs of correctness of Poly1305 and other cryptographic primitives using SMT-based program verifiers, including F* [64] and Dafny [18], use a combination of SMT automation and manual application of lemmas. On the plus side, SMT solvers are excellent at linear arithmetic, so these proofs delegate all associativity-commutativity (AC) reasoning about addition to SMT. Non-linear arithmetic in SMT solvers, even just AC-rewriting and distributivity, are, however, inefficient and unreliable—so much so that the prior efforts above (and other works too [40,41]) simply turn off support for non-linear arithmetic in the solver, in order not to degrade verification performance across the board due to poor interaction of theories. Instead, users need to explicitly invoke lemmas.[1]

For instance, here is a statement and proof of a lemma about Poly1305 in F*. The property and its proof do not really matter; the lines marked "*(∗argh! ∗)*" do. In this particular proof, working around the solver's inability to effectively reason about non-linear arithmetic, the programmer has spelled out basic facts about distributivity of multiplication and addition, by calling the library lemma distributivity_add_right, in order to guide the solver towards the proof. (Below, p44 and p88 represent $2^{44}$ and $2^{88}$ respectively)

```
let lemma_carry_limb_unrolled (a0 a1 a2 : nat) : Lemma (ensures (
   a0 % p44 + p44 * ((a1 + a0 / p44) % p44) + p88 * (a2 + ((a1 + a0 / p44) / p44))
   == a0 + p44 * a1 + p88 * a2)) =
 let z = a0 % p44 + p44 * ((a1 + a0 / p44) % p44)
          + p88 * (a2 + ((a1 + a0 / p44) / p44)) in
 distributivity_add_right p88 a2 ((a1 + a0 / p44) / p44); (* argh! *)
 pow2_plus 44 44;
 lemma_div_mod (a1 + a0 / p44) p44;
 distributivity_add_right p44 ((a1 + a0 / p44) % p44)
          (p44 * ((a1 + a0 / p44) / p44)); (* argh! *)
 assert (p44 * ((a1 + a0 / p44) % p44) + p88 * ((a1 + a0 / p44) / p44)
          == p44 * (a1 + a0 / p44) );
 distributivity_add_right p44 a1 (a0 / p44); (* argh! *)
 lemma_div_mod a0 p44
```

Even at this relatively small scale, needing to explicitly instantiate the distributivity lemma is verbose and error prone. Even worse, the user is blind while doing so: the program text does not display the current set of available facts nor

[1] Lemma (requires pre) (ensures post) is F* notation for the type of a computation proving pre $\Longrightarrow$ post—we omit pre when it is trivial. In F*'s standard library, math lemmas are proved using SMT with little or no interactions between problematic theory combinations. These lemmas can then be explicitly invoked in larger contexts, and are deleted during extraction.

the final goal. Proofs at this level of abstraction are painfully detailed in some aspects, yet also heavily reliant on the SMT solver to fill in the aspects of the proof that are missing.

Given enough time, the solver can sometimes find a proof without the additional hints, but this is usually rare and dependent on context, and almost never robust. In this particular example we find by varying Z3's random seed that, in an isolated setting, the lemma is proven automatically about 32% of the time. The numbers are much worse for more complex proofs, and where the context contains many facts, making this style quickly spiral out of control. For example, a proof of one of the main lemmas in Poly1305, poly_multiply, requires 41 steps of rewriting for associativity-commutativity of multiplication, and distributivity of addition and multiplication—making the proof much too long to show here.

**SMT and Tactics in Meta-F⋆.** The listing below shows the statement and proof of poly_multiply in Meta-F⋆, of which the lemma above was previously only a small part. Again, the specific property proven is not particularly relevant to our discussion. But, this time, the proof contains just two steps.

```
let poly_multiply (n p r h r0 r1 h0 h1 h2 s1 d0 d1 d2 h1 h2 hh : int) : Lemma
  (requires p > 0 ∧ r1 ≥ 0 ∧ n > 0 ∧ 4 * (n * n) == p + 5 ∧ r == r1 * n + r0 ∧
            h == h2 * (n * n) + h1 * n + h0 ∧ s1 == r1 + (r1 / 4) ∧ r1 % 4 == 0 ∧
            d0 == h0 * r0 + h1 * s1 ∧ d1 == h0 * r1 + h1 * r0 + h2 * s1 ∧
            d2 == h2 * r0 ∧ hh == d2 * (n * n) + d1 * n + d0)
  (ensures (h * r) % p == hh % p) =
  let r14 = r1 / 4 in
  let h_r_expand = (h2 * (n * n) + h1 * n + h0) * ((r14 * 4) * n + r0) in
  let hh_expand = (h2 * r0) * (n * n) + (h0 * (r14 * 4) + h1 * r0
                             + h2 * (5 * r14)) * n + (h0 * r0 + h1 * (5 * r14)) in
  let b = (h2 * n + h1) * r14 in
  modulo_addition_lemma hh_expand p b;
  assert (h_r_expand == hh_expand + b * (n * n * 4 + (−5)))
     by (canon_semiring int_csr) (* Proof of this step by Meta-F* tactic *)
```

First, we call a single lemma about modular addition from F⋆'s standard library. Then, we assert an equality annotated with a tactic (assert..by). Instead of encoding the assertion as-is to the SMT solver, it is preprocessed by the canon_semiring tactic. The tactic is presented with the asserted equality as its goal, in an environment containing not only all variables in scope but also hypotheses for the precondition of poly_multiply and the postcondition of the modulo_addition_lemma call (otherwise, the assertion could not be proven). The tactic will then canonicalize the sides of the equality, but notably only "up to" linear arithmetic conversions. Rather than fully canonicalizing the terms, the tactic just rewrites them into a sum-of-products canonical form, leaving all the remaining work to the SMT solver, which can then easily and robustly discharge the goal using linear arithmetic only.

This tactic works over terms in the commutative semiring of integers (int_csr) using proof-by-reflection [12,20,36,38]. Internally, it is composed of a simpler, also proof-by-reflection based tactic canon_monoid that works over monoids, which is then "stacked" on itself to build canon_semiring. The basic idea of proof-by-reflection is to reduce most of the proof burden to mechanical computation, obtaining much more efficient proofs compared to repeatedly applying lemmas. For canon_monoid, we begin with a type for monoids, a small AST representing monoid values, and a denotation for expressions back into the monoid type.

```
type monoid (a:Type) = { unit : a; mult : (a → a → a); (* + monoid laws ... *) }
type exp (a:Type) = | Unit : exp a | Var : a → exp a | Mult : exp a → exp a → exp a
(* Note on syntax: #a below denotes that a is an implicit argument *)
let rec denote (#a:Type) (m:monoid a) (e:exp a) : a =
  match e with
  | Unit → m.unit | Var x → x | Mult x y → m.mult (denote m x) (denote m y)
```

To canonicalize an exp, it is first converted to a list of operands (flatten) and then reflected back to the monoid (mldenote). The process is proven correct, in the particular case of equalities, by the monoid_reflect lemma.

```
val flatten : #a:Type → exp a → list a
val mldenote : #a:Type → monoid a → list a → a
let monoid_reflect (#a:Type) (m:monoid a) (e1 e2 : exp a)
              : Lemma (requires (mldenote m (flatten e1) == mldenote m (flatten e2)))
                      (ensures (denote m e1 == denote m e2)) = ...
```

At this stage, if the goal is $t_1 == t_2$, we require two monoidal expressions $e_1$ and $e_2$ such that $t_1 ==$ denote m $e_1$ and $t_2 ==$ denote m $e_2$. They are constructed by the tactic canon_monoid by inspecting the *syntax* of the goal, using Meta-F*'s reflection capabilities (detailed ahead in Sect. 3.3). We have no way to prove once and for all that the expressions built by canon_monoid correctly denote the terms, but this fact can be proven automatically at each application of the tactic, by simple unification. The tactic then applies the lemma monoid_reflect m $e_1 e_2$, and the goal is changed to mldenote m (flatten $e_1$) == mldenote m (flatten $e_2$). Finally, by normalization, each side will be canonicalized by running flatten and mldenote.

The canon_semiring tactic follows a similar approach, and is similar to existing reflective tactics for other proof assistants [9,38], except that it only canonicalizes up to linear arithmetic, as explained above. The full VC for poly_multiply contains many other facts, e.g., that p is non-zero so the division is well-defined and that the postcondition does indeed hold. These obligations remain in a "skeleton" VC that is also easily proven by Z3. This proof is much easier for the programmer to write and much more robust, as detailed ahead in Sect. 6.1. The proof of Poly1305's other main lemma, poly_reduce, is also similarly well automated.

**Tactic Proofs Without SMT.** Of course, one can verify poly_multiply in Coq, following the same conceptual proof used in Meta-F*, but relying on tactics only. Our proof (included in the appendix) is 27 lines long, two of which involve the use of Coq's ring tactic (similar to our canon_semiring tactic) and omega tactic for solving formulas in Presburger arithmetic. The remaining 25 lines include steps to destruct the propositional structure of terms, rewrite by equalities, enriching the context to enable automatic modulo rewriting (Coq does not fully automatically recognize equality modulo $p$ as an equivalence relation compatible with arithmetic operators). While a mature proof assistant like Coq has libraries and tools to ease this kind of manipulation, it can still be verbose.

In contrast, in Meta-F⋆ all of these mundane parts of a proof are simply dispatched to the SMT solver, which decides linear arithmetic efficiently, beyond the quantifier-free Presburger fragment supported by tactics like omega, handles congruence closure natively, etc.

## 2.2 Tactics for Entire VCs and Separation Logic

A different way to invoke Meta-F⋆ is over an entire VC. While the exact shape of VCs is hard to predict, users with some experience can write tactics that find and solve particular sub-assertions within a VC, or simply massage them into shapes better suited for the SMT solver. We illustrate the idea on proofs for heap-manipulating programs.

One verification method that has eluded F⋆ until now is separation logic, the main reason being that the pervasive "frame rule" requires instantiating existentially quantified heap variables, which is a challenge for SMT solvers, and simply too tedious for users. With Meta-F⋆, one can do better. We have written a (proof-of-concept) embedding of separation logic and a tactic (sl_auto) that performs heap frame inference automatically.

The approach we follow consists of designing the WP specifications for primitive stateful actions so as to make their footprint syntactically evident. The tactic then descends through VCs until it finds an existential for heaps arising from the frame rule. Then, by solving an equality between heap expressions (which requires canonicalization, for which we use a variant of canon_monoid targeting *commutative* monoids) the tactic finds the frames and instantiates the existentials. Notably, as opposed to other tactic frameworks for separation logic [4,45,49,51], this is *all* our tactic does before dispatching to the SMT solver, which can now be effective over the instantiated VC.

We now provide some detail on the framework. Below, 'emp' represents the empty heap, '•' is the separating conjunction and 'r ↦ v' is the heaplet with the single reference r set to value v.[2] Our development distinguishes between a "heap" and its "memory" for technical reasons, but we will treat the two as equivalent here. Further, defined is a predicate discriminating valid heaps (as in [52]), i.e., those built from separating conjunctions of *actually* disjoint heaps.

We first define the type of WPs and present the WP for the frame rule:

```
let pre = memory → prop (* predicate on initial heaps *)
let post a = a → memory → prop (* predicate on result values and final heaps *)
let wp a = post a → pre (* transformer from postconditions to preconditions *)

let frame_post (#a:Type) (p:post a) (m0:memory) : post a =
  λx m1 → defined (m0 • m1) ∧ p x (m0 • m1)
let frame_wp (#a:Type) (wp:wp a) (post:post a) (m:memory) =
  ∃m0 m1. defined (m0 • m1) ∧ m == (m0 • m1) ∧ wp (frame_post post m1) m0
```

[2] This differs from the usual presentation where these three operators are heap *predicates* instead of heaps.

Intuitively, frame_post p $m_0$ behaves as the postcondition p "framed" by $m_0$, i.e., frame_post p $m_0$ x $m_1$ holds when the two heaps $m_0$ and $m_1$ are disjoint and p holds over the result value x and the conjoined heaps. Then, frame_wp wp takes a postcondition p and initial heap m, and requires that m can be split into disjoint subheaps $m_0$ (the footprint) and $m_1$ (the frame), such that the postcondition p, when properly framed, holds over the footprint.

In order to provide specifications for primitive actions we start in small-footprint style. For instance, below is the WP for reading a reference:

```
let read_wp (#a:Type) (r:ref a) = λpost m0 → ∃x. m0 == r ↦ x ∧ post x m0
```

We then insert framing wrappers around such small-footprint WPs when exposing the corresponding stateful actions to the programmer, e.g.,

```
val (!) : #a:Type → r:ref a → STATE a (λ p m → frame_wp (read_wp r) p m)
```

To verify code written in such style, we annotate the corresponding programs to have their VCs processed by sl_auto. For instance, for the swap function below, the tactic successfully finds the frames for the four occurrences of the frame rule and greatly reduces the solver's work. Even in this simple example, not performing such instantiation would cause the solver to fail.

```
let swap_wp (r1 r2 : ref int) =
    λp m → ∃x y. m == (r1 ↦ x • r2 ↦ y) ∧ p () (r1 ↦ y • r2 ↦ x)
let swap (r1 r2 : ref int) : ST unit (swap_wp r1 r2) by (sl_auto ()) =
    let x = !r1 in let y = !r2 in r1 := y; r2 := x
```

The sl_auto tactic: (1) uses syntax inspection to unfold and traverse the goal until it reaches a frame_wp—say, the one for $!r_2$; (2) inspects frame_wp's first explicit argument (here read_wp $r_2$) to compute the references the current command requires (here $r_2$); (3) uses unification variables to build a memory expression describing the required framing of input memory (here $r_2 \mapsto ?u_1 \bullet ?u_2$) and instantiates the existentials of frame_wp with these unification variables; (4) builds a goal that equates this memory expression with frame_wp's third argument (here $r_1 \mapsto x \bullet r_2 \mapsto y$); and (5) uses a commutative monoids tactic (similar to Sect. 2.1) with the heap algebra (emp, $\bullet$) to canonicalize the equality and sort the heaplets. Next, it can solve for the unification variables component-wise, instantiating $?u_1$ to y and $?u_2$ to $r_1 \mapsto x$, and then proceed to the next frame_wp.

In general, after frames are instantiated, the SMT solver can efficiently prove the remaining assertions, such as the obligations about heap definedness. Thus, with relatively little effort, Meta-F* brings an (albeit simple version of a) widely used yet previously out-of-scope program logic (i.e., separation logic) into F*. To the best of our knowledge, the ability to *script* separation logic into an SMT-based program verifier, without any primitive support, is unique.

### 2.3 Metaprogramming Verified Low-Level Parsers and Serializers

Above, we used Meta-F* to manipulate VCs for user-written code. Here, we focus instead on generating verified code automatically. We loosely refer to the previous setting as using "tactics", and to the current one as "metaprogramming".

In most ITPs, tactics and metaprogramming are not distinguished; however in a program verifier like F*, where some proofs are not materialized at all (Sect. 4.1), proving VCs of existing terms is distinct from generating new terms.

Metaprogramming in F* involves programmatically generating a (potentially effectful) term (e.g., by constructing its syntax and instructing F* how to type-check it) and processing any VCs that arise via tactics. When applicable (e.g., when working in a domain-specific language), metaprogramming verified code can substantially reduce, or even eliminate, the burden of manual proofs.

We illustrate this by automating the generation of parsers and serializers from a type definition. Of course, this is a routine task in many mainstream metaprogramming frameworks (e.g., Template Haskell, camlp4, etc). The novelty here is that we produce imperative parsers and serializers extracted to C, with proofs that they are memory safe, functionally correct, and mutually inverse. This section is slightly simplified, more detail can be found the appendix.

We proceed in several stages. First, we program a library of pure, high-level parser and serializer combinators, proven to be (partial) mutual inverses of each other. A parser for a type t is represented as a function possibly returning a t along with the amount of input bytes consumed. The type of a serializer for a given p:parser t contains a refinement[3] stating that p is an inverse of the serializer. A package is a dependent record of a parser and an associated serializer.

```
let parser t = seq byte → option (t ∗ nat)
let serializer #t (p:parser t) = f:(t → seq byte){∀ x. p (f x) == Some (x, length (f x))}
type package t = { p : parser t ; s : serializer p }
```

Basic combinators in the library include constructs for parsing and serializing base values and pairs, such as the following:

```
val p_u8 : parse u8
val s_u8 : serializer p_u8
val p_pair : parser t1 → parser t2 → parser (t1 ∗ t2)
val s_pair : serializer p1 → serializer p2 → serializer (p_pair p1 p2)
```

Next, we define low-level versions of these combinators, which work over mutable arrays instead of byte sequences. These combinators are coded in the Low* subset of F* (and so can be extracted to C) and are proven to both be memory-safe and respect their high-level variants. The type for low-level parsers, parser_impl (p:parser t), denotes an imperative function that reads from an array of bytes and returns a t, behaving as the specificational parser p. Conversely, a serializer_impl (s:serializer p) writes into an array of bytes, behaving as s.

Given such a library, we would like to build verified, mutually inverse, low-level parsers and serializers for specific data formats. The task is mechanical, yet overwhelmingly tedious by hand, with many auxiliary proof obligations of a predictable structure: a perfect candidate for metaprogramming.

*Deriving Specifications from a Type Definition.* Consider the following F* type, representing lists of exactly 18 pairs of bytes.

[3] F* syntax for refinements is x:t $\{\phi\}$, denoting the type of all x of type t satisfying $\phi$.

```
type sample = nlist 18 (u8 * u8)
```

The first component of our metaprogram is gen_specs, which generates parser and serializer specifications from a type definition.

```
let ps_sample : package sample = _ by (gen_specs (`sample))
```

The syntax _ by $\tau$ is the way to call Meta-F* for code generation. Meta-F* will run the metaprogram $\tau$ and, if successful, replace the underscore by the result. In this case, the gen_specs (`sample) inspects the syntax of the sample type (Sect. 3.3) and produces the package below (seq_p and seq_s are sequencing combinators):

```
let ps_sample = { p = p_nlist 18 (p_u8 `seq_p` p_u8)
                ; s = s_nlist 18 (s_u8 `seq_s` s_u8) }
```

*Deriving Low-Level Implementations that Match Specifications.* From this pair of specifications, we can automatically generate Low* implementations for them:

```
let p_low : parser_impl ps_sample.p = _ by gen_parser_impl
let s_low : serializer_impl ps_sample.s = _ by gen_serializer_impl
```

which will produce the following low-level implementations:

```
let p_low = parse_nlist_impl 18ul (parse_u8_impl `seq_pi` parse_u8_impl)
let s_low = serialize_nlist_impl 18ul (serialize_u8_impl `seq_si` serialize_u8_impl)
```

For simple types like the one above, the generated code is fairly simple. However, for more complex types, using the combinator library comes with non-trivial proof obligations. For example, even for a simple enumeration, type color = Red | Green, the parser specification is as follows:

```
parse_synth (parse_bounded_u8 2)
            (λ x2 → mk_if_t (x2 = 0uy) (λ _ → Red) (λ _ → Green))
            (λ x → match x with | Green → 1uy | Red → 0uy)
```

We represent Red with 0uy and Green with 1uy. The parser first parses a "bounded" byte, with only two values. The parse_synth combinator then expects functions between the bounded byte and the datatype being parsed (color), which must be proven to be mutual inverses. This proof is conceptually easy, but for large enumerations nested deep within the structure of other types, it is notoriously hard for SMT solvers. Since the proof is inherently computational, a proof that destructs the inductive type into its cases and then normalizes is much more natural. With our metaprogram, we can produce the term and then discharge these proof obligations with a tactic *on the spot*, eliminating them from the final VC. We also explore simply tweaking the SMT context, again via a tactic, with good results. A quantitative evaluation is provided in Sect. 6.2.

## 3 The Design of Meta-F*

Having caught a glimpse of the use cases for Meta-F*, we now turn to its design. As usual in proof assistants (such as Coq, Lean and Idris), Meta-F* tactics work over a set of goals and apply primitive actions to transform them, possibly solving some goals and generating new goals in the process. Since this is standard, we will focus the most on describing the aspects where Meta-F* differs from other engines. We first describe how metaprograms are modelled as an effect (Sect. 3.1) and their runtime model (Sect. 3.2). We then detail some of Meta-F*'s syntax inspection and building capabilities (Sect. 3.3). Finally, we show how to perform some (lightweight) verification of metaprograms (Sect. 3.4) within F*.

### 3.1 An Effect for Metaprogramming

Meta-F* tactics are, at their core, programs that transform the "proof state", i.e. a set of goals needing to be solved. As in Lean [30] and Idris [22], we define a monad combining exceptions and stateful computations over a proof state, along with actions that can access internal components such as the type-checker. For this we first introduce abstract types for the proof state, goals, terms, environments, etc., together with functions to access them, some of them shown below.

```
type proofstate          val goals_of : proofstate → list goal
type goal                val goal_env : goal → env
type term                val goal_type : goal → term
type env                 val goal_solution : goal → term
```

We can now define our metaprogramming monad: tac. It combines F*'s existing effect for potential divergence (Div), with exceptions and stateful computations over a proofstate. The definition of tac, shown below, is straightforward and given in F*'s standard library. Then, we use F*'s effect extension capabilities [1] in order to elevate the tac monad and its actions to an effect, dubbed TAC.

```
type error = exn * proofstate (* error and proofstate at the time of failure *)
type result a = | Success : a → proofstate → result a | Failed : error → result a
let tac a = proofstate → Div (result a)
let t_return #a (x:a) = λps → Success x ps
let t_bind #a #b (m:tac a) (f:a → tac b) : tac b = λps → ... (* omitted, yet simple *)
let get () : tac proofstate = λps → Success ps ps
let raise #a (e:exn) : tac a = λps → Failed (e, ps)
new_effect { TAC with repr = tac ; return = t_return ; bind = t_bind
                            ; get = get ; raise = raise }
```

The new_effect declaration introduces *computation types* of the form TAC t wp, where t is the return type and wp a specification. However, until Sect. 3.4 we shall only use the derived form Tac t, where the specification is trivial. These computation types are distinct from their underlying monadic representation type tac t—users cannot directly access the proof state except via the actions. The simplest actions stem from the tac monad definition: get : unit → Tac proofstate returns the current proof state and raise: exn → Tac $\alpha$ fails with the given exception[4]. Failures can be handled using catch : (unit → Tac $\alpha$) → Tac (either exn $\alpha$), which resets the state on failure, including that of unification metavariables.

[4] We use greek letters $\alpha$, $\beta$, ... to abbreviate universally quantified type variables.

We emphasize two points here. First, there is no "set" action. This is to forbid metaprograms from arbitrarily replacing their proof state, which would be unsound. Second, the argument to catch must be thunked, since in F* impure un-suspended computations are evaluated before they are passed into functions.

The only aspect differentiating Tac from other user-defined effects is the existence of effect-specific primitive actions, which give access to the metaprogramming engine proper. We list here but a few:

```
val trivial : unit → Tac unit     val tc : term → Tac term     val dump : string → Tac unit
```

All of these are given an interpretation internally by Meta-F*. For instance, trivial calls into F*'s logical simplifier to check whether the current goal is a trivial proposition and discharges it if so, failing otherwise. The tc primitive queries the type-checker to infer the type of a given term in the current environment (F* types are a kind of terms, hence the codomain of tc is also term). This does not change the proof state; its only purpose is to return useful information to the calling metaprograms. Finally, dump outputs the current proof state to the user in a pretty-printed format, in support of user interaction.

Having introduced the Tac effect and some basic actions, writing metaprograms is as straightforward as writing any other F* code. For instance, here are two metaprogram combinators. The first one repeatedly calls its argument until it fails, returning a list of all the successfully-returned values. The second one behaves similarly, but folds the results with some provided folding function.

```
let rec repeat (τ : unit → Tac α) : Tac (list α) =
  match catch τ with | Inl _ → [] | Inr x → x :: repeat τ

let repeat_fold f e τ = fold_left f e (repeat τ)
```

These two small combinators illustrate a few key points of Meta-F*. As for all other F* effects, metaprograms are written in applicative style, without explicit return, bind, or lift of computations (which are inserted under the hood). This also works across different effects: repeat_fold can seamlessly combine the pure fold_left from F*'s list library with a metaprogram like repeat. Metaprograms are also type- and effect-inferred: while repeat_fold was not at all annotated, F* infers the polymorphic type $(\beta \rightarrow \alpha \rightarrow \beta) \rightarrow \beta \rightarrow (\text{unit} \rightarrow \text{Tac } \alpha) \rightarrow \text{Tac } \alpha$ for it.

It should be noted that, if lacking an effect extension feature, one could embed metaprograms simply via the (properly abstracted) tac monad instead of the Tac effect. It is just more convenient to use an effect, given we are working within an effectful program verifier already. In what follows, with the exception of Sect. 3.4 where we describe specifications for metaprograms, there is little reliance on using an effect; so, the same ideas could be applied in other settings.

### 3.2 Executing Meta-F* Metaprograms

Running metaprograms involves three steps. First, they are *reified* [1] into their underlying tac representation, i.e. as state-passing functions. User code cannot reify metaprograms: only F* can do so when about to process a goal.

Second, the reified term is applied to an initial proof state, and then simply evaluated according to F*'s dynamic semantics, for instance using F*'s existing normalizer. For intensive applications, such as proofs by reflection, we provide faster alternatives (Sect. 5). In order to perform this second step, the proof state, which up until this moments exists only internally to F*, must be *embedded* as a term, i.e., as abstract syntax. Here is where its abstraction pays off: since metaprograms cannot interact with a proof state except through a limited interface, it need not be *deeply* embedded as syntax. By simply wrapping the internal proofstate into a new kind of "alien" term, and making the primitives aware of this wrapping, we can readily run the metaprogram that safely carries its alien proof state around. This wrapping of proof states is a constant-time operation.

The third step is interpreting the primitives. They are realized by functions of similar types implemented within the F* type-checker, but over an internal tac monad and the concrete definitions for term, proofstate, etc. Hence, there is a translation involved on every call and return, switching between embedded representations and their concrete variants. Take dump, for example, with type string → Tac unit. Its internal implementation, implemented within the F* type-checker, has type string → proofstate → Div (result unit). When interpreting a call to it, the interpreter must *unembed* the arguments (which are representations of F* terms) into a concrete string and a concrete proofstate to pass to the internal implementation of dump. The situation is symmetric for the return value of the call, which must be *embedded* as a term.

### 3.3 Syntax Inspection, Generation, and Quotation

If metaprograms are to be reusable over different kinds of goals, they must be able to reflect on the goals they are invoked to solve. Like any metaprogramming system, Meta-F* offers a way to inspect and construct the syntax of F* terms. Our representation of terms as an inductive type, and the variants of quotations, are inspired by the ones in Idris [22] and Lean [30].

**Inspecting Syntax.** Internally, F* uses a locally-nameless representation [21] with explicit, delayed substitutions. To shield metaprograms from some of this internal bureaucracy, we expose a simplified view [61] of terms. Below we present a few constructors from the term_view type:

```
val inspect : term → Tac term_view    type term_view =
val pack : term_view → term             | Tv_BVar : v:dbvar → term_view
                                        | Tv_Var : v:name → term_view
                                        | Tv_FVar : v:qname → term_view
                                        | Tv_Abs : bv:binder → body:term → term_view
                                        | Tv_App : hd:term → arg:term → term_view
                                        ...
```

The term_view type provides the "one-level-deep" structure of a term: metaprograms must call inspect to reveal the structure of the term, one constructor at a time. The view exposes three kinds of variables: bound variables, Tv_BVar; named local variables Tv_Var; and top-level fully qualified names, Tv_FVar. Bound variables and local variables are distinguished since the internal abstract syntax is locally nameless. For metaprogramming, it is usually simpler to use a fully-named representation, so we provide inspect and pack functions that open and close binders appropriately to maintain this invariant. Since opening binders requires freshness, inspect has effect Tac.[5] As generating large pieces of syntax via the view easily becomes tedious, we also provide some ways of *quoting* terms:

**Static Quotations.** A static quotation `e is just a shorthand for statically calling the F⋆ parser to convert e into the abstract syntax of F⋆ terms above. For instance, `(f 1 2) is equivalent to the following,

```
pack (Tv_App (pack (Tv_App (pack (Tv_FVar "f"))
                           (pack (Tv_Const (C_Int 1)))))
             (pack (Tv_Const (C_Int 2))))
```

**Dynamic Quotations.** A second form of quotation is dquote: #a:Type → a → Tac term, an effectful operation that is interpreted by F⋆'s normalizer during metaprogram evaluation. It returns the syntax of its argument at the time dquote e is evaluated. Evaluating dquote e substitutes all the free variables in e with their current values in the execution environment, suspends further evaluation, and returns the abstract syntax of the resulting term. For instance, evaluating (λx → dquote (x + 1)) 16 produces the abstract syntax of 16 + 1.

**Anti-quotations.** Static quotations are useful for building big chunks of syntax concisely, but they are of limited use if we cannot combine them with existing bits of syntax. Subterms of a quotation are allowed to "escape" and be substituted by arbitrary expressions. We use the syntax `#t to denote an antiquoted t, where t must be an expression of type term in order for the quotation to be well-typed. For example, `(1 +`#e) creates syntax for an addition where one operand is the integer constant 1 and the other is the term represented by e.

**Unquotation.** Finally, we provide an effectful operation, unquote: #a:Type → t:term → Tac a, which takes a term representation t and an expected type for it a (usually inferred from the context), and calls the F⋆ type-checker to check and elaborate the term representation into a well-typed term.

## 3.4 Specifying and Verifying Metaprograms

Since we model metaprograms as a particular kind of effectful program within F⋆, which is a program verifier, a natural question to ask is whether F⋆ can specify and verify metaprograms. The answer is "yes, to a degree".

To do so, we must use the WP calculus for the TAC effect: TAC-computations are given computation types of the form TAC a wp, where a is the computation's result type and wp is a weakest-precondition transformer of type tacwp a = proofstate → (result a → prop) → prop. However, since WPs tend to not be very

[5] We also provide functions inspect_ln, pack_ln which stay in a locally-nameless representation and are thus pure, total functions.

intuitive, we first define two variants of the TAC effect: TacH in "Hoare-style" with pre- and postconditions and Tac (which we have seen before), which only specifies the return type, but uses trivial pre- and postconditions. The requires and ensures keywords below simply aid readability of pre- and postconditions—they are identity functions.

```
effect TacH (a:Type) (pre : proofstate → prop) (post : proofstate → result a → prop) =
        TAC a (λ ps post' → pre ps ∧ (∀ r. post ps r ⟹ post' r))
effect Tac (a:Type) = TacH a (requires (λ _ → ⊤)) (ensures (λ _ _ → ⊤))
```

Previously, we only showed the simple type for the raise primitive, namely exn → Tac $\alpha$. In fact, in full detail and Hoare style, its type/specification is:

```
val raise : e:exn→ TacH α (requires (λ _ → ⊤))
                          (ensures (λ ps r → r == Failed (e, ps)))
```

expressing that the primitive has no precondition, always fails with the provided exception, and does not modify the proof state. From the specifications of the primitives, and the automatically obtained Dijkstra monad, F$^\star$ can already prove interesting properties about metaprograms. We show a few simple examples.

The following metaprogram is accepted by F$^\star$ as it can conclude, from the type of raise, that the assertion is unreachable, and hence raise_flow can have a trivial precondition (as Tac unit implies).

```
let raise_flow () : Tac unit = raise SomeExn; assert ⊥
```

For cur_goal_safe below, F$^\star$ verifies that (given the precondition) the pattern match is exhaustive. The postcondition is also asserting that the metaprogram always succeeds without affecting the proof state, returning some unspecified goal. Calls to cur_goal_safe must statically ensure that the goal list is not empty.

```
let cur_goal_safe () : TacH goal (requires (λ ps → ¬(goals_of ps == [])))
                                 (ensures (λ ps r → ∃g. r == Success g ps)) =
    match goals_of (get ()) with | g :: _ → g
```

Finally, the divide combinator below "splits" the goals of a proof state in two at a given index n, and focuses a different metaprogram on each. It includes a runtime check that the given n is non-negative, and raises an exception in the TAC effect otherwise. Afterwards, the call to the (pure) List.splitAt function requires that n be statically known to be non-negative, a fact which can be proven from the specification for raise and the effect definition, which defines the control flow.

```
let divide (n:int) (tl : unit → Tac α) (tr : unit → Tac β) : Tac (α * β) =
    if n < 0 then raise NegativeN;
    let gsl, gsr = List.splitAt n (goals ()) in ...
```

This enables a style of "lightweight" verification of metaprograms, where expressive invariants about their state and control-flow can be encoded. The programmer can exploit dynamic checks (n < 0) and exceptions (raise) or static ones (preconditions), or a mixture of them, as needed.

Due to type abstraction, though, the specifications of most primitives cannot provide complete detail about their behavior, and deeper specifications (such as ensuring a tactic will correctly solve a goal) cannot currently be proven, nor even stated—to do so would require, at least, an internalization of the typing judgment of F*. While this is an exciting possibility [3], we have for now only focused on verifying basic safety properties of metaprograms, which helps users detect errors early, and whose proofs the SMT can handle well. Although in principle, one can also write tactics to discharge the proof obligations of metaprograms.

## 4 Meta-F*, Formally

We now describe the trust assumptions for Meta-F* (Sect. 4.1) and then how we reconcile tactics within a program verifier, where the exact shape of VCs is not given, nor known a priori by the user (Sect. 4.2).

### 4.1 Correctness and Trusted Computing Base (TCB)

As in any proof assistant, tactics and metaprogramming would be rather useless if they allowed to "prove" invalid judgments—care must be taken to ensure soundness. We begin with a taste of the specifics of F*'s static semantics, which influence the trust model for Meta-F*, and then provide more detail on the TCB.

**Proof Irrelevance in F*.** The following two rules for introducing and eliminating refinement types are key in F*, as they form the basis of its proof irrelevance.

$$\text{T-Refine}\quad \frac{\Gamma \vdash e : t \quad \Gamma \models \phi[e/x]}{\Gamma \vdash e : x{:}t\{\phi\}} \qquad\qquad \text{V-Refine}\quad \frac{\Gamma \vdash e : x{:}t\{\phi\}}{\Gamma \models \phi[e/x]}$$

The $\models$ symbol represents F*'s *validity judgment* [1] which, at a high-level, defines a proof-irrelevant, classical, higher-order logic. These validity hypotheses are usually collected by the type-checker, and then encoded to the SMT solver in bulk. Crucially, the irrelevance of validity is what permits efficient interaction with SMT solvers, since reconstructing F* terms from SMT proofs is unneeded.

As evidenced in the rules, validity and typing are mutually recursive, and therefore Meta-F* must also construct validity derivations. In the implementation, we model these validity goals as holes with a "squash" type [5,53], where squash $\phi = \_{:}\mathsf{unit}\{\phi\}$, i.e., a refinement of unit. Concretely, we model $\Gamma \models \phi$ as $\Gamma \vdash ?\mathsf{u} : \mathsf{squash}\ \phi$ using a unification variable. Meta-F* does not construct deep solutions to squashed goals: if they are proven valid, the variable ?u is simply solved by the unit value '()'. At any point, any such irrelevant goal can be sent to the SMT solver. Relevant goals, on the other hand, cannot be sent to SMT.

**Scripting the Typing Judgment.** A consequence of validity proofs not being materialized is that type-checking is undecidable in F*. For instance: does the unit value () solve the hole $\Gamma \vdash ?\mathsf{u} : \mathsf{squash}\ \phi$? Well, only if $\phi$ holds—a condition which no type-checker can effectively decide. This implies that the type-checker cannot, in general, rely on proof terms to reconstruct a proof. Hence, the primitives are designed to provide access to the typing judgment of F* directly, instead of building syntax for proof terms. One can think of F*'s type-checker as implementing one particular algorithmic heuristic of the typing and validity judgments—a heuristic which happens to work well in practice. For convenience, this default type-checking heuristic is also available to metaprograms: this is in fact precisely what the exact primitive does. Having programmatic access to the typing judgment also provides the flexibility to tweak VC generation as needed, instead of leaving it to the default behavior of F*. For instance, the refine_intro primitive implements T-REFINE. When applied, it produces two new goals, including that the refinement actually holds. At that point, a metaprogram can run any arbitrary tactic on it, instead of letting the F* type-checker collect the obligation and send it to the SMT solver in bulk with others.

**Trust.** There are two common approaches for the correctness of tactic engines: (1) the *de Bruijn criterion* [6], which requires constructing full proofs (or proof terms) and checking them at the end, hence reducing trust to an independent proof-checker; and (2) the LCF style, which applies backwards reasoning while constructing validation functions at every step, reducing trust to primitive, forward-style implementations of the system's inference rules.

As we wish to make use of SMT solvers within F*, the first approach is not easy. Reconstructing the proofs SMT solvers produce, if any, back into a proper derivation remains a significant challenge (even despite recent progress, e.g. [17,31]). Further, the logical encoding from F* to SMT, along with the solver itself, are already part of F*'s TCB: shielding Meta-F* from them would not significantly increase safety of the combined system.

Instead, we roughly follow the LCF approach and implement F*'s typing rules as the basic user-facing metaprogramming actions. However, instead of implementing the rules in forward-style and using them to validate (untrusted) backwards-style tactics, we implement them directly in backwards-style. That is, they run by breaking down goals into subgoals, instead of combining proven facts into new proven facts. Using LCF style makes the primitives part of the TCB. However, given the primitives are sound, any combination of them also is, and any user-provided metaprogram must be safe due to the abstraction imposed by the Tac effect, as discussed next.

**Correct Evolutions of the Proof State.** For soundness, it is imperative that tactics do not arbitrarily drop goals from the proof state, and only discharge them when they are solved, or when they can be solved by other goals tracked in the proof state. For a concrete example, consider the following program:

```
let f : int → int = _ by (intro (); exact (`42))
```

Here, Meta-F* will create an initial proof state with a single goal of the form $[\emptyset \vdash ?u_1 : \mathsf{int} \to \mathsf{int}]$ and begin executing the metaprogram. When applying the intro primitive, the proof state transitions as shown below.

$$[\emptyset \vdash ?u_1 : \mathsf{int} \to \mathsf{int}] \rightsquigarrow [x{:}\mathsf{int} \vdash ?u_2 : \mathsf{int}]$$

Here, a solution to the original goal has not yet been built, since it *depends* on the solution to the goal on the right hand side. When it is solved with, say, 42, we can solve our original goal with $\lambda x \rightarrow 42$. To formalize these dependencies, we say that a proof state $\phi$ *correctly evolves (via $f$) to $\psi$*, denoted $\phi \preceq_f \psi$, when there is a generic transformation $f$, called a *validation*, from solutions to all of $\psi$'s goals into correct solutions for $\phi$'s goals. When $\phi$ has $n$ goals and $\psi$ has $m$ goals, the validation $f$ is a function from $\mathsf{term}^m$ into $\mathsf{term}^n$. Validations may be composed, providing the transitivity of correct evolution, and if a proof state $\phi$ correctly evolves (in any amount of steps) into a state with no more goals, then we have fully defined solutions to all of $\phi$'s goals. We emphasize that validations are not constructed explicitly during the execution of metaprograms. Instead we exploit unification metavariables to instantiate the solutions automatically.

Note that validations may construct solutions for more than one goal, i.e., their codomain is not a single term. This is required in Meta-F*, where primitive steps may not only decompose goals into subgoals, but actually combine goals as well. Currently, the only primitive providing this behavior is join, which finds a maximal common prefix of the environment of two irrelevant goals, reverts the "extra" binders in both goals and builds their conjunction. Combining goals using join is especially useful for sending multiple goals to the SMT solver in a single call. When there are common obligations within two goals, joining them before calling the SMT solver can result in a significantly faster proof.

We check that every primitive action respects the $\preceq$ preorder. This relies on them modeling F*'s typing rules. For example, and unsurprisingly, the following rule for typing abstractions is what justifies the intro primitive:

$$\text{T-FUN}\quad \frac{\Gamma, x : t \vdash e : t'}{\Gamma \vdash \lambda(x : t).e \;:\; (x : t) \rightarrow t'}$$

Then, for the proof state evolution above, the validation function $f$ is the (mathematical, meta-level) function taking a term of type *int* (the solution for $?u_2$) and building syntax for its abstraction over $x$. Further, the intro primitive respects the correct-evolution preorder, by the very typing rule (T-Fun) from which it is defined. In this manner, every typing rule induces a syntax-building metaprogramming step. Our primitives come from this dual interpretation of typing rules, which ensures that logical consistency is preserved.

Since the $\preceq$ relation is a preorder, and every metaprogramming primitive we provide the user evolves the proof state according $\preceq$, it is trivially the case that the final proof state returned by a (successful) computation is a correct evolution of the initial one. That means that when the metaprogram terminates, one has indeed broken down the proof obligation correctly, and is left with a (hopefully) simpler set of obligations to fulfill. Note that since $\preceq$ is a preorder, Tac provides an interesting example of monotonic state [2].

### 4.2 Extracting Individual Assertions

As discussed, the logical context of a goal processed by a tactic is not always syntactically evident in the program. And, as shown in the List.splitAt call in divide from Sect. 3.4, some obligations crucially depend on the control-flow of the program. Hence, the proof state must crucially include these assumptions if proving the assertion is to succeed. Below, we describe how Meta-F$^\star$ finds proper contexts in which to prove the assertions, including control-flow information. Notably, this process is defined over logical formulae and does not depend at all on F$^\star$'s WP calculus or VC generator: we believe it should be applicable to any VC generator.

As seen in Sect. 2.1, the basic mechanism by which Meta-F$^\star$ attaches a tactic to a specific sub-goal is assert $\phi$ by $\tau$. Our encoding of this expression is built similarly to F$^\star$'s existing assert construct, which is simply sugar for a pure function _assert of type $\phi$:prop $\rightarrow$ Lemma (requires $\phi$) (ensures $\phi$), which essentially introduces a cut in the generated VC. That is, the term (assert $\phi$; e) roughly produces the verification condition $\phi \wedge (\phi \Longrightarrow \mathrm{VC}_e)$, requiring a proof of $\phi$ at this point, and assuming $\phi$ in the continuation. For Meta-F$^\star$, we aim to keep this style while allowing asserted formulae to be decorated with user-provided tactics that are tasked with proving or pre-processing them. We do this in three steps.

First, we define the following "phantom" predicate:

```
let with_tactic (φ : prop) (τ : unit → Tac unit) = φ
```

Here $\phi$ `with_tactic` $\tau$ simply associates the tactic $\tau$ with $\phi$, and is equivalent to $\phi$ by its definition. Next, we implement the assert_by_tactic lemma, and desugar assert $\phi$ by $\tau$ into assert_by_tactic $\phi$ $\tau$. This lemma is trivially provable by F$^\star$.

```
let assert_by_tactic (φ : prop) (τ : unit → Tac unit)
                    : Lemma (requires (φ `with_tactic` τ)) (ensures φ) = ()
```

Given this specification, the term (assert $\phi$ by $\tau$; e) roughly produces the verification condition $\phi$ `with_tactic` $\tau \wedge (\phi \Longrightarrow \mathrm{VC}_e)$, with a tagged left sub-goal, and $\phi$ as an hypothesis in the right one. Importantly, F$^\star$ keeps the with_tactic marker uninterpreted until the VC needs to be discharged. At that point, it may contain several annotated subformulae. For example, suppose the VC is VC0 below, where we distinguish an ambient context of variables and hypotheses $\Delta$:

(VC0) $\Delta \models$ X $\Longrightarrow$ ($\forall$ (x:t). R `with_tactic` $\tau_1$ $\wedge$ (R $\Longrightarrow$ S))

In order to run the $\tau_1$ tactic on R, it must first be "split out". To do so, all logical information "visible" for $\tau_1$ (i.e. the set of premises of the implications traversed and the binders introduced by quantifiers) must be included. As for any program verifier, these hypotheses include the control flow information, postconditions, and any other logical fact that is known to be valid at the program point where the corresponding assert R by $\tau_1$ was called. All of them are collected into $\Delta$ as the term is traversed. In this case, the VC for $R$ is:

(VC1) $\Delta$, _:X, x:t $\models$ R

Afterwards, this obligation is removed from the original VC. This is done by replacing it with $\top$, leaving a "skeleton" VC with all remaining facts.

(VC2) $\Delta \models \mathsf{X} \Longrightarrow (\forall\ (\mathsf{x{:}t}).\ \top \land (\mathsf{R} \Longrightarrow \mathsf{S}))$

The validity of VC1 and VC2 implies that of VC0. F* also recursively descends into R and S, in case there are more with_tactic markers in them. Then, tactics are run on the the split VCs (e.g., $\tau_1$ on VC1) to break them down (or solve them). All remaining goals, including the skeleton, are sent to the SMT solver.

Note that while the *obligation* to prove R, in VC1, is preprocessed by the tactic $\tau_1$, the *assumption* R for the continuation of the code, in VC2, is left as-is. This is crucial for tactics such as the canonicalizer from Sect. 2.1: if the skeleton VC2 contained an assumption for the canonicalized equality it would not help the SMT solver show the uncanonicalized postcondition.

However, not all nodes marked with with_tactic are proof obligations. Suppose X in the previous VC was given as (Y `with_tactic` $\tau_2$). In this case, one certainly does not want to attempt to prove Y, since it is an hypothesis. While it would be *sound* to prove it and replace it by $\top$, it is useless at best, and usually irreparably affects the system. Consider asserting the tautology ($\bot$`with_tactic`$\tau$) $\Longrightarrow \bot$.

Hence, F* splits such obligations only in strictly-positive positions. On all others, F* simply drops the with_tactic marker, e.g., by just unfolding the definition of with_tactic. For regular uses of the assert..by construct, however, all occurrences are strictly-positive. It is only when (expert) users use the with_tactic marker directly that the above discussion might become relevant.

Formally, the soundness of this whole approach is given by the following metatheorem, which justifies the splitting out of sub-assertions, and by the correctness of evolution detailed in Sect. 4.1. The proof of Theorem 1 is straightforward, and included in the appendix. We expect an analogous property to hold in other verifiers as well (in particular, it holds for first-order logic).

**Theorem 1.** *Let $E$ be a context with $\Gamma \vdash E : prop \Rightarrow prop$, and $\phi$ a squashed proposition such that $\Gamma \vdash \phi : prop$. Then the following holds:*

$$\frac{\Gamma \models E[\top] \quad \Gamma, \gamma(E) \models \phi}{\Gamma \models E[\phi]}$$

*where $\gamma(E)$ is the set of binders $E$ introduces. If $E$ is strictly-positive, then the reverse implication holds as well.*

## 5 Executing Metaprograms Efficiently

F* provides three complementary mechanisms for running metaprograms. The first two, F*'s call-by-name (CBN) interpreter and a (newly implemented) call-by-value (CBV) NbE-based evaluator, support strong reduction—henceforth we refer to these as "normalizers". In addition, we design and implement a new *native plugin* mechanism that allows both normalizers to interface with Meta-F* programs extracted to OCaml, reusing F*'s existing extraction pipeline for this purpose. Below we provide a brief overview of the three mechanisms.

### 5.1 CBN and CBV Strong Reductions

As described in Sect. 3.1, metaprograms, once reified, are simply F* terms of type proofstate → Div (result a). As such, they can be reduced using F*'s existing computation machinery, a CBN interpreter for strong reductions based on the Krivine abstract machine (KAM) [24,46]. Although complete and highly configurable, F*'s KAM interpreter is slow, designed primarily for converting types during dependent type-checking and higher-order unification.

Shifting focus to long-running metaprograms, such as tactics for proofs by reflection, we implemented an NbE-based strong-reduction evaluator for F* computations. The evaluator is implemented in F* and extracted to OCaml (as is the rest of F*), thereby inheriting CBV from OCaml. It is similar to Boespflug et al.'s [16] NbE-based strong-reduction for Coq, although we do not implement their low-level, OCaml-specific tag-elimination optimizations—nevertheless, it is already vastly more efficient than the KAM-based interpreter.

### 5.2 Native Plugins and Multi-language Interoperability

Since Meta-F* programs are just F* programs, they can also be extracted to OCaml and natively compiled. Further, they can be dynamically linked into F* as "plugins". Plugins can be directly called from the type-checker, as is done for the primitives, which is much more efficient than interpreting them. However, compilation has a cost, and it is not convenient to compile every single invocation. Instead, Meta-F* enables users to choose which metaprograms are to be plugins (presumably those expected to be computation-intensive, e.g. canon_semiring). Users can choose their native plugins, while still quickly scripting their higher-level logic in the interpreter.

This requires (for higher-order metaprograms) a form of multi-language interoperability, converting between representations of terms used in the normalizers and in native code. We designed a small multi-language calculus, with ML-style polymorphism, to model the interaction between normalizers and plugins and conversions between terms. See the appendix for details.

Beyond the notable efficiency gains of running compiled code vs. interpreting it, native metaprograms also require fewer embeddings. Once compiled, metaprograms work over the internal, *concrete* types for proofstate, term, etc., instead of over their F* representations (though still treating them abstractly). Hence, compiled metaprograms can call primitives without needing to embed their arguments or unembed their results. Further, they can call each other directly as well. Indeed, operationally there is little operational difference between a primitive and a compiled metaprogram used as a plugin.

Native plugins, however, are not a replacement for the normalizers, for several reasons. First, the overhead in compilation might not be justified by the execution speed-up. Second, extraction to OCaml erases types and proofs. As a result, the F* *interface* of the native plugins can only contain types that can also be expressed in OCaml, thereby excluding full-dependent types—internally, however, they can be dependently typed. Third, being OCaml programs, native plugins do not support reducing open terms, which is often required. However, when the programs treat their open arguments parametrically, relying on parametric polymorphism, the normalizers can pass such arguments *as-is*, thereby recovering open reductions in some cases. This allows us to use native datastructure implementations (e.g. List), which is much faster than using the normalizers, even for open terms. See the appendix for details.

# 6 Experimental Evaluation

We now present an experimental evaluation of Meta-F*. First, we provide benchmarks comparing our reflective canonicalizer from Sect. 2.1 to calling the SMT solver directly without any canonicalization. Then, we return to the parsers and serializers from Sect. 2.3 and show how, for VCs that arise, a domain-specific tactic is much more tractable than a SMT-only proof.

## 6.1 A Reflective Tactic for Partial Canonicalization

In Sect. 2.1, we have described the canon_semiring tactic that rewrites semiring expressions into sums of products. We find that this tactic significantly improves proof robustness. The table below compares the success rates and times for the poly_multiply lemma from Sect. 2.1. To test the robustness of each alternative, we run the tests 200 times while varying the SMT solver's random seed. The `smt`*i*`x` rows represent asking the solver to prove the lemma without any help from tactics, where $i$ represents the resource limit (`rlimit`) multiplier given to the solver. This `rlimit` is memory-allocation based and independent of the particular system or current load. For the interp and native rows, the canon_semiring tactic is used, running it using F*'s KAM normalizer and as a native plugin respectively—both with an `rlimit` of 1. For each setup, we display the success rate of verification, the average (CPU) time taken for the SMT queries (not counting the time for parsing/processing the theory) with its standard deviation, and the average total time (its standard deviation coincides with that of the queries). When applicable, the time for tactic execution (which is independent of the seed) is displayed. The `smt` rows show very poor success rates: even when upping the `rlimit` to a whopping 100x, over three quarters of the attempts fail. Note how the (relative) standard deviation increases with the

| | Rate | Queries | Tactic | Total |
|---|---|---|---|---|
| smt1x | 0.5% | $0.216 \pm 0.001$ | – | 2.937 |
| smt2x | 2% | $0.265 \pm 0.003$ | – | 2.958 |
| smt3x | 4% | $0.304 \pm 0.004$ | – | 3.022 |
| smt6x | 10% | $0.401 \pm 0.008$ | – | 3.155 |
| smt12x | 12.5% | $0.596 \pm 0.031$ | – | 3.321 |
| smt25x | 16.5% | $1.063 \pm 0.079$ | – | 3.790 |
| smt50x | 22% | $2.319 \pm 0.230$ | – | 5.030 |
| smt100x | 24% | $5.831 \pm 0.776$ | – | 8.550 |
| interp | 100% | $0.141 \pm 0.001$ | 1.156 | 4.003 |
| native | 100% | $0.139 \pm 0.001$ | 0.212 | 3.071 |

`rlimit`: this is due to successful runs taking rather random times, and failing ones exhausting their resources in similar times. The setups using the tactic show a clear increase in robustness: canonicalizing the assertion causes this proof to always succeed, even at the default `rlimit`. We recall that the tactic variants still leave goals for SMT solving, namely, the skeleton for the original VC and the canonicalized equality left by the tactic, easily dischargeable by the SMT solver through much more well-behaved linear reasoning. The last column shows that native compilation speeds up this tactic's execution by about 5x.

### 6.2 Combining SMT and Tactics for the Parser Generator

In Sect. 2.3, we presented a library of combinators and a metaprogramming approach to automate the construction of verified, mutually inverse, low-level parsers and serializers from type descriptions. Beyond generating the code, tactics are used to process and discharge proof obligations that arise when using the combinators.

We present three strategies for discharging these obligations, including those of bijectivity that arise when constructing parsers and serializers for enumerated types. First, we used F*'s default strategy to present all of these proofs directly to the SMT solver. Second, we programmed a ∼100 line tactic to discharge these proofs without relying on the SMT solver at all. Finally, we used a hybrid approach where a simple, 5-line tactic is used to prune the context of the proof removing redundant facts before presenting the resulting goals to the SMT solver.

| Size | SMT only | Tactic only | Hybrid |
|---|---|---|---|
| 4 | 178 | 17.3 | 6.6 |
| 7 | 468 | 38.3 | 9.8 |
| 10 | 690 | 63.0 | 19.4 |

The table alongside shows the total time in seconds for verifying metaprogrammed low-level parsers and serializers for enumerations of different sizes. In short, the hybrid approach scales the best; the tactic-only approach is somewhat slower; while the SMT-only approach scales poorly and is an order of magnitude slower. Our hybrid approach is very simple. With some more work, a more sophisticated hybrid strategy could be more performant still, relying on tactic-based normalization proofs for fragments of the VC best handled computationally (where the SMT solver spends most of its time), while using SMT only for integer arithmetic, congruence closure etc. However, with Meta-F*'s ability to manipulate proof contexts programmatically, our simple context-pruning tactic provides a big payoff at a small cost.

## 7 Related Work

Many SMT-based program verifiers [7,8,19,34,48], rely on user hints, in the form of assertions and lemmas, to complete proofs. This is the predominant style of proving used in tools like Dafny [47], Liquid Haskell [60], Why3 [33], and

F$^\star$ itself [58]. However, there is a growing trend to augment this style of semi-automated proof with interactive proofs. For example, systems like Why3 [33] allow VCs to be discharged using ITPs such as Coq, Isabelle/HOL, and PVS, but this requires an additional embedding of VCs into the logic of the ITP in question. In recent concurrent work, support for *effectful* reflection proofs was added to Why3 [50], and it would be interesting to investigate if this could also be done in Meta-F$^\star$. Grov and Tumas [39] present Tacny, a tactic framework for Dafny, which is, however, limited in that it only transforms source code, with the program verifier unchanged. In contrast, Meta-F$^\star$ combines the benefits of an SMT-based program verifier and those of tactic proofs within a single language.

Moving away from SMT-based verifiers, ITPs have long relied on separate languages for proof scripting, starting with Edinburgh LCF [37] and ML, and continuing with HOL, Isabelle and Coq, which are either extensible via ML, or have dedicated tactic languages [3,29,56,62]. Meta-F$^\star$ builds instead on a recent idea in the space of dependently typed ITPs [22,30,42,63] of reusing the object-language as the meta-language. This idea first appeared in Mtac, a Coq-based tactics framework for Coq [42,63], and has many generic benefits including reusing the standard library, IDE support, and type checker of the proof assistant. Mtac can additionally check the partial correctness of tactics, which is also sometimes possible in Meta-F$^\star$ but still rather limited (Sect. 3.4). Meta-F$^\star$'s design is instead more closely inspired by the metaprogramming frameworks of Idris [22] and Lean [30], which provide a deep embedding of terms that metaprograms can inspect and construct at will without dependent types getting in the way. However, F$^\star$'s effects, its weakest precondition calculus, and its use of SMT solvers distinguish Meta-F$^\star$ from these other frameworks, presenting both challenges and opportunities, as discussed in this paper.

Some SMT solvers also include tactic engines [27], which allow to process queries in custom ways. However, using SMT tactics from a program verifier is not very practical. To do so effectively, users must become familiar not only with the solver's language and tactic engine, but also with the translation from the program verifier to the solver. Instead, in Meta-F$^\star$, everything happens within a single language. Also, to our knowledge, these tactics are usually coarsely-grained, and we do not expect them to enable developments such as Sect. 2.2. Plus, SMT tactics do not enable metaprogramming.

Finally, ITPs are seeing increasing use of "hammers" such as Sledgehammer [14,15,54] in Isabelle/HOL, and similar tools for HOL Light and HOL4 [43], and Mizar [44], to interface with ATPs. This technique is similar to Meta-F$^\star$, which, given its support for a dependently typed logic is especially related to a recent hammer for Coq [26]. Unlike these hammers, Meta-F$^\star$ does not aim to reconstruct SMT proofs, gaining efficiency at the cost of trusting the SMT solver. Further, whereas hammers run in the background, lightening the load on a user otherwise tasked with completing the entire proof, Meta-F$^\star$ relies more heavily on the SMT solver as an end-game tactic in nearly all proofs.

## 8 Conclusions

A key challenge in program verification is to balance automation and expressiveness. Whereas tactic-based ITPs support highly expressive logics, the tactic author is responsible for all the automation. Conversely, SMT-based program verifiers provide good, scalable automation for comparatively weaker logics, but offer little recourse when verification fails. A design that allows picking the right tool, at the granularity of each verification sub-task, is a worthy area of research. Meta-F⋆ presents a new point in this space: by using hand-written tactics alongside SMT-automation, we have written proofs that were previously impractical in F⋆, and (to the best of our knowledge) in other SMT-based program verifiers.

**Acknowledgements.** We thank Leonardo de Moura and the Project Everest team for many useful discussions. The work of Guido Martínez, Nick Giannarakis, Monal Narasimhamurthy, and Zoe Paraskevopoulou was done, in part, while interning at Microsoft Research. Clément Pit-Claudel's work was in part done during an internship at Inria Paris. The work of Danel Ahman, Victor Dumitrescu, and Cătălin Hriţcu is supported by the MSR-Inria Joint Centre and the European Research Council under ERC Starting Grant SECOMP (1-715753).

## References

1. Ahman, D., et al.: Dijkstra monads for free. In: POPL (2017). https://doi.org/10.1145/3009837.3009878
2. Ahman, D., Fournet, C., Hriţcu, C., Maillard, K., Rastogi, A., Swamy, N.: Recalling a witness: foundations and applications of monotonic state. PACMPL **2**(POPL), 65:1–65:30 (2018). https://arxiv.org/abs/1707.02466
3. Anand, A., Boulier, S., Cohen, C., Sozeau, M., Tabareau, N.: Towards certified meta-programming with typed Template-Coq. In: Avigad, J., Mahboubi, A. (eds.) ITP 2018. LNCS, vol. 10895, pp. 20–39. Springer, Cham (2018). https://doi.org/10.1007/978-3-319-94821-8_2. https://template-coq.github.io/template-coq/
4. Appel, A.W.: Tactics for separation logic. Early Draft (2006). https://www.cs.princeton.edu/~appel/papers/septacs.pdf
5. Awodey, S., Bauer, A.: Propositions as [Types]. J. Log. Comput. **14**(4), 447–471 (2004). https://doi.org/10.1093/logcom/14.4.447
6. Barendregt, H., Geuvers, H.: Proof-assistants using dependent type systems. In: Handbook of Automated Reasoning, pp. 1149–1238. Elsevier Science Publishers B. V., Amsterdam (2001). http://dl.acm.org/citation.cfm?id=778522.778527
7. Barnett, M., Chang, B.-Y.E., DeLine, R., Jacobs, B., Leino, K.R.M.: Boogie: a modular reusable verifier for object-oriented programs. In: de Boer, F.S., Bonsangue, M.M., Graf, S., de Roever, W.-P. (eds.) FMCO 2005. LNCS, vol. 4111, pp. 364–387. Springer, Heidelberg (2006). https://doi.org/10.1007/11804192_17
8. Barnett, M., et al.: The Spec# programming system: challenges and directions. In: Meyer, B., Woodcock, J. (eds.) VSTTE 2005. LNCS, vol. 4171, pp. 144–152. Springer, Heidelberg (2008). https://doi.org/10.1007/978-3-540-69149-5_16
9. Barras, B., Grégoire, B., Mahboubi, A., Théry, L.: Chap. 25: The ring and field tactic families. Coq reference manual. https://coq.inria.fr/refman/ring.html

10. Berger, U., Schwichtenberg, H.: An inverse of the evaluation functional for typed lambda-calculus. In: LICS (1991). https://doi.org/10.1109/LICS.1991.151645
11. Bernstein, D.J.: The Poly1305-AES message-authentication code. In: Gilbert, H., Handschuh, H. (eds.) FSE 2005. LNCS, vol. 3557, pp. 32–49. Springer, Heidelberg (2005). https://doi.org/10.1007/11502760_3. https://cr.yp.to/mac/poly1305-20050329.pdf
12. Besson, F.: Fast reflexive arithmetic tactics the linear case and beyond. In: Altenkirch, T., McBride, C. (eds.) TYPES 2006. LNCS, vol. 4502, pp. 48–62. Springer, Heidelberg (2007). https://doi.org/10.1007/978-3-540-74464-1_4
13. Bhargavan, K., et al.: Everest: towards a verified, drop-in replacement of HTTPS. In: SNAPL (2017). http://drops.dagstuhl.de/opus/volltexte/2017/7119/pdf/LIPIcs-SNAPL-2017-1.pdf
14. Blanchette, J.C., Popescu, A.: Mechanizing the metatheory of Sledgehammer. In: Fontaine, P., Ringeissen, C., Schmidt, R.A. (eds.) FroCoS 2013. LNCS (LNAI), vol. 8152, pp. 245–260. Springer, Heidelberg (2013). https://doi.org/10.1007/978-3-642-40885-4_17
15. Blanchette, J.C., Böhme, S., Paulson, L.C.: Extending Sledgehammer with SMT solvers. JAR **51**(1), 109–128 (2013). https://doi.org/10.1007/s10817-013-9278-5
16. Boespflug, M., Dénès, M., Grégoire, B.: Full reduction at full throttle. In: Jouannaud, J.-P., Shao, Z. (eds.) CPP 2011. LNCS, vol. 7086, pp. 362–377. Springer, Heidelberg (2011). https://doi.org/10.1007/978-3-642-25379-9_26
17. Böhme, S., Weber, T.: Fast LCF-style proof reconstruction for Z3. In: Kaufmann, M., Paulson, L.C. (eds.) ITP 2010. LNCS, vol. 6172, pp. 179–194. Springer, Heidelberg (2010). https://doi.org/10.1007/978-3-642-14052-5_14
18. Bond, B., et al.: Vale: verifying high-performance cryptographic assembly code. In: USENIX Security (2017). https://www.usenix.org/conference/usenixsecurity17/technical-sessions/presentation/bond
19. Burdy, L., et al.: An overview of JML tools and applications. STTT **7**(3), 212–232 (2005). https://doi.org/10.1007/s10009-004-0167-4
20. Chaieb, A., Nipkow, T.: Proof synthesis and reflection for linear arithmetic. J. Autom. Reason. **41**(1), 33–59 (2008). https://doi.org/10.1007/s10817-008-9101-x
21. Charguéraud, A.: The locally nameless representation. J. Autom. Reason. **49**(3), 363–408 (2012). https://doi.org/10.1007/s10817-011-9225-2
22. Christiansen, D.R., Brady, E.: Elaborator reflection: extending Idris in Idris. In: ICFP (2016). https://doi.org/10.1145/2951913.2951932
23. Cohen, E., Moskal, M., Schulte, W., Tobies, S.: Local verification of global invariants in concurrent programs. In: Touili, T., Cook, B., Jackson, P. (eds.) CAV 2010. LNCS, vol. 6174, pp. 480–494. Springer, Heidelberg (2010). https://doi.org/10.1007/978-3-642-14295-6_42
24. Crégut, P.: Strongly reducing variants of the Krivine abstract machine. HOSC **20**(3), 209–230 (2007). https://doi.org/10.1007/s10990-007-9015-z
25. Cuoq, P., Kirchner, F., Kosmatov, N., Prevosto, V., Signoles, J., Yakobowski, B.: Frama-C: a software analysis perspective. In: Eleftherakis, G., Hinchey, M., Holcombe, M. (eds.) SEFM 2012. LNCS, vol. 7504, pp. 233–247. Springer, Heidelberg (2012). https://doi.org/10.1007/978-3-642-33826-7_16
26. Czajka, Ł., Kaliszyk, C.: Hammer for Coq: automation for dependent type theory. JAR **61**(1–4), 423–453 (2018). https://doi.org/10.1007/s10817-018-9458-4
27. de Moura, L., Passmore, G.O.: The strategy challenge in SMT solving. In: Bonacina, M.P., Stickel, M.E. (eds.) Automated Reasoning and Mathematics. LNCS (LNAI),

vol. 7788, pp. 15–44. Springer, Heidelberg (2013). https://doi.org/10.1007/978-3-642-36675-8_2. http://dl.acm.org/citation.cfm?id=2554473.2554475
28. de Moura, L., Bjørner, N.: Z3: an efficient SMT solver. In: Ramakrishnan, C.R., Rehof, J. (eds.) TACAS 2008. LNCS, vol. 4963, pp. 337–340. Springer, Heidelberg (2008). https://doi.org/10.1007/978-3-540-78800-3_24
29. Delahaye, D.: A tactic language for the system Coq. In: Parigot, M., Voronkov, A. (eds.) LPAR 2000. LNAI, vol. 1955, pp. 85–95. Springer, Heidelberg (2000). https://doi.org/10.1007/3-540-44404-1_7
30. Ebner, G., Ullrich, S., Roesch, J., Avigad, J., de Moura, L.: A metaprogramming framework for formal verification. PACMPL **1**(ICFP), 34:1–34:29 (2017). https://doi.org/10.1145/3110278
31. Ekici, B., et al.: SMTCoq: a plug-in for integrating SMT solvers into Coq. In: Majumdar, R., Kunčak, V. (eds.) CAV 2017, Part II. LNCS, vol. 10427, pp. 126–133. Springer, Cham (2017). https://doi.org/10.1007/978-3-319-63390-9_7
32. Erbsen, A., Philipoom, J., Gross, J., Sloan, R., Chlipala, A.: Simple high-level code for cryptographic arithmetic - with proofs, without compromises. In: IEEE S&P (2019). https://doi.org/10.1109/SP.2019.00005
33. Filliâtre, J.-C., Paskevich, A.: Why3 — where programs meet provers. In: Felleisen, M., Gardner, P. (eds.) ESOP 2013. LNCS, vol. 7792, pp. 125–128. Springer, Heidelberg (2013). https://doi.org/10.1007/978-3-642-37036-6_8. https://hal.inria.fr/hal-00789533/document
34. Flanagan, C., Leino, K.R.M., Lillibridge, M., Nelson, G., Saxe, J.B., Stata, R.: PLDI 2002: extended static checking for Java. SIGPLAN Not. **48**(4S), 22–33 (2013). https://doi.org/10.1145/2502508.2502520
35. Fromherz, A., Giannarakis, N., Hawblitzel, C., Parno, B., Rastogi, A., Swamy, N.: A verified, efficient embedding of a verifiable assembly language. PACMPL (POPL) (2019). https://github.com/project-everest/project-everest.github.io/raw/master/assets/vale-popl.pdf
36. Gonthier, G.: Formal proof—the four-color theorem. Not. AMS **55**(11), 1382–1393 (2008). https://www.ams.org/notices/200811/tx081101382p.pdf
37. Gordon, M.J., Milner, A.J., Wadsworth, C.P.: Edinburgh LCF: A Mechanised Logic of Computation. LNCS, vol. 78. Springer, Heidelberg (1979). https://doi.org/10.1007/3-540-09724-4
38. Grégoire, B., Mahboubi, A.: Proving equalities in a commutative ring done right in Coq. In: Hurd, J., Melham, T. (eds.) TPHOLs 2005. LNCS, vol. 3603, pp. 98–113. Springer, Heidelberg (2005). https://doi.org/10.1007/11541868_7
39. Grov, G., Tumas, V.: Tactics for the Dafny program verifier. In: Chechik, M., Raskin, J.-F. (eds.) TACAS 2016. LNCS, vol. 9636, pp. 36–53. Springer, Heidelberg (2016). https://doi.org/10.1007/978-3-662-49674-9_3
40. Hawblitzel, C., et al.: Ironclad apps: end-to-end security via automated full-system verification. In: OSDI (2014). https://www.usenix.org/conference/osdi14/technical-sessions/presentation/hawblitzel
41. Hawblitzel, C., et al.: Ironfleet: proving safety and liveness of practical distributed systems. CACM **60**(7), 83–92 (2017). https://doi.org/10.1145/3068608
42. Kaiser, J., Ziliani, B., Krebbers, R., Régis-Gianas, Y., Dreyer, D.: Mtac2: typed tactics for backward reasoning in Coq. PACMPL **2**(ICFP), 78:1–78:31 (2018). https://doi.org/10.1145/3236773
43. Kaliszyk, C., Urban, J.: Learning-assisted automated reasoning with Flyspeck. JAR **53**(2), 173–213 (2014). https://doi.org/10.1007/s10817-014-9303-3

44. Kaliszyk, C., Urban, J.: MizAR 40 for Mizar 40. JAR **55**(3), 245–256 (2015). https://doi.org/10.1007/s10817-015-9330-8
45. Krebbers, R., Timany, A., Birkedal, L.: Interactive proofs in higher-order concurrent separation logic. In: POPL (2017). http://dl.acm.org/citation.cfm?id=3009855
46. Krivine, J.-L.: A call-by-name lambda-calculus machine. Higher Order Symbol. Comput. **20**(3), 199–207 (2007). https://doi.org/10.1007/s10990-007-9018-9
47. Leino, K.R.M.: Dafny: an automatic program verifier for functional correctness. In: Clarke, E.M., Voronkov, A. (eds.) LPAR 2010. LNCS (LNAI), vol. 6355, pp. 348–370. Springer, Heidelberg (2010). https://doi.org/10.1007/978-3-642-17511-4_20. http://dl.acm.org/citation.cfm?id=1939141.1939161
48. Rustan, K., Leino, M., Nelson, G.: An extended static checker for modula-3. In: Koskimies, K. (ed.) CC 1998. LNCS, vol. 1383, pp. 302–305. Springer, Heidelberg (1998). https://doi.org/10.1007/BFb0026441
49. McCreight, A.: Practical tactics for separation logic. In: Berghofer, S., Nipkow, T., Urban, C., Wenzel, M. (eds.) TPHOLs 2009. LNCS, vol. 5674, pp. 343–358. Springer, Heidelberg (2009). https://doi.org/10.1007/978-3-642-03359-9_24
50. Melquiond, G., Rieu-Helft, R.: A Why3 framework for reflection proofs and its application to GMP's algorithms. In: Galmiche, D., Schulz, S., Sebastiani, R. (eds.) IJCAR 2018. LNCS (LNAI), vol. 10900, pp. 178–193. Springer, Cham (2018). https://doi.org/10.1007/978-3-319-94205-6_13
51. Nanevski, A., Morrisett, J.G., Birkedal, L.: Hoare type theory, polymorphism and separation. JFP **18**(5–6), 865–911 (2008). http://ynot.cs.harvard.edu/papers/jfpsep07.pdf
52. Nanevski, A., Vafeiadis, V., Berdine, J.: Structuring the verification of heap-manipulating programs. In: POPL (2010). https://doi.org/10.1145/1706299.1706331
53. Nogin, A.: Quotient types: a modular approach. In: Carreño, V.A., Muñoz, C.A., Tahar, S. (eds.) TPHOLs 2002. LNCS, vol. 2410, pp. 263–280. Springer, Heidelberg (2002). https://doi.org/10.1007/3-540-45685-6_18
54. Paulson, L.C., Blanchette, J.C.: Three years of experience with Sledgehammer, a practical link between automatic and interactive theorem provers. In: IWIL (2010). https://www21.in.tum.de/~blanchet/iwil2010-sledgehammer.pdf
55. Protzenko, J., et al.: Verified low-level programming embedded in F*. PACMPL **1**(ICFP), 17:1–17:29 (2017). https://doi.org/10.1145/3110261
56. Stampoulis, A., Shao, Z.: VeriML: typed computation of logical terms inside a language with effects. In: ICFP (2010). https://doi.org/10.1145/1863543.1863591
57. Swamy, N., Weinberger, J., Schlesinger, C., Chen, J., Livshits, B.: Verifying higher-order programs with the Dijkstra monad. In: PLDI (2013). https://www.microsoft.com/en-us/research/publication/verifying-higher-order-programs-with-the-dijkstra-monad/
58. Swamy, N., et al.: Dependent types and multi-monadic effects in F*. In: POPL (2016). https://www.fstar-lang.org/papers/mumon/
59. Vazou, N., Seidel, E.L., Jhala, R., Vytiniotis, D., Peyton Jones, S.L.: Refinement types for Haskell. In: ICFP (2014). https://goto.ucsd.edu/~nvazou/refinement_types_for_haskell.pdf
60. Vazou, N., et al.: Refinement reflection: complete verification with SMT. PACMPL **2**(POPL), 53:1–53:31 (2018). https://doi.org/10.1145/3158141
61. Wadler, P.: Views: a way for pattern matching to cohabit with data abstraction. In: POPL (1987). https://dl.acm.org/citation.cfm?doid=41625.41653

62. Wenzel, M.: The Isabelle/Isar reference manual (2017). http://isabelle.in.tum.de/doc/isar-ref.pdf
63. Ziliani, B., Dreyer, D., Krishnaswami, N.R., Nanevski, A., Vafeiadis, V.: Mtac: a monad for typed tactic programming in Coq. JFP **25** (2015). https://doi.org/10.1017/S0956796815000118
64. Zinzindohoué, J.-K., Bhargavan, K., Protzenko, J., Beurdouche, B.: HACL*: a verified modern cryptographic library. In: CCS (2017). http://eprint.iacr.org/2017/536

# 7

# Extended Call-by-Push-Value: Reasoning About Effectful Programs and Evaluation Order

Dylan McDermott(✉) and Alan Mycroft

Computer Laboratory, University of Cambridge, Cambridge, UK
{Dylan.McDermott,Alan.Mycroft}@cl.cam.ac.uk

**Abstract.** Traditionally, reasoning about programs under varying evaluation regimes (call-by-value, call-by-name etc.) was done at the meta-level, treating them as term rewriting systems. Levy's call-by-push-value (CBPV) calculus provides a more powerful approach for reasoning, by treating CBPV terms as a common intermediate language which captures both call-by-value and call-by-name, and by allowing equational reasoning about changes to evaluation order between or within programs.

We extend CBPV to additionally deal with call-by-need, which is non-trivial because of shared reductions. This allows the equational reasoning to also support call-by-need. As an example, we then prove that call-by-need and call-by-name are equivalent if nontermination is the only side-effect in the source language.

We then show how to incorporate an effect system. This enables us to exploit static knowledge of the potential effects of a given expression to augment equational reasoning; thus a program fragment might be invariant under change of evaluation regime only because of knowledge of its effects.

**Keywords:** Evaluation order · Call-by-need · Call-by-push-value · Logical relations · Effect systems

## 1 Introduction

Programming languages based on the $\lambda$-calculus have different semantics depending on the reduction strategy employed. Three common variants are call-by-value, call-by-name and call-by-need (with the third sometimes also referred to as "lazy evaluation" when data constructors defer evaluation of arguments until the data structure is traversed). Reasoning about such programs and their equivalence under varying reduction strategies can be difficult as we have to reason about meta-level reduction strategies and not merely at the object level.

Levy [17] introduced *call-by-push-value* (CBPV) to improve the situation. CBPV is a calculus with separated notions of value and computation. A characteristic feature is that each CBPV program encodes its own evaluation order. It is best seen as an *intermediate language* into which lambda-calculus-based *source-language* programs can be translated. Moreover, CBPV is powerful enough that programs employing call-by-value or call-by-name (or even a mixture) can be simply translated into it, giving an object-calculus way to reason about the meta-level concept of reduction order.

However, CBPV does not enable us to reason about call-by-need evaluation. An intuitive reason is that call-by-need has "action at a distance" in that reduction of one subterm causes reduction of all other subterms that originated as copies during variable substitution. Indeed call-by-need is often framed using mutable stores (graph reduction [32], or reducing a thunk which is accessed by multiple pointers [16]). CBPV does not allow these to be encoded.

This work presents *extended call-by-push-value* (ECBPV), a calculus similar to CBPV, but which can capture call-by-need reduction in addition to call-by-value and call-by-name. Specifically, ECBPV adds an extra primitive $M$ need$\underline{x}.\, N$ which runs $N$, with $M$ being evaluated the first time $\underline{x}$ is used. On subsequent uses of $\underline{x}$, the result of the first run is returned immediately. The term $M$ is evaluated at most once. We give the syntax and type system of ECBPV, together with an equational theory that expresses when terms are considered equal.

A key justification for an intermediate language that can express several evaluation orders is that it enables equivalences between the evaluation orders to be proved. If there are no (side-)effects at all in the source language, then call-by-need, call-by-value and call-by-name should be semantically equivalent. If the only effect is nondeterminism, then need and value (but not name) are equivalent. If the only effect is nontermination then need and name (but not value) are equivalent. We show that ECBPV can be used to prove such equivalences by proving the latter using an argument based on *Kripke logical relations of varying arity* [12].

These equivalences rely on the *language* being restricted to particular effects. However, one may wish to switch evaluation order for *subprograms* restricted to particular effects, even if the language itself does not have such a restriction. To allow reasoning to be applied to these cases, we add an *effect system* [20] to ECBPV, which allows the side-effects of subprograms to be statically estimated. This allows us to determine which parts of a program are invariant under changes in evaluation order. As we will see, support for call-by-need (and action at a distance more generally) makes describing an effect system significantly more difficult than for call-by-value.

*Contributions.* We make the following contributions:

- We describe *extended call-by-push-value*, a version of CBPV containing an extra construct that adds support for call-by-need. We give its syntax, type system, and equational theory (Sect. 2).
- We describe two translations from a lambda-calculus source language into ECBPV: one for call-by-name and one for call-by-need (the first such translation) (Sect. 3). We then show that, if the source language has nontermination as the only effect, call-by-name and call-by-need are equivalent.

- We refine the type system of ECBPV so that its types also carry effect information (Sect. 4). This allows equivalences between evaluation orders to be exploited, both at ECBPV and source level, when subprograms are statically limited to particular effects.

## 2 Extended Call-by-Push-Value

We describe an extension to call-by-push-value with support for call-by-need. The primary difference between ordinary CBPV and ECBPV is the addition of a primitive that allows computations to be added to the environment, so that they are evaluated only the first time they are used. Before describing this change, we take a closer look at CBPV and how it supports call-by-value and call-by-name.

CBPV stratifies terms into *values*, which do not have side-effects, and *computations*, which might. Evaluation order is irrelevant for values, so we are only concerned with how computations are sequenced. There is exactly one primitive that causes the evaluation of more than one computation, which is the computation $M\ \mathsf{to}\ x.\ N$. This means run the computation $M$, bind the result to $x$, and then run the computation $N$. (It is similar to `M >>= \x -> N` in Haskell.) The evaluation order is fixed: $M$ is always eagerly evaluated. This construct can be used to implement call-by-value: to apply a function, eagerly evaluate the argument and then evaluate the body of the function. No other constructs cause the evaluation of more than one computation.

To allow more control over evaluation order, CBPV allows computations to be thunked. The term $\mathsf{thunk}\,M$ is a value that contains the thunk of the computation $M$. Thunks can be duplicated (to allow a single computation to be evaluated more than once), and can be converted back into computations with $\mathsf{force}\,V$. This allows call-by-name to be implemented: arguments to functions are thunked computations. Arguments are used by forcing them, so that the computation is evaluated every time the argument is used. Effectively, there is a construct $M\ \mathsf{name}\ \underline{x}.\ N$, which evaluates $M$ each time the variable $\underline{x}$ is used by $N$, rather than eagerly evaluating. (The variable $\underline{x}$ is underlined here to indicate that it refers to a computation rather than a value: uses of it may have side-effects.)

To support call-by-need, extended call-by-push-value adds another construct $M\ \mathsf{need}\ \underline{x}.\ N$. This term runs the computation $N$, with the computation $M$ being evaluated the first time $\underline{x}$ is used. On subsequent uses of $\underline{x}$, the result of the first run is returned immediately. The computation $M$ is evaluated at most once. This new construct adds the "action at a distance" missing from ordinary CBPV.

We briefly mention that adding general mutable references to call-by-push-value would allow call-by-need to be encoded. However, reasoning about evaluation order would be difficult, and so we do not take this option.

## 2.1 Syntax

The syntax of extended call-by-push-value is given in Fig. 1. The highlighted parts are new here. The rest of the syntax is similar to CBPV.[1]

$$
\begin{aligned}
V, W &::= c \mid x \mid (V_1, V_2) \mid \mathsf{fst}\, V \mid \mathsf{snd}\, V \mid \mathsf{inl}\, V \mid \mathsf{inr}\, V \\
&\quad \mid \mathsf{case}\, V \,\mathsf{of}\, \{\mathsf{inl}\, x.\, W_1, \mathsf{inr}\, y.\, W_2\} \mid \mathsf{thunk}\, M \\
M, N &::= \underline{x} \mid \mathsf{force}\, V \mid \lambda\{i.\, M_i\}_{i \in I} \mid i`M \mid \lambda x.\, M \mid V`M \mid \mathsf{return}\, V \\
&\quad \mid M \,\mathsf{to}\, x.\, N \mid M \,\mathsf{need}\, \underline{x}.\, N \\
A, B &::= \mathbf{unit} \mid A_1 \times A_2 \mid A_1 + A_2 \mid \mathbf{U}\, \underline{C} \\
\underline{C}, \underline{D} &::= \textstyle\prod_{i \in I} \underline{C}_i \mid A \to \underline{C} \mid \mathbf{Fr}\, A \\
\Gamma &::= \diamond \mid \Gamma, x : A \mid \Gamma, \underline{x} : \mathbf{Fr}\, A
\end{aligned}
$$

**Fig. 1.** Syntax of ECBPV

We assume two sets of variables: *value variables* $x, y, \ldots$ and *computation variables* $\underline{x}, \underline{y}, \ldots$. While ordinary CBPV does not include computation variables, they do not of themselves add any expressive power to the calculus. The ability to use call-by-need in ECBPV comes from the need construct used to bind the variable.[2]

There are two kinds of terms, *value terms* $V, W$ which do not have side-effects (in particular, are strongly normalizing), and *computation terms* $M, N$ which might have side-effects. Value terms include constants $c$, and specifically the constant $()$ of type **unit**. There are no constant computation terms; value constants suffice (see Sect. 3 for an example). The value term $\mathsf{thunk}\, M$ suspends the computation $M$; the computation term $\mathsf{force}\, V$ runs the suspended computation $V$. Computation terms also include $I$-ary tuples $\lambda\{i.\, M_i\}_{i \in I}$ (where $I$ ranges over *finite* sets); the $i$th projection of a tuple $M$ is $i`M$. Functions send values to computations, and are computations themselves. Application is written $V`M$, where $V$ is the argument and $M$ is the function to apply. The term $\mathsf{return}\, V$ is a computation that just returns the value $V$, without causing any side-effects. Eager sequencing of computations is given by $M \,\mathsf{to}\, x.\, N$, which evaluates $M$ until it returns a value, then places the result in $x$ and evaluates $N$. For example, in $M \,\mathsf{to}\, x.\, \mathsf{return}\, (x, x)$, the term $M$ is evaluated once, and the result is duplicated. In $M \,\mathsf{to}\, x.\, \mathsf{return}\, ()$, the term $M$ is still evaluated once, but its result is never

---

[1] The only difference is that eliminators of product and sum types are value terms rather than computation terms (which makes value terms slightly more general). Levy [17] calls this CBPV with *complex values*.

[2] Computation variables are not strictly required to support call-by-need (since we can use $x : \mathbf{U}\,(\mathbf{Fr}\, A)$ instead of $\underline{x} : \mathbf{Fr}\, A$), but they simplify reasoning about evaluation order, and therefore we choose to include them.

used. Syntactically, both to and need (explained below) are right-associative (so $M_1$ to $x.\,M_2$ to $y.\,M_3$ means $M_1$ to $x.\,(M_2$ to $y.\,M_3))$.

The primary new construct is $M$ need $\underline{x}.\,N$. This term evaluates $N$. The first time $\underline{x}$ is evaluated (due to a use of $\underline{x}$ inside $N$) it behaves the same as the computation $M$. If $M$ returns a value $V$, then subsequent uses of $\underline{x}$ behave the same as return $V$. Hence only the first use of $\underline{x}$ will evaluate $M$. If $\underline{x}$ is not used then $M$ is not evaluated at all. The computation variable $\underline{x}$ bound inside the term is primarily used by eagerly sequencing it with other computations. For example,

$$M \ \mathsf{need}\ \underline{x}.\ \underline{x}\ \mathsf{to}\ y.\ \underline{x}\ \mathsf{to}\ z.\ \mathsf{return}\,(y, z)$$

uses $\underline{x}$ twice: once where the result is bound to $y$, and once where the result is bound to $z$. Only the first of these uses will evaluate $M$, so this term has the same semantics as $M$ to $x$. return$(x, x)$. The term $M$ need $\underline{x}$. return () does not evaluate $M$ at all, and has the same semantics as return ().

With the addition of need it is not in general possible to determine the order in which computations are executed statically. Uses of computation variables are given statically, but not all of these actually evaluate the corresponding computation dynamically. In general, the set of uses of computation variables that actually cause effects depends on run-time behaviour. This will be important when describing the effect system in Sect. 4.

The standard capture-avoiding substitution of value variables in value terms is denoted $V[x \mapsto W]$. We similarly have substitutions of value variables in computation terms, computation variables in value terms, and computation variables in computation terms. Finally, we define the call-by-name construct mentioned above as syntactic sugar for other CBPV primitives:

$$M\ \mathsf{name}\ \underline{x}.\,N \ :=\ \mathsf{thunk}\,M\ \text{`}\ \lambda y.\,N[\underline{x} \mapsto \mathsf{force}\,y]$$

where $y$ is not free in $N$.

Types are stratified into *value types* $A, B$ and *computation types* $\underline{C}, \underline{D}$. Value types include the unit type, products and sum types. (It is easy to add further base types; we omit Levy's empty types for simplicity.) Value types also include *thunk types* $\mathbf{U}\,\underline{C}$, which are introduced by thunk $M$ and eliminated by force $V$. Computation types include $I$-ary product types $\prod_{i \in I} \underline{C}_i$ for finite $I$, function types $A \to \underline{C}$, and *returner types* $\mathbf{Fr}\,A$. The latter are introduced by return $V$, and are the only types of computation that can appear on the left of either to or need (which are the eliminators of returner types). The type constructors $\mathbf{U}$ and $\mathbf{Fr}$ form an *adjunction* in categorical models. Finally, contexts $\Gamma$ map value variables to value types, and computation variables to computation types of the form $\mathbf{Fr}\,A$. This restriction is due to the fact that the only construct that binds computation variables is need, which only sequences computations of returner type. Allowing computation variables to be associated with other forms of computation type in typing contexts is therefore unnecessary. Typing contexts are ordered lists.

The syntax is parameterized by a *signature*, containing the constants $c$.

**Definition 1 (Signature).** *A signature $\mathcal{K}$ consists of a set $\mathcal{K}_A$ of constants of type $A$ for each value type $A$. All signatures contain $() \in \mathcal{K}_{\mathbf{unit}}$.*

### 2.2 Type System

The type system of extended call-by-push-value is a minor extension of the type system of ordinary call-by-push-value. Assume a fixed signature $\mathcal{K}$. There are two typing judgements, one for value types and one for computation types. The rules for the value typing judgement $\Gamma \vdash_{\mathrm{v}} V : A$ and the computation typing judgement $\Gamma \vdash M : \underline{C}$ are given in Fig. 2. Rules that add a new variable to the typing context implicitly require that the variable does not already appear in the context. The type system admits the usual weakening and substitution properties for both value and computation variables.

$$\boxed{\Gamma \vdash_{\mathrm{v}} V : A}$$

$$\frac{}{\Gamma \vdash_{\mathrm{v}} x : A}\ \text{if } (x : A) \in \Gamma \qquad \frac{}{\Gamma \vdash_{\mathrm{v}} c : A}\ \text{if } c \in \mathcal{K}_A \qquad \frac{\Gamma \vdash M : \underline{C}}{\Gamma \vdash_{\mathrm{v}} \mathsf{thunk}\, M : \mathbf{U}\,\underline{C}}$$

$$\frac{\Gamma \vdash_{\mathrm{v}} V_1 : A_1 \qquad \Gamma \vdash_{\mathrm{v}} V_2 : A_2}{\Gamma \vdash_{\mathrm{v}} (V_1, V_2) : A_1 \times A_2} \qquad \frac{\Gamma \vdash_{\mathrm{v}} V : A_1 \times A_2}{\Gamma \vdash_{\mathrm{v}} \mathsf{fst}\, V : A_1} \qquad \frac{\Gamma \vdash_{\mathrm{v}} V : A_1 \times A_2}{\Gamma \vdash_{\mathrm{v}} \mathsf{snd}\, V : A_2}$$

$$\frac{\Gamma \vdash_{\mathrm{v}} V : A_1}{\Gamma \vdash_{\mathrm{v}} \mathsf{inl}\, V : A_1 + A_2} \qquad \frac{\Gamma \vdash_{\mathrm{v}} V : A_2}{\Gamma \vdash_{\mathrm{v}} \mathsf{inr}\, V : A_1 + A_2}$$

$$\frac{\Gamma \vdash_{\mathrm{v}} V : A_1 + A_2 \qquad \Gamma, x : A_1 \vdash_{\mathrm{v}} W_1 : B \qquad \Gamma, x : A_2 \vdash_{\mathrm{v}} W_2 : B}{\Gamma \vdash_{\mathrm{v}} \mathsf{case}\, V\, \mathsf{of}\, \{\mathsf{inl}\, x.\, W_1, \mathsf{inr}\, y.\, W_2\} : B}$$

$$\boxed{\Gamma \vdash M : \underline{C}}$$

$$\frac{}{\Gamma \vdash \underline{x} : \mathbf{Fr}\, A}\ \text{if } (\underline{x} : \mathbf{Fr}\, A) \in \Gamma \qquad \frac{\Gamma \vdash_{\mathrm{v}} V : A}{\Gamma \vdash \mathsf{return}\, V : \mathbf{Fr}\, A} \qquad \frac{\Gamma \vdash_{\mathrm{v}} V : \mathbf{U}\,\underline{C}}{\Gamma \vdash \mathsf{force}\, V : \underline{C}}$$

$$\frac{(\Gamma \vdash M_i : \underline{C}_i)_{i \in I}}{\Gamma \vdash \lambda\{i.\, M_i\}_{i \in I} : \prod_{i \in I} \underline{C}_i} \qquad \frac{\Gamma \vdash M : \prod_{i \in I} \underline{C}_i}{\Gamma \vdash i`M : \underline{C}_i}$$

$$\frac{\Gamma, x : A \vdash M : \underline{C}}{\Gamma \vdash \lambda x.\, M : A \to \underline{C}} \qquad \frac{\Gamma \vdash_{\mathrm{v}} V : A \qquad \Gamma \vdash M : A \to \underline{C}}{\Gamma \vdash V`M : \underline{C}}$$

$$\frac{\Gamma \vdash M : \mathbf{Fr}\, A \qquad \Gamma, x : A \vdash N : \underline{C}}{\Gamma \vdash M\, \mathsf{to}\, x.\, N : \underline{C}} \qquad \frac{\Gamma \vdash M : \mathbf{Fr}\, A \qquad \Gamma, \underline{x} : \mathbf{Fr}\, A \vdash N : \underline{C}}{\Gamma \vdash M\, \mathsf{need}\, \underline{x}.\, N : \underline{C}}$$

**Fig. 2.** Typing rules for ECBPV

It should be clear that ECBPV is actually an extension of call-by-push-value. CBPV terms embed as terms that never use the highlighted forms. We translate call-by-need by encoding call-by-need functions as terms of the form

$$\lambda x'.\,(\mathsf{force}\, x')\ \mathsf{need}\ \underline{x}.\, M$$

where $x'$ is not free in $M$. This is a call-by-push-value function that accepts a thunk as an argument. The thunk is added to the context, and the body of the function is executed. The first time the argument is used (via $\underline{x}$), the computation inside the thunk is evaluated. Subsequent uses do not run the computation again. A translation based on this idea from a call-by-need source language is given in detail in Sect. 3.2.

### 2.3 Equational Theory

In this section, we present the *equational theory* of extended call-by-push-value. This is an extension of the equational theory for CBPV given by Levy [17] to support our new constructs. It consists of two judgement forms, one for values and one for computations:

$$\Gamma \vdash_{\mathrm{v}} V \equiv W : A \qquad \Gamma \vdash M \equiv N : \underline{C}$$

These mean both terms are well typed, and are considered equal by the equational theory. We frequently omit the context and type when they are obvious or unimportant.

The definition is given by the axioms in Fig. 3. Note that these axioms only hold when the terms they mention have suitable types, and when suitable constraints on free variables are satisfied. For example, the second sequencing axiom holds only if $\underline{x}$ is not free in $N$. These conditions are left implicit in the figure. The judgements are additionally reflexive (assuming the typing holds), symmetric and transitive. They are also closed under all possible congruence rules. There are no restrictions on congruence related to evaluation order. None are necessary because ECBPV terms make the evaluation order explicit: all sequencing of computations uses to and need. Finally, note that enriching the signature with additional constants will in general require additional axioms capturing their behaviour; Sect. 3 exemplifies this for constants $\bot_A$ representing nontermination.

For the equational theory to capture call-by-need, we might expect computation terms that are not of the form return $V$ to never be duplicated, since they should not be evaluated more than once. There are two exceptions to this. Such terms can be duplicated in the axioms that duplicate value terms (such as the $\beta$ laws for sum types). In this case, the syntax ensures such terms are thunked. This is correct because we should allow these terms to be executed once in each separate execution of a computation (and separate executions arise from duplication of thunks). We are only concerned with duplication *within* a single computation. Computation terms can also be duplicated across multiple elements of a tuple $\lambda\{i.\, M_i\}$ of computation terms. This is also correct, because only one component

$$\begin{aligned}
\Gamma \vdash_{\mathrm{v}} \ \mathsf{fst}\,(V_1, V_2) &\equiv V_1 \ : \ A_1 \\
\Gamma \vdash_{\mathrm{v}} \ \mathsf{snd}\,(V_1, V_2) &\equiv V_2 \ : \ A_2 \\
\Gamma \vdash_{\mathrm{v}} \ \mathsf{case}\,\mathsf{inl}\,V\,\mathsf{of}\,\{\mathsf{inl}\,x.\,W_1, \mathsf{inr}\,y.\,W_2\} &\equiv W_1[x \mapsto V] \ : \ B \\
\Gamma \vdash_{\mathrm{v}} \ \mathsf{case}\,\mathsf{inr}\,V\,\mathsf{of}\,\{\mathsf{inl}\,x.\,W_1, \mathsf{inr}\,y.\,W_2\} &\equiv W_2[y \mapsto V] \ : \ B \\
\Gamma \vdash \ \mathsf{force}(\mathsf{thunk}\,M) &\equiv M \ : \ \underline{C} \\
\Gamma \vdash \ i\,`\,\lambda\{i.\,M_i\}_{i \in I} &\equiv M_i \ : \ \underline{C}_i \\
\Gamma \vdash \ V\,`\,\lambda x.\,M &\equiv M[x \mapsto V] \ : \ \underline{C} \\
\Gamma \vdash \ \mathsf{return}\,V\,\mathsf{to}\,x.\,M &\equiv M[x \mapsto V] \ : \ \underline{C} \\
\Gamma \vdash \ \mathsf{return}\,V\,\mathsf{need}\,\underline{x}.\,M &\equiv M[\underline{x} \mapsto \mathsf{return}\,V] \ : \ \underline{C}
\end{aligned}$$

(a) $\beta$ laws

$$\begin{aligned}
\Gamma \vdash_{\mathrm{v}} \ () &\equiv V \ : \ \mathbf{unit} \\
\Gamma \vdash_{\mathrm{v}} \ (\mathsf{fst}\,V, \mathsf{snd}\,V) &\equiv V \ : \ A_1 \times A_2 \\
\Gamma \vdash_{\mathrm{v}} \ \mathsf{case}\,W\,\mathsf{of}\,\{\mathsf{inl}\,y.\,V[x \mapsto \mathsf{inl}\,y], \mathsf{inr}\,z.\,V[x \mapsto \mathsf{inr}\,z]\} &\equiv V[x \mapsto W] \ : \ B \\
\Gamma \vdash_{\mathrm{v}} \ \mathsf{thunk}(\mathsf{force}\,M) &\equiv M \ : \ \mathbf{U}\,\underline{C} \\
\Gamma \vdash \ \lambda\{i.\,i\,`\,M\}_{i \in I} &\equiv M \ : \ \textstyle\prod_{i \in I} \underline{C}_i \\
\Gamma \vdash \ \lambda x.\,x\,`\,M &\equiv M \ : \ A \to \underline{C} \\
\Gamma \vdash \ M\,\mathsf{to}\,x.\,\mathsf{return}\,x &\equiv M \ : \ \mathbf{Fr}\,A
\end{aligned}$$

(b) $\eta$ laws

$$\begin{aligned}
\Gamma \vdash \ M\,\mathsf{need}\,\underline{x}.\,\underline{x}\,\mathsf{to}\,y.\,N &\equiv M\,\mathsf{to}\,y.\,N[\underline{x} \mapsto \mathsf{return}\,y] \ : \ \underline{C} \\
\Gamma \vdash \ M\,\mathsf{need}\,\underline{x}.\,N &\equiv N \ : \ \underline{C}
\end{aligned}$$

$$\begin{aligned}
\Gamma \vdash \ \lambda\{i.\,M\,\mathsf{to}\,x.\,N_i\}_{i \in I} &\equiv M\,\mathsf{to}\,x.\,\lambda\{i.\,N_i\}_{i \in I} \ : \ \textstyle\prod_{i \in I} \underline{C}_i \\
\Gamma \vdash \ \lambda y.\,M\,\mathsf{to}\,x.\,N &\equiv M\,\mathsf{to}\,x.\,\lambda y.\,N \ : \ A \to \underline{C} \\
\Gamma \vdash \ \lambda\{i.\,M\,\mathsf{need}\,\underline{x}.\,N_i\}_{i \in I} &\equiv M\,\mathsf{need}\,\underline{x}.\,\lambda\{i.\,N_i\}_{i \in I} \ : \ \textstyle\prod_{i \in I} \underline{C}_i \\
\Gamma \vdash \ \lambda y.\,M\,\mathsf{need}\,\underline{x}.\,N &\equiv M\,\mathsf{need}\,\underline{x}.\,\lambda y.\,N \ : \ A \to \underline{C}
\end{aligned}$$

$$\begin{aligned}
\Gamma \vdash \ (M_1\,\mathsf{to}\,x.\,M_2)\,\mathsf{to}\,y.\,M_3 &\equiv M_1\,\mathsf{to}\,x.\,M_2\,\mathsf{to}\,y.\,M_3 \ : \ \underline{C} \\
\Gamma \vdash \ M_1\,\mathsf{to}\,x.\,M_2\,\mathsf{need}\,\underline{y}.\,M_3 &\equiv M_2\,\mathsf{need}\,\underline{y}.\,M_1\,\mathsf{to}\,x.\,M_3 \ : \ \underline{C} \\
\Gamma \vdash \ (M_1\,\mathsf{need}\,\underline{x}.\,M_2)\,\mathsf{to}\,y.\,M_3 &\equiv M_1\,\mathsf{need}\,\underline{x}.\,M_2\,\mathsf{to}\,y.\,M_3 \ : \ \underline{C} \\
\Gamma \vdash \ (M_1\,\mathsf{need}\,\underline{x}.\,M_2)\,\mathsf{need}\,\underline{y}.\,M_3 &\equiv M_1\,\mathsf{need}\,\underline{x}.\,M_2\,\mathsf{need}\,\underline{y}.\,M_3 \ : \ \underline{C}
\end{aligned}$$

(c) Sequencing axioms

**Fig. 3.** Equational theory of ECBPV

of a tuple can be used within a single computation (without thunking), so the effects still will not happen twice. (There is a similar consideration for functions, which can only be applied once.) The remainder of the axioms never duplicate need-bound terms that might have effects.

The majority of the axioms of the equational theory are standard. Only the axioms involving need are new; these are highlighted. The first new sequencing axiom (in Fig. 3c) is the crucial one. It states that if a computation will next evaluate $\underline{x}$, where $\underline{x}$ is a computation variable bound to $M$, then this is the same as evaluating $M$, and then using the result for subsequent uses of $\underline{x}$. In particular, this axiom (together with the $\eta$ law for **Fr**) implies that $M \ \mathsf{need}\ \underline{x}.\, \underline{x} \ \equiv\ M$.

The second sequencing axiom does *garbage collection* [22]: if a computation bound by need is not used (because the variable does not appear), then the binding can be dropped. This equation implies, for example, that

$$M_1 \ \mathsf{need}\ \underline{x}_1.\, M_2 \ \mathsf{need}\ \underline{x}_2.\, \cdots M_n \ \mathsf{need}\ \underline{x}_n.\ \mathsf{return}\,() \ \equiv\ \mathsf{return}\,()$$

The next four sequencing axioms (two from CBPV and two new) state that binding a computation with to or need commutes with the remaining forms of computation terms. These allow to and need to be moved to the outside of other constructs *except* thunks. The final four axioms (one from CBPV and three new) capture associativity and commutativity involving need and to; again these parallel the existing simple associativity axiom for to.

Note that associativity between different evaluation orders is not necessarily valid. In particular, we do not have

$$(M_1 \ \mathsf{to}\ x.\, M_2) \ \mathsf{need}\ \underline{y}.\, M_3 \quad \equiv \quad M_1 \ \mathsf{to}\ x.\, (M_2 \ \mathsf{need}\ \underline{x}.\, M_3)$$

(The first term might not evaluate $M_1$, the second always does.) This is usually the case when evaluation orders are mixed [26].

These final two groups allow computation terms to be placed in normal forms where bindings of computations are on the outside. (Compare this with the translation of source-language *answers* given in Sect. 3.2.) Finally, the $\beta$ law for need (in Fig. 3a) parallels the usual $\beta$ law for to: it gives the behaviour of computation terms that return values without having any effects.

The above equational theory induces a notion of *contextual equivalence* $\cong_{\text{ctx}}$ between ECBPV terms. Two terms are contextually equivalent when they have no observable differences in behaviour. When we discuss *equivalences between evaluation orders* in Sect. 3, $\cong_{\text{ctx}}$ is the notion of *equivalence between terms* that we consider.

Contextual equivalence is defined as follows. The *ground types* $G$ are the value types that do not contain thunks:

$$G ::= \mathbf{unit} \mid G_1 \times G_2 \mid G_1 + G_2$$

A *value-term context* $\mathcal{C}[-]$ is a computation term with a single hole (written $-$), which occurs in a position where a value term is expected. We write $\mathcal{C}[V]$ for the computation term that results from replacing the hole with $V$. Similarly, *computation-term contexts* $\underline{\mathcal{C}}[-]$ are computation terms with a single hole where a computation term is expected, and $\underline{\mathcal{C}}[M]$ is the term in which the hole is replaced by $M$. Contextual equivalence says that the terms cannot be distinguished by closed computations that return ground types. (Recall that $\diamond$ is the empty typing context.)

**Definition 2 (Contextual equivalence).** *There are two judgement forms of* contextual equivalence.

1. *Between value terms:* $\Gamma \vdash_{\mathrm{v}} V \cong_{\mathrm{ctx}} W : A$ *if* $\Gamma \vdash_{\mathrm{v}} V : A$, $\Gamma \vdash_{\mathrm{v}} W : A$, *and for all ground types* $G$ *and value-term contexts* $\mathcal{C}$ *such that* $\diamond \vdash \mathcal{C}[V] : \mathbf{Fr}\, G$ *and* $\diamond \vdash \mathcal{C}[W] : \mathbf{Fr}\, G$ *we have*

$$\diamond \vdash \mathcal{C}[V] \equiv \mathcal{C}[W] : \mathbf{Fr}\, G$$

2. *Between computation terms:* $\Gamma \vdash M \cong_{\mathrm{ctx}} N : \underline{C}$ *if* $\Gamma \vdash M : \underline{C}$, $\Gamma \vdash N : \underline{C}$, *and for all ground types* $G$ *and computation-term contexts* $\underline{\mathcal{C}}[-]$ *such that* $\diamond \vdash \underline{\mathcal{C}}[M] : \mathbf{Fr}\, G$ *and* $\diamond \vdash \underline{\mathcal{C}}[N] : \mathbf{Fr}\, G$ *we have*

$$\diamond \vdash \underline{\mathcal{C}}[M] \equiv \underline{\mathcal{C}}[N] : \mathbf{Fr}\, G$$

## 3 Call-by-Name and Call-by-Need

Extended call-by-push-value can be used to prove equivalences between evaluation orders. In this section we prove a classic example: if the only effect in the source language is nontermination, then call-by-name is equivalent to call-by-need. We do this in two stages.

First, we show that call-by-name is equivalent to call-by-need *within* ECBPV (Sect. 3.1). Specifically, we show that

$$M \;\mathsf{name}\; \underline{x}.\, N \;\cong_{\mathrm{ctx}}\; M \;\mathsf{need}\; \underline{x}.\, N$$

(Recall that $M \;\mathsf{name}\; \underline{x}.\, N$ is syntactic sugar for $\mathsf{thunk}\, M \text{ ` } \lambda y.\, N[\underline{x} \mapsto \mathsf{force}\, y]$.)

Second, an important corollary is that the meta-level reduction strategies are equivalent (Sect. 3.2). We show this by describing a lambda-calculus-based source language together with a call-by-name and a call-by-need operational semantics and giving sound (see Theorem 2) call-by-name and call-by-need translations into ECBPV. The former is based on the translation into the monadic metalanguage given by Moggi [25] (we expect Levy's translation [17] to work equally well). The call-by-need translation is new here, and its existence shows that ECBPV does indeed subsume call-by-need. We then show that given any source-language expression, the two translations give contextually equivalent ECBPV terms.

To model non-termination being our sole source-language effect, we use the ECBPV signature which contains a constant $\bot_A : \mathbf{U}\,(\mathbf{Fr}\, A)$ for each value type $A$, representing a thunked diverging computation. It is likely that our proofs still work if we have general fixed-point operators as constants, but for simplicity we do not consider this here. The constants $\bot_A$ enable us to define a diverging computation $\Omega_{\underline{C}}$ for each computation type $\underline{C}$:

$$\Omega_{\mathbf{Fr}A} := \mathsf{force}\,\bot_A \qquad \Omega_{\prod_{i\in I}\underline{C}_i} := \lambda\{i.\,\Omega_{\underline{C}_i}\}_{i\in I} \qquad \Omega_{A\to\underline{C}} := \lambda x.\,\Omega_{\underline{C}}$$

We characterise nontermination by augmenting the equational theory of Sect. 2.3 with the axiom

$$\Gamma \vdash \Omega_{\mathbf{Fr}A}\ \mathsf{to}\ x.\,M \ \equiv\ \Omega_{\underline{C}} \ :\ \underline{C} \qquad \text{(Omega)}$$

for each context $\Gamma$, value type $A$ and computation type $\underline{C}$. In other words, diverging as part of a larger computation causes the entire computation to diverge. This is the only change to the equational theory we need to represent nontermination. In particular, we do not add additional axioms involving need.

### 3.1 The Equivalence at the Object (Internal) Level

In this section, we show our primary result that

$$M\ \mathsf{name}\ \underline{x}.\,N \ \cong_{\mathrm{ctx}}\ M\ \mathsf{need}\ \underline{x}.\,N$$

As is usually the case for proofs of contextual equivalence, we use *logical relations* to get a strong enough inductive hypothesis for the proof to go through. However, unlike the usual case, it does not suffice to relate *closed* terms. To see why, consider a closed term $M$ of the form

$$\Omega_{\mathbf{Fr}A}\ \mathsf{need}\ \underline{x}.\,N_1\ \mathsf{to}\ y.\,N_2$$

If we relate only closed terms, then we do not learn anything about $N_1$ itself (since $\underline{x}$ may be free in it). We could attempt to proceed by considering the closed term $\Omega_{\mathbf{Fr}A}\ \mathsf{need}\ \underline{x}.\,N_1$. For example, if this returns a value $V$ then $\underline{x}$ cannot have been evaluated and $M$ should have the same behaviour as $\Omega_{\mathbf{Fr}A}\ \mathsf{need}\ \underline{x}.\,N_2[y \mapsto V]$. However, we get stuck when proving the last step. This is only a problem because $\Omega_{\mathbf{Fr}A}$ is a nonterminating computation: every terminating computation of returner type has the form $\mathsf{return}\,V$ (up to $\equiv$), and when these are bound using need we can eliminate the binding using the equation

$$\mathsf{return}\,V\ \mathsf{need}\ \underline{x}.\,M \equiv M[\underline{x} \mapsto \mathsf{return}\,V]$$

The solution is to relate terms that may have free computation variables (we do not need to consider free value variables). The free computation variables should be thought of as referring to nonterminating computations (because we can remove the bindings of variables that refer to terminating computations). We relate open terms using *Kripke logical relations of varying arity*, which were introduced by Jung and Tiuryn [12] to study lambda definability.

We need a number of definitions first. A context $\Gamma'$ *weakens* another context $\Gamma$, written $\Gamma' \rhd \Gamma$, whenever $\Gamma$ is a sublist of $\Gamma'$. For example, $(\Gamma, \underline{x} : \mathbf{Fr}\,A) \rhd \Gamma$. We define $\mathrm{Term}^{\Gamma}_{A}$ as the set of equivalence classes (up to the equational theory $\equiv$) of terms of value type $A$ in context $\Gamma$, and similarly define $\underline{\mathrm{Term}}_{\underline{D}}^{\Gamma}$ for computation types:

$$\mathrm{Term}_A^{\Gamma} := \{[V]_{\equiv} \mid \Gamma \vdash_{\mathrm{v}} V : A\} \qquad \underline{\mathrm{Term}}_{\underline{D}}^{\Gamma} := \{[M]_{\equiv} \mid \Gamma \vdash M : \underline{D}\}$$

Since weakening is admissible for both typing judgements, $\Gamma' \rhd \Gamma$ implies that $\mathrm{Term}_A^{\Gamma} \subseteq \mathrm{Term}_A^{\Gamma'}$ and $\underline{\mathrm{Term}}_{\underline{D}}^{\Gamma} \subseteq \underline{\mathrm{Term}}_{\underline{D}}^{\Gamma'}$ (note the contravariance).

A *computation context*, ranged over by $\Delta$, is a typing context that maps variables to computation types (i.e. has the form $\underline{x}_1 : \mathbf{Fr}\, A_1, \ldots, \underline{x}_n : \mathbf{Fr}\, A_n$). Variables in computation contexts refer to nonterminating computations for the proof of contextual equivalence. A *Kripke relation* is a family of binary relations indexed by computation contexts that respects weakening of terms:

**Definition 3 (Kripke relation).** *A* Kripke relation $R$ *over a value type* $A$ *(respectively a computation type* $\underline{D}$*) is a family of relations* $R^{\Delta} \subseteq \mathrm{Term}_A^{\Delta} \times \mathrm{Term}_A^{\Delta}$ *(respectively* $R^{\Delta} \subseteq \underline{\mathrm{Term}}_{\underline{D}}^{\Delta} \times \underline{\mathrm{Term}}_{\underline{D}}^{\Delta}$*) indexed by computation contexts* $\Delta$ *such that whenever* $\Delta' \rhd \Delta$ *we have* $R^{\Delta} \subseteq R^{\Delta'}$.

Note that we consider binary relations on equivalence classes of terms because we want to relate pairs of terms up to $\equiv$ (to prove contextual equivalence). The relations we define are *partial equivalence relations* (i.e. symmetric and transitive), though we do not explicitly use this fact.

We need the Kripke relations we define over computation terms to be closed under sequencing with nonterminating computations. (For the rest of this section, we omit the square brackets around equivalence classes.)

**Definition 4.** *A Kripke relation* $R$ *over a computation type* $\underline{C}$ *is* closed under sequencing *if each of the following holds:*

1. *If* $(\underline{x} : \mathbf{Fr}\, A) \in \Delta$ *and* $M, M' \in \underline{\mathrm{Term}}_{\underline{C}}^{\Delta, y:A}$ *then* $(\underline{x}\ \mathsf{to}\ y.\, M, \underline{x}\ \mathsf{to}\ y.\, M') \in R^{\Delta}$.
2. *The pair* $(\Omega_{\underline{C}}, \Omega_{\underline{C}})$ *is in* $R^{\Delta}$.
3. *For all* $(M, M') \in R^{\Delta, \underline{y}:\mathbf{Fr}A}$ *and* $N \in \{\Omega_{\mathbf{Fr}A}\} \cup \{\underline{x} \mid (\underline{x} : \mathbf{Fr}\, A) \in \Delta\}$*, all four of the following pairs are in* $R^{\Delta}$*:*

$$(N\ \mathsf{need}\ \underline{y}.\, M,\ N\ \mathsf{need}\ \underline{y}.\, M') \qquad (M[\underline{y} \mapsto N],\ M'[\underline{y} \mapsto N])$$
$$(M[\underline{y} \mapsto N],\ N\ \mathsf{need}\ \underline{y}.\, M') \qquad (N\ \mathsf{need}\ \underline{y}.\, M,\ M'[\underline{y} \mapsto N])$$

For the first case of the definition, recall that the computation variables in $\Delta$ refer to nonterminating computations. Hence the behaviour of $M$ and $M'$ are irrelevant (they are never evaluated), and we do not need to assume they are related.[3] The second case implies (using axiom Omega) that

$$(\Omega_{\mathbf{Fr}A}\ \mathsf{to}\ y.\, M, \Omega_{\mathbf{Fr}A}\ \mathsf{to}\ y.\, M') \in R^{\Delta}$$

[3] This is why it suffices to consider only computation contexts. If we had to relate $M$ to $M'$ then we would need to consider relations between terms with free value variables.

$$\boxed{R_A^\Delta \subseteq \mathrm{Term}_A^\Delta \times \mathrm{Term}_A^\Delta}$$

$$\begin{aligned}
R^\Delta_{\mathbf{unit}} &:= \{((), ())\} \\
R^\Delta_{A_1 \times A_2} &:= \{(V, V') \mid (\mathsf{fst}\, V, \mathsf{fst}\, V') \in R^\Delta_{A_1} \wedge (\mathsf{snd}\, V, \mathsf{snd}\, V') \in R^\Delta_{A_2}\} \\
R^\Delta_{A_1 + A_2} &:= \{(\mathsf{inl}\, V, \mathsf{inl}\, V') \mid (V, V') \in R^\Delta_{A_1}\} \cup \{(\mathsf{inr}\, V, \mathsf{inr}\, V') \mid (V, V') \in R^\Delta_{A_2}\} \\
R^\Delta_{\mathbf{U}\underline{C}} &:= \{(V, V') \mid (\mathsf{force}\, V, \mathsf{force}\, V') \in R^\Delta_{\underline{C}}\}
\end{aligned}$$

$$\boxed{R_{\underline{C}}^\Delta \subseteq \underline{\mathrm{Term}_{\underline{C}}^\Delta} \times \underline{\mathrm{Term}_{\underline{C}}^\Delta}}$$

$$\begin{aligned}
R_{\mathbf{Fr}A} &:= \text{the smallest closed-under-sequencing Kripke relation such that} \\
&\qquad (V, V') \in R^\Delta_A \;\Rightarrow\; (\mathsf{return}\, V, \mathsf{return}\, V') \in R^\Delta_{\mathbf{Fr}A} \\
R^\Delta_{\prod_{i \in I} \underline{C}_i} &:= \{(M, M') \mid \forall i \in I.\ (i`M, i`M') \in R^\Delta_{\underline{C}_i}\} \\
R^\Delta_{A \to \underline{C}} &:= \{(M, M') \mid \forall \Delta', V, V'.\ \Delta' \rhd \Delta \wedge (V, V') \in R^{\Delta'}_A \;\Rightarrow\; (V`M, V'`M') \in R^{\Delta'}_{\underline{C}}\}
\end{aligned}$$

**Fig. 4.** Definition of the logical relation

mirroring the first case. The third case is the most important. It is similar to the first (it is there to ensure that the relation is closed under the primitives used to combine computations). However, since we are showing that need is contextually equivalent to substitution, we also want these to be related. We have to consider computation variables in the definition (as possible terms $N$) only because of our use of Kripke logical relations. For ordinary logical relations, there would be no free variables to consider.

The key part of the proof of contextual equivalence is the definition of the Kripke logical relation, which is a family of relations indexed by value and computation types. It is defined in Fig. 4 by induction on the structure of the types. In the figure, we again omit square brackets around equivalence classes.

The definition of the logical relation on ground types (**unit**, sum types and product types) is standard. Since the only way to use a thunk is to force it, the definition on thunk types just requires the two forced computations to be related.

For returner types, we want any pair of computations that return related values to be related. We also want the relation to be closed under sequencing, in order to show the fundamental lemma (below) for to and need. We therefore define $R_{\mathbf{Fr}A}$ as the smallest such Kripke relation. For products of computation types the definition is similar to products of value types: we require that each of the projections are related. For function types, we require as usual that related arguments are sent to related results. For this to define a Kripke relation, we have to quantify over all computation contexts $\Delta'$ that weaken $\Delta$, because of the contravariance of the argument.

The relations we define are Kripke relations. Using the sequencing axioms of the equational theory, and the $\beta$ and $\eta$ laws for computation types, we can show that $R_{\underline{C}}$ is closed under sequencing for each computation type $\underline{C}$. These facts are important for the proof of the fundamental lemma.

*Substitutions* are given by the following grammar:

$$\sigma ::= \diamond \mid \sigma, x \mapsto V \mid \sigma, \underline{x} \mapsto M$$

We have a typing judgement $\Delta \vdash \sigma : \Gamma$ for substitutions, meaning in the context $\Delta$ the terms in $\sigma$ have the types given in $\Gamma$. This is defined as follows:

$$\frac{}{\Delta \vdash \diamond : \diamond} \qquad \frac{\Delta \vdash \sigma : \Gamma \qquad \Delta \vdash_{\mathrm{v}} V : A}{\Delta \vdash (\sigma, x \mapsto V) : (\Gamma, x : A)} \qquad \frac{\Delta \vdash \sigma : \Gamma \qquad \Delta \vdash M : \mathbf{Fr}\, A}{\Delta \vdash (\sigma, \underline{x} \mapsto M) : (\Gamma, \underline{x} : \mathbf{Fr}\, A)}$$

We write $V[\sigma]$ and $M[\sigma]$ for the applications of the substitution $\sigma$ to value terms $V$ and computation terms $M$. These are defined by induction on the structure of the terms. The key property of the substitution typing judgement is that if $\Delta \vdash \sigma : \Gamma$, then $\Gamma \vdash_{\mathrm{v}} V : A$ implies $\Delta \vdash_{\mathrm{v}} V[\sigma] : A$ and $\Gamma \vdash M : \underline{C}$ implies $\Delta \vdash M[\sigma] : \underline{C}$. The equational theory gives us an obvious pointwise equivalence relation $\equiv$ on well-typed substitutions. We define sets $\mathrm{Subst}_{\Gamma}^{\Delta}$ of equivalence classes of substitutions, and extend the logical relation by defining $R_{\Gamma}^{\Delta} \subseteq \mathrm{Subst}_{\Gamma}^{\Delta} \times \mathrm{Subst}_{\Gamma}^{\Delta}$:

$$\begin{aligned}
\mathrm{Subst}_{\Gamma}^{\Delta} &:= \{[\sigma]_{\equiv} \mid \Delta \vdash \sigma : \Gamma\} \\
R_{\diamond}^{\Delta} &:= \{(\diamond, \diamond)\} \\
R_{\Gamma, x:A}^{\Delta} &:= \{((\sigma, x \mapsto V), (\sigma', x \mapsto V')) \mid (\sigma, \sigma') \in R_{\Gamma}^{\Delta} \wedge (V, V') \in R_{A}^{\Delta}\} \\
R_{\Gamma, \underline{x}:\mathbf{Fr} A}^{\Delta} &:= \{((\sigma, \underline{x} \mapsto M), (\sigma', \underline{x} \mapsto M')) \mid (\sigma, \sigma') \in R_{\Gamma}^{\Delta} \wedge (M, M') \in R_{\mathbf{Fr} A}^{\Delta}\}
\end{aligned}$$

As usual, the logical relations satisfy a *fundamental lemma*.

**Lemma 1 (Fundamental)**

1. *For all value terms* $\Gamma \vdash_{\mathrm{v}} V : A$,

$$(\sigma, \sigma') \in R_{\Gamma}^{\Delta} \quad \Rightarrow \quad (V[\sigma], V[\sigma']) \in R_{A}^{\Delta}$$

2. *For all computation terms* $\Gamma \vdash M : \underline{C}$,

$$(\sigma, \sigma') \in R_{\Gamma}^{\Delta} \quad \Rightarrow \quad (M[\sigma], M[\sigma']) \in R_{\underline{C}}^{\Delta}$$

The proof is by induction on the structure of the terms. We use the fact that each $R_{\underline{C}}$ is closed under sequencing for the to and need cases. For the latter, we also use the fact that the relations respect weakening of terms.

We also have the following two facts about the logical relation. The first roughly is that name is related to need by the logical relation, and is true because of the additional pairs that are related in the definition of closed-under-sequencing (Definition 4).

**Lemma 2.** *For all computation terms* $\Gamma \vdash M : \mathbf{Fr}\, A$ *and* $\Gamma, \underline{x} : \mathbf{Fr}\, A \vdash N : \underline{C}$ *we have*

$$(\sigma, \sigma') \in R_{\Gamma}^{\Delta} \quad \Rightarrow \quad ((N[\underline{x} \mapsto M])[\sigma], (M \,\mathsf{need}\, \underline{x}.\, N)[\sigma']) \in R_{\underline{C}}^{\Delta}$$

The second fact is that related terms are contextually equivalent.

**Lemma 3**

1. *For all value terms* $\Gamma \vdash_{\mathrm{v}} V : A$ *and* $\Gamma \vdash_{\mathrm{v}} V' : A$*, if* $(V[\sigma], V'[\sigma']) \in R_{A}^{\Delta}$ *for all* $(\sigma, \sigma') \in R_{\Gamma}^{\Delta}$ *then*

$$\Gamma \vdash_{\mathrm{v}} V \cong_{\mathrm{ctx}} V' : A$$

2. *For all computation terms* $\Gamma \vdash M : \underline{C}$ *and* $\Gamma \vdash M' : \underline{C}$*, if* $(M[\sigma], M'[\sigma']) \in R_{\underline{C}}^{\Delta}$ *for all* $(\sigma, \sigma') \in R_{\Gamma}^{\Delta}$ *then*

$$\Gamma \vdash M \cong_{\mathrm{ctx}} M' : \underline{C}$$

This gives us enough to achieve the goal of this section.

**Theorem 1.** *For all computation terms* $\Gamma \vdash M : \mathbf{Fr}\, A$ *and* $\Gamma, \underline{x} : \mathbf{Fr}\, A \vdash N : \underline{C}$*, we have*

$$\Gamma \vdash M \,\mathsf{name}\, \underline{x}.\, N \cong_{\mathrm{ctx}} M \,\mathsf{need}\, \underline{x}.\, N : \underline{C}$$

### 3.2 The Meta-level Equivalence

In this section, we show that the equivalence between call-by-name and call-by-need also holds on the meta-level; this is a consequence of the object-level theorem, rather than something that is proved from scratch as it would be in a term rewriting system.

To do this, we describe a simple lambda-calculus-based source language with divergence as the only side-effect and give it a call-by-name and a call-by-need operational semantics. We then describe two translations from the source language into ECBPV. The first is a call-by-name translation based on the embedding of call-by-name in Moggi's [25] monadic metalanguage. The second is a call-by-need translation that uses our new constructs. The latter witnesses the fact that ECBPV does actually support call-by-need. Finally, we show that the two translations give contextually equivalent ECBPV terms.

The syntax, type system and operational semantics of the source language are given in Fig. 5. Most of this is standard. We include only booleans and function types for simplicity. In expressions, we include a constant $\mathsf{diverge}_A$ for each type $A$, representing a diverging computation. (As before, it should not be difficult to replace these with general fixed-point operators.) In typing contexts, we assume that all variables are distinct, and omit the required side-condition from the figure. There is a single set of variables $x, y, \ldots$; we implicitly map these to ECBPV value or computation variables as required.

| | |
|---|---|
| Types | $A, B ::= \mathbf{bool} \mid A \to B$ |
| Contexts | $\Gamma ::= \diamond \mid \Gamma, x : A$ |
| Expressions | $e ::= x \mid \mathsf{diverge}_A \mid \mathsf{true} \mid \mathsf{false} \mid \mathsf{if}\ e_1\ \mathsf{then}\ e_2\ \mathsf{else}\ e_3 \mid \lambda x.\, e \mid e_1\, e_2$ |

(a) Syntax

$$\frac{}{\Gamma \vdash x : A}\ \text{if } (x : A) \in \Gamma \qquad \frac{}{\Gamma \vdash \mathsf{diverge}_A : A}$$

$$\frac{}{\Gamma \vdash \mathsf{true} : \mathbf{bool}} \qquad \frac{}{\Gamma \vdash \mathsf{false} : \mathbf{bool}} \qquad \frac{\Gamma \vdash e_1 : \mathbf{bool} \qquad \Gamma \vdash e_2 : A \qquad \Gamma \vdash e_3 : A}{\Gamma \vdash \mathsf{if}\ e_1\ \mathsf{then}\ e_2\ \mathsf{else}\ e_3 : A}$$

$$\frac{\Gamma, x : A \vdash e : B}{\Gamma \vdash \lambda x.\, e : A \to B} \qquad \frac{\Gamma \vdash e_1 : A \to B \qquad \Gamma \vdash e_2 : A}{\Gamma \vdash e_1\, e_2 : B}$$

(b) Typing

$$\mathsf{if\ true\ then}\ e_2\ \mathsf{else}\ e_3 \overset{\text{name}}{\rightsquigarrow} e_2 \qquad \mathsf{diverge}_A \overset{\text{name}}{\rightsquigarrow} \mathsf{diverge}_A$$

$$\mathsf{if\ false\ then}\ e_2\ \mathsf{else}\ e_3 \overset{\text{name}}{\rightsquigarrow} e_3 \qquad \mathsf{if}\ \mathsf{diverge}_{\mathbf{bool}}\ \mathsf{then}\ e_2\ \mathsf{else}\ e_3 \overset{\text{name}}{\rightsquigarrow} \mathsf{diverge}_A$$

$$(\lambda x.\, e)\, e' \overset{\text{name}}{\rightsquigarrow} e[x \mapsto e'] \qquad \mathsf{diverge}_{A \to B}\, e' \overset{\text{name}}{\rightsquigarrow} \mathsf{diverge}_B$$

$$\frac{e_1 \overset{\text{name}}{\rightsquigarrow} e_1'}{\mathsf{if}\ e_1\ \mathsf{then}\ e_2\ \mathsf{else}\ e_3 \overset{\text{name}}{\rightsquigarrow} \mathsf{if}\ e_1'\ \mathsf{then}\ e_2\ \mathsf{else}\ e_3} \qquad \frac{e_1 \overset{\text{name}}{\rightsquigarrow} e_1'}{e_1\, e_2 \overset{\text{name}}{\rightsquigarrow} e_1'\, e_2}$$

(c) Call-by-name operational semantics

| | |
|---|---|
| Evaluation contexts | $E[-] ::= - \mid \mathsf{if}\ E[-]\ \mathsf{then}\ e_2\ \mathsf{else}\ e_3$ |
| | $\mid E[-]\, e_2 \mid (\lambda x.\, E[x])\, E'[-] \mid (\lambda x.\, E[-])\, e_2$ |
| Values | $v ::= \mathsf{true} \mid \mathsf{false} \mid \lambda x.\, e$ |
| Answers | $a ::= v \mid (\lambda x.\, a)\, e$ |

$$\mathsf{if\ true\ then}\ e_2\ \mathsf{else}\ e_3 \overset{\text{need}}{\rightsquigarrow} e_2$$

$$\mathsf{if\ false\ then}\ e_2\ \mathsf{else}\ e_3 \overset{\text{need}}{\rightsquigarrow} e_3$$

$$(\lambda x.\, E[x])\, v \overset{\text{need}}{\rightsquigarrow} (\lambda x.\, E[v])\, v$$

$$(\lambda x.\, a)\, e_1\, e_2 \overset{\text{need}}{\rightsquigarrow} (\lambda x.\, a\, e_2)\, e_1$$

$$(\lambda x.\, E[x])\, ((\lambda y.\, a)\, e) \overset{\text{need}}{\rightsquigarrow} (\lambda y.\, (\lambda x.\, E[x])\, a)\, e$$

$$\mathsf{diverge}_A \overset{\text{need}}{\rightsquigarrow} \mathsf{diverge}_A$$

$$E[\mathsf{diverge}_A] \overset{\text{need}}{\rightsquigarrow} \mathsf{diverge}_B$$

$$\frac{e \overset{\text{need}}{\rightsquigarrow} e'}{E[e] \overset{\text{need}}{\rightsquigarrow} E[e']}$$

(d) Call-by-need operational semantics

**Fig. 5.** The source language

The call-by-name operational semantics is straightforward; its small-step reductions are written $e \overset{\text{name}}{\rightsquigarrow} e'$.

The call-by-need operational semantics is based on Ariola and Felleisen [2]. The only differences between the source language and Ariola and Felleisen's calculus are the addition of booleans, $\mathsf{diverge}_A$, and a type system. It is likely that we can translate other call-by-need calculi, such as those of Launchbury [16] and Maraist et al. [22]. Call-by-need small-step reductions are written $e \overset{\text{need}}{\leadsto} e'$.

The call-by-need semantics needs some auxiliary definitions. An *evaluation context* $E[-]$ is a source-language expression with a single hole, picked from the grammar given in the figure. The hole in an evaluation context indicates where reduction is currently taking place: it says which part of the expression is currently *needed.* We write $E[e]$ for the expression in which the hole is replaced with $e$. A (source-language) *value* is the result of a computation (the word value should not be confused with the value terms of extended call-by-push-value). An *answer* is a value in some *environment*, which maps variables to expressions. These can be thought of as *closures.* The environment is encoded in an answer using application and lambda abstraction: the answer $(\lambda x.\, a)\, e$ means the answer $a$ where the environment maps $x$ to $e$. Encoding environments in this way makes the translation slightly simpler than if we had used a Launchbury-style [16] call-by-need language with explicit environments. In the latter case, the translation would need to encode the environments. Here they are already encoded inside expressions. Answers are terminal computations: they do not reduce.

The first two reduction axioms (on the left) of the call-by-need semantics (Fig. 5d) are obvious. The third axiom is the most important: it states that if the subexpression currently being evaluated is a variable $x$, and the environment maps $x$ to a source-language value $v$, then that use of $x$ can be replaced with $v$. Note that $E[v]$ may contain other uses of $x$; the replacement only occurs when the value is actually needed. This axiom roughly corresponds to the first sequencing axiom of the equational theory of ECBPV (in Fig. 3c). The fourth and fifth axioms of the call-by-need operational semantics rearrange the environment into a standard form. Both use a syntactic restriction to answers so that each expression has at most one reduct (this restriction is not needed to ensure that $\overset{\text{need}}{\leadsto}$ captures call-by-need). The rule on the right of the Fig. 5d states that the reduction relation is a congruence (a needed subexpression can be reduced).

The two translations from the source language to ECBPV are given in Fig. 6. The translation of types (Fig. 6a) is shared between call-by-name and call-by-need. The two translations differ only for contexts and expressions. Types $A$ are translated into value types $(\!|A|\!)$. The type **bool** becomes the two-element sum type **unit** + **unit**. The translation of a function type $A \to B$ is a thunked CBPV function type. The argument is a thunk of a computation that returns an $(\!|A|\!)$, and the result is a computation that returns a $(\!|B|\!)$.

For call-by-name (Fig. 6b), contexts $\Gamma$ are translated into contexts $(\!|\Gamma|\!)^{\text{name}}$ that contain thunks of computations. We could also have used contexts containing computation variables (omitting the thunks), but choose to use thunks to keep the translation as close as possible to previous translations into call-by-push-value. A well-typed expression $\Gamma \vdash e : A$ is translated into a ECBPV computation term $(\!|e|\!)^{\text{name}}$ that returns $(\!|A|\!)$, in context $(\!|\Gamma|\!)^{\text{name}}$. The translation

$$\llparenthesis \mathbf{bool} \rrparenthesis := \mathbf{unit} + \mathbf{unit} \qquad \llparenthesis A \to B \rrparenthesis := \mathbf{U}\,(\mathbf{U}\,(\mathbf{Fr}\,\llparenthesis A \rrparenthesis) \to \mathbf{Fr}\,\llparenthesis B \rrparenthesis)$$

(a) Translation $\llparenthesis A \rrparenthesis$ of types

Translation $\llparenthesis \Gamma \rrparenthesis^{\mathrm{name}}$ of typing contexts

$$\llparenthesis \diamond \rrparenthesis^{\mathrm{name}} := \diamond \qquad \llparenthesis \Gamma, x : A \rrparenthesis^{\mathrm{name}} := \llparenthesis \Gamma \rrparenthesis^{\mathrm{name}}, x : \mathbf{U}\,(\mathbf{Fr}\,\llparenthesis A \rrparenthesis)$$

Translation $\llparenthesis \Gamma \rrparenthesis^{\mathrm{name}} \vdash \llparenthesis e \rrparenthesis^{\mathrm{name}} : \mathbf{Fr}\,\llparenthesis A \rrparenthesis$ of expressions

$$\begin{aligned}
\llparenthesis x \rrparenthesis^{\mathrm{name}} &:= \mathsf{force}\, x \qquad \llparenthesis \mathsf{diverge}_A \rrparenthesis^{\mathrm{name}} := \mathsf{force}\, \bot_A \\
\llparenthesis \mathsf{true} \rrparenthesis^{\mathrm{name}} &:= \mathsf{return\, inl}\, () \qquad \llparenthesis \mathsf{false} \rrparenthesis^{\mathrm{name}} := \mathsf{return\, inr}\, () \\
\llparenthesis \mathsf{if}\ e_1\ \mathsf{then}\ e_2\ \mathsf{else}\ e_3 \rrparenthesis^{\mathrm{name}} &:= \llparenthesis e_1 \rrparenthesis^{\mathrm{name}}\ \mathsf{to}\ x.\ \mathsf{force}(\mathsf{case}\ x\ \mathsf{of} \\
&\qquad \{\mathsf{inl}\ z.\ \mathsf{thunk}\llparenthesis e_2 \rrparenthesis^{\mathrm{name}}, \mathsf{inr}\ z.\ \mathsf{thunk}\llparenthesis e_3 \rrparenthesis^{\mathrm{name}}\}) \\
\llparenthesis \lambda x.\, e \rrparenthesis^{\mathrm{name}} &:= \mathsf{return\, thunk}(\lambda x.\ \llparenthesis e \rrparenthesis^{\mathrm{name}}) \\
\llparenthesis e_1\, e_2 \rrparenthesis^{\mathrm{name}} &:= \llparenthesis e_1 \rrparenthesis^{\mathrm{name}}\ \mathsf{to}\ z.\ (\mathsf{thunk}\, \llparenthesis e_2 \rrparenthesis^{\mathrm{name}})\ \text{‘}\ (\mathsf{force}\, z)
\end{aligned}$$

(b) Call-by-name translation

Translation $\llparenthesis \Gamma \rrparenthesis^{\mathrm{need}}$ of typing contexts

$$\llparenthesis \diamond \rrparenthesis^{\mathrm{need}} := \diamond \qquad \llparenthesis \Gamma, x : A \rrparenthesis^{\mathrm{need}} := \llparenthesis \Gamma \rrparenthesis^{\mathrm{need}}, \underline{x} : \mathbf{Fr}\,\llparenthesis A \rrparenthesis$$

Translation $\llparenthesis \Gamma \rrparenthesis^{\mathrm{need}} \vdash \llparenthesis e \rrparenthesis^{\mathrm{need}} : \mathbf{Fr}\,\llparenthesis A \rrparenthesis$ of expressions

$$\begin{aligned}
\llparenthesis x \rrparenthesis^{\mathrm{need}} &:= \underline{x} \qquad \llparenthesis \mathsf{diverge}_A \rrparenthesis^{\mathrm{need}} := \mathsf{force}\, \bot_A \\
\llparenthesis \mathsf{true} \rrparenthesis^{\mathrm{need}} &:= \mathsf{return\, inl}\, () \qquad \llparenthesis \mathsf{false} \rrparenthesis^{\mathrm{need}} := \mathsf{return\, inr}\, () \\
\llparenthesis \mathsf{if}\ e_1\ \mathsf{then}\ e_2\ \mathsf{else}\ e_3 \rrparenthesis^{\mathrm{need}} &:= \llparenthesis e_1 \rrparenthesis^{\mathrm{need}}\ \mathsf{to}\ x.\ \mathsf{force}(\mathsf{case}\ x\ \mathsf{of} \\
&\qquad \{\mathsf{inl}\ z.\ \mathsf{thunk}\llparenthesis e_2 \rrparenthesis^{\mathrm{need}}, \mathsf{inr}\ z.\ \mathsf{thunk}\llparenthesis e_3 \rrparenthesis^{\mathrm{need}}\}) \\
\llparenthesis \lambda x.\, e \rrparenthesis^{\mathrm{need}} &:= \mathsf{return\, thunk}(\lambda x'.\ (\mathsf{force}\, x')\ \mathsf{need}\ \underline{x}.\ \llparenthesis e \rrparenthesis^{\mathrm{need}}) \\
\llparenthesis e_1\, e_2 \rrparenthesis^{\mathrm{need}} &:= \llparenthesis e_1 \rrparenthesis^{\mathrm{need}}\ \mathsf{to}\ z.\ (\mathsf{thunk}\, \llparenthesis e_2 \rrparenthesis^{\mathrm{need}})\ \text{‘}\ (\mathsf{force}\, z)
\end{aligned}$$

(c) Call-by-need translation

**Fig. 6.** Translation from the source language to ECBPV

of variables just forces the relevant variable in the context. The diverging computations $\mathsf{diverge}_A$ just use the diverging constants from our ECBPV signature. The translations of true and false are simple: they are computations that immediately return one of the elements of the sum type **unit** + **unit**. The translation of if $e_1$ then $e_2$ else $e_3$ first evaluates $\llparenthesis e_1 \rrparenthesis^{\mathrm{name}}$, then uses the result to choose between $\llparenthesis e_2 \rrparenthesis^{\mathrm{name}}$ and $\llparenthesis e_3 \rrparenthesis^{\mathrm{name}}$. Lambdas are translated into computations that just return a thunked computation. Finally, application first evaluates the computation that returns a thunk of a function, and then forces this function, passing it a thunk of the argument.

For call-by-need (Fig. 6c), contexts $\Gamma$ are translated into contexts $(\!|\Gamma|\!)^{\mathrm{need}}$, containing computations that return values. The computations in the context are all bound using need. An expression $\Gamma \vdash e : A$ is translated to a computation $(\!|e|\!)^{\mathrm{need}}$ that returns $(\!|A|\!)$ in the context $(\!|\Gamma|\!)^{\mathrm{need}}$. The typing is therefore similar to call-by-name. The key case is the translation of lambdas. These become computations that immediately return a thunk of a function. The function places the computation given as an argument onto the context using need, so that it is evaluated at most once, before executing the body. The remainder of the cases are similar to call-by-name.

Under the call-by-need translation, the expression $(\lambda x.\, e_1)\, e_2$ is translated into a term that executes the computation $(\!|e_1|\!)^{\mathrm{need}}$, and executes $(\!|e_2|\!)^{\mathrm{need}}$ only when needed. This is the case because, by the $\beta$ rules for thunks, functions, and returner types:

$$(\!|(\lambda x.\, e_1)\, e_2|\!)^{\mathrm{need}} \equiv (\!|e_2|\!)^{\mathrm{need}}\ \mathsf{need}\ \underline{x}.\ (\!|e_1|\!)^{\mathrm{need}}$$

As a consequence, translations of answers are particularly simple: they have the following form (up to $\equiv$):

$$M_1\ \mathsf{need}\ \underline{x}_1.\ M_2\ \mathsf{need}\ \underline{x}_2.\ \cdots M_n\ \mathsf{need}\ \underline{x}_n.\ \mathsf{return}\, V$$

which intuitively means the value $V$ in the environment mapping each $\underline{x}_i$ to $M_i$.

It is easy to see that both translations produce terms with the correct types. We prove that both translations are *sound*: if $e \overset{\mathrm{name}}{\rightsquigarrow} e'$ then $(\!|e|\!)^{\mathrm{name}} \equiv (\!|e'|\!)^{\mathrm{name}}$, and if $e \overset{\mathrm{need}}{\rightsquigarrow} e'$ then $(\!|e|\!)^{\mathrm{need}} \equiv (\!|e'|\!)^{\mathrm{need}}$. To do this for call-by-need, we first look at translations of evaluation contexts. The following lemma says the translation captures the idea that the hole in an evaluation context corresponds to the term being evaluated.

**Lemma 4.** *Define, for each evaluation context* $E[-]$, *the term* $\mathcal{E}_y(\!|E[-]|\!)^{\mathrm{need}}$ *by:*

$$\begin{aligned}
\mathcal{E}_y(\!|-|\!)^{\mathrm{need}} &:= \mathsf{return}\, y \\
\mathcal{E}_y(\!|\mathsf{if}\ E[-]\ \mathsf{then}\ e_2\ \mathsf{else}\ e_3|\!)^{\mathrm{need}} &:= \mathcal{E}(\!|E[-]|\!)^{\mathrm{need}}\ \mathsf{to}\ x.\ \mathsf{force}(\mathsf{case}\, x\ \mathsf{of} \\
&\qquad \{\mathsf{inl}\, z.\, \mathsf{thunk}(\!|e_2|\!)^{\mathrm{need}} \\
&\qquad ,\mathsf{inr}\, z.\, \mathsf{thunk}(\!|e_3|\!)^{\mathrm{need}}\}) \\
\mathcal{E}_y(\!|E[-]\, e_2|\!)^{\mathrm{need}} &:= \mathcal{E}_y(\!|E[-]|\!)^{\mathrm{need}}\ \mathsf{to}\ z.\ \mathsf{thunk}(\!|e_2|\!)^{\mathrm{need}}\ \text{`}\ \mathsf{force}\, z \\
\mathcal{E}_y(\!|(\lambda x.\, E[x])\, E'[-]|\!)^{\mathrm{need}} &:= \mathcal{E}_y(\!|E'[-]|\!)^{\mathrm{need}}\ \mathsf{need}\ \underline{x}.\ (\!|E[x]|\!)^{\mathrm{need}} \\
\mathcal{E}_y(\!|(\lambda x.\, E[-])\, e_2|\!)^{\mathrm{need}} &:= (\!|e_2|\!)^{\mathrm{need}}\ \mathsf{need}\ \underline{x}.\ \mathcal{E}_y(\!|E[-]|\!)^{\mathrm{need}}
\end{aligned}$$

*For each expression e we have:*

$$(\!|E[e]|\!)^{\mathrm{need}} \equiv (\!|e|\!)^{\mathrm{need}}\ \mathsf{to}\ y.\ \mathcal{E}_y(\!|E[-]|\!)^{\mathrm{need}}$$

This lemma omits the typing of expressions for presentational purposes. It is easy to add suitable constraints on typing. Soundness is now easy to show:

**Theorem 2 (Soundness).** *For any two well-typed source-language expressions $\Gamma \vdash e : A$ and $\Gamma \vdash e' : A$:*

1. *If* $e \overset{\text{name}}{\rightsquigarrow} e'$ *then* $(\!| e |\!)^{\text{name}} \equiv (\!| e' |\!)^{\text{name}}$.
2. *If* $e \overset{\text{need}}{\rightsquigarrow} e'$ *then* $(\!| e |\!)^{\text{need}} \equiv (\!| e' |\!)^{\text{need}}$.

Now that we have sound call-by-name and call-by-need translations, we can state the meta-level equivalence formally. Suppose we are given a possibly open source-language expression $\Gamma \vdash e : B$. Recall that the call-by-need translation uses a context containing computation variables (i.e. $(\!| \Gamma |\!)^{\text{need}}$) and the call-by-name translation uses a context containing value variables, which map to thunks of computations. We have two ECBPV computation terms of type $\mathbf{Fr}\,(\!| B |\!)$ in context $(\!| \Gamma |\!)^{\text{need}}$: one is just $(\!| e |\!)^{\text{need}}$, the other is $(\!| e |\!)^{\text{name}}$ with all of its variables substituted with thunked computations. The theorem then states that these are contextually equivalent.

**Theorem 3 (Equivalence between call-by-name and call-by-need).** *For all source-language expressions $e$ satisfying $\underline{x}_1 : A_1, \ldots, \underline{x}_n : A_n \vdash e : B$*

$$(\!| e |\!)^{\text{name}}[x_1 \mapsto \mathsf{thunk}\,\underline{x}_1, \ldots, x_n \mapsto \mathsf{thunk}\,\underline{x}_n] \quad \cong_{\text{ctx}} \quad (\!| e |\!)^{\text{need}}$$

*Proof.* The proof of this theorem is by induction on the typing derivation of $e$. The interesting case is lambda abstraction, where we use the internal equivalence between call-by-name and call-by-need (Theorem 1).

## 4 An Effect System for Extended Call-by-Push-Value

The equivalence between call-by-name and call-by-need in the previous section is predicated on the only effect in the language being nontermination. However, suppose the primitives of language have various effects (which means that in general the equivalence fails) but a given subprogram may be statically shown to have at most nontermination effects. In this case, we should be allowed to exploit the equivalence on the subprogram, interchanging call-by-need and call-by-name locally, even if the rest of the program uses other effects. In this section, we describe an *effect system* [20] for ECBPV, which statically estimates the side-effects of expressions, allowing us to exploit equivalences which hold only within subprograms. Effect systems can also be used for other purposes, such as proving the correctness of effect-dependent program transformations [7,29]. The ECBPV effect system also allows these.

Call-by-need makes statically estimating effects difficult. Computation variables bound using need might have effects on their first use, but on subsequent uses do not. Hence to precisely determine the effects of a term, we must track which variables have been used. McDermott and Mycroft [23] show how to achieve this for a call-by-need effect system; their technique can be adapted to ECBPV. Here we take a simpler approach. By slightly restricting the *effect algebras* we consider, we remove the need to track variable usage information, while still ensuring the effect information is not an underestimate (an underestimate would enable incorrect transformations). This can reduce the precision of the effect information obtained, but for our use case (determining equivalences between evaluation orders) this is not an issue, since we primarily care about which effects are used (rather than e.g. how many times they are used).

### 4.1 Effects

The effect system is parameterized by an *effect algebra*, which specifies the information that is tracked. Different effect algebras can be chosen for different applications. There are various forms of effect algebra. We follow Katsumata [15] and use *preordered monoids*, which are the most general.

**Definition 5 (Preordered monoid).** *A* preordered monoid $(\mathcal{F}, \leq, \cdot, 1)$ *consists of a monoid* $(\mathcal{F}, \cdot, 1)$ *and a preorder* $\leq$ *on* $\mathcal{F}$, *such that the binary operation* $\cdot$ *is monotone in each argument separately.*

Since we do not track variable usage information, we might misestimate the effect of a call-by-need computation variable evaluated for a second time (whose true effect is 1). To ensure this misestimate is an overestimate, we assume that the effect algebra is *pointed* (which is the case for most applications).

**Definition 6 (Pointed preordered monoid).** *A preordered monoid* $(\mathcal{F}, \leq, \cdot, 1)$ *is* pointed *if for all* $f \in \mathcal{F}$ *we have* $1 \leq f$.

The elements $f$ of the set $\mathcal{F}$ are called *effects*. Each effect abstractly represents some potential side-effecting behaviours. The order $\leq$ provides *approximation* of effects. When $f \leq f'$ this means behaviours represented by $f$ are included in those represented by $f'$. The binary operation $\cdot$ represents sequencing of effects, and 1 is the effect of a side-effect-free expression.

Traditional (*Gifford-style*) effect systems have some set $\Sigma$ of *operations* (for example, $\Sigma := \{\mathsf{read}, \mathsf{write}\}$), and use the preordered monoid $(\mathcal{P}\Sigma, \subseteq, \cup, \emptyset)$. In these cases, an effect $f$ is just a set of operations. If a computation has effect $f$ then $f$ contains all of the operations the computation *may* perform. They can therefore be used to enforce that computations do not use particular operations. Another example is the preordered monoid $(\mathbb{N}^+, \leq, +, 1)$, which can be used to count the number of possible results a nondeterministic computation can return (or to count the number of times an operation is used).

In our example, where we wish to establish whether the effects of an expression are restricted to nontermination for our main example, we use the two-element preorder $\{\mathsf{diveff} \leq \top\}$ with join for sequencing and $\mathsf{diveff}$ as the unit 1. The effect $\mathsf{diveff}$ means side-effects restricted to (at most) nontermination, and $\top$ means unrestricted side-effects. Thus we would enable the equivalence between call-by-name and call-by-need when the effect is $\mathsf{diveff}$, and not when it is $\top$. All of these examples are pointed. Others can be found in the literature.

$$\boxed{A <:_{\mathrm{v}} B}$$

$$\frac{}{\mathbf{unit} <:_{\mathrm{v}} \mathbf{unit}} \qquad \frac{A_1 <:_{\mathrm{v}} B_1 \qquad A_2 <:_{\mathrm{v}} B_2}{A_1 \times A_2 <:_{\mathrm{v}} B_1 \times B_2} \qquad \frac{A_1 <:_{\mathrm{v}} B_1 \qquad A_2 <:_{\mathrm{v}} B_2}{A_1 + A_2 <:_{\mathrm{v}} B_1 + B_2}$$

$$\frac{\underline{C} <: \underline{D}}{\mathbf{U}\,\underline{C} <:_{\mathrm{v}} \mathbf{U}\,\underline{D}}$$

$$\boxed{\underline{C} <: \underline{D}}$$

$$\frac{(\underline{C}_i <: \underline{D}_i)_{i \in I}}{\prod_{i \in I} \underline{C}_i <: \prod_{i \in I} \underline{D}_i} \qquad \frac{A <:_{\mathrm{v}} B \qquad \underline{C} <: \underline{D}}{(B \to \underline{C}) <: (A \to \underline{D})} \qquad \frac{A <:_{\mathrm{v}} B}{\langle f \rangle A <: \langle f' \rangle B} \text{ if } f \leq f'$$

**Fig. 7.** Subtyping in the ECBPV effect system

### 4.2 Effect System and Signature

The effect system includes effects within types. Specifically, each computation of returner type will have some side-effects when it is run, and hence each returner type $\mathbf{Fr}\,A$ is annotated with an element $f$ of $\mathcal{F}$. We write the annotated type as $\langle f \rangle A$. Formally we replace the grammar of ECBPV computation types (and similarly, the grammar of typing contexts) with

$$\underline{C}, \underline{D} ::= \prod_{i \in I} \underline{C}_i \mid A \to \underline{C} \mid \langle f \rangle A$$

$$\Gamma ::= \diamond \mid \Gamma, x : A \mid \Gamma, \underline{x} : \langle f \rangle A$$

(The highlighted parts indicate the differences.) The grammar used for value types is unchanged, except that it uses the new syntax of computation types.

The definition of ECBPV signature is similarly extended to contain the effect algebra as well as the set of constants:

**Definition 7 (Signature).** *A* signature $(\mathcal{F}, \mathcal{K})$ *consists of a pointed preordered monoid* $(\mathcal{F}, \leq, \cdot, 1)$ *of effects and, for each value type* $A$*, a set* $\mathcal{K}_A$ *of constants of type* $A$*, including* $() \in \mathcal{K}_{\mathbf{unit}}$.

We assume a fixed effect system signature for the remainder of this section.

Since types contain effects, which have a notion of subeffecting, there is a natural notion of subtyping. We define (in Fig. 7) two subtyping relations: $A <:_{\mathrm{v}} B$ for value types and $\underline{C} <: \underline{D}$ for computation types.

We treat the type constructor $\langle f \rangle$ as an operation on computation types by defining computation types $\langle f \rangle \underline{C}$.

$$\langle f \rangle \Big( \prod_{i \in I} \underline{C}_i \Big) := \prod_{i \in I} \langle f \rangle \underline{C}_i \qquad \langle f \rangle (A \to \underline{C}) := A \to \langle f \rangle \underline{C} \qquad \langle f \rangle (\langle f' \rangle A) := \langle f \cdot f' \rangle A$$

This is an *action* of the preordered monoid on computation types. Its purpose is to give the typing rule for sequencing of computations. The sequencing of a computation with effect $f$ with a computation of type $\underline{C}$ has type $\langle f \rangle \underline{C}$.

$$\frac{}{\Gamma \vdash \underline{x} : \langle f \rangle A} \text{ if } (\underline{x} : \langle f \rangle A) \in \Gamma \qquad \frac{\Gamma \vdash_{\mathrm{v}} V : A}{\Gamma \vdash \mathsf{return}\, V : \langle 1 \rangle A}$$

$$\frac{\Gamma \vdash M : \langle f \rangle A \qquad \Gamma, x : A \vdash N : \underline{C}}{\Gamma \vdash M \,\mathsf{to}\, x.\, N : \langle f \rangle \underline{C}} \qquad \frac{\Gamma \vdash M : \langle f \rangle A \qquad \Gamma, \underline{x} : \langle f \rangle A \vdash N : \underline{C}}{\Gamma \vdash M \,\mathsf{need}\, \underline{x}.\, N : \underline{C}}$$

$$\frac{\Gamma \vdash_{\mathrm{v}} V : A}{\Gamma \vdash_{\mathrm{v}} V : B} \text{ if } A <:_{\mathrm{v}} B \qquad \frac{\Gamma \vdash_{\mathrm{v}} M : \underline{C}}{\Gamma \vdash_{\mathrm{v}} N : \underline{D}} \text{ if } \underline{C} <: \underline{D}$$

**Fig. 8.** Effect system modifications to ECBPV

The typing judgements have exactly the same form as before (except for the new syntax of types). The majority of the typing rules, including all of the rules for value terms, are also unchanged. The only rules we change are those for computation variables, return, to and need, which are replaced with the first four rules in Fig. 8. We also add two subtyping rules, one for values and one for computations. These are the last two rules of Fig. 8.

The equational theory does not need to be changed to use it with the new effect system (except that the types appearing in each axiom now include effect information). For each axiom of the equational theory, the two terms still have the same type in the effect system. In particular, for the axiom

$$M \,\mathsf{need}\, \underline{x}.\, \underline{x} \,\mathsf{to}\, y.\, N \;\equiv\; M \,\mathsf{to}\, y.\, N[\underline{x} \mapsto \mathsf{return}\, y]$$

if $\Gamma \vdash M : \langle f \rangle A$ and $\Gamma, \underline{x} : \langle f \rangle A, y : A \vdash N : \underline{C}$ then the left-hand side has type $\langle f \rangle \underline{C}$. For the right-hand-side, we have $\Gamma, y : A \vdash N[\underline{x} \mapsto \mathsf{return}\, y] : \underline{C}$, because of the assumption that the preordered monoid is pointed (which implies $\mathsf{return}\, y$ can have *any* effect by subtyping, not just the unit effect 1). Hence the right-hand-side also has type $\langle f \rangle \underline{C}$. This axiom is the reason for our pointedness requirement. In particular, if we drop need from the language, the pointedness requirement is not required. Thus the rules we give also describe a fully general effect system for CBPV in which the effect algebra can be any preordered monoid.

### 4.3 Exploiting Effect-Dependent Equivalences

Our primary goal in adding an effect system to ECBPV is to exploit (local, effect-justified) equivalences between evaluation orders even without a whole-language restriction on effects. We sketch how to do this for our example.

When proving the equivalence between call-by-name and call-by-need in Sect. 3 we assumed that the only constants in the language were () and $\bot_A$ : $\mathbf{U}\,(\mathbf{Fr}\, A)$. To relax this restriction, we use the effect algebra with preorder $\{\mathsf{diveff} \leq \top\}$ described above, and change the type of $\bot_A$ from $\mathbf{U}\,(\mathbf{Fr}\, A)$ to $\mathbf{U}\,(\langle \mathsf{diveff} \rangle A)$. We can include other effectful constants, and give them the effect $\top$ (e.g. $\mathsf{write} : \mathbf{U}\,(V \to \langle \top \rangle \mathbf{unit})$).

The statement of the internal (object-level) equivalence becomes:

$$\text{if } \Gamma \vdash M : \langle\mathsf{diveff}\rangle A \text{ and } \Gamma, \underline{x} : \langle\mathsf{diveff}\rangle A \vdash N : \underline{C} \text{ then}$$
$$\Gamma \vdash M \ \mathsf{name}\ \underline{x}.\ N \cong_{\mathrm{ctx}} M \ \mathsf{need}\ \underline{x}.\ N : \underline{C}$$

The premise restricts the effect of $M$ to diveff so that nontermination is its only possible side-effect. To prove this equivalence, we need a logical relation for the effect system, which means we have to define a Kripke relation $R_{\langle f\rangle A}$ for each effect $f$. For $R_{\langle\mathsf{diveff}\rangle A}$ we use the same definition as before (the definition of $R_{\mathbf{Fr}A}$). The definition of $R_{\langle\top\rangle A}$ depends on the specific other effects included.

To state and prove a meta-level equivalence for a source language that includes other side-effects, we need to define an effect system for the source language. This would use the same effect algebra as the ECBPV effect system, and be such that the translation of source language expressions preserves effects. To do this for the source language of Sect. 3, we replace the syntax of function types with $\langle f\rangle A \xrightarrow{f'} B$, where $f$ is the effect of the argument (required due to lazy evaluation), and $f'$ is the latent effect of the function (the effect it has after application). The translation is then

$$(\!|\langle f\rangle A \xrightarrow{f'} B|\!) := \mathbf{U}\,(\mathbf{U}\,(\langle f\rangle(\!|A|\!)) \to \langle f'\rangle(\!|B|\!))$$

Just as for the object-level equivalence, the statement of the meta-level equivalence similarly requires the source-language expression to have the effect diveff. We omit the details here.

## 5 Related Work

*Metalanguages for Evaluation Order.* Call-by-push-value is similar to Moggi's monadic metalanguage [25], except for the distinction between computations and values. Both support several evaluation orders, but neither supports call-by-need. *Polarized* type theories [34] also take the approach of stratifying types into several kinds to capture multiple evaluation orders. Downen and Ariola [10] recently described how to capture call-by-need using polarity. They take a different approach to ours, by splitting up terms according to their evaluation order, rather than whether they might have effects. This means they have three kinds of type, resulting in a more complex language than ours. They also do not apply their language to reasoning about the differences between evaluation orders, which was the primary motivation for ECBPV. It is not clear whether their language can also be used for this purpose.

Multiple evaluation orders can also be captured in a Moggi-style language by using *joinads* instead of monads [28]. It is possible that there is some joinad structure implicit in extended call-by-push-value.

*Reasoning About Call-by-Need.* The majority of work on reasoning about call-by-need source languages has concentrated on operational semantics based on environments [16], graphs [30,32], and answers [2,3,9,22]. However, these do not compare call-by-need with other evaluation orders. The only type-based analysis of a lazy source language we know of apart from McDermott and Mycroft's effect system [23] is [31,33].

*Logical Relations.* Kripke logical relations have previously been applied to the problems of lambda definability [12] and normalization [1,11]. Previous proofs of contextual equivalence relate only closed terms. We were forced to relate open terms because of the need construct.

Reasoning about effects using logical relations often runs into a difficulty in ensuring the relations are closed under sequencing of computations. We are able to work around this due to our specific choice of effects. It is possible that considering other effects would require a technique such as Lindley and Stark's *leapfrog method* [18,19].

*Effect Systems.* Effect systems have a long history, starting with Gifford-style effect systems [20]. We use preordered monoids as effect algebras following Katsumata [15]. Almost all of the previous work on effect systems has concentrated on call-by-value only. Kammar and Plotkin [13,14] describe a Gifford-style call-by-push-value effect system, though their formulation does not generalise to other effect algebras. Our effect system is the first general effect system for a CBPV-like language. The only previous work on call-by-need effects is [23].

There has also been much work on reasoning about program transformations using effect systems, e.g. [4–8,29]. We expect it to be possible to recast much of this in terms of extended call-by-push-value, and therefore apply these transformations for various evaluation orders.

## 6 Conclusions and Future Work

We have described extended call-by-push-value, a calculus that can be used for reasoning about several evaluation orders. In particular, ECBPV supports call-by-need via the addition of the construct $M\ \mathsf{need}\ \underline{x}.\ N$. This allows us to prove that call-by-name and call-by-need reduction are equivalent if nontermination is the only effect in the source language, both inside the language itself, and on the meta-level. We proved the latter by giving two translations of a source language into ECBPV: one that captures call-by-name reduction, and one that captures call-by-need reduction. We also defined an effect system for ECBPV. The effect system statically bounds the side-effects of terms, allowing equivalences between evaluation orders to be used without restricting the entire language to particular effects. We close with a description of possible future work.

*Other Equivalences Between Evaluation Orders.* We have proved one example of an equivalence between evaluation orders using ECBPV, but there are others that we might also expect to hold. For example, we would expect call-by-need and call-by-value to be equivalent if the effects are restricted to nondeterminism, allocating state, and reading from state (but not writing). It should be possible to use ECBPV to prove these by defining suitable logical relations. More generally, it might be possible to characterize when particular equivalences hold in terms of the algebraic properties of the effects we restrict to.

*Denotational Semantics.* Using logical relations to prove contextual equivalence between terms directly is difficult. Adequate denotational semantics would allow us to reduce proofs of contextual equivalence to proofs of equalities in the model. Composing the denotational semantics with the call-by-need translation would also result in a call-by-need denotational semantics for the source language. Some potential approaches to describing the denotational semantics of ECBPV are Maraist et al.'s [21] translation into an affine calculus, combined with a semantics of linear logic [24], and also continuation-passing-style translations [27]. None of these consider side-effects however.

**Acknowledgements.** We gratefully acknowledge the support of an EPSRC studentship, and thank the anonymous reviewers for helpful comments.

## References


1. Altenkirch, T., Hofmann, M., Streicher, T.: Categorical reconstruction of a reduction free normalization proof. In: Pitt, D., Rydeheard, D.E., Johnstone, P. (eds.) CTCS 1995. LNCS, vol. 953, pp. 182–199. Springer, Heidelberg (1995). https://doi.org/10.1007/3-540-60164-3_27
2. Ariola, Z.M., Felleisen, M.: The call-by-need lambda calculus. J. Funct. Program. **7**(3), 265–301 (1997)
3. Ariola, Z.M., Maraist, J., Odersky, M., Felleisen, M., Wadler, P.: A call-by-need lambda calculus. In: Proceedings of the 22nd ACM SIGPLAN-SIGACT Symposium on Principles of Programming Languages, pp. 233–246. ACM (1995). https://doi.org/10.1145/199448.199507
4. Benton, N., Hofmann, M., Nigam, V.: Effect-dependent transformations for concurrent programs. In: Proceedings of the 18th International Symposium on Principles and Practice of Declarative Programming, pp. 188–201. ACM (2016). https://doi.org/10.1145/2967973.2968602
5. Benton, N., Kennedy, A.: Monads, effects and transformations. Electron. Notes Theor. Comput. Sci. **26**, 3–20 (1999). https://doi.org/10.1016/S1571-0661(05)80280-4
6. Benton, N., Kennedy, A., Hofmann, M., Nigam, V.: Counting successes: effects and transformations for non-deterministic programs. In: Lindley, S., McBride, C., Trinder, P., Sannella, D. (eds.) A List of Successes That Can Change the World. LNCS, vol. 9600, pp. 56–72. Springer, Cham (2016). https://doi.org/10.1007/978-3-319-30936-1_3
7. Benton, N., Kennedy, A., Russell, G.: Compiling standard ML to Java bytecodes. In: Proceedings of the Third ACM SIGPLAN International Conference on Functional Programming, pp. 129–140. ACM (1998). https://doi.org/10.1145/289423.289435

8. Birkedal, L., Sieczkowski, F., Thamsborg, J.: A concurrent logical relation. In: Cégielski, P., Durand, A. (eds.) 21st EACSL Annual Conference on Computer Science Logic, CSL 2012. Leibniz International Proceedings in Informatics (LIPIcs), vol. 16, pp. 107–121. Schloss Dagstuhl-Leibniz-Zentrum für Informatik, Dagstuhl (2012). https://doi.org/10.4230/LIPIcs.CSL.2012.107
9. Chang, S., Felleisen, M.: The call-by-need lambda calculus, revisited. In: Seidl, H. (ed.) ESOP 2012. LNCS, vol. 7211, pp. 128–147. Springer, Heidelberg (2012). https://doi.org/10.1007/978-3-642-28869-2_7
10. Downen, P., Ariola, Z.M.: Beyond polarity: towards a multi-discipline intermediate language with sharing. In: 27th EACSL Annual Conference on Computer Science Logic, CSL 2018, pp. 21:1–21:23 (2018). https://doi.org/10.4230/LIPIcs.CSL.2018.21
11. Fiore, M.: Semantic analysis of normalisation by evaluation for typed lambda calculus. In: Proceedings of the 4th ACM SIGPLAN International Conference on Principles and Practice of Declarative Programming, pp. 26–37. ACM (2002). https://doi.org/10.1145/571157.571161
12. Jung, A., Tiuryn, J.: A new characterization of lambda definability. In: Bezem, M., Groote, J.F. (eds.) TLCA 1993. LNCS, vol. 664, pp. 245–257. Springer, Heidelberg (1993). https://doi.org/10.1007/BFb0037110
13. Kammar, O.: Algebraic theory of type-and-effect systems. Ph.D. thesis, University of Edinburgh, UK (2014)
14. Kammar, O., Plotkin, G.D.: Algebraic foundations for effect-dependent optimisations. In: Proceedings of the 39th Annual ACM SIGPLAN-SIGACT Symposium on Principles of Programming Languages, pp. 349–360. ACM (2012). https://doi.org/10.1145/2103656.2103698
15. Katsumata, S.: Parametric effect monads and semantics of effect systems. In: Proceedings of the 41st ACM SIGPLAN-SIGACT Symposium on Principles of Programming Languages, pp. 633–645. ACM (2014). https://doi.org/10.1145/2535838.2535846
16. Launchbury, J.: A natural semantics for lazy evaluation. In: Proceedings of the 20th ACM SIGPLAN-SIGACT Symposium on Principles of Programming Languages, pp. 144–154. ACM (1993). https://doi.org/10.1145/158511.158618
17. Levy, P.B.: Call-by-push-value: a subsuming paradigm. In: Girard, J.-Y. (ed.) TLCA 1999. LNCS, vol. 1581, pp. 228–243. Springer, Heidelberg (1999). https://doi.org/10.1007/3-540-48959-2_17
18. Lindley, S.: Normalisation by evaluation in the compilation of typed functional programming languages. Ph.D. thesis, University of Edinburgh, UK (2005)
19. Lindley, S., Stark, I.: Reducibility and $\top\top$-lifting for computation types. In: Urzyczyn, P. (ed.) TLCA 2005. LNCS, vol. 3461, pp. 262–277. Springer, Heidelberg (2005). https://doi.org/10.1007/11417170_20
20. Lucassen, J.M., Gifford, D.K.: Polymorphic effect systems. In: Proceedings of the 15th ACM SIGPLAN-SIGACT Symposium on Principles of Programming Languages, pp. 47–57. ACM (1988). https://doi.org/10.1145/73560.73564
21. Maraist, J., Odersky, M., Turner, D.N., Wadler, P.: Call-by-name, call-by-value, call-by-need, and the linear lambda calculus. In: Proceedings of the Eleventh Annual Mathematical Foundations of Programming Semantics Conference, pp. 370–392 (1995). https://doi.org/10.1016/S0304-3975(98)00358-2
22. Maraist, J., Odersky, M., Wadler, P.: The call-by-need lambda calculus. J. Funct. Program. **8**(3), 275–317 (1998). https://doi.org/10.1017/S0956796898003037
23. McDermott, D., Mycroft, A.: Call-by-need effects via coeffects. Open Comput. Sci. **8**, 93–108 (2018). https://doi.org/10.1515/comp-2018-0009

24. Melliès, P.A.: Categorical semantics of linear logic. In: Interactive Models of Computation and Program Behaviour, Panoramas et Synthèses 27, Société Mathématique de France (2009)
25. Moggi, E.: Notions of computation and monads. Inf. Comput. **93**(1), 55–92 (1991). https://doi.org/10.1016/0890-5401(91)90052-4
26. Munch-Maccagnoni, G.: Models of a non-associative composition. In: Muscholl, A. (ed.) FoSSaCS 2014. LNCS, vol. 8412, pp. 396–410. Springer, Heidelberg (2014). https://doi.org/10.1007/978-3-642-54830-7_26
27. Okasaki, C., Lee, P., Tarditi, D.: Call-by-need and continuation-passing style. LISP Symbolic Comput. **7**(1), 57–81 (1994). https://doi.org/10.1007/BF01019945
28. Petricek, T., Syme, D.: Joinads: a retargetable control-flow construct for reactive, parallel and concurrent programming. In: Rocha, R., Launchbury, J. (eds.) PADL 2011. LNCS, vol. 6539, pp. 205–219. Springer, Heidelberg (2011). https://doi.org/10.1007/978-3-642-18378-2_17
29. Tolmach, A.: Optimizing ML using a hierarchy of monadic types. In: Leroy, X., Ohori, A. (eds.) TIC 1998. LNCS, vol. 1473, pp. 97–115. Springer, Heidelberg (1998). https://doi.org/10.1007/BFb0055514
30. Turner, D.A.: A new implementation technique for applicative languages. Softw. Pract. Experience **9**(1), 31–49 (1979). https://doi.org/10.1002/spe.4380090105
31. Turner, D.N., Wadler, P., Mossin, C.: Once upon a type. In: Proceedings of the Seventh International Conference on Functional Programming Languages and Computer Architecture, pp. 1–11. ACM (1995). https://doi.org/10.1145/224164.224168
32. Wadsworth, C.: Semantics and Pragmatics of the Lambda-Calculus. University of Oxford (1971)
33. Wansbrough, K., Peyton Jones, S.: Once upon a polymorphic type. In: Proceedings of the 26th ACM SIGPLAN-SIGACT Symposium on Principles of Programming Languages, pp. 15–28. ACM (1999). https://doi.org/10.1145/292540.292545
34. Zeilberger, N.: The logical basis of evaluation order and pattern-matching. Ph.D. thesis, Carnegie Mellon University, Pittsburgh, PA, USA (2009)

# 8

# Coinduction in Uniform: Foundations for Corecursive Proof Search with Horn Clauses

Henning Basold[1(✉)], Ekaterina Komendantskaya[2(✉)], and Yue Li[2]

[1] CNRS, ENS Lyon, Lyon, France
henning.basold@ens-lyon.fr
[2] Heriot-Watt University, Edinburgh, UK
{ek19,yl55}@hw.ac.uk

**Abstract.** We establish proof-theoretic, constructive and coalgebraic foundations for proof search in coinductive Horn clause theories. Operational semantics of coinductive Horn clause resolution is cast in terms of *coinductive uniform proofs*; its constructive content is exposed via soundness relative to an intuitionistic first-order logic with recursion controlled by the later modality; and soundness of both proof systems is proven relative to a novel coalgebraic description of complete Herbrand models.

**Keywords:** Horn clause logic · Coinduction · Uniform proofs · Intuitionistic logic · Coalgebra · Fibrations · Löb modality

## 1 Introduction

*Horn clause logic* is a Turing complete and constructive fragment of first-order logic, that plays a central role in verification [22], automated theorem proving [52, 53, 57] and type inference. Examples of the latter can be traced from the Hindley-Milner type inference algorithm [55, 73], to more recent uses of Horn clauses in Haskell type classes [26, 51] and in refinement types [28, 43]. Its popularity can be attributed to well-understood fixed point semantics and an efficient semi-decidable resolution procedure for automated proof search.

According to the standard fixed point semantics [34, 52], given a set $P$ of Horn clauses, the *least Herbrand model* for $P$ is the set of all (finite) ground atomic formulae *inductively entailed* by $P$. For example, the two clauses below define the set of natural numbers in the least Herbrand model.

$$\kappa_{\mathbf{nat}0} : \mathbf{nat}\, 0$$
$$\kappa_{\mathbf{nat}s} : \forall x.\, \mathbf{nat}\, x \to \mathbf{nat}\, (s\, x)$$

This work is supported by the European Research Council (ERC) under the EU's Horizon 2020 programme (CoVeCe, grant agreement No. 678157) and by the EPSRC research grants EP/N014758/1, EP/K031864/1-2.

Formally, the least Herbrand model for the above two clauses is the set of ground atomic formulae obtained by taking a (forward) closure of the above two clauses. The model for **nat** is given by $\mathcal{N} = \{\mathbf{nat}\, 0,\ \mathbf{nat}\,(s\, 0),\ \mathbf{nat}\,(s\,(s\, 0)), \ldots\}$.

We can also view Horn clauses coinductively. The *greatest complete Herbrand model* for a set $P$ of Horn clauses is the largest set of finite and infinite ground atomic formulae *coinductively entailed* by $P$. For example, the greatest complete Herbrand model for the above two clauses is the set

$$\mathcal{N}^{\infty} = \mathcal{N} \cup \{\mathbf{nat}\,(s\,(s\,(\cdots))))\},$$

obtained by taking a backward closure of the above two inference rules on the set of all finite and infinite ground atomic formulae. The *greatest Herbrand model* is the largest set of *finite* ground atomic formulae *coinductively entailed* by $P$. In our example, it would be given by $\mathcal{N}$ already. Finally, one can also consider the *least complete Hebrand model*, which interprets entailment inductively but over potentially infinite terms. In the case of **nat**, this interpretation does not differ from $\mathcal{N}$. However, finite paths in coinductive structures like transition systems, for example, require such semantics.

The need for coinductive semantics of Horn clauses arises in several scenarios: the Horn clause theory may explicitly define a coinductive data structure or a coinductive relation. However, it may also happen that a Horn clause theory, which is not explicitly intended as coinductive, nevertheless gives rise to infinite inference by resolution and has an interesting coinductive model. This commonly happens in type inference. We will illustrate all these cases by means of examples.

*Horn Clause Theories as Coinductive Data Type Declarations.* The following clause defines, together with $\kappa_{\mathbf{nat}0}$ and $\kappa_{\mathbf{nat}s}$, the type of streams over natural numbers.

$$\kappa_{\mathbf{stream}} : \forall x y.\, \mathbf{nat}\, x \wedge \mathbf{stream}\, y \rightarrow \mathbf{stream}\,(\mathrm{scons}\, x\, y)$$

This Horn clause does not have a meaningful inductive, i.e. least fixed point, model. The greatest Herbrand model of the clauses is given by

$$\mathcal{S} = \mathcal{N}^{\infty} \cup \{\mathbf{stream}(\mathrm{scons}\, x_0\, (\mathrm{scons}\, x_1\, \cdots)) \mid \mathbf{nat}\, x_0, \mathbf{nat}\, x_1, \ldots \in \mathcal{N}^{\infty}\}$$

In trying to prove, for example, the goal $(\mathbf{stream}\, x)$, a goal-directed proof search may try to find a substitution for $x$ that will make $(\mathbf{stream}\, x)$ valid relative to the coinductive model of this set of clauses. This search by resolution may proceed by means of an infinite reduction $\underline{\mathbf{stream}\, x} \overset{\kappa_{\mathbf{stream}}:[\mathrm{scons}\ y\ x'/x]}{\rightsquigarrow}$ $\mathbf{nat}\, y \wedge \mathbf{stream}\, x' \overset{\kappa_{\mathbf{nat}0}:[0/y]}{\rightsquigarrow} \underline{\mathbf{stream}\, x'} \overset{\kappa_{\mathbf{stream}}:[\mathrm{scons}\ y'\ x''/x']}{\rightsquigarrow} \cdots$, thereby generating a stream $Z$ of zeros via composition of the computed substitutions: $Z = (\mathrm{scons}\, 0\, x')[\mathrm{scons}\, 0\, x''/x'] \cdots$. Above, we annotated each resolution step with the label of the clause it resolves against and the computed substitution. A method to compute an answer for this infinite sequence of reductions was given by Gupta et al. [41] and Simon et al. [69]: the underlined loop gives rise to the circular unifier $x = \mathrm{scons}\,0\,x$ that corresponds to the infinite term $Z$. It is proven that, if a loop and a corresponding circular unifier are detected, they provide an answer that is sound relative to the greatest complete Herbrand model of the clauses. This approach is known under the name of CoLP.

*Horn Clause Theories in Type Inference.* Below clauses give the typing rules of the simply typed λ-calculus, and may be used for type inference or type checking:

$$\kappa_{t1} : \forall x\,\Gamma\,a.\,\mathbf{var}\,x \wedge \mathbf{find}\,\Gamma\,x\,a \;\rightarrow \mathbf{typed}\,\Gamma\,x\,a$$
$$\kappa_{t2} : \forall x\,\Gamma\,a\,m\,b.\,\mathbf{typed}\,[x : a|\Gamma]\,m\,b \rightarrow \mathbf{typed}\,\Gamma\,(\lambda\,x\,m)\,(a \rightarrow b)$$
$$\kappa_{t3} : \forall\Gamma\,a\,m\,n\,b.\,\mathbf{typed}\,\Gamma\,m\,(a \rightarrow b) \wedge \mathbf{typed}\,\Gamma\,n\,a \rightarrow \mathbf{typed}\,\Gamma\,(\mathrm{app}\,m\,n)\,b$$

It is well known that the $Y$-combinator is not typable in the simply-typed λ-calculus and, in particular, self-application $\lambda x.\,x\,x$ is not typable either. However, by switching off the occurs-check in Prolog or by allowing circular unifiers in CoLP [41,69], we can resolve the goal "$\mathbf{typed}\,[]\,(\lambda\,x\,(\mathrm{app}\,x\,x))\,a$" and would compute the circular substitution: $a = b \rightarrow c, b = b \rightarrow c$ suggesting that an infinite, or circular, type may be able to type this λ-term. A similar trick would provide a typing for the $Y$-combinator. Thus, a coinductive interpretation of the above Horn clauses yields a theory of infinite types, while an inductive interpretation corresponds to the standard type system of the simply typed λ-calculus.

*Horn Clause Theories in Type Class Inference.* Haskell type class inference does not require circular unifiers but may require a cyclic resolution inference [37,51]. Consider, for example, the following mutually defined data structures in Haskell.

```
data OddList  a  =  OCons a (EvenList  a)
data EvenList a  =  Nil | ECons a (OddList a)
```

This type declaration gives rise to the following equality class instance declarations, where we leave the, here irrelevant, body out.

```
instance(Eq a, Eq (EvenList a)) => Eq (OddList a) where
instance(Eq a, Eq (OddList  a)) => Eq (EvenList a) where
```

The above two type class instance declarations have the shape of Horn clauses. Since the two declarations mutually refer to each other, an instance inference for, e.g., **Eq** (OddList **Int**) will give rise to an infinite resolution that alternates between the subgoals **Eq** (OddList **Int**) and **Eq** (EvenList **Int**). The solution is to terminate the computation as soon as the cycle is detected [51], and this method has been shown sound relative to the greatest Herbrand models in [36]. We will demonstrate this later in the proof systems proposed in this paper.

The diversity of these coinductive examples in the existing literature shows that there is a practical demand for coinductive methods in Horn clause logic, but it also shows that no unifying proof-theoretic approach exists to allow for a generic use of these methods. This causes several problems.

**Problem 1. The existing proof-theoretic coinductive interpretations of cycle and loop detection are unclear, incomplete and not uniform.**

**Table 1. Examples of greatest (complete) Herbrand models for Horn clauses** $\gamma_1$, $\gamma_2$, $\gamma_3$. The signatures are $\{a\}$ for the clause $\gamma_1$ and $\{a, f\}$ for the others.

| Horn clauses | $\gamma_1 : \forall x. p\,x \to p\,x$ | $\gamma_2 : \forall x. p(f\,x) \to p\,x$ | $\gamma_3 : \forall x. p\,x \to p(f\,x)$ |
|---|---|---|---|
| Greatest Herbrand model: | $\{p\,a\}$ | $\{p(a), p(f\,a), p(f(f\,a)), \ldots\}$ | $\emptyset$ |
| Greatest complete Herbrand model: | $\{p\,a\}$ | $\{p(a), p(f\,a), p(f(f\,a), \ldots, p(f(f \ldots)\}$ | $\{p(f(f \ldots)\}$ |
| CoLP substitution for query $p\,a$ | *id* | fails | fails |
| CoLP substitution for query $p\,x$ | *id* | $x = f\,x$ | $x = f\,x$ |

To see this, consider Table 1, which exemplifies three kinds of circular phenomena in Horn clauses: The clause $\gamma_1$ is the easiest case. Its coinductive models are given by the finite set $\{p\,a\}$. On the other extreme is the clause $\gamma_3$ that, just like $\kappa_{\mathbf{stream}}$, admits only an infinite formula in its coinductive model. The intermediate case is $\gamma_2$, which could be interpreted by an infinite set of finite formulae in its greatest Herbrand model, or may admit an infinite formula in its greatest complete Herbrand model. Examples like $\gamma_1$ appear in Haskell type class resolution [51], and examples like $\gamma_2$ in its experimental extensions [37]. Cycle detection would only cover computations for $\gamma_1$, whereas $\gamma_2$, $\gamma_3$ require some form of loop detection[1]. However, CoLP's loop detection gives confusing results here. It correctly fails to infer $p\,a$ from $\gamma_3$ (no unifier for subgoals $p\,a$ and $p\,(f\,a)$ exists), but incorrectly fails to infer $p\,a$ from $\gamma_2$ (also failing to unify $p\,a$ and $p\,(f\,a)$). The latter failure is misleading bearing in mind that $p\,a$ is in fact in the coinductive model of $\gamma_2$. Vice versa, if we interpret the CoLP answer $x = f\,x$ as a declaration of an infinite term $(f\,f\,\ldots)$ in the model, then CoLP's answer for $\gamma_3$ and $p\,x$ is exactly correct, however the same answer is badly incomplete for the query involving $p\,x$ and $\gamma_2$, because $\gamma_2$ in fact admits other, finite, formulae in its models. And in some applications, e.g. in Haskell type class inference, a finite formula would be the only acceptable answer for any query to $\gamma_2$.

This set of examples shows that loop detection is too coarse a tool to give an operational semantics to a diversity of coinductive models.

**Problem 2. Constructive interpretation of coinductive proofs in Horn clause logic is unclear.** Horn clause logic is known to be a constructive fragment of FOL. Some applications of Horn clauses rely on this property in a crucial way. For example, inference in Haskell type class resolution is constructive: when a certain formula $F$ is inferred, the Haskell compiler in fact constructs a proof term that inhabits $F$ seen as type. In our earlier example **Eq** (OddList **Int**) of the Haskell type classes, Haskell in fact captures the cycle by a fixpoint term $t$ and proves that $t$ inhabits the type **Eq** (OddList **Int**).

[1] We follow the standard terminology of [74] and say that two formulae $F$ and $G$ form a cycle if $F = G$, and a loop if $F[\theta] = G[\theta]$ for some (possibly circular) unifier $\theta$.

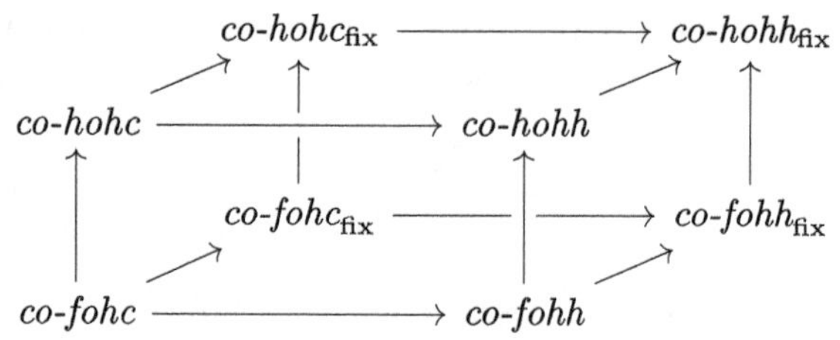


**Fig. 1.** Cube of logics covered by CUP

Although we know from [36] that these computations are sound relative to greatest Herbrand models of Horn clauses, the results of [36] do not extend to Horn clauses like $\gamma_3$ or $\kappa_{\mathbf{stream}}$, or generally to Horn clauses modelled by the greatest *complete* Herbrand models. This shows that there is not just a need for coinductive proofs in Horn clause logic, but *constructive* coinductive proofs.

**Problem 3. Incompleteness of circular unification for irregular coinductive data structures.** Table 1 already showed some issues with incompleteness of circular unification. A more famous consequence of it is the failure of circular unification to capture irregular terms. This is illustrated by the following Horn clause, which defines the infinite stream of successive natural numbers.

$$\kappa_{\mathbf{from}} : \forall x\, y.\, \mathbf{from}\, (s\, x)\, y \to \mathbf{from}\, x\, (\mathrm{scons}\, x\, y)$$

The reductions for $\mathbf{from}\, 0\, y$ consist only of irregular (non-unifiable) formulae:

$$\mathbf{from}\ 0\ y \overset{\kappa_{\mathbf{from}}:[\mathrm{scons}\ 0\ y'/y]}{\rightsquigarrow} \mathbf{from}\ (s\, 0)\ y' \overset{\kappa_{\mathbf{from}}:[\mathrm{scons}\ (s\, 0)\ y''/y']}{\rightsquigarrow} \ldots$$

The composition of the computed substitutions would suggest an infinite term as answer: $\mathbf{from}\, 0\, (\mathrm{scons}\ 0\ (\mathrm{scons}\ (s\, 0)\ \ldots))$. However, circular unification no longer helps to compute this answer, and CoLP fails. Thus, there is a need for more general operational semantics that allows irregular coinductive structures.

### A New Theory of Coinductive Proof Search in Horn Clause Logic

In this paper, we aim to give a principled and *general* theory that resolves the three problems above. This theory establishes a *constructive* foundation for coinductive resolution and allows us to give proof-theoretic characterisations of the approaches that have been proposed throughout the literature.

To solve Problem 1, we follow the footsteps of the *uniform proofs* by Miller et al. [53,54], who gave a general proof-theoretic account of resolution in first-order Horn clause logic (*fohc*) and three extensions: first-order hereditary Harrop clauses (*fohh*), higher-order Horn clauses (*hohc*), and higher-order hereditary Harrop clauses (*hohh*). In Sect. 3, we extend uniform proofs with a general coinduction proof principle. The resulting framework is called *coinductive uniform proofs (CUP)*. We show how the coinductive extensions of the four logics of Miller et al., which we name *co-fohc*, *co-fohh*, *co-hohc* and *co-hohh*, give a precise proof-theoretic characterisation to the different kinds of coinduction described in the literature. For example, coinductive proofs involving the clauses $\gamma_1$ and $\gamma_2$ belong to *co-fohc* and *co-fohh*, respectively. However, proofs involving clauses like $\gamma_3$ or $\kappa_{\mathbf{stream}}$ require in addition fixed point terms to express infinite data. These extentions are denoted by *co-fohc*$_{\text{fix}}$, *co-fohh*$_{\text{fix}}$, *co-hohc*$_{\text{fix}}$ and *co-hohh*$_{\text{fix}}$.

Section 3 shows that this yields the cube in Fig. 1, where the arrows show the increase in logical strength. The invariant search for regular infinite objects done in CoLP is fully described by the logic *co-fohc*$_{\text{fix}}$, including proofs for clauses like $\gamma_3$ and $\kappa_{\mathbf{stream}}$. An important consequence is that CUP is complete for $\gamma_1$, $\gamma_2$, and $\gamma_3$, e.g. $p\,a$ is provable from $\gamma_2$ in CUP, but not in CoLP.

In tackling Problem 3, we will find that the irregular proofs, such as those for $\kappa_{\mathbf{from}}$, can be given in *co-hohh*$_{\text{fix}}$. The stream of successive numbers can be defined as a higher-order fixed point term $s_{\text{fr}} = \text{fix}\; f.\, \lambda x.\, \text{scons}\, x\, (f\,(s\,x))$, and the proposition $\forall x.\, \mathbf{from}\, x\, (s_{\text{fr}}\, x)$ is provable in *co-hohh*$_{\text{fix}}$. This requires the use of higher-order syntax, fixed point terms and the goals of universal shape, which become available in the syntax of Hereditary Harrop logic.

In order to solve Problem 2 and to expose the constructive nature of the resulting proof systems, we present in Sect. 4 a coinductive extension of first-order intuitionistic logic and its sequent calculus. This extension ($\mathbf{iFOL}_{\blacktriangleright}$) is based on the so-called later modality (or Löb modality) known from provability logic [16, 71], type theory [8, 58] and domain theory [20]. However, our way of using the later modality to control recursion in first-order proofs is new and builds on [13, 14]. In the same section we also show that CUP is sound relative to $\mathbf{iFOL}_{\blacktriangleright}$, which gives us a handle on the constructive content of CUP. This yields, among other consequences, a constructive interpretation of CoLP proofs.

Section 5 is dedicated to showing soundness of both coinductive proof systems relative to *complete Herbrand models* [52]. The construction of these models is carried out by using coalgebras and category theory. This frees us from having to use topological methods and will simplify future extensions of the theory to, e.g., encompass typed logic programming. It also makes it possible to give original and constructive proofs of soundness for both CUP and $\mathbf{iFOL}_{\blacktriangleright}$ in Sect. 5. We finish the paper with discussion of related and future work.

## Originality of the Contribution

The results of this paper give a comprehensive characterisation of coinductive Horn clause theories from the point of view of proof search (by expressing coinductive proof search and resolution as coinductive uniform proofs), constructive proof theory (via a translation into an intuitionistic sequent calculus), and coalgebraic semantics (via coinductive Herbrand models and constructive soundness results). Several of the presented results have never appeared before: the coinductive extension of uniform proofs; characterisation of coinductive properties of Horn clause theories in higher-order logic with and without fixed point operators; coalgebraic and fibrational view on complete Herbrand models; and soundness of an intuitionistic logic with later modality relative to complete Herbrand models.

## 2 Preliminaries: Terms and Formulae

In this section, we set up notation and terminology for the rest of the paper. Most of it is standard, and blends together the notation used in [53] and [11].

**Definition 1.** We define the sets $\mathbb{T}$ of *types* and $\mathbb{P}$ of *proposition types* by the following grammars, where $\iota$ and $o$ are the *base type* and *base proposition type.*

$$\mathbb{T} \ni \sigma, \tau ::= \iota \,|\, \sigma \to \tau \qquad\qquad \mathbb{P} \ni \rho ::= o \,|\, \sigma \to \rho, \quad \sigma \in \mathbb{T}$$

We adapt the usual convention that $\to$ binds to the right.

$$\frac{c : \tau \in \Sigma}{\Gamma \vdash c : \tau} \qquad \frac{x : \tau \in \Gamma}{\Gamma \vdash x : \tau} \qquad \frac{\Gamma \vdash M : \sigma \to \tau \qquad \Gamma \vdash N : \sigma}{\Gamma \vdash M\,N : \tau}$$

$$\frac{\Gamma, x : \sigma \vdash M : \tau}{\Gamma \vdash \lambda x.\, M : \sigma \to \tau} \qquad \frac{\Gamma, x : \tau \vdash M : \tau}{\Gamma \vdash \mathrm{fix}\, x.\, M : \tau}$$

**Fig. 2.** Well-formed terms

$$\frac{(p : \tau_1 \to \cdots \to \tau_n \to o) \in \Pi \qquad \Gamma \vdash M_1 : \tau_1 \qquad \cdots \qquad \Gamma \vdash M_n : \tau_n}{\Gamma \Vdash p\, M_1 \cdots M_n}$$

$$\frac{}{\Gamma \Vdash \top} \qquad \frac{\Gamma \Vdash \varphi \qquad \Gamma \Vdash \psi \qquad \Box \in \{\wedge, \vee, \to\}}{\Gamma \Vdash \varphi \,\Box\, \psi} \qquad \frac{\Gamma, x : \tau \Vdash \varphi}{\Gamma \Vdash \forall x : \tau.\, \varphi} \qquad \frac{\Gamma, x : \tau \Vdash \varphi}{\Gamma \Vdash \exists x : \tau.\, \varphi}$$

**Fig. 3.** Well-formed formulae

**Definition 2.** A *term signature* $\Sigma$ is a set of pairs $c : \tau$, where $\tau \in \mathbb{T}$, and a *predicate signature* is a set $\Pi$ of pairs $p : \rho$ with $\rho \in \mathbb{P}$. The elements in $\Sigma$ and $\Pi$ are called *term symbols* and *predicate symbols*, respectively. Given term and predicate signatures $\Sigma$ and $\Pi$, we refer to the pair $(\Sigma, \Pi)$ as *signature.* Let Var be a countable set of variables, the elements of which we denote by $x, y, \ldots$ We call a finite list $\Gamma$ of pairs $x : \tau$ of variables and types a *context.* The set $\Lambda_\Sigma$ of *(well-typed) terms* over $\Sigma$ is the collection of all $M$ with $\Gamma \vdash M : \tau$ for some context $\Gamma$ and type $\tau \in \mathbb{T}$, where $\Gamma \vdash M : \tau$ is defined inductively in Fig. 2. A term is called *closed* if $\vdash M : \tau$, otherwise it is called *open.* Finally, we let $\Lambda_\Sigma^-$ denote the set of all terms $M$ that do not involve fix.

**Definition 3.** Let $(\Sigma, \Pi)$ be a signature. We say that $\varphi$ is a *(first-order) formula* in context $\Gamma$, if $\Gamma \Vdash \varphi$ is inductively derivable from the rules in Fig. 3.

**Definition 4.** The *reduction relation* $\longrightarrow$ on terms in $\Lambda_\Sigma$ is given as the compatible closure (reduction under applications and binders) of $\beta$- and fix-reduction:

$$(\lambda x.\, M)N \longrightarrow M\,[N/x] \qquad \mathrm{fix}\, x.\, M \longrightarrow M\,[\mathrm{fix}\, x.\, M/x]$$

We denote the reflexive, transitive closure of $\longrightarrow$ by $\twoheadrightarrow$. Two terms $M$ and $N$ are called *convertible*, if $M \equiv N$, where $\equiv$ is the equivalence closure of $\longrightarrow$. Conversion of terms extends to formulae in the obvious way: if $M_k \equiv M'_k$ for $k = 1, \ldots, n$, then $p\, M_1 \cdots M_n \equiv p\, M'_1 \cdots M'_n$.

We will use in the following that the above calculus features subject reduction and confluence, cf. [61]: if $\Gamma \vdash M : \tau$ and $M \equiv N$, then $\Gamma \vdash N : \tau$; and $M \equiv N$ iff there is a term $P$, such that $M \twoheadrightarrow P$ and $N \twoheadrightarrow P$.

The *order* of a type $\tau \in \mathbb{T}$ is given as usual by $\mathrm{ord}(\iota) = 0$ and $\mathrm{ord}(\sigma \to \tau) = \max\{\mathrm{ord}(\sigma) + 1, \mathrm{ord}(\tau)\}$. If $\mathrm{ord}(\tau) \leq 1$, then the arity of $\tau$ is given by $\mathrm{ar}(\iota) = 0$ and $\mathrm{ar}(\iota \to \tau) = \mathrm{ar}(\tau) + 1$. A signature $\Sigma$ is called *first-order*, if for all $f : \tau \in \Sigma$ we have $\mathrm{ord}(\tau) \leq 1$. We let the arity of $f$ then be $\mathrm{ar}(\tau)$ and denote it by $\mathrm{ar}(f)$.

**Definition 5.** The set of *guarded base terms* over a first-order signature $\Sigma$ is given by the following type-driven rules.

$$\frac{x : \tau \in \Gamma \qquad \mathrm{ord}(\tau) \leq 1}{\Gamma \vdash_g x : \tau} \qquad \frac{f : \tau \in \Sigma}{\Gamma \vdash_g f : \tau} \qquad \frac{\Gamma \vdash_g M : \sigma \to \tau \qquad \Gamma \vdash_g N : \sigma}{\Gamma \vdash_g M\, N : \tau}$$

$$\frac{f : \sigma \in \Sigma \qquad \mathrm{ord}(\tau) \leq 1 \qquad \Gamma, x : \tau, y_1 : \iota, \ldots, y_{\mathrm{ar}(\tau)} : \iota \vdash_g M_i : \iota \qquad 1 \leq i \leq \mathrm{ar}(f)}{\Gamma \vdash_g \mathrm{fix}\, x.\, \lambda \vec{y}.\, f\, \vec{M} : \tau}$$

General *guarded terms* are terms $M$, such that all fix-subterms are guarded base terms, which means that they are generated by the following grammar.

$$G ::= M \ (\text{with } \vdash_g M : \tau \text{ for some type } \tau) \mid c \in \Sigma \mid x \in \mathrm{Var} \mid G\, G \mid \lambda x. G$$

Finally, $M$ is a *first-order* term over $\Sigma$ with $\Gamma \vdash M : \tau$ if $\mathrm{ord}(\tau) \leq 1$ and the types of all variables occurring in $\Gamma$ are of order 0. We denote the set of guarded first-order terms $M$ with $\Gamma \vdash M : \iota$ by $\Lambda_\Sigma^{G,1}(\Gamma)$ and the set of guarded terms in $\Gamma$ by $\Lambda_\Sigma^G(\Gamma)$. If $\Gamma$ is empty, we just write $\Lambda_\Sigma^{G,1}$ and $\Lambda_\Sigma^G$, respectively.

Note that an important aspect of guarded terms is that no free variable occurs under a fix-operator. *Guarded base terms* should be seen as specific fixed point terms that we will be able to unfold into potentially infinite trees. *Guarded terms* close guarded base terms under operations of the simply typed $\lambda$-calculus.

**Example 6.** Let us provide a few examples that illustrate (first-order) guarded terms. We use the first-order signature $\Sigma = \{\mathrm{scons}\colon \iota \to \iota \to \iota, s\colon \iota \to \iota, 0 : \iota\}$.

1. Let $s_{\mathrm{fr}} = \mathrm{fix}\, f.\, \lambda x.\, \mathrm{scons}\ x\ (f\ (s\ x))$ be the function that computes the streams of numerals starting at the given argument. It is easy to show that $\vdash_g s_{\mathrm{fr}} : \iota \to \iota$ and so $s_{\mathrm{fr}}\ 0 \in \Lambda_\Sigma^{G,1}$.

2. For the same signature $\Sigma$ we also have $x : \iota \vdash_g x : \iota$. Thus $x \in \Lambda_\Sigma^{G,1}(x : \iota)$ and $s\,x \in \Lambda_\Sigma^{G,1}(x : \iota)$.
3. We have $x : \iota \to \iota \vdash_g x\,0 : \iota$, but $(x\ 0) \notin \Lambda_\Sigma^{G,1}(x : \iota \to \iota)$.

The purpose of guarded terms is that these are productive, that is, we can reduce them to a term that either has a function symbol at the root or is just a variable. In other words, guarded terms have head normal forms: We say that a term $M$ is in *head normal form*, if $M = f\,\overrightarrow{N}$ for some $f \in \Sigma$ or if $M = x$ for some variable $x$. The following lemma is a technical result that is needed to show in Lemma 8 that all guarded terms have a head normal form.

**Lemma 7.** *Let $M$ and $N$ be guarded base terms with $\Gamma, x : \sigma \vdash_g M : \tau$ and $\Gamma \vdash_g N : \sigma$. Then $M\,[N/x]$ is a guarded base term with $\Gamma \vdash_g M\,[N/x] : \tau$.*

**Lemma 8.** *If $M$ is a first-order guarded term with $M \in \Lambda_\Sigma^{G,1}(\Gamma)$, then $M$ reduces to a unique head normal form. This means that either (i) there is a unique $f \in \Sigma$ and terms $N_1, \ldots, N_{\mathrm{ar}(f)}$ with $\Gamma \vdash_g N_k : \iota$ and $M \twoheadrightarrow f\,\overrightarrow{N}$, and for all $L$ if $M \twoheadrightarrow f\,\overrightarrow{L}$, then $\overrightarrow{N} \equiv \overrightarrow{L}$; or (ii) $M \twoheadrightarrow x$ for some $x : \iota \in \Gamma$.*

We end this section by introducing the notion of an atom and refinements thereof. This will enable us to define the different logics and thereby to analyse the strength of coinduction hypotheses, which we promised in the introduction.

**Definition 9.** A formula $\varphi$ of the shape $\top$ or $p\,M_1 \cdots M_n$ is an *atom* and a

- *first-order atom*, if $p$ and all the terms $M_i$ are first-order;
- *guarded atom*, if all terms $M_i$ are guarded; and
- *simple atom*, if all terms $M_i$ are non-recursive, that is, are in $\Lambda_\Sigma^-$.

First-order, guarded and simple atoms are denoted by $\mathrm{At}_1$, $\mathrm{At}_\omega^g$ and $\mathrm{At}_\omega^s$. We denote conjunctions of these predicates by $\mathrm{At}_1^g = \mathrm{At}_1 \cap \mathrm{At}_\omega^g$ and $\mathrm{At}_1^s = \mathrm{At}_1 \cap \mathrm{At}_\omega^s$.

Note that the restriction for $\mathrm{At}_\omega^g$ only applies to fixed point terms. Hence, any formula that contains terms without fix is already in $\mathrm{At}_\omega^g$ and $\mathrm{At}_\omega^g \cap \mathrm{At}_\omega^s = \mathrm{At}_\omega^s$. Since these notions are rather subtle, we give a few examples

**Example 10.** We list three examples of first-order atoms.

1. For $x : \iota$ we have **stream** $x \in \mathrm{At}_1$, but there are also "garbage" formulae like "**stream** $(\mathrm{fix}\, x. x)$" in $\mathrm{At}_1$. Examples of atoms that are not first-order are $p\,M$, where $p : (\iota \to \iota) \to o$ or $x : \iota \to \iota \vdash M : \tau$.
2. Our running example "**from** $0\ (s_{\mathrm{fr}}\ 0)$" is a first-order guarded atom in $\mathrm{At}_1^g$.
3. The formulae in $\mathrm{At}_1^s$ may not contain recursion and higher-order features. However, the atoms of Horn clauses in a logic program fit in here.

## 3 Coinductive Uniform Proofs

This section introduces the eight logics of the coinductive uniform proof framework announced and motivated in the introduction. The major difference of uniform proofs with, say, a sequent calculus is the "uniformity" property, which means that the choice of the application of each proof rule is deterministic and all proofs are in normal form (cut free). This subsumes the operational semantics of resolution, in which the proof search is always goal directed. Hence, the main challenge, that we set out to solve in this section, is to extend the uniform proof framework with coinduction, while preserving this valuable operational property.

We begin by introducing the different goal formulae and definite clauses that determine the logics that were presented in the cube for coinductive uniform proofs in the introduction. These clauses and formulae correspond directly to those of the original work on uniform proofs [53] with the only difference being that we need to distinguish atoms with and without fixed point terms. The general idea is that goal formulae ($G$-formulae) occur on the right of a sequent, thus are the *goal* to be proved. Definite clauses ($D$-formulae), on the other hand, are selected from the context as assumptions. This will become clear once we introduce the proof system for coinductive uniform proofs.

**Definition 11.** Let $D_i$ be generated by the following grammar with $i \in \{1, \omega\}$.

$$D_i ::= \mathrm{At}_i^s \mid G \to D \mid D \wedge D \mid \forall x : \tau .\, D$$

**Table 2.** D- and G-formulae for coinductive uniform proofs.

| | Definite Clauses | Goals |
|---|---|---|
| *co-fohc* | $D_1$ | $G ::= \mathrm{At}_1^s \mid G \wedge G \mid G \vee G \mid \exists x : \tau .\, G$ |
| *co-hohc* | $D_\omega$ | $G ::= \mathrm{At}_\omega^s \mid G \wedge G \mid G \vee G \mid \exists x : \tau .\, G$ |
| *co-fohh* | $D_1$ | $G ::= \mathrm{At}_1^s \mid G \wedge G \mid G \vee G \mid \exists x : \tau .\, G \mid D \to G \mid \forall x : \tau .\, G$ |
| *co-hohh* | $D_\omega$ | $G ::= \mathrm{At}_\omega^s \mid G \wedge G \mid G \vee G \mid \exists x : \tau .\, G \mid D \to G \mid \forall x : \tau .\, G$ |

The sets of definite clauses ($D$-formulae) and goals ($G$-formulae) of the four logics *co-fohc*, *co-fohh*, *co-hohc*, *co-hohh* are the well-formed formulae of the corresponding shapes defined in Table 2. For the variations *co-fohh*$_{\mathrm{fix}}$ etc. of these logics with fixed point terms, we replace upper index "$s$" with "$g$" everywhere in Table 2. A $D$-formula of the shape $\forall \vec{x}.\, A_1 \wedge \cdots \wedge A_n \to A_0$ is called *$H$-formula* or *Horn clause* if $A_k \in \mathrm{At}_1^s$, and *$H^g$-formula* if $A_k \in \mathrm{At}_1^g$. Finally, a *logic program* (or *program*) $P$ is a set of $H$-formulae. Note that any set of $D$-formulae in *fohc* can be transformed into an intuitionistically equivalent set of $H$-formulae [53].

We are now ready to introduce the coinductive uniform proofs. Such proofs are composed of two parts: an outer coinduction that has to be at the root of a proof tree, and the usual the usual uniform proofs by Miller et al. [54]. The latter are restated in Fig. 4. Of special notice is the rule DECIDE that mimics the operational behaviour of resolution in logic programming, by choosing a clause $D$ from the given program to resolve against. The coinduction is started by the rule CO-FIX in Fig. 5. Our proof system mimics the typical recursion with a guard condition found in coinductive programs and proofs [5,8,19,31,40]. This guardedness condition is formalised by applying the guarding modality $\langle \_ \rangle$ on the formula being proven by coinduction and the proof rules that allow us to distribute the guard over certain logical connectives, see Fig. 5. The guarding modality may be discharged only if the guarded goal was resolved against a clause in the initial program or any hypothesis, except for the coinduction hypotheses. This is reflected in the rule DECIDE$\langle\rangle$, where we may only pick a clause from $P$, and is in contrast to the rule DECIDE, in which we can pick *any* hypothesis. The proof may only terminate with the INITIAL step if the goal is no longer guarded.

Note that the CO-FIX rule introduces a goal as a new hypothesis. Hence, we have to require that this goal is also a definite clause. Since coinduction hypotheses play such an important role, they deserve a separate definition.

**Definition 12.** Given a language $L$ from Table 2, a formula $\varphi$ is a *coinduction goal* of $L$ if $\varphi$ simultaneously is a $D$- and a $G$-formula of $L$.

Note that the coinduction goals of *co-fohc* and *co-fohh* can be transformed into equivalent $H$- or $H^g$-formulae, since any coinduction goal is a $D$-formula.

Let us now formally introduce the coinductive uniform proof system.

$$\frac{\Sigma; P; \Delta \overset{D}{\Rightarrow} A \quad D \in P \cup \Delta}{\Sigma; P; \Delta \Longrightarrow A}\ \text{DECIDE} \qquad \frac{A \equiv A'}{\Sigma; P; \Delta \overset{A'}{\Rightarrow} A}\ \text{INITIAL} \qquad \frac{}{\Sigma; P; \Delta \Longrightarrow \top}\ \top R$$

$$\frac{\Sigma; P; \Delta \overset{D}{\Rightarrow} A \qquad \Sigma; P; \Delta \Longrightarrow G}{\Sigma; P; \Delta \xRightarrow{G \to D} A}\ {\to}L \qquad \frac{\Sigma; P, D; \Delta \Longrightarrow G}{\Sigma; P; \Delta \Longrightarrow D \to G}\ {\to}R$$

$$\frac{\Sigma; P; \Delta \overset{D_x}{\Rightarrow} A \qquad x \in \{1, 2\}}{\Sigma; P; \Delta \xRightarrow{D_1 \wedge D_2} A}\ \wedge L \qquad \frac{\Sigma; P; \Delta \Longrightarrow G_1 \qquad \Sigma; P; \Delta \Longrightarrow G_2}{\Sigma; P; \Delta \Longrightarrow G_1 \wedge G_2}\ \wedge R$$

$$\frac{\Sigma; P; \Delta \xRightarrow{D[N/x]} A \qquad \varnothing \vdash_g N : \tau}{\Sigma; P; \Delta \xRightarrow{\forall x.\, D} A}\ \forall L \qquad \frac{c : \tau, \Sigma; P; \Delta \Longrightarrow G[c/x] \qquad c : \tau \notin \Sigma}{\Sigma; P; \Delta \Longrightarrow \forall x : \tau.\, G}\ \forall R$$

$$\frac{\Sigma; P; \Delta \Longrightarrow G[N/x] \qquad \varnothing \vdash_g N : \tau}{\Sigma; P; \Delta \Longrightarrow \exists x : \tau.\, G}\ \exists R \qquad \frac{\Sigma; P; \Delta \Longrightarrow G_x \qquad x \in \{1, 2\}}{\Sigma; P; \Delta \Longrightarrow G_1 \vee G_2}\ \vee R$$

**Fig. 4.** Uniform proof rules

$$\frac{\Sigma; P; \varphi \Longrightarrow \langle\varphi\rangle}{\Sigma; P \looparrowright \varphi}\ \text{CO-FIX}$$

$$\frac{\Sigma; P; \Delta \overset{D}{\Rightarrow} A \quad D \in P}{\Sigma; P; \Delta \Longrightarrow \langle A\rangle}\ \text{DECIDE}\langle\rangle \qquad \frac{c : \tau, \Sigma; P; \Delta \Longrightarrow \langle\varphi\,[c/x]\rangle \quad c : \tau \notin \Sigma}{\Sigma; P; \Delta \Longrightarrow \langle\forall x : \tau.\,\varphi\rangle}\ \forall R\langle\rangle$$

$$\frac{\Sigma; P; \Delta \Longrightarrow \langle\varphi_1\rangle \quad \Sigma; P; \Delta \Longrightarrow \langle\varphi_2\rangle}{\Sigma; P; \Delta \Longrightarrow \langle\varphi_1 \wedge \varphi_2\rangle}\ \wedge R\langle\rangle \qquad \frac{\Sigma; P; \Delta, \varphi_1 \Longrightarrow \langle\varphi_2\rangle}{\Sigma; P; \Delta \Longrightarrow \langle\varphi_1 \to \varphi_2\rangle}\ \to R\langle\rangle$$

**Fig. 5.** Coinductive uniform proof rules

**Definition 13.** Let $P$ and $\Delta$ be finite sets of, respectively, definite clauses and coinduction goals, over the signature $\Sigma$, and suppose that $G$ is a goal and $\varphi$ is a coinduction goal. A *sequent* is either a *uniform provability sequent* of the form $\Sigma; P; \Delta \Longrightarrow G$ or $\Sigma; P; \Delta \overset{D}{\Rightarrow} A$ as defined in Fig. 4, or it is a *coinductive uniform provability sequent* of the form $\Sigma; P \looparrowright \varphi$ as defined in Fig. 5. Let $L$ be a language from Table 2. We say that $\varphi$ is *coinductively provable* in $L$, if $P$ is a set of $D$-formulae in $L$, $\varphi$ is a coinduction goal in $L$ and $\Sigma; P \looparrowright \varphi$ holds.

The logics we have introduced impose different syntactic restrictions on $D$- and $G$-formulae, and will therefore admit coinduction goals of different strength. This ability to explicitly use stronger coinduction hypotheses within a goal-directed search was missing in CoLP, for example. And it allows us to account for different coinductive properties of Horn clauses as described in the introduction. We finish this section by illustrating this strengthening.

The first example is one for the logic *co-fohc*, in which we illustrate the framework on the problem of type class resolution.

**Example 14.** Let us restate the Haskell type class inference problem discussed in the introduction in terms of Horn clauses:

$$\kappa_{\mathrm{i}} : \mathbf{eq}\ \mathrm{i}$$
$$\kappa_{\mathrm{odd}} : \forall x.\, \mathbf{eq}\ x \wedge \mathbf{eq}\ (\mathrm{even}\ x) \to \mathbf{eq}\ (\mathrm{odd}\ x)$$
$$\kappa_{\mathrm{even}} : \forall x.\, \mathbf{eq}\ x \wedge \mathbf{eq}\ (\mathrm{odd}\ x) \to \mathbf{eq}\ (\mathrm{even}\ x)$$

To prove **eq** (odd i) for this set of Horn clauses, it is sufficient to use this formula directly as coinduction hypothesis, as shown in Fig. 6. Note that this formula is indeed a coinduction goal of *co-fohc*, hence we find ourselves in the simplest scenario of coinductive proof search. In Table 1, $\gamma_1$ is a representative for this kind of coinductive proofs with simplest atomic goals.

It was pointed out in [37] that Haskell's type class inference can also give rise to irregular corecursion. Such cases may require the more general coinduction

$$\dfrac{\dfrac{\dfrac{\dfrac{\dfrac{}{\Sigma;P;\varphi \xrightarrow{\varphi} \mathbf{eq}\ (\text{odd i})}\ \text{INITIAL}}{\vdots}\ \text{DECIDE}}{\Sigma;P;\varphi \xrightarrow{\kappa_{\text{even}}} \mathbf{eq}\ (\text{even i})}\ \forall L}{\Sigma;P;\varphi \Rightarrow \mathbf{eq}\ (\text{even i})}\ \text{DECIDE}}{\spadesuit}$$

$$\dfrac{\dfrac{\dfrac{\dfrac{\dfrac{\dfrac{}{\Sigma;P;\varphi \xrightarrow{\mathbf{eq}\ (\text{odd i})} \mathbf{eq}\ (\text{odd i})}\ \text{INITIAL} \qquad \dfrac{\dfrac{\dfrac{}{\Sigma;P;\varphi \xrightarrow{\kappa_{\text{i}}} \mathbf{eq}\ \text{i}}\ \text{INITIAL}}{\Sigma;P;\varphi \Rightarrow \mathbf{eq}\ \text{i}}\ \text{DECIDE} \qquad \spadesuit}{\Sigma;P;\varphi \Longrightarrow \mathbf{eq}\ \text{i} \wedge\ \mathbf{eq}\ (\text{even i})}\ \wedge R}{\Sigma;P;\varphi \xrightarrow{\mathbf{eq}\ \text{i}\wedge\ \mathbf{eq}\ (\text{even i})\to\mathbf{eq}\ (\text{odd i})} \mathbf{eq}\ (\text{odd i})}\ \to L}{\Sigma;P;\varphi \xrightarrow{\kappa_{\text{odd}}} \mathbf{eq}\ (\text{odd i})}\ \forall L}{\Sigma;P;\varphi \Longrightarrow \langle\mathbf{eq}\ (\text{odd i})\rangle}\ \text{DECIDE}\langle\rangle}{\Sigma;P \looparrowright \mathbf{eq}\ (\text{odd i})}\ \text{CO-FIX}$$

**Fig. 6.** The *co-fohc* proof for Horn clauses arising from Haskell Type class examples. $\varphi$ abbreviates the coinduction hypothesis **eq** (odd i). Note its use in the branch ♠.

hypothesis (e.g. universal and/or implicative) of *co-fohh* or *co-hohh*. The below set of Horn clauses is a simplified representation of a problem given in [37]:

$$\begin{aligned}
&\kappa_{\text{i}} : \mathbf{eq}\ \text{i} \\
&\kappa_{s} : \forall x.\,(\mathbf{eq}\ x) \wedge \mathbf{eq}\ (s\ (g\ x)) \to \mathbf{eq}\ (s\ x) \\
&\kappa_{g} : \forall x.\,\mathbf{eq}\ x \qquad\qquad\qquad\quad\ \to \mathbf{eq}\ (g\ x)
\end{aligned}$$

Trying to prove **eq** $(s$ i$)$ by using **eq** $(s$ i$)$ directly as a coinduction hypothesis is deemed to fail, as the coinductive proof search is irregular and this coinduction hypothesis would not be applicable in any guarded context. But it is possible to prove **eq** $(s$ i$)$ as a corollary of another theorem: $\forall x.\,(\mathbf{eq}\ x) \to \mathbf{eq}\ (s\ x)$. Using this formula as coinduction hypothesis leads to a successful proof, which we omit here. From this more general goal, we can derive the original goal by instantiating the quantifier with i and eliminating the implication with $\kappa_{\text{i}}$. This second derivation is sound with respect to the models, as we show in Theorem 34.

We encounter $\gamma_2$ from Table 1 in a similar situation: To prove $p\,a$, we first have to prove $\forall x.\,p\ x$ in *co-fohh*, and then obtain $p\ a$ as a corollary by appealing to Theorem 34. The next example shows that we can cover all cases in Table 1 by providing a proof in *co-hohh*$_{\text{fix}}$ that involves irregular recursive terms.

**Example 15.** Recall the clause $\forall x\ y.\,\mathbf{from}\ (s\ x)\ y \to \mathbf{from}\ x\ (\text{scons}\ x\ y)$ that we named $\kappa_{\mathbf{from}}$ in the introduction. Proving $\exists y.\,\mathbf{from}\ 0\ y$ is again not possible directly. Instead, we can use the term $s_{\text{fr}} = \text{fix}\ f.\,\lambda x.\,\text{scons}\ x\ (f\ (s\ x))$ from Example 6 and prove $\forall x.\,\mathbf{from}\ x\ (s_{\text{fr}}\ x)$ coinductively, as shown in Fig. 7. This formula gives a coinduction hypothesis of sufficient generality. Note that the correct coinduction hypothesis now requires the fixed point definition of an infinite stream of successive numbers and universal quantification in the goal. Hence the need for the richer language of *co-hohh*$_{\text{fix}}$. From this more general goal we can derive our initial goal $\exists\, y.\textbf{from}\ 0\ y$ by instantiating $y$ with $s_{\text{fr}}\ 0$.

$$\dfrac{\dfrac{\dfrac{\overline{c, \Sigma; P; \varphi \xRightarrow{\textbf{from}\ (s\ c)\ (s_{\text{fr}}\ (s\ c))} \textbf{from}\ (s\ c)\ (s_{\text{fr}}\ (s\ c))}\ \text{INITIAL}}{c, \Sigma; P; \varphi \xRightarrow{\varphi} \textbf{from}\ (s\ c)\ (s_{\text{fr}}\ (s\ c))}\ \forall L}{c, \Sigma; P; \varphi \Longrightarrow \textbf{from}\ (s\ c)\ (s_{\text{fr}}\ (s\ c))}\ \text{DECIDE}}{\spadesuit}$$

$$\dfrac{\dfrac{\dfrac{\dfrac{\overline{c, \Sigma; P; \varphi \xRightarrow{\textbf{from}\ c\ (\text{scons}\ c\ (s_{\text{fr}}\ (s\ c)))} \textbf{from}\ c\ (s_{\text{fr}}\ c)}\ \text{INITIAL} \qquad \spadesuit}{c, \Sigma; P; \varphi \xRightarrow{\textbf{from}\ (s\ c)\ (s_{\text{fr}}\ (s\ c)) \to \textbf{from}\ c\ (\text{scons}\ c\ (s_{\text{fr}}\ (s\ c)))} \textbf{from}\ c\ (s_{\text{fr}}\ c)}\ \to L}{c, \Sigma; P; \varphi \xRightarrow{\kappa_{\textbf{from}}} \textbf{from}\ c\ (s_{\text{fr}}\ c)}\ \forall L\ (2\ \text{times})}{c, \Sigma; P; \varphi \Longrightarrow \langle \textbf{from}\ c\ (s_{\text{fr}}\ c) \rangle}\ \text{DECIDE}\langle\rangle$$

$$\dfrac{\dfrac{c, \Sigma; P; \varphi \Longrightarrow \langle \textbf{from}\ c\ (s_{\text{fr}}\ c) \rangle}{\Sigma; P; \varphi \Longrightarrow \langle \forall x.\, \textbf{from}\ x\ (s_{\text{fr}}\ x) \rangle}\ \forall R\langle\rangle}{\Sigma; P \looparrowright \forall x.\, \textbf{from}\ x\ (s_{\text{fr}}\ x)}\ \text{CO-FIX}$$

**Fig. 7.** The *co-hohh*$_{\text{fix}}$ proof for $\varphi = \forall x.\, \textbf{from}\ x\ (s_{\text{fr}}\ x)$. Note that the last step of the leftmost branch involves $\textbf{from}\ c\ (\text{scons}\ c\ (s_{\text{fr}}\ (s\ c))) \equiv \textbf{from}\ c\ (s_{\text{fr}}\ c)$.

There are examples of coinductive proofs that require a fixed point definition of an infinite stream, but do not require the syntax of higher-order terms or hereditary Harrop formulae. Such proofs can be performed in the *co-fohc*$_{\text{fix}}$ logic. A good example is a proof that the stream of zeros satisfies the Horn clause theory defining the predicate **stream** in the introduction. The goal (**stream** $s_0$), with $s_0 = \text{fix}\, x.\, \text{scons}\ 0\ x$ can be proven directly by coinduction. Similarly, one can type self-application with the infinite type $a = \text{fix}\, t.\, t \to b$ for some given type $b$. The proof for **typed** $[x : a]$ (app $x$ $x$) $b$ is then in *co-fohc*$_{\text{fix}}$. Finally, the clause $\gamma_3$ is also in this group. More generally, circular unifiers obtained from CoLP's [41] loop detection yield immediately guarded fixed point terms, and thus CoLP corresponds to coinductive proofs in the logic *co-fohc*$_{\text{fix}}$. A general discussion of Horn clause theories that describe infinite objects was given in [48], where the above logic programs were identified as being productive.

## 4 Coinductive Uniform Proofs and Intuitionistic Logic

In the last section, we introduced the framework of coinductive uniform proofs, which gives an operational account to proofs for coinductively interpreted logic programs. Having this framework at hand, we need to position it in the existing ecosystem of logical systems. The goal of this section is to prove that coinductive uniform proofs are in fact constructive. We show this by first introducing an extension of intuitionistic first-order logic that allows us to deal with recursive

$$\frac{\Gamma \Vdash \Delta \qquad \varphi \in \Delta}{\Gamma \mid \Delta \vdash \varphi}\ (\textbf{Proj}) \qquad \frac{\Gamma \mid \Delta \vdash \varphi' \qquad \varphi \equiv \varphi'}{\Gamma \mid \Delta \vdash \varphi}\ (\textbf{Conv}) \qquad \frac{\Gamma \Vdash \Delta}{\Gamma \mid \Delta \vdash \top}\ (\top\textbf{-I})$$

$$\frac{\Gamma \mid \Delta \vdash \varphi \qquad \Gamma \mid \Delta \vdash \psi}{\Gamma \mid \Delta \vdash \varphi \wedge \psi}\ (\wedge\textbf{-I}) \qquad \frac{\Gamma \mid \Delta \vdash \varphi_1 \wedge \varphi_2 \qquad i \in \{1,2\}}{\Gamma \mid \Delta \vdash \varphi_i}\ (\wedge_i\textbf{-E})$$

$$\frac{\Gamma \mid \Delta \vdash \varphi_i \qquad \Gamma \Vdash \varphi_j \qquad j \neq i}{\Gamma \mid \Delta \vdash \varphi_1 \vee \varphi_2}\ (\vee_i\textbf{-I}) \qquad \frac{\Gamma \mid \Delta, \varphi_1 \vdash \psi \qquad \Gamma \mid \Delta, \varphi_2 \vdash \psi}{\Gamma \mid \Delta, \varphi_1 \vee \varphi_2 \vdash \psi}\ (\vee\textbf{-E})$$

$$\frac{\Gamma \mid \Delta, \varphi \vdash \psi}{\Gamma \mid \Delta \vdash \varphi \to \psi}\ (\to\textbf{-I}) \qquad \frac{\Gamma \mid \Delta \vdash \varphi \to \psi \qquad \Gamma \mid \Delta \vdash \varphi}{\Gamma \mid \Delta \vdash \psi}\ (\to\textbf{-E})$$

$$\frac{\Gamma, x : \tau \mid \Delta \vdash \varphi \qquad x \notin \Gamma}{\Gamma \mid \Delta \vdash \forall x : \tau .\, \varphi}\ (\forall\textbf{-I}) \qquad \frac{\Gamma \mid \Delta \vdash \forall x : \tau .\, \varphi \qquad M : \tau \in \Lambda^{G}_{\Sigma}(\Gamma)}{\Gamma \mid \Delta \vdash \varphi[M/x]}\ (\forall\textbf{-E})$$

$$\frac{M : \tau \in \Lambda^{G}_{\Sigma}(\Gamma) \quad \Gamma \mid \Delta \vdash \varphi[M/x]}{\Gamma \mid \Delta \vdash \exists x : \tau .\, \varphi}\ (\exists\textbf{-I}) \qquad \frac{\Gamma \Vdash \psi \quad \Gamma, x : \tau \mid \Delta, \varphi \vdash \psi \quad x \notin \Gamma}{\Gamma \mid \Delta, \exists x : \tau .\, \varphi \vdash \psi}\ (\exists\textbf{-E})$$

**Fig. 8.** Intuitionistic rules for standard connectives

proofs for coinductive predicates. Afterwards, we show that coinductive uniform proofs are sound relative to this logic by means of a proof tree translation. The model-theoretic soundness proofs for both logics will be provided in Sect. 5.

We begin by introducing an extension of intuitionistic first-order logic with the so-called *later modality*, written $\blacktriangleright$. This modality is the essential ingredient that allows us to equip proofs with a controlled form of recursion. The later modality stems originally from provability logic, which characterises transitive, well-founded Kripke frames [30,72], and thus allows one to carry out induction without an explicit induction scheme [16]. Later, the later modality was picked up by the type-theoretic community to control recursion in coinductive programming [8,9,21,56,58], mostly with the intent to replace syntactic guardedness checks for coinductive definitions by type-based checks of well-definedness.

Formally, the logic $\mathbf{iFOL}_{\blacktriangleright}$ is given by the following definition.

**Definition 16.** The formulae of $\mathbf{iFOL}_{\blacktriangleright}$ are given by Definition 3 and the rule:

$$\frac{\Gamma \Vdash \varphi}{\Gamma \Vdash \blacktriangleright \varphi}$$

Conversion extends to these formulae in the obvious way. Let $\varphi$ be a formula and $\Delta$ a sequence of formulae in $\mathbf{iFOL}_{\blacktriangleright}$. We say $\varphi$ is *provable in context* $\Gamma$ *under the assumptions* $\Delta$ in $\mathbf{iFOL}_{\blacktriangleright}$, if $\Gamma \mid \Delta \vdash \varphi$ holds. The *provability relation* $\vdash$ is thereby given inductively by the rules in Figs. 8 and 9.

$$\frac{\Gamma \mid \Delta \vdash \varphi}{\Gamma \mid \Delta \vdash \blacktriangleright \varphi}\ (\textbf{Next}) \qquad \frac{\Gamma \mid \Delta \vdash \blacktriangleright(\varphi \to \psi)}{\Gamma \mid \Delta \vdash \blacktriangleright \varphi \to \blacktriangleright \psi}\ (\textbf{Mon}) \qquad \frac{\Gamma \mid \Delta, \blacktriangleright \varphi \vdash \varphi}{\Gamma \mid \Delta \vdash \varphi}\ (\textbf{Löb})$$

**Fig. 9.** Rules for the later modality

The rules in Fig. 8 are the usual rules for intuitionistic first-order logic and should come at no surprise. More interesting are the rules in Fig. 9, where the rule **(Löb)** introduces recursion into the proof system. Furthermore, the rule **(Mon)** allows us to to distribute the later modality over implication, and consequently over conjunction and universal quantification. This is essential in the translation in Theorem 18 below. Finally, the rule **(Next)** gives us the possibility to proceed without any recursion, if necessary.

Note that so far it is not possible to use the assumption $\blacktriangleright \varphi$ introduced in the **(Löb)**-rule. The idea is that the formulae of a logic program provide us the obligations that we have to prove, possibly by recursion, in order to prove a coinductive predicate. This is cast in the following definition.

**Definition 17.** Given an $H^g$-formula $\varphi$ of the shape $\forall \vec{x}.\,(A_1 \wedge \cdots \wedge A_n) \to \psi$, we define its *guarding* $\overline{\varphi}$ to be $\forall \vec{x}.\,(\blacktriangleright A_1 \wedge \cdots \wedge \blacktriangleright A_n) \to \psi$. For a logic program $P$, we define its guarding $\overline{P}$ by guarding each formula in $P$.

The translation given in Definition 17 of a logic program into formulae that admit recursion corresponds unfolding a coinductive predicate, cf. [14]. We show now how to transform a coinductive uniform proof tree into a proof tree in $\mathbf{iFOL}_{\blacktriangleright}$, such that the recursion and guarding mechanisms in both logics match up.

**Theorem 18.** *If $P$ is a logic program over a first-order signature $\Sigma$ and the sequent $\Sigma; P \looparrowright \varphi$ is provable in co-hohh$_{\text{fix}}$, then $\overline{P} \vdash \varphi$ is provable in* $\mathbf{iFOL}_{\blacktriangleright}$.

To prove this theorem, one uses that each coinductive uniform proof tree starts with an initial tree that has an application of the CO-FIX-rule at the root and that eliminates the guard by using the rules in Fig. 5. At the leaves of this tree, one finds proof trees that proceed only by means of the rules in Fig. 4. The initial tree is then translated into a proof tree in $\mathbf{iFOL}_{\blacktriangleright}$ that starts with an application of the **(Löb)**-rule, which corresponds to the CO-FIX-rule, and that simultaneously transforms the coinduction hypothesis and applies introduction rules for conjunctions etc. This ensures that we can match the coinduction hypothesis with the guarded formulae of the program $P$.

The results of this section show that it is irrelevant whether the guarding modality is used on the right (CUP-style) or on the left ($\mathbf{iFOL}_{\blacktriangleright}$-style), as the former can be translated into the latter. However, CUP uses the guarding on the right to preserve proof uniformity, whereas $\mathbf{iFOL}_{\blacktriangleright}$ extends a general sequent calculus. Thus, to obtain the reverse translation, we would have to have an admissible cut rule in CUP. The main ingredient to such a cut rule is the ability to prove several coinductive statements simultaneously. This is possible in CUP by proving the conjunction of these statements. Unfortunately, we cannot eliminate such a conjunction into one of its components, since this would require non-deterministic guessing in the proof construction, which in turn breaks uniformity. Thus, we leave a solution of this problem for future work.

# 5 Herbrand Models and Soundness

In Sect. 4 we showed that coinductive uniform proofs are sound relative to the intuitionistic logic $\mathbf{iFOL}_{\blacktriangleright}$. This gives us a handle on the constructive nature of coinductive uniform proofs. Since $\mathbf{iFOL}_{\blacktriangleright}$ is a non-standard logic, we still need to provide semantics for that logic. We do this by interpreting in Sect. 5.4 the formulae of $\mathbf{iFOL}_{\blacktriangleright}$ over the well-known (complete) Herbrand models and prove the soundness of the accompanying proof system with respect to these models. Although we obtain soundness of coinductive uniform proofs over Herbrand models from this, this proof is indirect and does not give a lot of information about the models captured by the different calculi *co-fohc* etc. For this reason, we will give in Sect. 5.3 a direct soundness proof for coinductive uniform proofs. We also obtain coinduction invariants from this proof for each of the calculi, which allows us to describe their proof strength.

## 5.1 Coinductive Herbrand Models and Semantics of Terms

Before we come to the soundness proofs, we introduce in this section (complete) Herbrand models by using the terminology of final coalgebras. We then utilise this description to give operational and denotational semantics to guarded terms. These semantics show that guarded terms allow the description and computation of potentially infinite trees.

The coalgebraic approach has been proven very successful both in logic and programming [1,75,76]. We will only require very little category theoretical vocabulary and assume that the reader is familiar with the category **Set** of sets and functions, and functors, see for example [12,25,50]. The terminology of algebras and coalgebras [4,47,64,65] is given by the following definition.

**Definition 19.** A *coalgebra* for a functor $F\colon \mathbf{Set} \to \mathbf{Set}$ is a map $c\colon X \to FX$. Given coalgebras $d : Y \to FY$ and $c\colon X \to FX$, we say that a map $h : Y \to X$ is a *homomorphism* $d \to c$ if $Fh \circ d = c \circ h$. We call a coalgebra $c\colon X \to FX$ *final*, if for every coalgebra $d$ there is a unique homomorphism $h\colon d \to c$. We will refer to $h$ as the *coinductive extension* of $d$.

The idea of (complete) Herbrand models is that a set of Horn clauses determines for each predicate symbol a set of potentially infinite terms. Such terms are (potentially infinite) trees, whose nodes are labelled by function symbols and whose branching is given by the arity of these function symbols. To be able to deal with open terms, we will allow such trees to have leaves labelled by variables. Such trees are a final coalgebra for a functor determined by the signature.

**Definition 20.** Let $\Sigma$ be first-order signature. The *extension* of a first-order signature $\Sigma$ is a (polynomial) functor [38] $[\![\Sigma]\!] : \mathbf{Set} \to \mathbf{Set}$ given by

$$[\![\Sigma]\!](X) = \coprod_{f \in \Sigma} X^{\mathrm{ar}(f)},$$

where $\mathrm{ar}\colon \Sigma \to \mathbb{N}$ is defined in Sect. 2 and $X^n$ is the $n$-fold product of $X$. We define for a set $V$ a functor $[\![\Sigma]\!]+V\colon \mathbf{Set} \to \mathbf{Set}$ by $([\![\Sigma]\!]+V)(X) = [\![\Sigma]\!](X)+V$, where $+$ is the coproduct (disjoint union) in **Set**.

To make sense of the following definition, we note that we can view $\Pi$ as a signature and we thus obtain its extension $[\![\Pi]\!]$. Moreover, we note that the final coalgebra of $[\![\Sigma]\!] + V$ exists because $[\![\Sigma]\!]$ is a polynomial functor.

**Definition 21.** Let $\Sigma$ be a first-order signature. The *coterms* over $\Sigma$ are the final coalgebra $\mathrm{root}_V : \Sigma^\infty(V) \to [\![\Sigma]\!](\Sigma^\infty(V)) + V$. For brevity, we denote the coterms with no variables, i.e. $\Sigma^\infty(\emptyset)$, by $\mathrm{root}: \Sigma^\infty \to [\![\Sigma]\!](\Sigma^\infty)$, and call it the *(complete) Herbrand universe* and its elements *ground* coterms. Finally, we let the *(complete) Herbrand base* $\mathcal{B}^\infty$ be the set $[\![\Pi]\!](\Sigma^\infty)$.

The construction $\Sigma^\infty(V)$ gives rise to a functor $\Sigma^\infty : \mathbf{Set} \to \mathbf{Set}$, called the *free completely iterative monad* [5]. If there is no ambiguity, we will drop the injections $\kappa_i$ when describing elements of $\Sigma^\infty(V)$. Note that $\Sigma^\infty(V)$ is final with property that for every $s \in \Sigma^\infty(V)$ either there are $f \in \Sigma$ and $\overrightarrow{t} \in (\Sigma^\infty(V))^{\mathrm{ar}(f)}$ with $\mathrm{root}_V(s) = f(\overrightarrow{t})$, or there is $x \in V$ with $\mathrm{root}_V(s) = x$. Finality allows us to specify unique maps into $\Sigma^\infty(V)$ by giving a coalgebra $X \to [\![\Sigma]\!](X) + V$. In particular, one can define for each $\theta : V \to \Sigma^\infty$ the substitution $t[\theta]$ of variables in the coterm $t$ by $\theta$ as the coinductive extension of the following coalgebra.

$$\Sigma^\infty(V) \xrightarrow{\mathrm{root}_V} [\![\Sigma]\!](\Sigma^\infty(V)) + V \xrightarrow{[\mathrm{id}, \mathrm{root} \circ \theta]} [\![\Sigma]\!](\Sigma^\infty(V))$$

Now that we have set up the basic terminology of coalgebras, we can give semantics to guarded terms from Definition 5. The idea is that guarded terms guarantee that we can always compute with them so far that we find a function symbol in head position, see Lemma 8. This function symbol determines then the label and branching of a node in the tree generated by a guarded term. If the computation reaches a constant or a variable, then we stop creating the tree at the present branch. This idea is captured by the following lemma.

**Lemma 22.** *There is a map* $[\![-]\!]_1 : \Lambda^{G,1}_\Sigma(\Gamma) \to \Sigma^\infty(\Gamma)$ *that is unique with*

1. *if* $M \equiv N$, *then* $[\![M]\!]_1 = [\![N]\!]_1$, *and*
2. *for all* $M$, *if* $M \longrightarrow\!\!\!\!\rightarrow f\,\overrightarrow{N}$ *then* $\mathrm{root}_\Gamma([\![M]\!]_1) = f\big(\overrightarrow{[\![N]\!]_1}\big)$, *and if* $M \longrightarrow\!\!\!\!\rightarrow x$ *then* $\mathrm{root}_\Gamma([\![M]\!]_1) = x$.

*Proof (sketch).* By Lemma 8, we can define a coalgebra on the quotient of guarded terms by convertibility $c : \Lambda^{G,1}_\Sigma(\Gamma)/\!\equiv\; \to [\![\Sigma]\!]\Big(\Lambda^{G,1}_\Sigma(\Gamma)/\!\equiv\Big) + \Gamma$ with $c[M] = f[\overrightarrow{N}]$ if $M \longrightarrow\!\!\!\!\rightarrow f\,\overrightarrow{N}$ and $c[M] = x$ if $M \longrightarrow\!\!\!\!\rightarrow x$. This yields a homomorphism $h : \Lambda^{G,1}_\Sigma(\Gamma)/\!\equiv\; \to \Sigma^\infty(\Gamma)$ and we can define $[\![-]\!]_1 = h \circ [-]$. The rest follows from uniqueness of $h$.

### 5.2 Interpretation of Basic Intuitionistic First-Order Formulae

In this section, we give an interpretation of the formulae in Definition 3, in which we restrict ourselves to guarded terms. This interpretation will be relative to models in the complete Herbrand universe. Since we later extend these models to Kripke models to be able to handle the later modality, we formulate these models already now in the language of fibrations [17,46].

**Definition 23.** Let $p\colon \mathbf{E} \to \mathbf{B}$ be a functor. Given an object $I \in \mathbf{B}$, the *fibre* $\mathbf{E}_I$ above $I$ is the category of objects $A \in \mathbf{E}$ with $p(A) = I$ and morphisms $f\colon A \to B$ with $p(f) = \mathrm{id}_I$. The functor $p$ is a *(split) fibration* if for every morphism $u\colon I \to J$ in $\mathbf{B}$ there is functor $u^*\colon \mathbf{E}_J \to \mathbf{E}_I$, such that $\mathrm{id}_I^* = \mathrm{Id}_{\mathbf{E}_I}$ and $(v \circ u)^* = u^* \circ v^*$. We call $u^*$ the *reindexing along* $u$.

To give an interpretation of formulae, consider the following category **Pred**.

$$\mathbf{Pred} = \begin{cases} \text{objects :} & (X,P) \ \text{with}\, X \in \mathbf{Set} \text{ and } P \subseteq X \\ \text{morphisms :} & f : (X,P) \to (Y,Q) \text{ is a map } f : X \to Y \text{ with } f(P) \subseteq Q \end{cases}$$

The functor $\mathbb{P}\colon \mathbf{Pred} \to \mathbf{Set}$ with $\mathbb{P}(X,P) = X$ and $\mathbb{P}(f) = f$ is a split fibration, see [46], where the reindexing functor for $f\colon X \to Y$ is given by taking preimages: $f^*(Q) = f^{-1}(Q)$. Note that each fibre $\mathbf{Pred}_X$ is isomorphic to the complete lattice of predicates over $X$ ordered by set inclusion. Thus, we refer to this fibration as the *predicate fibration.*

Let us now expose the logical structure of the predicate fibration. This will allow us to conveniently interpret first-order formulae over this fibration, but it comes at the cost of having to introduce a good amount of category theoretical language. However, doing so will pay off in Sect. 5.4, where we will construct another fibration out of the predicate fibration. We can then use category theoretical results to show that this new fibration admits the same logical structure and allows the interpretation of the later modality.

The first notion we need is that of fibred products, coproducts and exponents, which will allow us to interpret conjunction, disjunction and implication.

**Definition 24.** A fibration $p\colon \mathbf{E} \to \mathbf{B}$ has *fibred finite products* $(\mathbf{1}, \times)$, if each fibre $\mathbf{E}_I$ has finite products $(\mathbf{1}_I, \times_I)$ and these are preserved by reindexing: for all $f\colon I \to J$, we have $f^*(\mathbf{1}_J) = \mathbf{1}_I$ and $f^*(A \times_J B) = f^*(A) \times_I f^*(B)$. Fibred finite coproducts and exponents are defined analogously.

The fibration $\mathbb{P}$ is a so-called first-order fibration, which allows us to interpret first-order logic, see [46, Def. 4.2.1].

**Definition 25.** A fibration $p\colon \mathbf{E} \to \mathbf{B}$ is a *first-order fibration* if[2]

- $\mathbf{B}$ has finite products and the fibres of $p$ are preorders;
- $p$ has fibred finite products $(\top, \wedge)$ and coproducts $(\bot, \vee)$ that distribute;
- $p$ has fibred exponents $\to$; and
- $p$ has existential and universal quantifiers $\exists_{I,J} \dashv \pi_{I,J}^* \dashv \forall_{I,J}$ for all projections $\pi_{I,J}\colon I \times J \to I$.

A *first-order $\lambda$-fibration* is a first-order fibration with Cartesian closed base $\mathbf{B}$.

2 Technically, the quantifiers should also fulfil the Beck-Chevalley and Frobenius conditions, and the fibration should admit equality. Since these are fulfilled in all our models and we do not need equality, we will not discuss them here.

The fibration $\mathbb{P}\colon \mathbf{Pred} \to \mathbf{Set}$ is a first-order $\lambda$-fibration, as all its fibres are posets and $\mathbf{Set}$ is Cartesian closed; $\mathbb{P}$ has fibred finite products $(\top, \cap)$, given by $\top_X = X$ and intersection; fibred distributive coproducts $(\emptyset, \cup)$; fibred exponents $\Rightarrow$, given by $(P \Rightarrow Q) = \{\vec{t} \mid \text{if } \vec{t} \in P, \text{then } \vec{t} \in Q\}$; and universal and existential quantifiers given for $P \in \mathbf{Pred}_{X\times Y}$ by

$$\forall_{X,Y} P = \{x \in X \mid \forall y \in Y.\, (x,y) \in P\} \quad \exists_{X,Y} P = \{x \in X \mid \exists y \in Y.\, (x,y) \in P\}.$$

The purpose of first-order fibrations is to capture the essentials of first-order logic, while the $\lambda$-part takes care of higher-order features of the term language. In the following, we interpret types, contexts, guarded terms and formulae in the fibration $\mathbb{P}\colon \mathbf{Pred} \to \mathbf{Set}$: We define for types $\tau$ and context $\Gamma$ sets $[\![\tau]\!]$ and $[\![\Gamma]\!]$; for guarded terms $M$ with $\Gamma \vdash M : \tau$ we define a map $[\![M]\!]\colon [\![\Gamma]\!] \to [\![\tau]\!]$ in $\mathbf{Set}$; and for a formula $\Gamma \Vdash \varphi$ we give a predicate $[\![\varphi]\!] \in \mathbf{Pred}_{[\![\Gamma]\!]}$.

The semantics of types and contexts are given inductively in the Cartesian closed category $\mathbf{Set}$, where the base type $\iota$ is interpreted as coterms, as follows.

$$[\![\iota]\!] = \Sigma^\infty \qquad\qquad [\![\emptyset]\!] = \mathbf{1}$$
$$[\![\tau \to \sigma]\!] = [\![\sigma]\!]^{[\![\tau]\!]} \qquad\qquad [\![\Gamma, x : \tau]\!] = [\![\Gamma]\!] \times [\![\tau]\!]$$

We note that a coterm $t \in \Sigma^\infty(V)$ can be seen as a map $(\Sigma^\infty)^V \to \Sigma^\infty$ by applying a substitution in $(\Sigma^\infty)^V$ to $t$: $\sigma \mapsto t[\sigma]$. In particular, the semantics of a guarded first-order term $M \in \Lambda_\Sigma^{G,1}(\Gamma)$ is equivalently a map $[\![M]\!]_1\colon [\![\Gamma]\!] \to \Sigma^\infty$. We can now extend this map inductively to $[\![M]\!]\colon [\![\Gamma]\!] \to [\![\tau]\!]$ for all guarded terms $M \in \Lambda_\Sigma^G(\Gamma)$ with $\Gamma \vdash M : \tau$ by

$$\begin{aligned}
[\![M]\!](\gamma)(\vec{t}) &= [\![M\,\vec{x}]\!]_1([\vec{x} \mapsto \vec{t}]) \qquad \vdash_g M : \tau \text{ with } \mathrm{ar}(\tau) = |\vec{t}| = |\vec{x}| \\
[\![c]\!](\gamma)(\vec{t}) &= c\,\vec{t} \\
[\![x]\!](\gamma) &= \gamma(x) \\
[\![M\,N]\!](\gamma) &= [\![M]\!](\gamma)([\![N]\!](\gamma)) \\
[\![\lambda x.\, M]\!](\gamma)(t) &= [\![M]\!](\gamma[x \mapsto t])
\end{aligned}$$

**Lemma 26.** *The mapping $[\![-]\!]$ is a well-defined function from guarded terms to functions, such that $\Gamma \vdash M : \tau$ implies $[\![M]\!]\colon [\![\Gamma]\!] \to [\![\tau]\!]$.*

Since $\mathbb{P}\colon \mathbf{Pred} \to \mathbf{Set}$ is a first-order fibration, we can interpret inductively all logical connectives of the formulae from Definition 3 in this fibration. The only case that is missing is the base case of predicate symbols. Their interpretation will be given over a Herbrand model that is constructed as the largest fixed point of an operator over all predicate interpretations in the Herbrand base. Both the operator and the fixed point are the subjects of the following definition.

**Definition 27.** We let the set of *interpretations* $\mathcal{I}$ be the powerset $\mathcal{P}(\mathcal{B}^\infty)$ of the complete Herbrand base. For $I \in \mathcal{I}$ and $p \in \Pi$, we denote by $I|_p$ the interpretation of $p$ in $I$ (the fibre of $I$ above $p$)

$$I|_p = \{\vec{t} \in (\Sigma^\infty)^{\mathrm{ar}(p)} \mid p(\vec{t}) \in I\}.$$

Given a set $P$ of $H^g$-formulae, we define a monotone map $\Phi_P : \mathcal{I} \to \mathcal{I}$ by

$$\Phi_P(I) = \{[\![\psi]\!]_1[\theta] \mid (\forall \vec{x}.\ \bigwedge_{k=1}^n \varphi_k \to \psi) \in P, \theta : |\vec{x}| \to \Sigma^\infty, \forall k.\ [\![\varphi_k]\!]_1[\theta] \in I\},$$

where $[\![-]\!]_1[\theta]$ is the extension of semantics and substitution from coterms to the Herbrand base by functoriality of $[\![\Pi]\!]$. The *(complete) Herbrand model* $\mathcal{M}_P$ of $P$ is the largest fixed point of $\Phi_P$, which exists because $\mathcal{I}$ is a complete lattice.

Given a formula $\varphi$ with $\Gamma \Vdash \varphi$ that contains only guarded terms, we define the semantics of $\varphi$ in **Pred** from an interpretation $I \in \mathcal{I}$ inductively as follows.

$$[\![\Gamma \Vdash p\,\vec{M}]\!]_I = \left([\![\vec{M}]\!]\right)^*(I|_p)$$

$$[\![\Gamma \Vdash \top]\!]_I = \top_{[\![\Gamma]\!]}$$

$$[\![\Gamma \Vdash \varphi \,\Box\, \psi]\!]_I = [\![\Gamma \Vdash \varphi]\!]_I \,\Box\, [\![\Gamma \Vdash \psi]\!]_I \qquad \Box \in \{\wedge, \vee, \to\}$$

$$[\![\Gamma \Vdash Qx : \tau.\,\varphi]\!]_I = Q_{[\![\Gamma]\!],[\![\tau]\!]}\ [\![\Gamma, x : \tau \Vdash \varphi]\!]_I \qquad Q \in \{\forall, \exists\}$$

**Lemma 28.** *The mapping* $[\![-]\!]_I$ *is a well-defined function from formulae to predicates, such that* $\Gamma \Vdash \varphi$ *implies* $[\![\varphi]\!]_I \subseteq [\![\Gamma]\!]$ *or, equivalently,* $[\![\varphi]\!]_I \in \mathbf{Pred}_{[\![\Gamma]\!]}$.

This concludes the semantics of types, terms and formulae. We now turn to show that coinductive uniform proofs are sound for this interpretation.

## 5.3 Soundness of Coinductive Uniform Proofs for Herbrand Models

In this section, we give a direct proof of soundness for the coinductive uniform proof system from Sect. 3. Later, we will obtain another soundness result by combining the proof translation from Theorem 18 with the soundness of $\mathbf{iFOL}_\blacktriangleright$ (Theorems 39 and 42). The purpose of giving a direct soundness proof for uniform proofs is that it allows the extraction of a coinduction invariant, see Lemma 32.

The main idea is as follows. Given a formula $\varphi$ and a uniform proof $\pi$ for $\Sigma; P \looparrowright \varphi$, we construct an interpretation $I \in \mathcal{I}$ that validates $\varphi$, i.e. $[\![\varphi]\!]_I = \top$, and that is contained in the complete Herbrand model $\mathcal{M}_P$. Combining these two facts, we obtain that $[\![\varphi]\!]_{\mathcal{M}_P} = \top$, and thus the soundness of uniform proofs.

To show that the constructed interpretation $I$ is contained in $\mathcal{M}_P$, we use the usual coinduction proof principle, as it is given in the following definition.

**Definition 29.** An *invariant for* $K \in \mathcal{I}$ is a set $I \in \mathcal{I}$, such that $K \subseteq I$ and $I$ is a $\Phi_P$-invariant, that is, $I \subseteq \Phi_P(I)$. If $K$ has an invariant, then $K \subseteq \mathcal{M}_P$.

Thus, our goal is now to construct an interpretation together with an invariant. This invariant will essentially collect and iterate all the substitutions that appear in a proof. For this we need the ability to compose substitutions of coterms, which we derive from the monad [5] $(\Sigma^\infty, \eta, \mu)$ with $\mu : \Sigma^\infty \Sigma^\infty \Rightarrow \Sigma^\infty$.

**Definition 30.** A *(Kleisli-)substitution* $\theta$ from $V$ to $W$, written $\theta : V \twoheadrightarrow W$, is map $V \to \Sigma^\infty(W)$. Composition of $\theta : V \twoheadrightarrow W$ and $\delta : U \twoheadrightarrow V$ is given by

$$\theta \circledcirc \delta = U \xrightarrow{\delta} \Sigma^\infty(V) \xrightarrow{\Sigma^\infty(\theta)} \Sigma^\infty(\Sigma^\infty(W)) \xrightarrow{\mu_W} \Sigma^\infty(W).$$

The notions in the following definition will allow us to easily organise and iterate the substitutions that occur in a uniform proof.

**Definition 31.** Let $S$ be a set with $S = \{1, \dots, n\}$ for some $n \in \mathbb{N}$. We call the set $S^*$ of lists over $S$ the set of *substitution identifiers.* Suppose that we have substitutions $\theta_0 \colon V \twoheadrightarrow \emptyset$ and $\theta_k \colon V \twoheadrightarrow V$ for each $k \in S$. Then we can define a map $\Theta \colon S^* \to (\Sigma^\infty)^V$, which turns each substitution identifier into a substitution, by iteration from the right:

$$\Theta(\varepsilon) = \theta_0 \quad \text{and} \quad \Theta(w : k) = \Theta(w) \circledcirc \theta_k$$

After introducing these notations, we can give the outline of the soundness proof for uniform proofs relative to the complete Herbrand model. Given an $H^g$-formula $\forall \vec{x}\,.\,\varphi$, we note that a uniform proof $\pi$ for $\Sigma; P \looparrowright \forall \vec{x}\,.\,\varphi$ starts with

$$\cfrac{\cfrac{\vec{c} : \iota, \Sigma; P; \Delta \Longrightarrow \langle \varphi[\vec{c}/\vec{x}] \rangle \qquad \vec{c} : \iota \notin \Sigma}{\Sigma; P; \forall \vec{x}\,.\,\varphi \Longrightarrow \langle \forall \vec{x}\,.\,\varphi \rangle}\ \forall R\langle\rangle}{\Sigma; P \looparrowright \forall \vec{x}\,.\,\varphi}\ \text{CO-FIX}$$

where the eigenvariables in $\vec{c}$ are all distinct. Let $\Sigma^c$ be the signature $\vec{c} : \iota, \Sigma$ and $C$ the set of variables in $\vec{c}$. Suppose the following is a valid subtree of $\pi$.

$$\cfrac{\cfrac{\Sigma^c; P; \Delta \xRightarrow{\varphi[\vec{N}/\vec{x}]} A}{\Sigma^c; P; \Delta \xRightarrow{\forall \vec{x}\,.\,\varphi \in \Delta} A}\ \forall L}{\Sigma^c; P; \Delta \Longrightarrow A}\ \text{DECIDE}$$

This proof tree gives rise to a substitution $\delta \colon C \twoheadrightarrow C$ by $\delta(c) = [\![N_c]\!]$, which we call an *agent* of $\pi$. We let $D \subseteq \mathrm{At}_1^g$ be the set of atoms that are proven in $\pi$:

$$D = \{A \mid \Sigma^c; P; \Delta \Longrightarrow \langle A \rangle \text{ or } \Sigma^c; P; \Delta \Longrightarrow A \text{ appears in } \pi\}$$

From the agents and atoms in $\pi$ we extract an invariant for the goal formula.

**Lemma 32.** *Suppose that $\varphi$ is an $H^g$-formula of the form $\forall \vec{x}\,.\,A_1 \wedge \cdots \wedge A_n \to A_0$ and that there is a proof $\pi$ for $\Sigma; P \looparrowright \varphi$. Let $D$ be the proven atoms in $\pi$ and $\theta_0, \dots, \theta_s$ be the agents of $\pi$. Define $A_k^c = A_k[\vec{c}/\vec{x}]$ and suppose further that $I_1$ is an invariant for $\{A_k^c[\Theta(\varepsilon)] \mid 1 \leq k \leq n\}$. If we put*

$$I_2 = \bigcup_{w \in S^*} D\,[\Theta\,(w)]$$

*then $I_1 \cup I_2$ is an invariant for $A_0^c[\Theta(\varepsilon)]$.*

Once we have Lemma 32 the following soundness theorem is easily proven.

**Theorem 33.** *If $\varphi$ is an $H^g$-formula and $\Sigma; P \looparrowright \varphi$, then $[\![\varphi]\!]_{\mathcal{M}_P} = \top$.*

Finally, we show that extending logic programs with coinductively proven lemmas is sound. This follows easily by coinduction.

**Theorem 34.** *Let $\varphi$ be an $H^g$-formula of the shape $\forall \vec{x}.\, \psi_1 \to \psi_2$, such that, for all substitutions $\theta$ if $[\![\psi_1]\!]_1[\theta] \in \mathcal{M}_{P,\varphi}$, then $[\![\psi_1]\!]_1[\theta] \in \mathcal{M}_P$. Then $\Sigma; P \looparrowright \varphi$ implies $\mathcal{M}_{P \cup \{\varphi\}} = \mathcal{M}_P$, that is, $P \cup \{\varphi\}$ is a conservative extension of $P$ with respect to the Herbrand model.*

As a corollary we obtain that, if there is a proof for $\Sigma; P \looparrowright \varphi$, then a proof for $\Sigma; P, \varphi \looparrowright \psi$ is sound with respect to $\mathcal{M}_P$. Indeed, by Theorem 34 we have that $\mathcal{M}_P = \mathcal{M}_{P \cup \varphi}$ and by Theorem 33 that $\Sigma; P, \varphi \looparrowright \psi$ is sound with respect to $\mathcal{M}_{P \cup \{\varphi\}}$. Thus, the proof of $\Sigma; P, \varphi \looparrowright \psi$ is also sound with respect to $\mathcal{M}_P$. We use this property implicitly in our running examples, and refer the reader to [15, 49] for proofs, further examples and discussion.

### 5.4 Soundness of iFOL$_\blacktriangleright$ over Herbrand Models

In this section, we demonstrate how the logic **iFOL$_\blacktriangleright$** can be interpreted over Herbrand models. Recall that we obtained a fixed point model from the monotone map $\Phi_P$ on interpretations. In what follows, it is crucial that we construct the greatest fixed point of $\Phi_P$ by iteration, c.f. [6, 32, 77]: Let **Ord** be the class of all ordinals equipped with their (well-founded) order. We denote by $\mathbf{Ord}^{\mathrm{op}}$ the class of ordinals with their reversed order and define a monotone function $\overleftarrow{\Phi_P} \colon \mathbf{Ord}^{\mathrm{op}} \to \mathcal{I}$, where we write the argument ordinal in the subscript, by

$$\left(\overleftarrow{\Phi_P}\right)_\alpha = \bigcap\nolimits_{\beta<\alpha} \Phi_P\left(\overleftarrow{\Phi_P}_\beta\right).$$

Note that this definition is well-defined because $<$ is well-founded and because $\Phi_P$ is monotone, see [14]. Since $\mathcal{I}$ is a complete lattice, there is an ordinal $\alpha$ such that $\overleftarrow{\Phi_P}_\alpha = \Phi_P\left(\overleftarrow{\Phi_P}_\alpha\right)$, at which point $\overleftarrow{\Phi_P}_\alpha$ is the largest fixed point $\mathcal{M}_P$ of $\Phi_P$. In what follows, we will utilise this construction to give semantics to **iFOL$_\blacktriangleright$**.

The fibration $\mathbb{P} \colon \mathbf{Pred} \to \mathbf{Set}$ gives rise to another fibration as follows. We let $\overline{\mathbf{Pred}}$ be the category of functors (monotone maps) with fixed predicate domain:

$$\overline{\mathbf{Pred}} = \begin{cases} \text{objects:} & u \colon \mathbf{Ord}^{\mathrm{op}} \to \mathbf{Pred}, \text{such that } \mathbb{P} \circ u \text{ is constant} \\ \text{morphisms:} & u \to v \text{ are natural transformations } f \colon u \Rightarrow v, \\ & \text{such that } \mathbb{P}f \colon \mathbb{P} \circ u \Rightarrow \mathbb{P} \circ v \text{ is the identity} \end{cases}$$

The fibration $\overline{\mathbb{P}}$: $\mathbf{Pred} \to \mathbf{Set}$ is defined by evaluation at any ordinal (here 0), i.e. by $\overline{\mathbb{P}}(u) = \mathbb{P}(u(0))$ and $\overline{\mathbb{P}}(f) = (\mathbb{P}f)_0$, and reindexing along $f \colon X \to Y$ by applying the reindexing of $\mathbb{P}$ point-wise, i.e. by $f^{\#}(u)_\alpha = f^*(u_\alpha)$.

Note that there is a (full) embedding $K \colon \mathbf{Pred} \to \overline{\mathbf{Pred}}$ that is given by $K(X, P) = (X, \overline{P})$ with $\overline{P}_\alpha = P$. One can show [14] that $\overline{\mathbb{P}}$ is again a first-order fibration and that it models the later modality, as in the following theorem.

**Theorem 35.** *The fibration $\overline{\mathbb{P}}$ is a first-order fibration. If necessary, we denote the first-order connectives by $\dot{\top}$, $\dot{\wedge}$ etc. to distinguish them from those in* **Pred**. *Otherwise, we drop the dots. Finite (co)products and quantifiers are given pointwise, while for $X \in$* **Set** *and $u, v \in \overline{\mathbf{Pred}}_X$ exponents are given by*

$$(v \mathrel{\dot{\Rightarrow}} u)_\alpha = \bigcap\nolimits_{\beta\leq\alpha} (v_\beta \Rightarrow u_\beta).$$

*There is a fibred functor* $\blacktriangleright\colon \overline{\mathbf{Pred}} \to \overline{\mathbf{Pred}}$ *with* $\overline{\pi} \circ \blacktriangleright = \overline{\pi}$ *given on objects by*

$$(\blacktriangleright u)_\alpha = \bigcap\nolimits_{\beta<\alpha} u_\beta$$

*and a natural transformation* next: $\mathrm{Id} \Rightarrow \blacktriangleright$ *from the identity functor to* $\blacktriangleright$. *The functor* $\blacktriangleright$ *preserves reindexing, products, exponents and universal quantification:* $\blacktriangleright(f^{\#}u) = f^{\#}(\blacktriangleright u)$, $\blacktriangleright(u \wedge v) = \blacktriangleright u \wedge \blacktriangleright v$, $\blacktriangleright(u^v) \to (\blacktriangleright u)^{\blacktriangleright v}$, $\blacktriangleright(\overline{\forall}_n u) = \overline{\forall}_n(\blacktriangleright u)$. *Finally, for all* $X \in \mathbf{Set}$ *and* $u \in \overline{\mathbf{Pred}}_X$, *there is* löb: $(\blacktriangleright u \dot{\Rightarrow} u) \to u$ *in* $\overline{\mathbf{Pred}}_X$.

Using the above theorem, we can extend the interpretation of formulae to $\mathbf{iFOL}_\blacktriangleright$ as follows. Let $u\colon \mathbf{Ord}^{\mathrm{op}} \to \mathcal{I}$ be a descending sequence of interpretations. As before, we define the restriction of $u$ to a predicate symbol $p \in \Pi$ by $\left(u|_p\right)_\alpha = u_\alpha|_p = \{\vec{t} \mid p(\vec{t}) \in u_\alpha\}$. The semantics of formulae in $\mathbf{iFOL}_\blacktriangleright$ as objects in $\overline{\mathbf{Pred}}$ is given by the following iterative definition.

$$\begin{aligned}
[\![\Gamma \Vdash p\,\vec{M}]\!]_u &= \left(\overrightarrow{[\![M]\!]}\right)^{\#}(u|_p) && \\
[\![\Gamma \Vdash \top]\!]_u &= \dot{\top}_{[\![\Gamma]\!]} && \\
[\![\Gamma \Vdash \varphi \,\square\, \psi]\!]_u &= [\![\Gamma \Vdash \varphi]\!]_u \,\square\, [\![\Gamma \Vdash \psi]\!]_u && \square \in \{\wedge, \vee, \to\} \\
[\![\Gamma \Vdash Qx : \tau.\, \varphi]\!]_u &= Q_{[\![\Gamma]\!],[\![\tau]\!]}\, [\![\Gamma, x : \tau \Vdash \varphi]\!]_u && Q \in \{\forall, \exists\} \\
[\![\Gamma \Vdash \blacktriangleright \varphi]\!]_u &= \blacktriangleright [\![\Gamma \Vdash \varphi]\!]_u &&
\end{aligned}$$

The following lemma is the analogue of Lemma 28 for the interpretation of formulae without the later modality.

**Lemma 36.** *The mapping* $[\![-]\!]_u$ *is a well-defined map from formulae in* $\mathbf{iFOL}_\blacktriangleright$ *to sequences of predicates, such that* $\Gamma \Vdash \varphi$ *implies* $[\![\varphi]\!]_u \in \overline{\mathbf{Pred}}_{[\![\Gamma]\!]}$.

**Lemma 37.** *All rules of* $\mathbf{iFOL}_\blacktriangleright$ *are sound with respect to the interpretation* $[\![-]\!]_u$ *of formulae in* $\overline{\mathbf{Pred}}$, *that is, if* $\Gamma \mid \Delta \vdash \varphi$, *then* $\left(\bigwedge_{\psi\in\Delta}[\![\psi]\!]_u \dot{\Rightarrow} [\![\varphi]\!]_u\right) = \dot{\top}$. *In particular,* $\Gamma \vdash \varphi$ *implies* $[\![\varphi]\!]_u = \dot{\top}$.

The following lemma shows that the guarding of a set of formulae is valid in the chain model that they generate.

**Lemma 38.** *If* $\varphi$ *is an H-formula in P, then* $[\![\overline{\varphi}]\!]_{\overleftarrow{\Phi_P}} = \dot{\top}$.

Combining this with soundness from Lemma 37, we obtain that provability in $\mathbf{iFOL}_\blacktriangleright$ relative to a logic program $P$ is sound for the model of $P$.

**Theorem 39.** *For all logic programs P, if* $\Gamma \mid \overline{P} \vdash \varphi$ *then* $[\![\varphi]\!]_{\overleftarrow{\Phi_P}} = \dot{\top}$.

The final result of this section is to show that the descending chain model, which we used to interpret formulae of $\mathbf{iFOL}_\blacktriangleright$, is sound and complete for the fixed point model, which we used to interpret the formulae of coinductive uniform proofs. This will be proved in Theorem 42 below. The easiest way to prove this result is by establishing a functor $\overline{\mathbf{Pred}} \to \mathbf{Pred}$ that maps the chain $\overleftarrow{\Phi_P}$ to the model $\mathcal{M}_P$, and that preserves and reflects truth of first-order formulae (Proposition 41). We will phrase the preservation of truth of first-order formulae by a functor by appealing to the following notion of fibrations maps, cf. [46, Def. 4.3.1].

**Definition 40.** Let $p\colon \mathbf{E} \to \mathbf{B}$ and $q\colon \mathbf{D} \to \mathbf{A}$ be fibrations. A *fibration map* $p \to q$ is a pair $(F\colon \mathbf{E} \to \mathbf{D}, G\colon \mathbf{B} \to \mathbf{A})$ of functors, s.t. $q \circ F = G \circ p$ and $F$ preserves Cartesian morphisms: if $f\colon X \to Y$ in $\mathbf{E}$ is Cartesian over $p(f)$, then $F(f)$ is Cartesian over $G(p(f))$. $(F, G)$ is a map of *first-order ($\lambda$-)fibrations*, if $p$ and $q$ are first-order ($\lambda$-)fibrations, and $F$ and $G$ preserve this structure.

Let us now construct a first-order $\lambda$-fibration map $\overline{\mathbf{Pred}} \to \mathbf{Pred}$. We note that since every fibre of the predicate fibration is a complete lattice, for every chain $u \in \overline{\mathbf{Pred}}_X$ there exists an ordinal $\alpha$ at which $u$ stabilises. This means that there is a limit $\lim u$ of $u$ in $\mathbf{Pred}_X$, which is the largest subset of $X$, such that $\forall \alpha.\ \lim u \subseteq u_\alpha$. This allows us to define a map $L\colon \overline{\mathbf{Pred}} \to \mathbf{Pred}$ by

$$L(X, u) = (X, \lim u)$$
$$L(f\colon (X, u) \to (Y, v)) = f.$$

In the following proposition, we show that $L$ gives us the ability to express first-order properties of limits equivalently through their approximating chains. This, in turn, provides soundness and completeness for the interpretation of the logic $\mathbf{iFOL}_{\blacktriangleright}$ over descending chains with respect to the largest Herbrand model.

**Proposition 41.** *$L\colon \overline{\mathbf{Pred}} \to \mathbf{Pred}$, as defined above, is a map of first-order fibrations. Furthermore, $L$ is right-adjoint to the embedding $K\colon \mathbf{Pred} \to \overline{\mathbf{Pred}}$. Finally, for each $p \in \Pi$ and $u \in \overline{\mathbf{Pred}}_{\mathcal{B}^\infty}$, we have $L\big(u|_p\big) = L(u)|_p$.*

We get from Proposition 41 soundness and completeness of $\overleftarrow{\Phi_P}$ for Herbrand models. More precisely, if $\varphi$ is a formula of plain first-order logic ($\blacktriangleright$-free), then its interpretation in the coinductive Herbrand model is true if and only if its interpretation over the chain approximation of the Herbrand model is true.

**Theorem 42.** *If $\varphi$ is $\blacktriangleright$-free (Definition 3) then $[\![\varphi]\!]_{\overleftarrow{\Phi_P}} = \dot{\top}$ if and only if $[\![\varphi]\!]_{\mathcal{M}_P} = \top$.*

*Proof (sketch).* First, one shows for all $\blacktriangleright$-free formulae $\varphi$ that $L([\![\varphi]\!]_{\overleftarrow{\Phi_P}}) = [\![\varphi]\!]_{\mathcal{M}_P}$ by induction on $\varphi$ and using Proposition 41. Using this identity and $K \dashv L$, the result is then obtained from the following adjoint correspondence.

$$\frac{\dot{\top} = K(\top) \longrightarrow [\![\varphi]\!]_{\overleftarrow{\Phi_P}} \quad \text{in } \overline{\mathbf{Pred}}}{\top \longrightarrow L([\![\varphi]\!]_{\overleftarrow{\Phi_P}}) = [\![\varphi]\!]_{\mathcal{M}_P} \quad \text{in } \mathbf{Pred}}$$

□

## 6 Conclusion, Related Work and the Future

In this paper, we provided a comprehensive theory of resolution in coinductive Horn-clause theories and coinductive logic programs. This theory comprises of a uniform proof system that features a form of guarded recursion and that provides operational semantics for proofs of coinductive predicates. Further, we showed how to translate proofs in this system into proofs for an extension of intuitionistic FOL with guarded recursion, and we provided sound semantics for both proof systems in terms of coinductive Herbrand models. The Herbrand models and semantics were thereby presented in a modern style that utilises coalgebras and fibrations to provide a conceptual view on the semantics.

*Related Work.* It may be surprising that automated *proof search for coinductive predicates* in first-order logic does not have a coherent and comprehensive theory, even after three decades [3,60], despite all the attention that it received as programming [2,29,42,44] and proof [33,35,39,40,45,59,64–67] method. The work that comes close to algorithmic proof search is the system CIRC [63], but it cannot handle general coinductive predicates and corecursive programming. Inductive and coinductive data types are also being added to SMT solvers [24,62]. However, both CIRC and SMT solving are inherently based on classical logic and are therefore not suited to situations where proof objects are relevant, like programming, type class inference or (dependent) type theory. Moreover, the proposed solutions, just like those in [41,69] can only deal with regular data, while our approach also works for irregular data, as we saw in the **from**-example.

This paper subsumes Haskell type class inference [37,51] and exposes that the inference presented in those papers corresponds to coinductive proofs in *co-fohc* and *co-hohh*. Given that the proof systems proposed in this paper are constructive and that uniform proofs provide proofs (type inhabitants) in normal form, we could give a propositions-as-types interpretation to all eight coinductive uniform proof systems. This was done for *co-fohc* and *co-hohh* in [37], but we leave the remaining cube from the introduction for future work.

*Future Work.* There are several directions that we wish to pursue in the future. First, we know that CUP is incomplete for the presented models, as it is intuitionistic and it lacks an admissible cut rule. The first can be solved by moving to Kripke/Beth-models, as done by Clouston and Goré [30] for the propositional part of $\mathbf{iFOL}_{\blacktriangleright}$. However, the admissible cut rule is more delicate. To obtain such a rule one has to be able to prove several propositions simultaneously by coinduction, as discussed at the end of Sect. 4. In general, completeness of recursive proof systems depends largely on the theory they are applied to, see [70] and [18]. However, techniques from cyclic proof systems [27,68] may help. We also aim to extend our ideas to other situations like higher-order Horn clauses [28,43] and interactive proof assistants [7,10,23,31], typed logic programming, and logic programming that mix inductive and coinductive predicates.

**Acknowledgements.** We would like to thank Damien Pous and the anonymous reviewers for their valuable feedback.

## References


1. Abbott, M., Altenkirch, T., Ghani, N.: Containers: constructing strictly positive types. TCS **342**(1), 3–27 (2005). https://doi.org/10.1016/j.tcs.2005.06.002
2. Abel, A., Pientka, B., Thibodeau, D., Setzer, A.: Copatterns: programming infinite structures by observations. In: POPL 2013, pp. 27–38 (2013). https://doi.org/10.1145/2429069.2429075
3. Aczel, P.: Non-well-founded sets. Center for the Study of Language and Information, Stanford University (1988)
4. Aczel, P.: Algebras and coalgebras. In: Backhouse, R., Crole, R., Gibbons, J. (eds.) Algebraic and Coalgebraic Methods in the Mathematics of Program Construction. LNCS, vol. 2297, pp. 79–88. Springer, Heidelberg (2002). https://doi.org/10.1007/3-540-47797-7_3
5. Aczel, P., Adámek, J., Milius, S., Velebil, J.: Infinite trees and completely iterative theories: a coalgebraic view. TCS **300**(1–3), 1–45 (2003). https://doi.org/10.1016/S0304-3975(02)00728-4
6. Adámek, J.: On final coalgebras of continuous functors. Theor. Comput. Sci. **294**(1/2), 3–29 (2003). https://doi.org/10.1016/S0304-3975(01)00240-7
7. P.L. group on Agda: Agda Documentation. Technical report, Chalmers and Gothenburg University (2015). http://wiki.portal.chalmers.se/agda/, version 2.4.2.5
8. Appel, A.W., Melliès, P.A., Richards, C.D., Vouillon, J.: A very modal model of a modern, major, general type system. In: POPL, pp. 109–122. ACM (2007). https://doi.org/10.1145/1190216.1190235
9. Atkey, R., McBride, C.: Productive coprogramming with guarded recursion. In: ICFP, pp. 197–208. ACM (2013). https://doi.org/10.1145/2500365.2500597
10. Baelde, D., et al.: Abella: a system for reasoning about relational specifications. J. Formaliz. Reason. **7**(2), 1–89 (2014). https://doi.org/10.6092/issn.1972-5787/4650
11. Barendregt, H., Dekkers, W., Statman, R.: Lambda Calculus with Types. Cambridge University Press, Cambridge (2013)
12. Barr, M., Wells, C.: Category Theory for Computing Science. Prentice Hall International Series in Computer Science, 2nd edn. Prentice Hall, Upper Saddle River (1995). http://www.tac.mta.ca/tac/reprints/articles/22/tr22abs.html
13. Basold, H.: Mixed inductive-coinductive reasoning: types, programs and logic. Ph.D. thesis, Radboud University Nijmegen (2018). http://hdl.handle.net/2066/190323
14. Basold, H.: Breaking the Loop: Recursive Proofs for Coinductive Predicates in Fibrations. ArXiv e-prints, February 2018. https://arxiv.org/abs/1802.07143
15. Basold, H., Komendantskaya, E., Li, Y.: Coinduction in uniform: foundations for corecursive proof search with horn clauses. Extended version of this paper. CoRR abs/1811.07644 (2018). http://arxiv.org/abs/1811.07644
16. Beklemishev, L.D.: Parameter free induction and provably total computable functions. TCS **224**(1–2), 13–33 (1999). https://doi.org/10.1016/S0304-3975(98)00305-3
17. Bénabou, J.: Fibered categories and the foundations of naive category theory. J. Symb. Logic **50**(1), 10–37 (1985). https://doi.org/10.2307/2273784
18. Berardi, S., Tatsuta, M.: Classical system of Martin-Löf's inductive definitions is not equivalent to cyclic proof system. In: Esparza, J., Murawski, A.S. (eds.) FoSSaCS 2017. LNCS, vol. 10203, pp. 301–317. Springer, Heidelberg (2017). https://doi.org/10.1007/978-3-662-54458-7_18

19. Birkedal, L., Møgelberg, R.E.: Intensional type theory with guarded recursive types qua fixed points on universes. In: LICS, pp. 213–222. IEEE Computer Society (2013). https://doi.org/10.1109/LICS.2013.27
20. Birkedal, L., Møgelberg, R.E., Schwinghammer, J., Støvring, K.: First steps in synthetic guarded domain theory: step-indexing in the topos of trees. In: Proceedings of LICS 2011, pp. 55–64. IEEE Computer Society (2011). https://doi.org/10.1109/LICS.2011.16
21. Bizjak, A., Grathwohl, H.B., Clouston, R., Møgelberg, R.E., Birkedal, L.: Guarded dependent type theory with coinductive types. In: Jacobs, B., Löding, C. (eds.) FoSSaCS 2016. LNCS, vol. 9634, pp. 20–35. Springer, Heidelberg (2016). https://doi.org/10.1007/978-3-662-49630-5_2. https://arxiv.org/abs/1601.01586
22. Bjørner, N., Gurfinkel, A., McMillan, K., Rybalchenko, A.: Horn clause solvers for program verification. In: Beklemishev, L.D., Blass, A., Dershowitz, N., Finkbeiner, B., Schulte, W. (eds.) Fields of Logic and Computation II. LNCS, vol. 9300, pp. 24–51. Springer, Cham (2015). https://doi.org/10.1007/978-3-319-23534-9_2
23. Blanchette, J.C., Meier, F., Popescu, A., Traytel, D.: Foundational nonuniform (co)datatypes for Higher-Order Logic. In: LICS 2017, pp. 1–12. IEEE Computer Society (2017). https://doi.org/10.1109/LICS.2017.8005071
24. Blanchette, J.C., Peltier, N., Robillard, S.: Superposition with datatypes and codatatypes. In: Galmiche, D., Schulz, S., Sebastiani, R. (eds.) IJCAR 2018. LNCS (LNAI), vol. 10900, pp. 370–387. Springer, Cham (2018). https://doi.org/10.1007/978-3-319-94205-6_25
25. Borceux, F.: Handbook of Categorical Algebra. Basic Category Theory, vol. 1. Cambridge University Press, Cambridge (2008)
26. Bottu, G., Karachalias, G., Schrijvers, T., Oliveira, B.C.D.S., Wadler, P.: Quantified class constraints. In: Haskell Symposium, pp. 148–161. ACM (2017). https://doi.org/10.1145/3122955.3122967
27. Brotherston, J., Simpson, A.: Sequent calculi for induction and infinite descent. J. Log. Comput. **21**(6), 1177–1216 (2011). https://doi.org/10.1093/logcom/exq052
28. Burn, T.C., Ong, C.L., Ramsay, S.J.: Higher-order constrained horn clauses for verification. PACMPL **2**(POPL), 11:1–11:28 (2018). https://doi.org/10.1145/3158099
29. Capretta, V.: General Recursion via Coinductive Types. Log. Methods Comput. Sci. **1**(2), July 2005. https://doi.org/10.2168/LMCS-1(2:1)2005
30. Clouston, R., Goré, R.: Sequent calculus in the topos of trees. In: Pitts, A. (ed.) FoSSaCS 2015. LNCS, vol. 9034, pp. 133–147. Springer, Heidelberg (2015). https://doi.org/10.1007/978-3-662-46678-0_9
31. Coquand, T.: Infinite objects in type theory. In: Barendregt, H., Nipkow, T. (eds.) TYPES 1993. LNCS, vol. 806, pp. 62–78. Springer, Heidelberg (1994). https://doi.org/10.1007/3-540-58085-9_72
32. Cousot, P., Cousot, R.: Constructive versions of Tarski's fixed point theorems. Pac. J. Math. **82**(1), 43–57 (1979). http://projecteuclid.org/euclid.pjm/1102785059
33. Dax, C., Hofmann, M., Lange, M.: A proof system for the linear time $\mu$-calculus. In: Arun-Kumar, S., Garg, N. (eds.) FSTTCS 2006. LNCS, vol. 4337, pp. 273–284. Springer, Heidelberg (2006). https://doi.org/10.1007/11944836_26
34. van Emden, M., Kowalski, R.: The semantics of predicate logic as a programming language. J. Assoc. Comput. Mach. **23**, 733–742 (1976). https://doi.org/10.1145/321978.321991
35. Endrullis, J., Hansen, H.H., Hendriks, D., Polonsky, A., Silva, A.: A coinductive framework for infinitary rewriting and equational reasoning. In: RTA 2015, pp. 143–159 (2015). https://doi.org/10.4230/LIPIcs.RTA.2015.143

36. Farka, F., Komendantskaya, E., Hammond, K.: Coinductive soundness of corecursive type class resolution. In: Hermenegildo, M.V., Lopez-Garcia, P. (eds.) LOPSTR 2016. LNCS, vol. 10184, pp. 311–327. Springer, Cham (2017). https://doi.org/10.1007/978-3-319-63139-4_18
37. Fu, P., Komendantskaya, E., Schrijvers, T., Pond, A.: Proof relevant corecursive resolution. In: Kiselyov, O., King, A. (eds.) FLOPS 2016. LNCS, vol. 9613, pp. 126–143. Springer, Cham (2016). https://doi.org/10.1007/978-3-319-29604-3_9
38. Gambino, N., Kock, J.: Polynomial functors and polynomial monads. Math. Proc. Cambridge Phil. Soc. **154**(1), 153–192 (2013). https://doi.org/10.1017/S0305004112000394
39. Giesl, J., et al.: Analyzing program termination and complexity automatically with AProVE. J. Autom. Reason. **58**(1), 3–31 (2017). https://doi.org/10.1007/s10817-016-9388-y
40. Giménez, E.: Structural recursive definitions in type theory. In: Larsen, K.G., Skyum, S., Winskel, G. (eds.) ICALP 1998. LNCS, vol. 1443, pp. 397–408. Springer, Heidelberg (1998). https://doi.org/10.1007/BFb0055070
41. Gupta, G., Bansal, A., Min, R., Simon, L., Mallya, A.: Coinductive logic programming and its applications. In: Dahl, V., Niemelä, I. (eds.) ICLP 2007. LNCS, vol. 4670, pp. 27–44. Springer, Heidelberg (2007). https://doi.org/10.1007/978-3-540-74610-2_4
42. Hagino, T.: A typed lambda calculus with categorical type constructors. In: Pitt, D.H., Poigné, A., Rydeheard, D.E. (eds.) Category Theory and Computer Science. LNCS, vol. 283, pp. 140–157. Springer, Heidelberg (1987). https://doi.org/10.1007/3-540-18508-9_24
43. Hashimoto, K., Unno, H.: Refinement type inference via horn constraint optimization. In: Blazy, S., Jensen, T. (eds.) SAS 2015. LNCS, vol. 9291, pp. 199–216. Springer, Heidelberg (2015). https://doi.org/10.1007/978-3-662-48288-9_12
44. Howard, B.T.: Inductive, coinductive, and pointed types. In: Harper, R., Wexelblat, R.L. (eds.) Proceedings of ICFP 1996, pp. 102–109. ACM (1996). https://doi.org/10.1145/232627.232640
45. Hur, C.K., Neis, G., Dreyer, D., Vafeiadis, V.: The power of parameterization in coinductive proof. In: Proceedings of POPL 2013, pp. 193–206. ACM (2013). https://doi.org/10.1145/2429069.2429093
46. Jacobs, B.: Categorical Logic and Type Theory. Studies in Logic and the Foundations of Mathematics, vol. 141. North Holland, Amsterdam (1999)
47. Jacobs, B.: Introduction to Coalgebra: Towards Mathematics of States and Observation. Cambridge Tracts in Theoretical Computer Science, vol. 59. Cambridge University Press, Cambridge (2016). https://doi.org/10.1017/CBO9781316823187. http://www.cs.ru.nl/B.Jacobs/CLG/JacobsCoalgebraIntro.pdf
48. Komendantskaya, E., Li, Y.: Productive corecursion in logic programming. J. TPLP (ICLP 2017 post-proc.) **17**(5–6), 906–923 (2017). https://doi.org/10.1017/S147106841700028X
49. Komendantskaya, E., Li, Y.: Towards coinductive theory exploration in horn clause logic: Position paper. In: Kahsai, T., Vidal, G. (eds.) Proceedings 5th Workshop on Horn Clauses for Verification and Synthesis, HCVS 2018, Oxford, UK, 13th July 2018, vol. 278, pp. 27–33 (2018). https://doi.org/10.4204/EPTCS.278.5
50. Lambek, J., Scott, P.J.: Introduction to Higher-Order Categorical Logic. Cambridge University Press, Cambridge (1988)
51. Lämmel, R., Peyton Jones, S.L.: Scrap your boilerplate with class: extensible generic functions. In: ICFP 2005, pp. 204–215. ACM (2005). https://doi.org/10.1145/1086365.1086391

52. Lloyd, J.W.: Foundations of Logic Programming, 2nd edn. Springer, Heidelberg (1987). https://doi.org/10.1007/978-3-642-83189-8
53. Miller, D., Nadathur, G.: Programming with Higher-order logic. Cambridge University Press, Cambridge (2012)
54. Miller, D., Nadathur, G., Pfenning, F., Scedrov, A.: Uniform proofs as a foundation for logic programming. Ann. Pure Appl. Logic **51**(1–2), 125–157 (1991). https://doi.org/10.1016/0168-0072(91)90068-W
55. Milner, R.: A theory of type polymorphism in programming. J. Comput. Syst. Sci. **17**(3), 348–375 (1978). https://doi.org/10.1016/0022-0000(78)90014-4
56. Møgelberg, R.E.: A type theory for productive coprogramming via guarded recursion. In: CSL-LICS, pp. 71:1–71:10. ACM (2014). https://doi.org/10.1145/2603088.2603132
57. Nadathur, G., Mitchell, D.J.: System description: Teyjus—a compiler and abstract machine based implementation of λProlog. CADE-16. LNCS (LNAI), vol. 1632, pp. 287–291. Springer, Heidelberg (1999). https://doi.org/10.1007/3-540-48660-7_25
58. Nakano, H.: A modality for recursion. In: LICS, pp. 255–266. IEEE Computer Society (2000). https://doi.org/10.1109/LICS.2000.855774
59. Niwinski, D., Walukiewicz, I.: Games for the $\mu$-Calculus. TCS **163**(1&2), 99–116 (1996). https://doi.org/10.1016/0304-3975(95)00136-0
60. Park, D.: Concurrency and automata on infinite sequences. In: Deussen, P. (ed.) GI-TCS 1981. LNCS, vol. 104, pp. 167–183. Springer, Heidelberg (1981). https://doi.org/10.1007/BFb0017309
61. Plotkin, G.D.: LCF considered as a programming language. Theor. Comput. Sci. **5**(3), 223–255 (1977). https://doi.org/10.1016/0304-3975(77)90044-5
62. Reynolds, A., Kuncak, V.: Induction for SMT solvers. In: D'Souza, D., Lal, A., Larsen, K.G. (eds.) VMCAI 2015. LNCS, vol. 8931, pp. 80–98. Springer, Heidelberg (2015). https://doi.org/10.1007/978-3-662-46081-8_5
63. Roşu, G., Lucanu, D.: Circular coinduction: a proof theoretical foundation. In: Kurz, A., Lenisa, M., Tarlecki, A. (eds.) CALCO 2009. LNCS, vol. 5728, pp. 127–144. Springer, Heidelberg (2009). https://doi.org/10.1007/978-3-642-03741-2_10
64. Rutten, J.: Universal coalgebra: a theory of systems. TCS **249**(1), 3–80 (2000). https://doi.org/10.1016/S0304-3975(00)00056-6
65. Sangiorgi, D.: Introduction to Bisimulation and Coinduction. Cambridge University Press, New York (2011)
66. Santocanale, L.: A calculus of circular proofs and its categorical semantics. In: Nielsen, M., Engberg, U. (eds.) FoSSaCS 2002. LNCS, vol. 2303, pp. 357–371. Springer, Heidelberg (2002). https://doi.org/10.1007/3-540-45931-6_25
67. Santocanale, L.: $\mu$-bicomplete categories and parity games. RAIRO - ITA **36**(2), 195–227 (2002). https://doi.org/10.1051/ita:2002010
68. Shamkanov, D.S.: Circular proofs for the Gödel-Löb provability logic. Math. Notes **96**(3), 575–585 (2014). https://doi.org/10.1134/S0001434614090326
69. Simon, L., Bansal, A., Mallya, A., Gupta, G.: Co-logic programming: extending logic programming with coinduction. In: Arge, L., Cachin, C., Jurdziński, T., Tarlecki, A. (eds.) ICALP 2007. LNCS, vol. 4596, pp. 472–483. Springer, Heidelberg (2007). https://doi.org/10.1007/978-3-540-73420-8_42
70. Simpson, A.: Cyclic arithmetic is equivalent to Peano arithmetic. In: Esparza, J., Murawski, A.S. (eds.) FoSSaCS 2017. LNCS, vol. 10203, pp. 283–300. Springer, Heidelberg (2017). https://doi.org/10.1007/978-3-662-54458-7_17
71. Smoryński, C.: Self-Reference and Modal Logic. Universitext. Springer, New York (1985). https://doi.org/10.1007/978-1-4613-8601-8

72. Solovay, R.M.: Provability interpretations of modal logic. Israel J. Math. **25**(3), 287–304 (1976). https://doi.org/10.1007/BF02757006
73. Sulzmann, M., Stuckey, P.J.: HM(X) type inference is CLP(X) solving. J. Funct. Program. **18**(2), 251–283 (2008). https://doi.org/10.1017/S0956796807006569
74. Terese: Term Rewriting Systems. Cambridge University Press, Cambridge (2003)
75. Turner, D.A.: Elementary strong functional programming. In: Hartel, P.H., Plasmeijer, R. (eds.) FPLE 1995. LNCS, vol. 1022, pp. 1–13. Springer, Heidelberg (1995). https://doi.org/10.1007/3-540-60675-0_35
76. van den Berg, B., de Marchi, F.: Non-well-founded trees in categories. Ann. Pure Appl. Logic **146**(1), 40–59 (2007). https://doi.org/10.1016/j.apal.2006.12.001
77. Worrell, J.: On the final sequence of a finitary set functor. Theor. Comput. Sci. **338**(1–3), 184–199 (2005). https://doi.org/10.1016/j.tcs.2004.12.009

# Permissions

All chapters in this book were first published by Springer; hereby published with permission under the Creative Commons Attribution License or equivalent. Every chapter published in this book has been scrutinized by our experts. Their significance has been extensively debated. The topics covered herein carry significant findings which will fuel the growth of the discipline. They may even be implemented as practical applications or may be referred to as a beginning point for another development.

The contributors of this book come from diverse backgrounds, making this book a truly international effort. This book will bring forth new frontiers with its revolutionizing research information and detailed analysis of the nascent developments around the world.

We would like to thank all the contributing authors for lending their expertise to make the book truly unique. They have played a crucial role in the development of this book. Without their invaluable contributions this book wouldn't have been possible. They have made vital efforts to compile up to date information on the varied aspects of this subject to make this book a valuable addition to the collection of many professionals and students.

This book was conceptualized with the vision of imparting up-to-date information and advanced data in this field. To ensure the same, a matchless editorial board was set up. Every individual on the board went through rigorous rounds of assessment to prove their worth. After which they invested a large part of their time researching and compiling the most relevant data for our readers.

The editorial board has been involved in producing this book since its inception. They have spent rigorous hours researching and exploring the diverse topics which have resulted in the successful publishing of this book. They have passed on their knowledge of decades through this book. To expedite this challenging task, the publisher supported the team at every step. A small team of assistant editors was also appointed to further simplify the editing procedure and attain best results for the readers.

Apart from the editorial board, the designing team has also invested a significant amount of their time in understanding the subject and creating the most relevant covers. They scrutinized every image to scout for the most suitable representation of the subject and create an appropriate cover for the book.

The publishing team has been an ardent support to the editorial, designing and production team. Their endless efforts to recruit the best for this project, has resulted in the accomplishment of this book. They are a veteran in the field of academics and their pool of knowledge is as vast as their experience in printing. Their expertise and guidance has proved useful at every step. Their uncompromising quality standards have made this book an exceptional effort. Their encouragement from time to time has been an inspiration for everyone.

The publisher and the editorial board hope that this book will prove to be a valuable piece of knowledge for researchers, students, practitioners and scholars across the globe.

# List of Contributors

**Pierre Boutillier**
Harvard Medical School, Boston, USA

**Ioana Cristescu**
Inria Rennes - Bretagne Atlantique, Rennes, France

**Jérôme Feret**
DI-ENS (INRIA/ÉNS/CNRS/PSL), Paris, France

**Ismail Kuru and Colin S. Gordon**
Drexel University, Philadelphia, USA

**Danel Ahman**
University of Ljubljana, Ljubljana, Slovenia

**Victor Dumitrescu**
MSR-Inria Joint Centre, Paris, France

**Nick Giannarakis and Zoe Paraskevopoulou**
Princeton University, Princeton, USA

**Chris Hawblitzel, Nikhil Swamy, Jonathan Protzenko and Tahina Ramananandro**
Microsoft Research, Redmond, USA

**Monal Narasimhamurthy**
University of Colorado Boulder, Boulder, USA

**Clément Pit-Claudel**
MIT CSAIL, Cambridge, USA

**Aseem Rastogi**
Microsoft Research, Bangalore, India

**Glen Mével, Cătălin Hriţcu and François Pottier**
Inria, Paris, France

**Jacques-Henri Jourdan**
CNRS, LRI, Univ. Paris Sud, Université Paris Saclay, Orsay, France

**Carsten Fuhs**
Department of Computer Science and Information Systems, Birkbeck, University of London, London, UK

**Cynthia Kop**
Department of Software Science, Radboud University Nijmegen, Nijmegen, The Netherlands

**Matthieu Journault and Abdelraouf Ouadjaout**
Sorbonne Université, CNRS, Laboratoire d'Informatique de Paris 6, LIP6, 75005 Paris, France

**Antoine Miné**
Sorbonne Université, CNRS, Laboratoire d'Informatique de Paris 6, LIP6, 75005 Paris, France
Institut universitaire de France, Paris, France

**Nikita Chopra, Rekha Pai and Deepak D'Souza**
Indian Institute of Science, Bangalore, India

**Henning Basold**
CNRS, ENS Lyon, Lyon, France

**Ekaterina Komendantskaya and Yue Li**
Heriot-Watt University, Edinburgh, UK

# Index

## R



## S



## U



## V



## W

Printed in the USA
CPSIA information can be obtained
at www.ICGtesting.com
JSHW061033121023
50109JS00004B/14

9 781647 253714